"Hugh Crago weaves together recent research on brain function with the lives of story-makers beginning with toddlers' babbling, moving through childhood, adolescence, and adulthood, as each stage brings with it changes in the ways stories are told and the motivations that inspire the telling. This book makes an invaluable contribution to our understanding of the importance of stories in human life."

—Cristina Bruns, Chapman University, USA

"This important and thought-provoking contribution to the world of ideas is an extremely well-written book. While unusually cross-disciplinary, it is also easy to read. Adults who are young at heart will be entranced by this voyage of discovery into why it is that we all love stories and what they mean to our lives."

—Jessica Milner Davis, University of Sydney, Australia

What we have here is a product of a lifetime of originality . . . It is coherent, logical, and inspiring—positively glittering with ideas. The mix of theory, science, literary reference, anecdote and empiricism is difficult to resist.

—Peter Hunt, Emeritus Professor, University of Cardiff

We live in a world of stories; yet few of us pause to ask what stories actually are, why we consume them so avidly, and what they do for story makers and their audiences. This book focuses on the experiences that good stories generate: feelings of purposeful involvement, elevation, temporary loss of self, vicarious emotion, and relief of tension. The author examines what drives writers to create stories and why readers fall under their spell; why some children grow up to be writers; and how the capacity for creating and comprehending stories develops from infancy right through into old age.

Entranced by Story applies recent research on brain function to literary examples ranging from the *Iliad* and *Wuthering Heights* to *Harold and the Purple Crayon*, providing a ground-breaking exploration of the biological and neurological basis of the literary experience. Blending research, theory, and biographical anecdote, the author shows how it is the unique structure of the human brain, with its layering of sophisticated cognitive capacities upon archaic, emotion-driven functions, which best explains the mystery of story.

Hugh Crago has taught literature, human development and counselling in Australia, and recently retired as Senior Lecturer in Counselling at the University of Western Sydney. He is co-author of *Prelude to Literacy: A Preschool Child's Encounter with Picture and Story*, author of *A Circle Unbroken: The Hidden Emotional Patterns that Shape Our Lives*, and many articles on children's literature, social change, welfare policy, family therapy and counsellor training. He currently maintains a private practice in Blackheath, near Sydney, and contributes a regular column to *Psychotherapy in Australia* magazine.

ENTRANCED BY STORY

Children's Literature and Culture
Jack Zipes, *Founding Series Editor*
Philip Nel, *Series Editor*

For a complete series list, please go to routledge.com

Into the Closet
Cross-Dressing and the Gendered Body in Children's Literature
Victoria Flanagan

Russian Children's Literature and Culture
Edited by Marina Balina and Larissa Rudova

The Outside Child In and Out of the Book
Christine Wilkie-Stibbs

Representing Africa in Children's Literature
Old and New Ways of Seeing
Vivian Yenika-Agbaw

The Fantasy of Family
Nineteenth-Century Children's Literature and the Myth of the Domestic Ideal
Liz Thiel

From Nursery Rhymes to Nationhood
Children's Literature and the Construction of Canadian Identity
Elizabeth A. Galway

The Family in English Children's Literature
Ann Alston

Enterprising Youth
Social Values and Acculturation in Nineteenth-Century American Children's Literature
Monika Elbert

Constructing Adolescence in Fantastic Realism
Alison Waller

Crossover Fiction
Global and Historical Perspectives
Sandra L. Beckett

The Crossover Novel
Contemporary Children's Fiction and Its Adult Readership
Rachel Falconer

Shakespeare in Children's Literature
Gender and Cultural Capital
Erica Hateley

Critical Approaches to Food in Children's Literature
Edited by Kara K. Keeling and Scott T. Pollard

Neo-Imperialism in Children's Literature About Africa
A Study of Contemporary Fiction
Yulisa Amadu Maddy and Donnarae MacCann

Death, Gender and Sexuality in Contemporary Adolescent Literature
Kathryn James

Fundamental Concepts of Children's Literature Research
Literary and Sociological Approaches
Hans-Heino Ewers

Children's Fiction about 9/11
Ethnic, Heroic and National Identities
Jo Lampert

The Place of Lewis Carroll in Children's Literature
Jan Susina

Power, Voice and Subjectivity in Literature for Young Readers
Maria Nikolajeva

"Juvenile" Literature and British Society, 1850–1950
The Age of Adolescence
Charles Ferrall and Anna Jackson

Picturing the Wolf in Children's Literature
Debra Mitts-Smith

New Directions in Picturebook Research
Edited by Teresa Colomer, Bettina Kümmerling-Meibauer, Cecilia Silva-Díaz

The Role of Translators in Children's Literature
Invisible Storytellers
Gillian Lathey

The Children's Book Business
Lessons from the Long Eighteenth Century
Lissa Paul

Humor in Contemporary Junior Literature
Julie Cross

Innocence, Heterosexuality, and the Queerness of Children's Literature
Tison Pugh

Reading the Adolescent Romance
Sweet Valley and the Popular Young Adult Romance Novel
Amy S. Pattee

Irish Children's Literature and Culture
New Perspectives on Contemporary Writing
Edited by Valerie Coghlan and Keith O'Sullivan

Beyond Pippi Longstocking
Intermedial and International Perspectives on Astrid Lindgren's Works
Edited by Bettina Kümmerling-Meibauer and Astrid Surmatz

Contemporary English-Language Indian Children's Literature:
Representations of Nation, Culture, and the New Indian Girl
Michelle Superle

Re-visioning Historical Fiction
The Past through Modern Eyes
Kim Wilson

The Myth of Persephone in Girls' Fantasy Literature
Holly Virginia Blackford

Pinocchio, Puppets and Modernity
The Mechanical Body
Edited by Katia Pizzi

Crossover Picturebooks
A Genre for All Ages
Sandra L. Beckett

Peter Pan's Shadows in the Literary Imagination
Kirsten Stirling

Landscape in Children's Literature
Jane Suzanne Carroll

Colonial India in Children's Literature
Supriya Goswami

Children's Culture and the Avant-Garde
Painting in Paris, 1890–1915
Marilynn Olson

Textual Transformations in Children's Literature
Adaptations, Translations, Reconsiderations
Edited by Benjamin Lefebvre

The Nation in Children's Literature
Nations of Childhood
Edited by Kit Kelen and Björn Sundmark

Subjectivity in Asian Children's Literature and Film
Global Theories and Implications
Edited by John Stephens

Children's Literature, Domestication, and Social Foundation
Narratives of Civilization and Wilderness
Layla AbdelRahim

Charles Dickens and the Victorian Child
Romanticizing and Socializing the Imperfect Child
Amberyl Malkovich

Second-Generation Memory and Contemporary Children's Literature
Ghost Images
Anastasia Ulanowicz

Contemporary Dystopian Fiction for Young Adults
Brave New Teenagers
Edited by Carrie Hintz, Balaka Basu, and Katherine R. Broad

Jews and Jewishness in British Children's Literature
Madelyn J. Travis

Genocide in Contemporary Children's and Young Adult Literature
Cambodia to Darfur
Jane M. Gangi

Children and Cultural Memory in Texts of Childhood
Edited by Heather Snell and Lorna Hutchison

Picturebooks
Representation and Narration
Edited by Bettina Kümmerling-Meibauer

Children's Literature and New York City
Edited by Pádraic Whyte and Keith O'Sullivan

Entranced by Story
Brain, Tale and Teller, from Infancy to Old Age
Hugh Crago

ENTRANCED BY STORY

Brain, Tale and Teller, from Infancy to Old Age

HUGH CRAGO

Routledge
Taylor & Francis Group
NEW YORK AND LONDON

First published 2014
by Routledge
711 Third Avenue, New York, NY 10017

and by Routledge
2 Park Square, Milton Park, Abingdon, Oxon OX14 4RN

Routledge is an imprint of the Taylor & Francis Group, an informa business

Library of Congress Cataloging in Publication Data
A catalog record has been requested for this book.

ISBN13: 978-0-415-74170-5 (hbk)
ISBN13: 978-1-315-81515-2 (ebk)

Typeset in Minion
by IBT Global.

For Maureen

Peer: *Hvor var jeg som meg selv, som den hele, den sanne?*

Solveig: *I min tro, i mitt håp og i min klaerlighet.*

Contents

Series Editor's Foreword

The Children's Literature and Culture series is dedicated to promoting original research in children's literature, children's culture, and childhood studies. We use the term "children" in the broadest sense, spanning from earliest childhood up through adolescence. The already capacious term "culture" encompasses media (radio, film, television, video games, blogs, websites, social networking sites), material culture (toys, games, products), acculturation (processes of socialization), and of course literature, including all types of crossover works. Since children's literature is defined by its audience, this series seeks to foster scholarship on the full range of children's literature's many genres and subgenres: fairy tales, folk tales, comics, graphic novels, picture books, novels, poetry, didactic tales, nonsense, fantasy, realism, mystery, horror, fan fiction, and others.

Founded by Jack Zipes in 1994, Routledge's Children's Literature and Culture is the longest-running series devoted to the study of children's literature and culture from a national and international perspective. In 2011, expanding its focus to include childhood studies, the series also seeks to explore the legal, historical, and philosophical conditions of different childhoods. An advocate for scholarship from around the globe, the series recognizes innovation and encourages interdisciplinarity. In Zipes' words, "the goal of the Children's Literature and Culture series is to enhance research in this field and, at the same time, point to new directions that bring together the best scholarly work throughout the world."

Philip Nel

Acknowledgments

Writing can be a lonely enterprise. I remember those who in different ways, and at different times in my life, have provided much-needed encouragement: John Ryan, Valerie and Brian Alderson, Nancy Chambers, Iain McCalman, John Moorhead, Peter Hunt, Sanjay Sircar, Dave Straton, Hilary McPhee, Brian Stagoll, Gabrielle Lord, Sue Austin, Jessica Milner Davis and Penny Gardner. In the increasingly despairing final stages of a six year journey, I was grateful to Yvette Nielsen, Linda Johnston, Kara Goodsell and Stephanie Brennan. Special thanks to Helen Thomas, who offered wonderfully honest moment-by-moment reactions to each draft chapter, and Meeray Ghaly, who designed a cover graphic that captured the true spirit of the book. After failing to interest thirty agents and twenty publishers over five years, I acknowledge with gratitude Phil Nel, Series Editor, and Emily Ross, Commissioning Editor, for supporting the inclusion of *Entranced by Story* in Routledge's Children's Literature and Childhood Studies monographs series.

None of these people has had to live with me. Maureen Crago has, and I know how much my involvement in this book has cost her. Her pleasure when it was finally accepted for publication touched me deeply. *Entranced by Story* would never have been possible without her steadying presence, honesty, and many fruitful suggestions. The University of Western Sydney allowed me a few months of professional development leave in 2009, during which I completed an early draft of this book: most of it has been written in my own time, with no institutional support. Finally, I want to thank Gerhard Hassler and his staff at Café Memento, Blackheath, over more than a dozen years in which I was left undisturbed to enter 'writer's trance' for an hour or so several times a week, sustained by Gerhard's excellent coffee, and his personal warmth and wit.

Bloomsbury Publishers kindly granted me permission to quote from Jennifer Donnelly's Preface, 'Why You Should Read This', to their Bloomsbury Classics reprint of Emily Bronte's *Wuthering Heights* (2006).

Hugh Crago, Blackheath, NSW, Australia, 2013

Introduction

Entranced by Story

As I write this, *Entranced by Story* has just started its journey towards publication. Apart from a chapter or two, the book exists only as ideas in my head, and lots of notes. I know the direction I'm going in, but how the pieces will fit together and what precisely they will add up to, is something that I do not know. Not yet. '*Listen! It's time to begin!*' exclaims Hans Andersen at the start of 'The Snow Queen', adding '*And when we come to the end we shall know more than we do now!*' It sounds arch, and maybe a bit patronising. But Andersen, a true story maker, knew what he was talking about—in a very real sense, we don't 'compose' or 'make up' stories, we *discover* them, and we rarely know what they mean until we've completed them—and not always then.

I start work on each new chapter with some spark of inspiration, some intriguing fact, vivid memory, or suggestive metaphor. The spark stays with me for a while, as long as a few days, until I can start to put it into words—or better, to *paint some words around it* (that's what it feels more like). There is a sense of excitement about doing this, as the words start to flow and one idea leads to another. Time slips away without my being conscious of it: in a kind of trance, I have written several pages, perhaps a thousand words. Then the flow dries up. I stop, feeling pleased with what I've done so far, yet frustrated and impatient because I know there is more, but I don't know what it is yet. A day or a week later, the next bit comes. It wells up from somewhere when it is ready—it won't come simply because I want it to, although I've noticed that a good coffee will often help to restore my confidence that I'm *going somewhere* and that, in the end, I will *arrive*.

If I go with the inspiration when it's pulsing and sparking, then the writing comes easily. Even though it may simply be a restatement of what I already know, or what I've said previously in print, it *feels* new-born. It is as if something important is *making itself* inside of me, something that needs to come out, and will come out in its own time—a sense of *inevitability* is involved. If I delay too long in getting the new bit down in words, then the spark dies, the energy diminishes, I lose confidence and if I try to write in that state, it's a struggle, and it doesn't feel like fun anymore. If I 'strike while the iron is hot', the writing happens by itself. I feel as if I am merely assisting in a process that originates *outside* of me, just as Homer believed (or half-believed) that a goddess was speaking through him—*Menen aeide, Thea!*—when he struck his lyre and chanted those famous lines about the heroes Achilles and Agamemnon and their quarrel before the high-walled, windy city of Troy.

Homer was *telling* a story, while my book is simply a non-fiction book *about* stories. Yet the composition process I've been describing is in its essentials identical with the process by which stories are created. They seem to come from outside us, or bubble up from the unknown depths of some inner well; they seem to come of their own volition, in their own time; and composing them *feels* like being the first ever to burst into the sparkling expanse of the Pacific (even though an earlier explorer probably got there years ago). And it is curiously similar, although not quite the same, when we read, or hear, or watch, a story that someone else has created. Story making and story reading are apparently very different activities, yet they can evoke similar *experiences.*

****

I wrote what you have just read in 2006. I'm now going to 'fast forward' much closer to the present, with *Entranced by Story* complete in its final draft, and from this vantage point (as if looking down from the high walls of a great city) I can offer you an overview of what this book will be grappling with. It will not be a detailed, chapter-by-chapter summary, but it will introduce the key questions I'm going to explore, and anticipate the main conclusions I'll reach.

****

Hilary Mantel's novel *Wolf Hall* is about Thomas Cromwell, the man who became King Henry VIII's trusted 'fixer' after the fall of Sir Thomas More. Years ago I read Mantel's *A Place of Greater Safety* (a long novel about the French Revolution) with a mixture of fascination and dread, because it confronted me with the voices and thoughts of the very same men who were responsible for the Terror of 1793—the antecedent of Stalin's terrible purges, and of Hitler's 'final solution'. I don't want to repeat that experience, so I hold off on reading *Wolf Hall* for several years. Most of all, I don't want to find out that Thomas More might be less of a hero than I always believed ('*I die the King's good servant, but God's first*').

When I finally buy *Wolf Hall*, I twice put it down after just a few pages (it starts with the boy Cromwell being brutally kicked by his blacksmith father, and left to bleed into his own vomit). Temporarily, I can't bear to live in this world. Hilary Mantel writes in the present tense, and almost entirely in dialogue—reading *Wolf Hall* is like hearing the sound track of a movie without the visuals. In the 'thrilling adventure stories' I read as a boy, the author always told you who said what (*'You don't say!' exclaimed Jim. 'Yes', was Ted's rejoinder, 'I most certainly do!'*) I find it irritating to have to keep checking on who said what, and at times I have the sneaking feeling (which, I tell myself, I shouldn't, because Mantel is a *famous novelist* who has won the *Booker Prize*) that she should have been more like those hack authors I read as a child. I can't see what she might gain by making me guess all the time which of the novel's *several* 'Thomases' the current speaker is.

Yet when I start reading again, I do become absorbed—almost too absorbed. I can't, any longer, be comfortably sure that Cromwell is a pragmatic manipulator without any human feelings. I'm so close in to him now that I find it painful, and I find myself full of the same dread that I felt when reading *A Place of Greater Safety*. The dread persists, even though I know (from history) what's going to happen—the King is going to get his way, Anne Boleyn will become Queen, but fail to bear the son the King is set upon having. Quite soon, she will be sent to her death, and replaced by a new favourite. Cromwell will duck and weave and survive—at least for now. Hilary Mantel, whose own experiences of pain, shame and failure she presents with blunt honesty in her memoir *Giving Up the Ghost*, has persuaded me to care about a 'baddie', to see the world as he sees it, and to realise that he is not a monster, but a human being like myself. Monsters are scarier when we see them only from the outside—but it's a lot more comforting to see them that way.

****

I've just given a personal example of what it's like to be an entranced reader—the way I (and so many other readers) get caught up in a story, *lifted out* of ourselves, *merging* with its characters. The way we read faster and faster, *rushing on* to the end—sometimes wanting to get there, sometimes dreading it. Why was it that when I studied literature in high school, and then at university, such experiences were bracketed, almost as if they did not exist? Readers talk about them to other readers ('I stayed up all night, I just had to turn another page . . . '), but teachers and academics didn't seem to. Instead, they taught us to ask questions about what we read, to analyse patterns and themes, to compare characters with 'real life' (and hence to decide whether they were realistic or melodramatic), to set up hierarchies of value, where 'great works' predictably won out over the bestsellers that I (and others) secretly enjoyed more—at least, I did back then, and if I'm honest, sometimes still do.

I proved to be quite good at doing what my professors wanted, and in my twenties I even taught literature myself—but I was never fully convinced. In the course of researching and writing this book, I have gradually come to see that literary criticism is neurologically the product of one side of the human brain—whereas the *experience* of story arises on the *other* side. In the terms I'll introduce in Chapter 2, critics and academic scholars are mostly *interrogators*, dominated by the brain's left hemisphere, whereas writers are *performers*, under the spell of the right hemisphere. So, too, are enthralled readers—except that their performances are acted out solely in the theatre of their own minds, not put into print for others to read.

My university teachers acted as if it were naïve to connect writers' lives with the stories they wrote. Welleck and Warren told us in their *Theory of Literature* (1942) that to get too preoccupied with themes and characters as reflections of writers' own experiences was a 'biographical fallacy'.[1] Instead, we must respond to 'texts' as if they existed independently of their creators. Writers had their own version of this, too. They described their creative process as something that was partly or wholly mysterious to them. They spoke of stories 'coming to them'. They talked of characters 'developing a life of their own' or 'taking over', as if they (the authors) had no control over these things. Yet they clearly valued the *inspired* state in which they wrote—a state in which they could be unaware of other people, and lose touch with time. Why did many academics show so little interest in what drove writers to write, or in how authors described their own writing process? I didn't know, but I felt deeply that a vital part of the 'literary experience' was not being acknowledged, except of course by biographers.

As a child, I was an avid reader, and I devoured all kinds of books, regardless of their literary merit—stories intended for children like myself, stories intended for adults (but readable by a child) and a few stories (like William Golding's *Lord of the Flies* and the now-forgotten *Lucifer and the Child* by 1930s novelist Ethel Mannin) that were *about* children, but not *for* them. I read these before I was emotionally mature, and consequently experienced complex emotions of horror and shame, almost as if I'd been touched by an adult in an inappropriate way. As an adult, I continued to read children's books alongside adult ones, but found that this was regarded as very odd. Most of my literary colleagues found children's literature (then starting to establish a precarious academic respectability) a bit embarrassing, not something any 'real' scholar would be bothered with. It was as if adults were denying or minimising the significance of their own childhoods. 'Simple stories', dominated by 'mere plot' were regarded as somehow undignified and unimportant (though E. M. Forster put a case for them in his *Aspects of the Novel*). Yet such stories were what most adults actually read for pleasure. Studying bestsellers and thrillers could be justified on sociological grounds—'cultural studies' was just beginning then, and Q. D. Leavis had acknowledged that popular fiction could be undeniably powerful. But nobody seemed too concerned with how stories could get inside people's heads and (sometimes) stay there life long. This was 'psychology' and it had nothing to do with literature. The Postmodern theories of the latter part of the twentieth century had little more to say on this subject than the New Criticism of the first part. Nor, with a couple of rare exceptions, did academic psychologists. They couldn't conduct controlled experiments on the reading or writing process, so what was the point in investigating them?

****

More than sixty years ago, and several years before *The Lion, the Witch and the Wardrobe*, C. S. Lewis published an essay 'On Stories'.[2] Lewis wrote powerfully and persuasively, using his personal experiences of stories like Henry Rider Haggard's *King Solomon's Mines* to talk about those hard-to-define qualities that make some stories so memorable. Yet despite his encyclopedic knowledge of literature from the epic poetry of ancient Greece to twentieth-century science fiction, Lewis didn't achieve his quest. Unable to draw on insights from *outside* literature, he was unable to 'nail' the mystery of story. That mystery—the one I am going to explore in this book—lies in the complex interaction of the brain's two hemispheres, and between the archaic layers of the brain (with their automatic capacities for fear, rage, lust, grief, and joy) and the newer capacities of the cerebral cortex (capacities for self-conscious artistry, for selection, for comparison and evaluation).

Of course, our present knowledge of the evolution and functioning of different parts of the brain was not available to Lewis—how could it be? Yet even in 1947, he could have drawn on a partial version of this knowledge—Sigmund Freud's realisation that one part of our mind can hold, and act on, feelings and beliefs of which another part is *unconscious*. Freud himself (who died in 1939), Melanie Klein (who revised and extended Freud's powerful ideas), and John Bowlby, who formulated Attachment Theory—all were living and writing in Lewis' adulthood, but Lewis regarded them with deep suspicion.[3] In a very similar way, many creative artists distrust psychoanalysis and psychotherapy, fearing that self-exploration may destroy the artistic quest that gives purpose and meaning to their lives, makes them 'special'. Director and script-writer David Lynch described how he once asked a psychiatrist whether the process of therapy might affect his creativity. When the psychiatrist replied that yes, it might, Lynch 'shook his hand and left'.[4]

Psychoanalysis has produced its own approach to literature, of course, starting with Freud's essay on daydreaming and creativity. Since then, we have had Jung's discussions of archetypal characters and narrative patterns (most recently taken up in by Christopher Booker in his blockbuster exploration *The Seven Basic Plots*), Simon Lesser's *Fiction and the Unconscious* (1957), and Norman Holland's *5 Readers Reading* (1975). The latter played an important part in the brief flowering of something called 'Reader Response Criticism'—a way of approaching poetry, drama and narrative fiction that, as Holland had asked, took the *experience* of literature seriously, instead of sidelining it. We are not passive 'consumers' of story, said reader response scholars, but *create* our own experience of stories (and other literary works) in an active way, almost as their authors do. And the experiences that we create, with the help of our own memories, are essentially *emotional* experiences.[5]

At the end of each of the first two episodes of HBO's swords-sex-and-sorcery series *Game of Thrones*, based on George Martin's *A Song of Ice and Fire*, I experienced what I can only describe as *grief* and *rage*. 'I'm not watching any more of this', I thought (I did, though). Stories can arouse very powerful feelings indeed, and when, instead of offering the consoling resolutions that we crave, they humiliate or even decapitate our favourite characters, we react in the most primitive way, wanting to 'dump' the story itself. These feelings alone should alert us to the central truth of the psychoanalytic position taken by Holland—that literature speaks to fantasies and feelings that are deeply rooted in all of us from childhood, invites us to participate in those fantasies and feelings, and offers us a particular kind of pleasure in doing so, even (sometimes) when the experience is painful or distressing. At the time I first read Holland, I was still fighting off such insights. Since then, I have accepted many of them, in part thanks to my own experience (in my fifties) as a patient in psychoanalytic psychotherapy.

Yet there was something intractable about the story experience that psychoanalytic theory seemed to complicate without really explaining. In my early thirties I'd read Julian Jaynes' *The Origin of Consciousness in the Breakdown of the Bicameral Mind*—an extraordinarily bold and imaginative book to come from the pen of a Princeton psychology professor.[6] Despite my scepticism about some of his conclusions, I felt intuitively that Jaynes was onto something. He was not writing about stories, of course, but he offered a broad framework for understanding how the structure of the human brain itself might explain many of the puzzles of human culture and human experience. As so often in my writing life, I was haunted as much by the bits of Jaynes I *hadn't* been able to understand as by the bits I thought I'd grasped. His ideas lay dormant inside me for another thirty years, until, having already drafted most of my own book, I discovered Iain McGilchrist's recent revisiting of Jayne's territory in his authoritative and provocative *The Master and His Emissary*.[7]

Jaynes had written his *Bicameral Mind* in the early days of so-called 'split brain experiments'—in which scientists had for the first time communicated with each hemisphere of a living person's brain, after the accidental or surgical severing of the *corpus callosum* (the thick band of neuronal matter that normally connects the right and left hemispheres and allows them to communicate constantly and almost instantaneously). Between Jaynes' speculations (published in 1976) and McGilchrist's work (which appeared in 2009), years of research had modified some of what the scientists of Jaynes' time thought they had found, and established more certainty about the very different ways in which the two 'halves' of the human cerebral cortex perceive, and represent, the world—something I'll outline in more detail shortly.

Now, I thought, we finally have a secure base on which to erect a theory of how literature works, but more particularly, to address the special qualities of *story*—a particular literary form that reliably evokes particular experiences in readers, listeners or viewers. McGilchrist himself taught literature at various stages of his career, and clearly values it greatly, but his book addresses it only tangentially, as part of a sweeping survey of the way the left hemisphere has gradually come to dominate human consciousness and society. In *Entranced by Story*, I have tried to make an intelligent application of McGilchrist's conclusions to the issue of the making, and meaning, of stories. However, I've also been influenced by other seminal contributions to our understanding of the human brain and how it works.

In 1990, Paul D. MacLean (a specialist in the neurology of reptiles) proposed that the human brain comprises three strata, three distinct 'brains'.[8] These are layered upon (and around) one another in the order in which they evolved, the most recent (in evolutionary terms) on top, and the oldest at the bottom. The oldest stratum of all is the brain stem, or 'reptile brain' (sometimes called the 'R-complex' or 'dinosaur brain'). As the name suggests, we share this with forms of life as primitive as lizards, snakes and tortoises. Its functions appear to be associated with instincts like reproduction, hunger, thirst and self-preservation (in the form of 'fight, flight or freeze' behaviours). While the reptile brain is very limited in what it can do, it does govern both *mimicry* (one animal copies the actions of another) and *purposeful repetition*. In later chapters, we'll see how imitation is crucial to the impulse to create stories, and how repetition is one of the most basic techniques of story making. Lizards don't make up stories—but when we humans do, we draw on capacities that seem to be hard-wired into the most primitive parts of our brains.[9]

MacLean's second layer, much more recent in evolutionary terms, is the limbic system or 'mammal brain', which has grown around the reptile brain. All mammals, from mice and rabbits to the great apes and human beings, have a limbic system. In some ways, the organs of the mammal brain extend and elaborate those of the reptile brain. The limbic system, too, plays a part in survival-level behaviour. But it also enables what we call 'warm-blooded' instincts: the pull to care for one's offspring, for example, or the attachment felt by a mating pair—transcending the reptile compulsion to mate with any partner available. When we humans write anthropomorphic stories for children—stories in which other creatures speak, dress and act as if human—it is mostly *mammals* that we choose as characters. Hence Aesop's fables, or Beatrix Potter's famous tales of mice, rabbits, guinea pigs and foxes. Something in us reaches out to mammals, perhaps because we recognise that like us, they have *feelings*, even if they do not *think about* them in the same way that we do. Geologist Richard Fortey points out that we have selectively bred pets so that their faces start to resemble our own (breeding the prominent snout out of dogs, for example), and picture books and cartoons for young children exhibit a form of the same process: Disney's animal heroes are much more 'human' than Beatrix Potter's, and the baby seals appeal so strongly because of their 'general babyness'.[10]

Only the brain's third, and (in evolutionary terms) newest layer is able to reflect upon its own experience. Cats, dogs and horses *experience* emotions, as anyone who has a pet knows, but so far as we know, they probably do not think about what they are feeling, wonder what it means, or ask what has caused it. This function we humans owe to the cerebral cortex, by far the bulkiest part of the human brain, which enfolds the reptile and mammal brains (as a pearl grows around a tiny fragment of sand or grit in an oyster) but is still joined with them in a dense network of intercommunication. Where the reptile brain can process information at the level of 'Is this new thing in my environment a threat?' or 'Is this creature a potential mate?', the mammal brain can process not only the new arrival's external appearance, but also, to a degree, its internal (emotional) state, by reading its body language and expression. It can evaluate how *dangerous* a potential adversary may be, how *desirable* a potential mate may be (exercising what evolutionists call 'sexual selection'). As any pet owner is aware, a mammal's past experience of people, places and things (and the pleasant or unpleasant feelings associated with them) feed into its brain, permitting individualised responses, all at a level inaccessible to conscious thought, and accomplished in an instant. All of this goes on in humans also.

In its turn, the cerebral cortex, the 'human brain', *thinks about* the information offered it by more primitive brain organs. Not only can we put *words* to our feeling, we can consciously *remember* whether we have felt similarly in the past, and we can even consider whether or not it is *sensible* for us to act on that feeling right now. The frontal lobes of the cortex, among other functions, have the capacity to *inhibit* impulses to action coming from 'lower down' in the brain. Yet, in a further complication, the cortex is not a single entity: it contains two distinct hemispheres with distinct ways of processing experience—mostly working cooperatively, but on occasion almost like two different 'people' within each of us. A lateralised brain is not unique to humans: farmyard hens use the right side of their brains to detect danger, and the left to search for food.[11] But in human beings, the two hemispheres have evolved complex, multi-dimensional specialisations, and here I follow McGilchrist's recent summary of what we know about these differences. It is right hemisphere that seems to represent and enhance the functions of the older 'brains', while the left hemisphere adds a new set of functions—most notably, language itself, along with cause-effect reasoning, and the capacity to become a 'spectator' of one's own actions and feelings.

In the last twenty years, neurological research has moved in new directions. We have discovered just how much duplication of functions there can be within the brain—between reptile and mammal brains, between the cortex and older 'brains', even between the two hemispheres themselves. However, MacLean's notion of a 'triune' brain—three brains in one—remains a useful shortcut to understanding for non-experts. Accretion (adding on) is the means by which life, even at cellular level, builds complexity.[12]There is abundant evidence for the principle that human culture *builds on and elaborates what is already there, adding new structures, rather than eliminating older ones.* A computer analogy may help: a modern PC offers us the old 'keyboard shortcuts' *and* point-and-click options via a mouse. Touch-screen activation is now rapidly supplementing mouse-driven drag-and-drop functions. Our machine offers us two or even three ways of achieving the same end, some 'older' and some 'newer'.

In this book, I have used the term 'Old Brain' as a convenient label for the instinctive behaviour patterns that have evolved in earlier forms of life, and which continue to function in humans too—the archaic functions of the reptile and mammal brains, which Freud thought of as 'drives' and located in the 'Id'. Insofar as the right hemisphere carries forward many of these automatic functions, I have considered it, too, part of the Old Brain. Strictly, the right hemisphere (and particularly its frontal lobe) embodies sophisticated functions which are beyond the capacity of other animals, and consequently it could equally be claimed to be part of the 'New Brain'. Nevertheless, it is the right hemisphere which (in humans as in hens) warns us of *danger* via the primitive emotion of *fear*, and hence channels survival instincts. (The right hemisphere can also be suffused with *grief*—which in humans we might think of as *existential sadness*, a key emotion for story makers, which we'll revisit in Chapter 2.) It sees the world in 'wholes', not parts, in 'wide shot' (the 'wood' *and* the 'trees'). The right hemisphere offers us an instant judgment, a 'sureness', based on the *gestalts* (patterns) that it perceives, and the feelings that flood it. It notices, and values, *relationships*—between people, between inanimate objects. It thinks by associating images and feelings that 'belong together'—again, building complexity by accretion. The world of the right hemisphere is a 'here and now' world, a 'present tense' world without past or future. The 'self' of which the right hemisphere is aware is a self that is embedded within the world—not separate from it. What it experiences, coloured by emotion, seems intrinsically true and real, with 'no end, and no beginning'. Instead of *time*, the right hemisphere apprehends *space*, and later in this book, we'll see how this survives in the way that fairy tales use space to represent time.

By contrast, the left hemisphere of the cortex 'zooms in' with a close focus on particular *parts* of the environment, then builds up a picture of the world based on its 'research'. It tends to see individual trees, but not the 'wood'. It is able to *talk about* emotions (represent them in language) but not to *feel* them. It makes distinctions and draws boundaries—for example, between 'real' and 'not real', between 'child readers' and 'adult readers'. It builds complexity by categorizing, contrasting and arranging, rather than by accretion. It distinguishes past from present (*This happened to me once before but it isn't happening now*) and, as we'll see, is responsible for insisting that stories have *beginnings* and *endings*. The left hemisphere is the location of an 'observing self'—a self that is distinct from the world in which it is embedded, a self that can stand back and *reflect on itself.* My shorthand term for all these capacitiesis the 'New Brain'—with the proviso, as already noted, that the left hemisphere does not have a monopoly on 'newness'.

Both hemispheres are essential to story making—but in very different ways. For although the hemispheres send information back and forth all the time, and can if necessary duplicate many of each other's functions, they retain their separate identities to some extent, in the same way that the reptile and mammal brains do. Thus the human brain can usefully be thought of as a bit like the European Union—a federation of unique, individual states with their own languages and monetary systems which have cautiously merged some of their individual powers and jurisdictions via a common parliament and a common currency (of course such analogies cannot be pushed too far). Alternatively, we could see the two hemisphere brain as embodying the same principle of 'checks and balances' as the U.S. constitution: it can sometimes ensure more rational outcomes and guard against risk, but it can also result in inaction and *irrational* outcomes.

It is the triune brain with its bicameral cortex that is responsible for many of the features of story that make it so fascinating—and so puzzling. Why do we *react* to stories almost as if they were 'real' when in fact we 'know' they are not? Why do many people confuse the actors who play fictional characters with the characters themselves? Why do writers claim that their stories 'have nothing to do with their own lives' when in fact their works have *everything* to do with their own lives? Why do we reject some works of fiction as 'incredible' or 'unrealistic' when real human lives contain things just as incredible—or even more incredible? All of these things make sense in terms of the brain structures and functions we've been discussing. In particular, such puzzles come about because under certain conditions the functions of the New Brain are temporarily suspended, and for a short time, the Old Brain holds sway.

****

In 1928 an inspirational teacher named Ernest Raymond wrote a little book called *Through Literature to Life*, which infectiously conveyed the author's enthusiasm for reading (closer to our own time, Roger Sale's *Fairy Tales and After* and Francis Spufford's *The Child that Books Built* have done something similar).[13] I could perhaps have titled my own book *Through Life to Literature*. Literature necessarily reflects the patterns of human lives—both conscious and unconscious—and only makes full sense when considered in this wider context. I shall also argue that stories, like all art, arise out of their creators' persistent, powerful emotions and inner quests, and that in this sense cannot be properly appreciated without awareness of the individual lives from which they spring. I'll show how the central experiences both of composing stories and 'remaking' them (as readers, listeners and viewers) *simulate biological experiences*—falling in love, giving birth, perhaps even letting go of life—and elicit the same emotions.

For much of my adulthood, psychology has been dominated by the cognitive paradigm. But, just as cognitive behavioural therapy fails to engage with the stubborn core of many human problems, so the assertion that story is a 'way of knowing' (true enough as far as it goes) seems somehow empty. Several times over the past twenty years, I struggled mightily to read Jerome Bruner's influential *Actual Minds, Possible Worlds*, of which the following extract is typical:

> 'Story must construct two landscapes simultaneously. One is the landscape of action, where the arguments are the constituents of action: agent, intention or goal, situation, instrument, something corresponding to a "story grammar". The other landscape is the landscape of consciousness: what those involved in the action know, think, or feel, or do not know, think, or feel. The two landscapes are essential and distinct: it is the difference between Oedipus sharing Jocasta's bed before and after he learns from the messenger that she is his mother.'[14]

This kind of analysis represents the brain's left hemisphere trying to make sense out of something created by the right. Not surprisingly, given how very differently the two hemispheres approach the world, the attempt is unsatisfactory. What Bruner calls the 'landscape of action' is how the right hemisphere apprehends the world; the 'landscape of consciousness' draws more upon the capacities of the left hemisphere to stand back from experience and observe it, but in practice (whether we are writing a story, or reading one) our *experience* of story involves little (if any) awareness of two different 'landscapes'. Bruner's abstractions come alive only when he briefly alludes to a *real* story—the tragedy of Oedipus, who has sex with his mother without realising who she is. Here is precisely the point: stories exist because they *convey meaning analogically*, without the necessity for analysis or conscious thinking. As soon as we attempt to convert that communication into 'digital' form (words, abstract concepts), it loses its power—the coach turns back into a pumpkin, the coachmen diminish into rats. While Mark Turner's more recent *The Literary Mind* acknowledges that stories communicate analogically, it is, despite its many literary examples, about cognitive processes rather than about literature, and 'story grammars', from Vladimir Propp's to the more recent contributions of 'narratology', illuminate much, but similarly fail to grapple with the *experiences* stories generate.[15]

Implicit in the cognitive paradigm is the assumption that it is the *thoughts* originated by the cerebral cortex that trigger our *feelings*, which in turn propel us into *actions*. This is as selective and misleading when applied to human beings' experience of literature as it is selective and misleading when applied to the kinds of human struggles that psychotherapy deals with. Any patient in therapy knows that *feelings* often come first, and *thoughts* then attach themselves to those feelings—that's precisely why it is so hard to 'manage' or 'control' feelings (the goal of therapy, according to the cognitive paradigm), and it's also why, for many of us, it is only within *a human relationship* (with a trusted therapist, or sometimes a trusted friend or partner) that we can feel safe enough to explore those seemingly overwhelming, out-of-control feelings, and, finally, reach some understanding of them, and in turn, greater control over them. In the experience of 'entranced reading' it is also *feelings* that are basic to our experience. Only after a story has stirred up our emotions will we start reflecting on them in a conscious way ('Why do I hate that woman, when she's only a made-up person in a story?'): right hemisphere activity precedes (by nano-seconds) the activity of the left.

Jaak Panksepp, Ukrainian-born American investigator of the brains of animals, has devoted much of his scientific life to uncovering the neural pathways located in the older parts of the brain, through which primary emotions flow.[16] His work makes it clear that the Old Brain contains the neuronal circuitry necessary to produce fear or rage even *before* some actual enemy arouses those feelings. In mammals who care for their young, newer emotions (in evolutionary terms) come on stream, playful joy, intense care for another being (which we humans might call 'love') and separation anxiety—the dreadful sense of aloneness and abandonment we experience when we are cut off from a loved one in some way. Particular combinations of brain chemicals are necessary for animals—and for us—to experience these feelings. In a final demonstration that emotions are primary and cognitions secondary, Panksepp reminds us that encephalic children (humans born without a cerebral cortex) can experience fear, anger, joy, and sadness *even though they have no 'thinking' brain at all.*[17]

We also know (and McGilchrist's summary of research into the separate functions of the two hemispheres confirms this) that in the human brain it is the right hemisphere that, as it were, 'conducts' these primitive emotions, because of its closer neuronal connection with the older layers of the brain that lie beneath the cortex. The right hemisphere seems to have evolved before the left, and is also somewhat larger than the left. Human evolution seems to be partly a matter of the left hemisphere gradually 'catching up' with the right, and then (perhaps) surpassing or dominating it. The same thing clearly happens in the development of the individual human being: many of the right hemisphere's capacities are present from birth, and they dominate the child's mental life until around two years of age. But the left hemisphere rapidly catches up, a process that continues through childhood and adolescence. We now know that the very last stages of brain maturation are not completed until well into middle adulthood, with the right hemisphere also acquiring new and more sophisticated capacities for which the word 'wisdom' seems more appropriate than 'knowledge'.

How all of this fits with the nature of story, and story making, is the subject that will unfold in the pages that follow, but at this point I will say that story—as a literary form, as a particular kind of experience—*originates in the right hemisphere*, and *offers a right hemisphere experience* to its listeners, readers or viewers. It is not a matter of the right hemisphere 'being creative' or 'governing creativity' (as is sometimes believed): both hemispheres are 'creative' in their own ways, just as both are 'conscious' in their own ways. Rather, the left hemisphere communicates digitally, putting together words and concepts to *represent* experience. In contrast, the right hemisphere creates *analogies* to experiences—instead of talking about joy, it *tells us a story that evokes joy*, just as a piece of music automatically evokes sadness, elation or blissful peace. Instead of telling us, the right hemisphere *shows* us. Psychotherapists talk of 'projective identification', where patients act so as to evoke in the therapist powerful, largely unconscious, feelings which they (patients) are unable to put into words. Story does the same: it creates in us experiences that communicate what the story maker has felt, but without making this explicit. What story offers us—a simulated world in which characters engage in actions, feel things, suffer and (perhaps) triumph—represents the right hemisphere's unique view of the world, a world that is whole, coherent, full of vivid sense impressions, replete with feeling, and imbued with intense significance. We become absorbed into this world, merge with its characters, 'live' the story—rather than observing it, or thinking about it, which would be the left hemisphere's mode.

Stories 'work' because they simulate the experience we all had in infancy, before the left hemisphere started to build a conscious self, separate from the world, able to observe it and reflect upon it. Australian novelist Patrick White said that childhood is 'the purest well from which the creative writer draws'.[18] But it is not only writers who grieve for the loss of that childhood vision and try to re-create it—most of us do. So the story impulse *originates* in the right hemisphere—producing little worlds that seem to be *going somewhere* even though they may never arrive anywhere (because we wake up, turn the TV off, or put the book down). But that is only half of the process of story making.

Adults' anecdotes about what happened to them at work that day may be of some interest to their partners or their friends; young children's stories may seem cute or even fascinating to their parents (though most parents seem to ignore them)—but neither will ever compel the interest of a wider audience. Just as the left hemisphere seems to have evolved first the capacities necessary for finding food (distinguishing the potentially edible from the inedible), then the skills necessary for making and using tools (picking out the *best* flints for chipping, and carefully shaping their cutting edge), and last but not least, the 'tool' of language itself, which enables us to communicate our thoughts and feelings to others in a myriad complex, sophisticated ways—so the left hemisphere of the cortex is ultimately responsible for turning shapeless, dream-like sequences of events into strongly patterned narratives that command interest and attention from people we do not know, and will never know, even, perhaps, from people in a future we will never inhabit.

Although Chapters 1 to 4 of this book trace the evolution of story making from infancy through to late adolescence, its span extends all the way to old age. And although it contains many references to children's authors and their stories (mainly ones that the critical left hemisphere would disapprove of), it is not a book 'about children's literature'. *It is a book about Story*—and, in the spirit of the right hemisphere, it takes a broad view of its subject, so that infant 'songstries' (see Chapter 1) are compared with Homer's *Iliad*, and fiction specifically addressed to children appears in the context of stories few children could read or understand. The right hemisphere sees what *is*, not what it thinks 'should be', and it is the left hemisphere that erects categories like 'children's literature' and 'adult literature', and then spends a lot of time and energy arguing about the differences. The significant distinction is that between the world views of the two hemispheres: *that* is real.

A word about the evidence on which this book is based: published studies of early childhood story making and response to stories are listed in the endnotes to Chapters 1 and 2. Where possible, I have cross-referenced young children's recorded responses to stories with similar thoughts and feelings expressed by adults (thirty biographies of writers were surveyed in this regard) in order to highlight the continuity of such experiences across the entire life span. My examples of stories composed by three year olds, nine year olds and adolescents are obviously a tiny selection from what is available, but they are typical in key ways. Where the nature of Story is concerned, there is a remarkable amount of common ground to be found, across genders, nationalities, times and places. Likewise, the parallels between the experience of the 'entranced reader' and the 'inspired writer' are, to my mind, inescapable. So, while 'hard' evidence of my conclusions—such as the scientific left hemisphere demands—is elusive, I hope that *Entranced by Story* makes up for this, not only in breadth of reference but also in 'depth'—the ability to recognise underlying patterns beneath surface differences.

I could go on and on (a sure sign that my right hemisphere is composing this chapter, even while I *think* I am in charge of it), but I'd rather leave the 'tale' to speak for itself. So, back to Hans Andersen. *Are we ready to begin? When we come to the end, we shall know more than we do now!*

Chapter One
'Bothe Blysse and Blunder'
How Stories Begin

'Where werre and wrake and wonder *Bi sythes hatz wont therinne,* *And oft bothe blysse and blunder* *Ful skete hath skyfted synne.'*	*'War and woe and wonder* *In turn have ruled our land.* *Both joy and dreadful danger:* *They're not at our command.*[1]

Creativity in the Crib

Sometime in the late 1950s, Ruth Weir's twenty-one-month-old son Anthony would chatter away quietly to himself when left alone in his cot for his day-time rest, or prior to going to sleep at night. Many toddlers do this, but few parents pay much attention to it. It sounds cute but it doesn't seem to make much sense, and mothers are usually too busy to sit and listen carefully—let alone record their child's 'babble'. Ruth Hirsch Weir, however, was a student of child language, and where other parents would hear their toddler uttering a random assortment of 'proper words', mixed with apparently meaningless sounds, Ruth Weir's tape recorder helped her to hear much more. 'There is linguistic sense in the child's nonsense: that is our conclusion', she wrote triumphantly at the end of her scholarly book *Language in the Crib.*[2]

Ruth Weir's audio tapes made it possible for her to write down, word for word, and sound for sound, exactly what her little boy had said in his pre-sleep 'babble'. Once this was done, something emerged that very clearly was not random, for certain words and phrases appeared repeatedly, often in the same order. It was not meaningless either, for even when the words did not make sense, *patterns of sound* were evident. Easiest to pick out, for those of us who are not experts in linguistics, are examples of 'rhyme'. Consistently, Anthony utters a word, and then (it seems) thinks of a word that 'sounds the same': sometimes the vowel is the same, sometimes both the vowel and one or more of the consonants are repeated ('full rhyme' in traditional literary terminology). Anthony is composing a kind of poetry—a primitive song. In one monologue, he makes the apparently nonsensical statement, 'blanket like a lipstick'. Now, a blanket is *not* 'like a lipstick' in any obvious way. But Weir noticed that the consonant sequences 'b-l' and 'k-t' in 'blanket' are *reversed* in 'lipstick' (where 'l-p' followed by 't-k'). The connecting phrase, 'like a' also contains the 'l . . . k' sequence from 'blanket'. It would seem that one set of sounds *suggested* the other to Anthony, and, in a way that seems playful yet almost purposeful, the child followed that suggestion. Of course, if 'blanket like a lipstick' were the only example, we could dismiss it as pure coincidence. However, Ruth Weir is able to multiply such examples. Anthony is *experimenting* with sound patterns, and not only sound patterns but grammatical patterns: trying them out, repeating them, reversing them, substituting new elements for the existing ones. If we think of a theme-plus-variations in music, this is exactly what Anthony is composing, only his 'notes' are the sounds of spoken English, and in fact, clear metrical patterns are evident in his monologue.

Little children play because it's fun, but their play also has a function. The 'function', however, is unconscious and instinctive. It can only be understood for what it is by the outside observer, not by the child who is doing the playing—or composing. When we listen back to a recording of Anthony, as his mother did, we can sometimes guess at the function his composition may have had for him. In one long, complex, pre-sleep composition which Weir analyses in depth, Anthony repeats the phrase 'daddy dance' several times, returning to it almost in the way that a theme returns in what musicians call a 'rondo' (the third movement of Beethoven's 'Waldstein' piano sonata is a well-known example). Anthony's phrase 'Daddy dance' exhibits the same repeated sound-patterns that we have just been discussing: the initial consonant-vowel combination (/dae/) appears in both words. But this particular phrase is not just sound-play, it *means something* in terms of the child's own life. According to Ruth Weir, Anthony's father rarely, if ever, danced. So perhaps 'Daddy dancing' was something the little boy had paid particular attention to because it was a once-off. We cannot be sure. Yet in the monologue, the phrase is linked with other references to 'daddy', almost to a 'daddy preoccupation'. While we cannot know exactly what concerned Anthony, he is clearly musing on, remembering, wondering about—his father.

All of us (child or adult) talk about something repeatedly *because it is important to us*, or because in some way it is *problematic*. Perhaps there is a conflict between what we want and what we can have. Let's imagine a possible conflict for Anthony: *Daddy danced once—it was fun—why doesn't he do it again? Is it my fault?* If there is such a conflict, we 'try' to deal with that conflict by worrying away at it (as a puppy worries a bone or a toy). I put the word 'try' in quotation marks because the trying is not really a conscious thing, but more of an unconscious urge, or instinct. We play with a number of different positions in relation to the conflict, openly acknowledging the thing that 'worries' us, then insisting that 'it doesn't worry us at all'. Antony is *shaping* his troubled feelings about Daddy into something—something that will perhaps offer him release, or satisfaction. Here, at the earliest beginnings of language, we can observe the start of this impulse to take a painful or perplexing subject and 'work it' into something ordered and meaningful, as a sculptor works a chunk of stone into a shape we recognise as a woman, or a lion. Is it possible that *an underlying emotional concern may fuel the narratives of young children, even though that concern is never explicitly voiced?*

What does it mean that a tiny child like Anthony can create something that embodies form, yet not have any awareness of that form, no conscious control over the process of its creation? This is a question that I believe cannot fully be answered from within the world of human art, or from within the human world itself. Think about the way a spider spins her web, for example. A spider has no 'mind' as we understand it, only pre-programmed instincts. Yet, without conscious purpose or planning, *the spider's web takes shape as a complex, often symmetrical structure*, with strong formal features that human observers can perceive.[3] That seems to be what is happening in Anthony's monologues. Now of course, a human child does have a brain, but at birth, the survival-oriented, pattern-geared right hemisphere is more 'operational' than its left, because a baby must first of all survive, and in order to do so, it needs the capacities of the Old Brain. It needs to *express its feelings*, and hence gain adult attention; and it needs to *perceive patterns* in the behaviour of the adults who care for it. By eighteen months, the left hemisphere has gained ground and is maturing rapidly, bringing with it the beginnings of language.

Given this early imbalance between the hemispheres, it shouldn't surprise us, then, that the earliest 'art form' that a toddler composes might take the form of *patterned sound*, for experts theorise that before human beings spoke, they 'sang' (much as birds and whales do). Music may be the right hemisphere's 'first language'.[4] (It may also be the last: Alzheimer's sufferers continue to respond to music after their capacity for speech has disappeared.) Nor should it surprise us that a toddler's compositions might express feelings—since emotion is also the province of the right hemisphere. Anthony's left hemisphere is maturing, and so *words* are part of the song—but as yet, the meaning of the song is inherent in its pattern. Trying to select out and analyse any particular group of words in the song will not do us much good, because the right hemisphere does not work that way. We need to look at the structure of the whole. 'Daddy dance' returns several times: that is the clue that alerts us to the possible meaning of Anthony's 'song'. But this is to anticipate. For now, we need to ask whether the principles that Weir deduced from one toddler can be generalised to other children, and other situations. I believe they can.

Sing a TV Broke, O Goddess!

In 1989, Katherine Nelson and several academic colleagues published a study of the numerous pre-sleep monologues of a little girl, Emily, between the ages of twenty-one months and three years. As with Anthony's 'Daddy dance', the centre of many of Emily's compositions is something puzzling or *charged with emotion*, even when their content seems mundane to us She does not tell us what she is feeling, she *shows* us in the pattern of her 'song'. In the following extract, Emily is distressed by a broken TV set, so she 'worries away at it':

> 'My broke my t-[i.e. 'TV']
> (re) pairman fix *it*
> maybe (re) pairman fix *that*
> fix *it*
> [*low voice*] (Poppy that)
> fix the car
> car not broken
> but the T-TV broke
> [*several lines omitted*]
> Emmy's repairman fixes her TV for her
> But the boys, the boy goes
> that's his TV
> why can't go my play get his TV?
> Doctor (Margot) some tee times
> that boy goes my bed that
> someone watches TV
> but the boy was bro- [*whispers*] broken broken
> have a tank
> I broken'
> [*remainder of this section omitted*][5]

Notice how Emily cycles back and back to the broken TV, hinting that she *herself* may have broken it (as indeed she may have believed she had), repeating in a dramatic whisper, 'broken, broken', and perhaps even identifying herself as 'broken'. The full significance of this concern with broken objects is something we'll explore in our next chapter. For now, I am simply emphasising that this child comes back and back over something *because it is problematic or distressing.* Emily's composition seems to alternate statements relating to 'brokenness' and statements about repairing the damage ('fixing'), and in this pattern we can see what is perhaps the earliest narrative structure: an alternation of opposites. In the quotation I placed at the head of this chapter (taken from the medieval romance, *Sir Gawain and the Green Knight*), the same alternation is present, from 'blysse' (which means roughly what it means today) to 'blunder' (which means 'misfortune' or 'disaster'). The poet is reminding us that in human history, good times are followed by bad times, and bad times by good. For Emily, 'broken' is followed by 'fix it'. For other children it might be 'go out' and 'come back home', or 'get hurt' and 'feel better'.

Anthony and Emily were doing something that many other small children have done, unnoticed and unreported by their parents, and later forgotten even by themselves. One who did not forget was the Scots author Robert Louis Stevenson, who in his mid-thirties was to write that greatest of all adventure stories, *Treasure Island*. A highly intelligent and extremely sensitive child, Stevenson remembered his childhood games and fantasies in great detail. Among the activities he records was this one, although unfortunately, he does not tell us how old he was:

> 'But the time when my mind displayed most activity was after I was put to bed and before I fell asleep. I remember these periods more distinctly and I believe *further back than any other part of my childhood*. I would lie awake *declaiming aloud to myself* my views of the universe *in something that I called singing although I have no ear*, and in a measure of my own although at that time I can have known nothing of verse. One of these *Songstries*, for so I named my evening exercises, was taken down by my father from behind the door, and I have seen it within the last few years. It dealt summarily with the Fall of Man, taking a view most inimical to Satan; but what is truly odd, it fell into a loose, irregular measure with a tendency toward the ten-syllable heroic line. *This*, as I am sure I can then have heard little or nothing but hymn metres, *seems to show a leaning in the very constitution of the language to that form of verse*; or was it but a trick of the ear, inherited from eighteenth century ancestors?' [italics mine][6]

We know that little Stevenson was exposed to a great deal of vivid sermonising about Sin and Hell from his nurse, Cummy, and that he was taken to church every Sunday, so it is natural enough that the subject of his 'songstry' was 'the fall of Man'. Today, this seems very odd and extremely precocious, but like Anthony and Emily, like the 'Trackton' children recorded by Shirley Brice Heath,[7] Stevenson simply used whatever he heard around him as raw material for his language play. The 'loose, irregular measure' (that is, metre, or rhythm) is typical of modern children too. Stevenson calls his compositions 'songstries', and these compositions *do* fall somewhere between song and story, between chant and conversation. In delivering them, the voice rises and falls, and 'characters' within the child's 'story' often speak in distinct, higher-pitched or more dramatic tones than the main 'narrative'. It appears that these young improvisers are, in a general sort of way, imitating the voices of adults when they tell stories, or read them aloud, but as Stevenson himself notices, they are not simply copying what they have heard. Like the spider's web, the songstry seems to come of its own accord, shaping itself as it goes along, and wandering in and out of strict rhythmical patterns. Left to itself, this is how the brain's right hemisphere, at this stage of development, expresses itself. I can think of no better term for these monologues than the one Stevenson himself coined. 'Songstries' they are, and although that is not the term modern psycholinguists use, I propose to adopt it in this book.

As Freud notoriously recognised, children in the first two years of life have powerful feelings, feelings that organise their reactions and shape their 'pretend play', even though as yet they have only an embryonic 'self'. Hence, the earliest 'stories' children create are driven by feelings, organised around feelings, *but have no recognisable 'hero' or 'heroine'*. For a story to have a clear protagonist, its teller must have a sense of self, and right-hemisphere dominated toddlers do not yet experience themselves as completely separate from the world around them. And although feelings *organise* toddlers' stories, they are rarely named as such, for to name our feelings, we need the fuller capacities of the left hemisphere, which are not yet available to a very young child. Antony does not say, 'I wish my daddy would dance again!'. Emily does not say, 'I feel bad because I might have broken my TV', but the form of their compositions *shows* us what they wish or fear, just as a child's play with dolls or toys will *show* a sensitive observer what the child's most pressing fears and wishes are. The right hemisphere *shows*; the left *tells*.

Relatively few parents read to their children as early as twenty-four months, but most of the carefully observed children we are meeting in this chapter had heard many stories. They had had multiple opportunities to internalise the shape of what scholars call a 'well formed story'. A well formed story has a beginning, a middle and an ending—a formula that Aristotle recommended in his *Poetics* more than two thousand years ago. A well formed story begins by introducing a protagonist (the 'hero') and one or more subsidiary characters, develops through a sequence of events that follow one another in time and are logically connected, and then concludes in a way that unmistakably tells us that 'the story is over'. Aristotle was thinking of the great dramas of Athens, like *Oedipus Rex* and *Antigone,* which ended tragically. In the stories our own culture has produced for children, conclusions are usually reassuring—whatever may have gone wrong is set to rights. Either way, there is a clear ending—as in the fairy tale formula, 'And they lived happily ever after'. Yet the young children we have observed here *do not seem to reproduce that sort of structure*. Their compositions do not begin in a clear way, nor do they end reassuringly. Were they imitating stories they had heard, but imperfectly?[8] Or were they creating something else? What was this 'something', and where did it come from? We have looked at the kind of composition that Anthony and Emily created 'in the crib', weaving words and sounds together into a set of variations on a theme. Let's turn now to the sorts of compositions that children create a little later, at three or four years of age—probably the age Stevenson was when his father took down his 'songstry' about the Fall of Man. By three and a half, many children are capable of making up 'a story' when asked to do so by an adult. Yet what most of them make up still does not correspond particularly closely to the stories they have heard, or seen on television.

The Earliest Narrative Structure?

'Once upon a time there was a birdie
One day a hawt [*hawk*] flew out of the sky and at [*ate*] the birdie
Oh, poor little birdie!
The next day a bid bodie [*big Bogie*] came out from behind the hill
And at up the hawt from [*for*] eating up the little birdie.'[9]

New Zealand novelist and poet Janet Frame was three-and-a-bit-years-old at the time she told this story, and her parents helped her to remember it by quoting it back at her, complete with her childish pronunciations. Janet's composition begins confidently with the fairy tale formula, 'Once upon a time', with which she is clearly familiar, and progresses through two stages—an action, and a reversal: the hawk eats the birdie, and then a Bogey eats the hawk (notice how, as in Anthony's songstries, the *sound* of 'birdie' suggests 'Bodie'). The story ends there, with 'blunder' followed by 'bliss' (sort of!). Adults like Janet's parents can recognise this as well formed story, and appreciate its precocity. But the average child's 'stories' at this age do not end so neatly or exhibit such an obvious structure. Instead, they consist of much longer sequences of 'happenings', in which each new event reverses the previous one. This more typical structure is clearly demonstrated in stories by two different four-year-olds quoted by Lucy Sprague Mitchell, who in the 1920s called on adults writing for young children to take more notice of preschoolers' spontaneous story making, and to incorporate its features when writing for them. The comments in square brackets are my own.

[Story One]

'Once there was a table
and he was taking a walk [*initial situation*]
and he fell into a pond of water [*situation reversed: misfortune*]
and an alligator bit him [*elaboration of reversal*]
and then he came up out of the pond of water [*misfortune rectified*]
and he stepped into a trap that some hunters had set for him, [*situation reversed: new misfortune*]
and turned a somersault on his nose.' [*continuation of the previous, or perhaps intended as a reversal*]

[Story Two]

There was a new engine and it didn't have any headlight [*initial situation: misfortune stated*]
its light wasn't open in its headlight [*misfortune restated*]
so its engineer went and put some fire in the wires and made a light. [*situation reversed: misfortune rectified*]

And then it saw a lot of other engines on the track in front of it. [*new situation, misfortune implied*]
So when it wanted to puff smoke and go fast it told its engineer
and he put some coal in the coal car. [*situation reversed: misfortune rectified*]
And then the other engines told their engineers to put coal in their coal cars [*restatement of reversal, with new protagonists*]
and then they all could go [*restatement as conclusion*][10]

Lucy Mitchell saw a big difference between these two stories. The hero of the first is a 'table', but soon the events seem to be happening to a human or an animal; and the incidents are not linked in any logical way. It is more like a dream than a 'proper story'. By contrast, she thought that the second storyteller was able to make 'scientific' (by which she meant 'cause-effect') connections between things (the engineer puts 'fires in the wires' to make the engine's light 'open'). Clearly, the second 4-year-old's story represents a higher level of maturity in the left hemisphere—but at a structural level the stories are virtually identical: *both* stories describe a series of situations and reversals.[11] The pattern is also prominent in fairy tales. Red Riding Hood's grandmother may be hungry, so Red Riding Hood is sent to visit her with some tasty food; a Queen has no child, then unexpectedly, she gives birth to one. Red Riding Hood is about to be eaten; the woodcutter rescues her; and so on. The difference between fairytales and the average three- or four-year-old's narrative, however, is that fairy tales (like little Janet Frame's story, and the second of Lucy Mitchell's four-year-olds) conclude in a way that we adults *recognise as an ending*, rather than a temporary pause in an ongoing sequence (as in the first Mitchell story).

Psychoanalyst Otto Kernberg believed that infants initially categorise experiences into those that feel pleasant and those that feel uncomfortable or painful.[12] Could it be that, years later, a child is still powerfully influenced by this early template, organising experience into the alternation of 'good' and 'bad', 'nice' and 'nasty'? Earlier in the twentieth century, the French psychologist Henri Wallon had argued that *les couples* (paired opposites, like a statement and its reversal) represented the earliest cognitive structure—in other words, young children construct stories dialectically, in the same way that they organise all their experiences: 'either this or that', 'either good or bad'. Perhaps this is the earliest of the myriad *categories* which the left hemisphere will later set up.[13]

We surmise that the most primitive layers of the brain—certainly the 'reptile brain' and probably the mammal brain too—are essentially timeless, aware only of immediate events and impressions in the 'here and now'. Corresponding with this, the earliest 'Old Brain stories' (like those of Anthony and Emily) lack clear introductions and conclusions. Each 'ending' leads straight into a new beginning. As the capabilities of the cerebral cortex (and particularly, of the left hemisphere) gradually come on stream in the growing child, so too does the capacity to comprehend what an 'end' means. Children can then begin to produce 'proper endings', a step towards producing narratives that adults recognise as well formed stories. A story with a beginning and an end is the first major modification that young children make in the Old Brain narrative pattern which appears to be their default setting. At first, the endings may still seem unrelated to what has come before. Three year olds declaim 'the End', on the model of adult-composed stories, without really understanding how a conclusion is the logical outcome of the events that have preceded it. But they have taken their first step on their way to an understanding of what conclusion actually means. *Children imitate [repeat] the form before they can comprehend the meaning.*

The evidence we have offered so far in this chapter suggests that perhaps young children possess inbuilt templates for arranging sounds, then words and finally, incidents, into patterned structures, just as spiders are born with the instinct to spin their webs in consistent, organised ways. These structures do not come solely from the children's attempts to reproduce or copy the structures of the 'proper stories' that adults present to them (although a minority of children, like Janet Frame, may be able to do so). An innate structure seems to come first, its 'meaning' inherent in its very pattern, and seemingly dictated by something of emotional significance to the child 'narrator'. These are Old Brain narratives, creations dominated by the right hemisphere. By the ages of four or five, as the left hemisphere begins to catch up with the right, this early structure is beginning to be modified in the direction Aristotle considered so basic to story making.

As I hinted earlier, this mysterious business becomes clearer if we search for evidence from outside the verbal world of human beings. Take, for example, the play of young mammals—from rodents right through to young wolves and lion cubs.[14] One youngster runs away, encouraging the other to chase him/her; the roles are then reversed, with the chaser running away, and the pursued becoming the pursuer. As Brian Boyd points out, story (like all art forms) is a sophisticated form of play, and animal play can be seen as a two-part 'composition' performed in actions rather than represented in words.[15] Something here confirms Wallon's ideas about binary structures. Sophisticated human play, such as a football game, has much the same structure. It is an endless chain of pursuits and reversals, as one team gains temporary possession of the ball and attempts to score, until the other regains the ball and takes the movement back into their opponents' half of the field.

Or, think of a puppy wanting its human owner to throw a ball. The puppy runs towards the ball where it lies on the ground, and look up expectantly, whines, wags its tail, or makes other signals to say that it wants the ball to be thrown. If the owner fails to take the hint, the puppy may act differently, first running away from the ball, and then running back towards it. Is this, fundamentally, what children are doing in their little 'songstries' when they state, then reverse; or state, then repeat? Like the puppy, they are, first and foremost, engaging in enjoyable play. Yet, just as in a football match, they are also striving for mastery, to tackle something that challenges them. They move towards understanding something by saying it 'out in the clear' ('my broke my TV'), but then they 'unsay it', or say the opposite ('maybe 'pairman fix *that*'), perhaps to reassure themselves. The 'game' surges first one way, and then the other. 'The engine doesn't have a light . . . that's bad. I wish it did . . . here's how it could be 'fixed' . . . Oh-oh, the other engines missed out . . . that's bad . . . ' and so on, and on.

In Old Brain narratives, *actions are more important than who is doing them, or whom they are done to*: 'protagonists' can shift several times in the course of a short composition (a 'table' may turn into a human being, a 'bear' into a boy). It is common for preschool narrators to begin their compositions in the third person ('Once there was a bear who lived with his Mommy . . . ') because they know that most stories are told in the third person. However, within a very short time, the narrator abruptly shifts to the first person, and the 'bear' is nowhere to be seen ('But I got tired, so I went to sleep'). This fact shows us very clearly that only a single point of view is involved in Old Brain narratives, no matter how many characters there appear to be, and that all characters are really versions of (variations of) the protagonist.[16] This is exactly what seems to be happening in Iris Murdoch's final novel *Jackson's Dilemma*, when the author's own confused, despairing feelings permeate every one of her fictional characters, as we'll see in chapter seven.

In most songstries, *there is hardly any description* of anyone or anything. *There is no inner life: nobody thinks or feels* anything. Expressed emotion is absent, or extremely rare. Yet, as we've seen, emotion (in the broad sense of 'affective arousal') seems to propel the construction of story. This becomes clearer from the third year of life onwards, although, as we saw earlier in this chapter, underlying emotion may also drive the compositions of younger children—it is simply that with younger children, there may be no words that signal emotion.[17] Logical connections between one event and another, one character and another, may be missing: but underneath the surface of the narrative, with its dizzying alterations of protagonist, scene and incident, we are going to find an emotionally-charged theme, which will remain the same, even though it may wear many disguises.

This is precisely what happens in dreams. Despite their bizarre images and bewildering juxtapositions, dreams make sense: but only when we can decode the underlying pattern, a pattern which, very often, will have some emotional significance for the dreamer. Last night, I dreamed I was in a room containing a large wood stove, which was burning fiercely, piled high with more logs despite the comparatively warm night. On waking it was easy to see that my right hemisphere had come up with this image because I had been too hot under my blankets. Later the same night, a different dream 'scene' offered me a different representation of 'something wrong', a sequence in which my wife,

I, and a young woman crawled along a flimsy, narrow bridge over a river, and the young woman fell in, my wife and I attempting to hold her head above the water. Once again there was danger or discomfort, but this time embodied, not in a single image, but in *a series of dramatic actions*. This is what dreams do: they represent experiences and feelings as primitive 'narratives' which contain a consistent pattern, but do not ever make its meaning explicit, for dreams, like songstries, communicate in the manner of the unaided right hemisphere.

Without specific knowledge of a particular child and his or her circumstances, we can rarely be certain of what the underlying 'theme' of a songstry is. This is why parents' regular, disciplined, dispassionate observations of their own children (on which much of the next chapter will also be based) are so important. Nobody else is in a position to know what may be important to *this* preschooler, what has recently happened in her life, what she may be distressed or puzzled about. Of course, there are many occasions when even parents or caregivers do not know what is going on. The themes of many songstries will forever remain mysterious to us. But in the story told by Lucy Mitchell's second four-year-old, there is a clear concern with having power, of being able to 'keep up' with others—not a surprising theme for any four-year-old to be expressing, though not every four-year-old is going to share that concern to the same degree.

To better understand the nature of Old Brain narratives, we need now to make a dizzying leap back through millennia, from modern children's loosely-constructed, spontaneous 'chants' to a great work of art, a monument to a long tradition of heroic songs composed by sophisticated adult artists whose only seeming resemblance to modern preschool children rests in the fact that they could neither read nor write.

From Emily to Achilles

Homer's *Iliad*, the 'Song of Ilion', stands like a great, weatherworn portal at the very beginning of Western literature.[18] Like the Lion Gate at Mycenae with its enormous, unmortared stones, the *Iliad* suggests a world we have lost, and the exact details of how it was constructed remain a mystery. The Ionian Greek in which it was first written down (who knows how long after it had first been declaimed to live audiences by professional 'song-weavers') was as different from the classical Greek of fifth-century Athens as eighteenth-century English—the English of Henry Fielding's *Tom Jones*—is from ours. Even the names are confusing: the epic is called the 'Iliad' in English, because '[W]ilion' or '[W]ilios' was one name by which the Greeks referred to the city the Hittite Empire knew as 'Wilusia'. But it was also called 'Troia' [Troy], the name we usually use in English. It is possible that one name referred to the city, and the other to the region governed from that city (much as 'Washington brokers peace deal' means, 'The *United States* brokers peace deal').

We all know that the *Iliad* is about the great fight between the Greeks and the Trojans, but Homer refers to the Greeks as the *Archaioi* (Archaians) or *Argeioi* ('Argives') and calls their opponents, the Trojans, *Dardanoi*, a name preserved in 'the Dardanelles', our modern name for the region. In English, we commonly say that it was Paris, a Trojan prince, who abducted Helen, thus provoking the Trojan War, yet in the poem, Paris is more often called 'Aleksandros'—a Greek name. Homer himself, who we think of as the author of the poem, was almost certainly not the person who actually wrote down the version we now know as the *Iliad*—a person who may even have been a woman. And whoever Homer actually was, if he ever existed, we know virtually nothing about him—or her. The great story exists regardless of who 'made' it—just as many great stories since have outlived their creators, and inspired sequels and imitations by others, whose names are long forgotten.

All of these puzzles and conundrums are in one way or another related to the fact that the *Iliad* originated as an oral epic—a long story in verse which was not memorised word for word, but improvised by a 'singer' or *rhapsodos* (song-weaver), in the days before writing existed. Such narratives were passed down by one singer to another, across many generations, but because they were never written down, their details constantly altered. The real Siege of Troy (and we now have reason to believe that there probably was one, although it was almost certainly very different from the one described in the *Iliad*) occurred centuries before the writing down of the story as we have it now. Doubled and tripled names, and many inconsistencies, all point to a story that has been passed down orally over hundreds of years, and adapted to make it fit the time, place and audience of each individual performance.

Such long narratives of 'the deeds of men' were always told in verse, not prose. Why? Verse was traditionally considered 'higher' and more dignified than the looser, more colloquial language of everyday speech. It was thought of as divine in origin (that is, it came from the Gods, in fact, it was *dictated by Gods* to the 'singer'). If music was indeed the 'first language of the right hemisphere', as McGilchrist suggests, it would make sense that verse would be viewed as 'God-given', something older and holier than the common speech of men. But above all, from the performer's point of view, verse is *easy to remember*—a regular metre not only gives shape to each line but also serves to remind the singer of what comes next.

A couple of contemporary analogies may help. Today's rap artists also 'chant' their songs over a steady beat, and (unlike Greek *aoidoi*) employ a regular, simple *rhyme* as well. Of course, an epic song is immeasurably more complex and sophisticated than a set of rap lyrics, yet the comparison has its uses. Both forms are delivered 'live', and the audience's response may influence the performance. Rappers half-sing, half-speak their lyrics, and this is probably how the *rhapsodoi* 'sang' as well, accompanying themselves with regular strumming on the lyre. As we've seen, half-singing, half-talking is how preschool children declaim their spontaneous 'songstries'. Today's TV reporters also 'chant': the short lines into which the teleprompter breaks sentences leads to 'singsong' diction, with accents sometimes falling on unimportant words. And this sort of 'verse', flowing onwards with its predictable phrases, is also *trance-inducing*. Both singer and listener enter an altered state of consciousness, where 'woven words' create a sort of spell, compelling attention, and binding teller and audience together so that the story becomes 'real' for the duration of the performance.

These days, ancient Greek has almost completely disappeared from the school and university curriculum. The vast majority of us encounter *The Iliad* only in translation, and English verse is so different in technique and effect that translating Homer into English is like substituting unyielding steel for the sheen of softer bronze. An English translation that works in its own terms, for its own times, can be revelatory. When the Romantic poet John Keats read Chapman's seventeenth-century version of the *Iliad*, he compared his sense of awe to the feelings of the Spanish conquistador Cortez,

> 'When with eagle eyes,
> He stared at the Pacific, and all his men
> Looked at each other with a wild surmise—
> Silent upon a peak in Darien.'

Balboa, not Cortez, was the first Spaniard to 'stare at the Pacific', but Keats had either misremembered the facts, or, more probably, opted for 'Cortez' because its two syllables fitted his metre, whereas 'Balboa' would have left him with an extra syllable, crippling the 'swing' of the verse. And that principle (that the musical form sometimes dictates the content, rather than the other way around) was something that profoundly affected Homer's original Greek composition too. Our own equivalent of Chapman, perhaps, is Stanley Lombardo. Listening to Lombardo read aloud his own version of the *Iliad* is a powerful experience which—to the degree any mere translation can accomplish—'lifts us out' of our own time and place, and into another, while at the same time highlighting the humour, the surprising informality and the rapid-fire action that we moderns can relate to in Homer, for all the alienness of his setting and his assumptions.

For indeed, the world of the Achaians is remote and alien from ours in many ways. Gods—immortal, although not 'all-powerful' by any means—appear suddenly beside humans, speak out of clouds, or 'morph' for short periods into human shape. Homer's human heroes, who otherwise comport themselves not unlike some of today's highly paid sporting stars, regard these Godly encounters as an honour, although not always a welcome one. When the Immortals decree that a hero must die, he calmly accepts his fate, for when death comes, a true hero must above all face death with *panache* and dignity, so that his brave deeds or splendid final words will be sung for centuries after his end. The opening lines of the *Iliad* instantly convey the relative status of heroes and Gods:

'Sing rage through me, Oh Goddess—
Achilles' fateful rage that brought
The Greeks such heavy loss,
Sent so many down to darkness,
Their bodies fit for nothing but to serve
As food for dogs, or carrion:
For thus the will of Zeus was done.
Begin your song with how
Great Agamemnon first fell out
With near-divine Achilles,
And tell us which of the Immortal Gods
It was who caused their fight.'[19]

It is an Immortal Goddess who is to 'sing' the great story *through* the poet the audience see in front of them. And, even though its stated subject is a conflict between two men, a very *human* conflict over a desirable young woman, this conflict and its consequences are ultimately instigated not by their own rivalrous feelings, but by another Immortal, Apollo. Apollo 'puts into them' the feelings of jealousy and rage that they then act out on one another. As Julian Jaynes showed, we glimpse a state of consciousness in which feelings may be stirred up within us by a Presence completely external to us, in which *we may not 'own' our own thoughts and feelings at all*—in the same way as the *rhapsodos* does not 'own' the words that come from his mouth during a performance. In the Trojan War, first the Greeks seem to prevail, then the Trojans, not because one side or the other is stronger or more cunning, but because particular Gods have intervened, and lent courage, cleverness or abnormal strength to individual heroes on either side. So greatly have things changed that a mental state that we moderns equate with schizophrenia seems to have been 'normal' for Homer's people, at least, if we take him literally. However, Homer's assumption that it was a Goddess who sang the *Iliad* rather than him is something that we will encounter again and again throughout this book—as modern story makers, too, speak of stories 'coming to them' or 'insisting on being told'. They don't believe any Goddess is involved, but nor are they simply being metaphorical: it really does feel to them as if their inspiration comes from outside themselves. This kind of consciousness has not been left behind with the ancient Greeks. It represents the experience of the brain's right hemisphere, operating in temporary independence of the left—not just in little children, but also in fully mature, conscious adults.

Homer's huge epic, more than fifteen thousand lines long, does not even contain the story of the 'Wooden Horse', the one incident that most people now associate with the Trojan War—for that incident happened *after* the events narrated in the *Iliad*, and is actually told in *The Odyssey.* At the end of the *Iliad*, the Siege of Troy is still unfinished, the war not yet won—although once Achilles has killed Hector, the great Trojan hero, the doom of the city is already sealed. Nor does the *Iliad* begin with the Judgment of Paris, which modern readers consider the 'logical' starting point of the entire narrative. It is not that the *Iliad* is shapeless or truncated: it has a shape of its own, with its own logic. The cycle of tales concerning Troy could begin at any point, because a singer could rely upon most listeners already knowing the great deeds of Hector, Achilles, Agamemnon, and 'Wily Odysseus', hero of *The Odyssey.*

Like other epic songs that are handed down in preliterate cultures, the *Iliad* is constructed partly of 'formulas'—standard, memorised phrases that could be used again and again. 'Agamemnon, ruler of men' is one such formula; 'black ships', 'rosy-fingered Dawn' and 'wine-dark sea' are further examples. Many of them consist of a noun with its attached descriptor, the whole forming a phrase of two or three words that contains the correct number of long and short syllables to make up half of a Greek hexameter line—sometimes a whole one. (Keats' 'stout Cortez' was a deliberate imitation of this sort of formula. Keats, incidentally, did not mean that Cortez was 'fat'. An older meaning of 'stout' was 'bold', and English poets made frequent use of archaic words and meanings, for exactly the same reasons that Homer did: *because they fitted the metre,* or provided variety). Homeric 'formulas' were memorised and handed down from one singer to another because they could be readily slotted into place as lines of verse were declaimed. Other formulas ('Answering this, he said' or 'He spoke winged words') connected one speaker's words with the next, for the *Iliad* is full of speeches, lively and passionate. In fact, it could be said that the *Iliad* is largely made up of *actions* and *conversations.* Sometimes the formulas contain a complete action: a hero's death in battle, for example, is conveyed by 'he bit the cold bronze' (as in our colloquialism, 'bit the dust').

The formulas filled in part of a verse line automatically, rather as a mobile phone in 'TXT' mode anticipates the word you intend as soon as you select an initial letter or two. This may have given the 'singer of tales' a slight breathing space to think ahead to the next half line, and so on. Oral-formulaic composition is neither recited word for word, from memory, nor completely improvised. The epic 'singer of tales' retold a *familiar* story, using a combination of traditional, memorised phrases and 'new' (or at least, non-formulaic) expressions. That combination would carry the narrative forward along a well worn path, in a slow, stately progression. As with the improvised grace-notes and ornaments in Baroque music, there was room for each performer's creativity and judgment—but within firm parameters of predictability. For example, unique to the *Iliad* and the *Odyssey* is a particular kind of description, the long 'Homeric simile', in which one thing is likened to another in an elaborate, highly pictorial comparison. Each new performance would be different, yes, but no singer would dare to alter the main outlines of the story itself.

Often, the poet of the *Iliad* makes a fairly short, simple statement, then simply adds another statement to the first, with no connecting words whatever. Thus, instead of saying, 'Achilles ran swiftly *so that* he could reach the ships', Homer's Greek will literally say, 'Fleet-footed Achilles ran; he reached the ships'. This method of sentence construction, called 'paratactic' by grammarians, is typical of oral composition. Homer may produce long 'verse paragraphs', but for the most part their overall structure is very simple. 'He did this, he did that: this happened, that happened; he spoke, she answered'. The *Iliad* is, by our standards, extremely *repetitive*. It says something, then it says the same thing again, in different words. Set-piece scenes (a quarrel between heroes, or a stranger being entertained to dinner, or a conversation between a God and a mortal) appear again and again. When anyone is instructed to take a message to someone else, the message is first told to the messenger, and then repeated word for word by the messenger to the recipient—even though every listener would already know what the messenger was going to say. This, too, is part of the way that oral composition works. Just as each wave of the incoming tide starts to recede, but is overtaken by the next, so the oral poet moves his narrative slowly forward, covering and re-covering the same ground. Pre-school songstries do not do this, exactly, but they do employ a lot of repetition, and for the same reason. When you are not sure what to say next, repeating something you've already said fills in the space, and gives you time to think of what might follow. It also 'thickens' the composition, by adding emphasis. It might even be said that repetition is the earliest form of description.

Children who have heard numerous stories read aloud to them are also able to employ 'formulas': three-year-old Janet Frame knew how to begin her story with 'Once upon a time'. Other children have memorised formulas like 'But it was too late', or 'Everything was quiet'. They can introduce new incidents with 'Then' or 'So', or 'Next day'. They may press into service entire chunks of memorised material from stories that are already familiar to them. Often, the chunk does not fit its new context all that well, and that, too, is similar to Homer, whose formulas may at times fill metrical requirements at the cost of realism (although 'realism' as we understand it isn't really in question, as we'll shortly see). Hypothetically, a particular hero might be described as 'well armed' when in fact, he is not, at that moment, wearing any armour or carrying a weapon. In other words, the needs of the verse form temporarily override the appropriateness of the meaning (as in Anthony's 'blanket like a lipstick', pattern comes first, and meaning is less important). This is not wholly a matter of technical considerations, however. It is part of the world-view of Homer (and other oral poets) that although individual heroes are being celebrated in song, and although specific deeds and words are associated with them, *what they have in common with other heroes is at least as important as what distinguishes them as individuals*. It is going much too far to say that any hero is interchangeable with any other, but the attributes of heroes, and the types of actions they perform, often *are* interchangeable. Their 'heroic status' is ultimately what is affirmed by the epic. Homer's formulas tell us about universals, not particulars. Scholar Moses Finley put it well: 'All maidens had lovely hair. Ships were hollow, lyres were shrill, all singers achieved fame, and all singers bestowed fame on men and gods'.[20]

The preschool narrators we met earlier in this chapter use hardly any adjectives at all. But fairy tales, of which we'll have more to say in our next two chapters, use adjectives in a similar way to Homer. A witch is always 'wicked', a princess is always 'beautiful', and so on. *This is how things are, this is the nature of the world*—that is what we are being told. At the age of two or three, we think, a child actually *perceives* people and things in this 'essentialist' way: good or bad, pretty or ugly, happy or unhappy. That is, in part, why young children respond strongly to fairy tales, even when they cannot yet fully understand them.[21] The ability to see 'shades of grey', to perceive human beings as a mix of good and bad, beautiful and ugly, comes only later, as the New Brain continues to mature. As in three year old songstries, logical discussions of possible courses of action are largely absent in Homer: 'Instead there are *arguments* in which each side seeks to overpower the other by threats, and to win over the assembled multitude by emotional appeal, by harangue, or by warning'.[22] In other words, Homeric arguments are simply a verbal form of combat—exactly as in modern parliamentary 'debate'. They are about survival, not truth, superiority, not good sense.

In the *Iliad*, and other heroic epics, there is a great deal more description than in preschool children's spontaneous compositions, but by our standards, this description is very selectively deployed. Armour, weapons, feasts and ceremonies of various kinds are described over and over again, but many other things—more important to our modern way of thinking—are not described at all. We are never told, for example, what Achilles, Odysseus, Paris or Hector actually *look* like, beyond formulaic phrases like 'swift-running' or 'red-haired'. The great city of Ilion is never described; it is simply 'windy', 'well-built', or 'high-walled'. In the *Iliad*, directions, distances, and speeds are vague in the extreme. Numbers of men and ships are reported in fine detail, but the numbers seem implausible, and the details do not add up to a coherent picture. Homer's descriptions are not designed to evoke the visual appearance of particular people, places and events in the minds of his listeners, as modern descriptions are. Instead, they are there to lend lustre to key events that are central to the heroic life. That a particular hero or petty King brings with him '40 black ships' (each presumably crowded with warriors) is a statement about his *importance*, not a statement of fact, or one with any real military significance. All of this is *description according to the right hemisphere*, for the latter is concerned with the essence of things rather than with the exact details of their surface appearance (which is the concern of the left hemisphere). Similarly, the battles that rage on the plain before Troy, with first the Achaians and then the Trojans achieving temporary mastery, are not factual accounts of an actual sequence of battles. Instead, they are designed to exemplify the *essence* of battle, and to showcase brave and pathetic deaths. Such a purpose fits a sweeping narrative in which fortunes change regularly, and the winners become the losers. Yet can we not, on this great canvas, see some similarity to the structure of situation/reversal that we have observed in the stories of three-year-olds in our own culture? Could it be that even in Homer's great epic, the form, the structure, has partly dictated the content, rather than the other way around?

The *Iliad* ends, not with Odysseus' improbable strategy of the Wooden Horse, and the subsequent capture of Troy, but with the funeral games for Achilles' closest friend Patroclos, and the burial by the Trojans of their great hero, Hector. A small child retelling a story of significance to her leaves out a lot of the original, but focusses on its *emotional* 'high points'.[23] So does Homer in retelling the story of the siege of Troy. When twentieth-century authors (from the critically-despised Enid Blyton to the critically-approved Rosemary Sutcliff) have retold the *Iliad* in English for today's children, their versions have almost invariably chosen a different beginning and ending point to Homer's.[24] The story has been re-arranged, so that it begins in the *logical* place (for a modern audience), with the Judgment of Paris, and the Trojan prince's subsequent abduction of Helen; and it ends with the *logical* conclusion: the wooden horse, the capture and burning of the city, and the reunion of Helen with Menelaus of Sparta. There seems some deep-seated pressure here to correct what is 'wrong' with Homer's epic, to put events in their rightful, chronological order, and to end the story in a 'decisive' way, as 'proper stories' end. Is this only happening because our era believes that children need 'simple' stories with clear beginnings and endings? Well, no. The literate narrators of later antiquity, writing for adults, felt the same need to make the *Iliad* into a 'proper story' as Blyton and Sutcliff, writing for today's children, do. What we are seeing here is the left hemisphere of the brain 'taking over' and 'correcting' a right hemisphere-dictated narrative—turning something endless and shapeless into a well formed story.

Where We've Come From, Where We're Going

Whoever he or she was, the poet of the *Iliad* was a highly-trained artist, consciously aware of what he (or she) was doing. Preschool composers of 'song-stries' are finding their way, with very limited resources of language and understanding, and without any training whatsoever, except exposure to the songs, stories and conversations that surround them. I am not equating the two as art. I am suggesting that there are compositional principles in common, which owe their existence to the nature of oral narrative. Clearly, there is a yawning gulf between what literate people have come to expect in a story and the nature of oral storytelling. Whether the oral narrators are peasants telling fairy tales, preschool children sleepily spinning words into patterns, or a great *aoidos* declaiming an epic song from a distant heroic age, oral composition taps something deep and disturbing, something that obstinately slips away from the conscious, reflecting mind of the left hemisphere. This 'something' stems from the survival-oriented reptile and mammal brains, carried forward by the right hemisphere. I call it Old Brain storytelling.

Old Brain storytelling lacks a sense of time. Its structure is an endless series of actions and reversals, it is driven by emotion but rarely articulates that emotion in words, and its characters shift and change. It produces dreams. It is largely responsible for the songstries chanted by preschool children like Anthony, Emma or the little R. L. Stevenson, compositions which are only partly under their conscious control. It dictates most of the structure and many of the conventional features of fairy tales. Its patterns constitute 'deep magic from the dawn of time',[25] about which our rational left hemispheres *could* ask logical questions, but which more often, we simply accept, swept along by these patterns that seem so compelling, so inevitable, that in Coleridge's famous phrase, we 'suspend disbelief', and follow them wherever they lead, with rapt attention—*entranced.* In chapter five, we will return to the way that the 'oral style' remains a potent force, even in the psychological novels of the modern era.

In our next chapter, we'll see how narratives intended especially for young children pose threats and challenges to children in the fourth year of life, despite the authors' attempts to avoid such distress. We'll see, too, how the maturing cerebral cortex of the child assists her to defend against the threats offered by fictional damage, loss, and negation. Yet, just as Homer's great armies surge back and forth before Troy, so children's victories over the 'deep magic' of the Old Brain are only temporary. It will continue to be this way as we grow up. Indeed, it will remain this way for the rest of our lives.

Chapter Two

'A Hole in the World'

Self and Story in the Preschool Years

Most adults who have read or told a story to children are immediately struck by their young listeners' intense absorption. Children demand to hear the same story again and again, and greet predictable events and repeated words with glee. When the adult reader is also a trusted person, such as a parent, older sibling or preschool teacher, the whole story experience becomes part of a positive, loving relationship, in which the child feels secure and special. But this is not a necessary prerequisite for the story experience. Preschoolers will sit on their own for hours watching a series of cartoons, even when much of the dialogue is obscure to them. They bounce excitedly up and down when the heroes are zapping the evildoers. They squeal with laughter when a character is squashed, only to emerge once more in his familiar shape. All the indications are that the experience is wholly positive. Most adults conclude that 'kids love stories' and leave it at that. In this chapter, however, we will explore other reasons for children to be so absorbed, other causes for their demands to hear stories again and again.

Children Become Worth Noticing

Along with being photographed more often and shown around to more relatives than their younger siblings, firstborn children have also been the main subjects of those parents who have kept detailed diaries of their children's development in the early years of life. Keeping such records daily is so demanding that few parents feel able to undertake it for more than one child at a time, and even fewer have the energy to extend their endeavours to subsequent siblings. Diaries of this kind seem first to have appeared in the late eighteenth century, and flourished during the nineteenth.[1] Children became 'worth noticing', and not just worth noticing, but (for a few adults, at least) worth close, sustained attention. Sara Coleridge, daughter of the poet, kept a diary of 'the little darling', as she referred to her son, between 1832 and 1838, and in 1839 Charles Darwin kept a record of his first child, William ('Doddy'). As we saw in the last chapter, Robert Louis Stevenson's father listened intently to some of his son's 'songstries', and tried to write at least one of them down word for word. Early in our own century, the Swiss-German artist Paul Klee made a number of careful observations of his little son, and preserved quantities of the boy's drawings (as Klee's own parents had kept his). Some of these early diaries offered observations of a child's reaction to tales told or read, but it was not until the second half of the twentieth century that librarians' enthusiasm for 'children's literature' (as it was now called) prompted a small number of mothers[2] to keep diaries specifically devoted to their child's responses to *fiction*. The new, story-oriented diaries covered periods from a few months to six or more years, and the parent-observers focused most of their attention on what their children said and did in response to published picture books—illustrated stories created by adults specifically for children, and embodying adult ideas about what children 'like' and 'need'. Their diaries provide a deep vein which we can mine for evidence of preschool children's developing ability to grasp and internalise key features of well-formed stories. In addition, the diarists provide a wealth of information about children's emotional reactions to pictures and stories, and significant insights into the development of the self in early childhood. Yet the published diaries have found hardly any readers among scholars of literature, and none at all, it would seem, among developmental psychologists, or even psychoanalytic developmentalists—who might have been expected to be keenly interested in them.

In 1954, US-trained New Zealand librarian Dorothy Neal White published *Books Before Five*, a gracefully written blend of child observation and critical reflection which inspired a number of similar studies over the following forty years. Notable among these are Dorothy Butler's (1979), Maureen Crago's (1983), Shelby Wolf and Shirley Brice Heath's (1992) and most recently, Virginia Lowe's (2006).[3] They hoped their children's responses would confirm their own view that 'quality' children's books would generate a richer, deeper impact on young children than hack writing or stereotyped pictures. Commendably, some of the diarists were honest enough to admit that the evidence they'd gathered did not always support their ideals. From the 1960s onwards, diaries with a different focus started to appear. These were kept by academic researchers of child language development and early literacy. Ruth Weir's study of her son Anthony, quoted in our last chapter, was one of the earliest. These language and literacy-focussed diarists occasionally included striking responses by their own children to adult-created stories, but for the most part, such responses were of little interest to them.[4] Anthropological studies like Shirley Brice Heath's *Ways with Words* focussed mainly on the politics of child language in its cultural context, although Heath did include important observations about the strikingly different ways that children in different ethnic and socio-economic settings are introduced to stories.[5]

Even in their published form, few of these diaries make for easy reading. Whether their compilers were primarily concerned with language development or with the child's responses to fiction, most offer a dense mass of detailed evidence, and it is often difficult to see the wood for the trees. However, by taking a different perspective from most of the diarists, I've attempted to draw out some of the intriguing patterns that are implicit in the information they have gathered. Nearly all the 'literary' diarists marvel at the intuitive way in which young children use concepts and experiences from their daily lives to help them make meaning out of story events and settings which would otherwise be quite alien to them. Simultaneously, the children draw on stories to better understand their own existence: it is a two-way process. Adult observers notice when their child uses 'book language' to describe the real world (often in ways that seem enormously charming to bookish adults); they describe the ways their child incorporates story characters and events into its spontaneous play. All the diarists note the thirst that young children have for *repetition*—the same love of the repeated word and phrase we noticed in both songstries and Homer. They note how children as young as two respond to the sudden *reversal* of the expected. Parent diaries describe the way that young children learn to 'read' pictures over several years, moving from the simple identification of individual objects and creatures within a picture ('That's a dinosaur!' 'That's a Daddy!') to interpreting a complex scene as a whole—a process that is paralleled in the child's developing ability to grasp an entire story plot, rather than responding only to individual incidents. The diarists recognise when their child suddenly 'knows better' than a story character, and is able to tell him off, or laugh at his silliness—evidence that the child has learned to participate in a story, and yet simultaneously stand 'outside' it, recognising it as 'made up' and commenting on its characters—a capacity that all mature reading and movie-viewing depends upon. So, despite the fact that the published studies span several different countries and half a century, there is important common ground. And nowhere is this more true than in the children's obvious distress and discomfort in response to pictures and story events that seem to pose a *threat* to them. As we shall see throughout this chapter, not only is threat a powerful organiser of children's responses to individual stories and pictures, but at a more fundamental level, it is linked inextricably with the nature of story itself. To put it very baldly, story depends heavily upon 'trouble': the right hemisphere of the human brain taps directly into the Old Brain's hypervigilance to potential danger—something skilful thriller-writers learn to incorporate early in any new story:

> 'The vehicle comes to a silent stop. The figure within leans over into the back to pick up an object and pulls out an Anschutz 525 from under a rug. The loaded magazine makes the gun heavy.
>
> Getting out of the car, the driver stretches, sniffs the rain, then vanishes into the deep darkness.'[6]

Notice how this passage from Gabrielle Lord's recent adult thriller mentions not only the obvious menace of an assault rifle, but also the misty darkness that has lent advantage to attackers from the Neolithic to the Battle of the Bulge. In the dark, nothing is certain and people blur into murderers—or even monsters.

Young Children Notice Loss and Damage

As far back as Dorothy White in the late 1940s, parent diarists noticed how their children sometimes seemed worried by illustrations that showed only parts of a person—so that a character seemed to have 'lost' a head or an arm. Carol, the nearly two-and-a-half-year-old child observed in White's *Books Before Five*, paid close attention to a picture of a little boy swimming, his legs invisible beneath the water. She asked where his legs had gone. White, like several other diarists, saw this primarily as an instance of a young child's failure to understand perspective. The apparent calmness of Carol's question did not suggest underlying distress—but it was there, conveyed by the comments and questions repeatedly elicited by this and similar pictures. Similarly, Carol's little friend Ann could not cope with an illustration where the chest and head of a pictured figure were 'cut off' by the top of the page. 'Where is that mummy's head?' she demanded.[7] Even at this tender age, a child is aware that the head is a very important part of one's body—a part that one can't afford to lose. The apparent severing of a head poses a massive threat indeed. (In Chapter 7, we'll see how the image of a severed head can express, for adult writers, something deeply disturbing about their ability to 'detach themselves' from life and even lose touch with their own bodies.)

Other diarists report similar instances, beginning at twenty-one months,[8] but just how far back that heightened sensibility to 'missing parts' extends becomes clear when we tap a completely different source of information, unconnected with books and reading, and probably quite unknown to our story-oriented diarists—the observations of psychoanalyst Melanie Klein. In her essay, 'The Behaviour of Young Infants', first published while White was working on *Books Before Five*, Klein reports several incidents where something broken or damaged provoked distress in a small boy (almost certainly her own son).[9] The earliest of these incidents occurred at just eight months: 'He cried when he dropped a glass—and another time a cup—and it broke. Soon he was so disturbed by the sight of broken things, irrespective of who had caused the damage, that his mother at once put them out of his sight.'[10]

It may seem a big leap from this little boy's intense reaction to a broken cup, to three-year-old Ann and Carol's insistent questioning of the 'incomplete figures' in their book illustrations, yet there is a continuity. By the third year of life, many children—those whom clinicians would see as displaying a Type A attachment style—have learned to avoid openly revealing their disquiet. Instead, they use language to defend themselves against it.[11] They ask apparently calm, cognitively oriented questions that only hint at their very real concerns. But why should any child, whether at eight months or at thirty months, be concerned about something broken? What might this behaviour mean? One possibility is that if an object (or a pictured object) appears broken or damaged, this triggers existential anxiety—a sense of the vulnerability of the child's own body. Dead creatures elicit a very similar reaction from young children. In 1812, the year Napoleon's *Grande Armée* commenced its disastrous retreat from Moscow, British mother Catherine Stanley observed that one of her sons 'Shewed a strong antipathy to a dead bird on touching it and afterwards to anything like fur or feathers, but by giving him a dog of fur to play with, he forgot it by degrees.[12]

The cold, stiff plumage of the dead bird—so different from the feel of a warm, live creature—shocks this little boy. We are all living beings, and feel a 'visceral clutch' at a reminder that the gift of life can be withdrawn. Hence, the abnormal state of a familiar object seems to rank alongside 'broken', 'damaged' and 'incomplete' objects and creatures as triggers of distress to young children. Yet in order to understand fully what is going on, we have to follow Melanie Klein a step further. Klein thought that her little boy became so distressed and fearful *because he believed that he himself had caused the damage* to the cup or glass (even if it had actually been damaged by somebody else). An infant, Klein maintained, does not distinguish the external world from the inner world of his own wishes, fears and rages. Piaget, a pioneering observer of children's cognitive development, concluded much the same, referring to young children's 'egocentricity' which only gradually diminishes as they begin to understand that their position in the universe is actually far less central and important than they thought it was. The sun, they realise, does *not* go down 'so we can go to sleep'.[13]

For a very young child, the relationship between 'inside' and 'outside', between internal world and external world, is both fluid and two-way. Just as children may believe they have caused damage to some external object, so, when they are faced with something disturbing outside of them, they may assume that the disturbance is *inside* them. A broken toy may signal their own 'brokenness',[14] just as a dead bird may (so we surmise) suggest their own death—insofar as they can comprehend such a concept. All of this comes together in the dramatic conclusion to Klein's case study. Now fifteen months old, the same boy dropped a favourite humming top to the floor while playing with it, and its two halves came apart:

> 'He cried, was inconsolable and would not go back into the room where the incident had happened. When at last his mother succeeded in taking him there to show him that the top had been put together again, he refused to look at it, and ran out of the room (even on the next day he did not want to go near the toy cupboard where the humming top was kept). Moreover, several hours after the incident, he refused to eat his tea. A little later on, however, it happened that his mother took up his toy dog and said, 'What a nice little doggie.' The boy brightened up, picked up the dog and kept on walking from one person to another, expecting them to say, 'Nice little doggie'. It was clear that he identified himself with the toy dog, and therefore that the affection shown to it reassured him about the harm which he felt he had inflicted on the humming top.'[15]

If the 'nice doggie' could comfort him, then the new, alarming form of the spinning top may have told him that he, too, was 'broken' or vulnerable to damage. A sharp awareness of mutability creates a powerful need for some bulwark against it, for a God who 'changeth not', for a 'place of greater safety'.[16] So far as we know, children's understanding of death develops very gradually; the age of seven has been identified as pivotal, yet it could be argued that for some, a mature concept of death may not emerge until well into adulthood.[17] There can be little doubt, though, that glimpses of mutability—incidents of loss, damage and negation like those we have been discussing—form a foundation for later concepts of death.

However, there is another aspect of Klein's top-and-dog incident that is, as scientists say, 'counter-intuitive'—less accessible to the logical reasoning of the left hemisphere. Why is the little boy consoled by the toy dog, yet refuses even to *look* at the repaired spinning top? If the child has broken the toy through his own angry, destructive impulses, why can't he believe he can 'make the toy whole again' in a similar magical way? Why does he need the 'nice doggie' to restore his equanimity? Consider this adult analogy. Many adults, when their marriage ends, feel the 'brokenness' so strongly that their only way of assuaging the pain is to substitute a new partner as soon as possible. Secure in the arms of a new lover, ideals of love and permanence can be resurrected, and painful damage temporarily forgotten. A *new* 'whole' relationship has replaced the old 'broken' one. For them, the new partner is the 'nice doggie' that reassured Klein's fifteen month old, or the 'dog of fur' which comforted Catherine Stanley's little son. Shortly, we will see how young children's fierce disapproval of a story that ends inconclusively or unsatisfactorily leads them to manufacture new 'endings' of their own, endings which offer temporary reassurance but cannot eliminate the profound disturbance caused by the story's original ending. For these children, 'broken' *must* be 'fixed', and 'lost' *must* be 'found', and in this—as we'll see throughout this book—they are not very different from the rest of us. Stories exist, in part, because of our overwhelming need to replace, repair and re-make a world (and a self) in which there is, as it were, a gaping hole.

The Unbearable Brokenness of Being

Even when nothing is overtly broken or damaged, existential anxieties can be aroused quite readily in some children by words alone. Hearing her mother talk about the moon, and 'great distances, a long, long way away, and about suns we have never seen' provoked Carol White, now four-and-a-half years old, to exclaim: 'We won't go on talking about this any more'.[18] Her mother's words must have evoked a vast, incomprehensible universe, in which Carol's tiny, individual identity was swallowed up. Does it seem ridiculous to read so much into a small child's chance remark? Well, consider a similar statement made by an adult, which articulates the same feelings much more clearly and fully:

> 'I don't like thinking about eternity. You think about time, and the end of time, and then you think what's beyond the end of time, and it gives you a sort of gasping-for-breath feeling . . . I don't like it, it's too big and overwhelming . . . I don't like hearing sad stories if I can't help to put things right . . . The feeling of impotence that comes when a story of suffering is related, is one of the hardest things to hear, that I know.'[19]

Perhaps surprisingly, the writer here is Enid Blyton at twenty-seven, writing in the magazine *Teacher's World* more than a decade before she became the most popular children's author of her time. Notice how she goes straight from 'I don't like thinking about eternity' to 'I don't like hearing sad stories'. To her right hemisphere, the two are clearly similar, and so (we may reasonably assume) are they for little Carol. The far reaches of the universe, and the pettiness of human beings, are not something she—or anyone—can alter. For Carol, they constitute a threat against which there is no defence except to turn away from the whole subject.

Another telling example is provided by two different children's reactions to Crocket Johnson's classic American picture book, *Harold and the Purple Crayon* (1955). Harold has a magic crayon: everything he draws with it becomes real. If he is shut inside a room, he simply draws an open door on the wall, and walks out through it. If he needs a bridge, he draws one and walks across it. The purple line that he draws continues from each page of the book to the next. A crisis occurs, however, after Harold has drawn a mountain and climbed up one side of it: 'But as he looked down over the other side he slipped—And there wasn't any other side of the mountain. He was falling, in thin air.'[20] Johnson does not allow this frightening situation to persist. On the very next page, Harold, who has fortunately kept hold of his magic crayon, draws a balloon, and 'grabs onto it'. Yet the author's inclusion of this reassuring reversal of misfortune *failed to comfort* two observed children.[21] Both girls displayed strong reactions at the point where the magic 'line' comes to an abrupt halt in the middle of empty, white space, even though, having heard the story before, they 'knew' that Harold would escape his predicament. Both the picture and the abrupt negativity of the words 'there *wasn't any* other side' signal damage and loss, and in response, the children's reactions suggest anxiety. Up to this point in the story, Harold has always been able to 'put things right'; now, suddenly, he cannot. Like Harold with his crayon, a young child can feel invincible and immortal—whatever goes wrong can be magically fixed. But when the 'line runs out', this comforting feeling is shockingly removed.

That adults spontaneously construct like images, similarly associated with existential anxiety, is clear from an account of two dreams experienced by adult novelist Patrick O'Brian. In the first of the dreams, when O'Brian was about forty-one, he dreamed he was on a cliff overlooking the sea, and his second wife Mary said, 'I'm sorry, Patrick, I'm afraid I'm slipping'. Mary was O'Brian's major source of creative inspiration and support, a 'life line' if ever there was one, and the dream points to a deep fear of losing her. The imagery of the dream comes direct from the Old Brain. Losing Mary is a threat to his survival (invoking the reptile brain), a loss of connection to his mate (invoking the mammal brain), both represented pictorially. To the right hemisphere, a frightening drop from a cliff *shows us* the frightening loss of a loved one, where the left hemisphere would *tell us* in words that the cliff drop 'stands for' or 'resembles' the loss. In a second dream, forty years later when O'Brian was in his early eighties, and now the bestselling author of *Master and Commander* and its many successors, he was standing on a castle wall above 'a sheer drop of 1000 feet to an estuary'. He remembered 'a voice telling me about it in the silence—the horror of the void'. Here the basic images are repeated in slightly different form—not surprisingly, since his Mary became seriously ill and died early in that very year, 1989.[22]

It is not hard to see how such imagery might begin with an infant's experience of reaching out for its mother and finding 'nothing there', and how a more mature fear of death—the death of a loved one, or one's own death—may resonate with that earlier emptiness. And in fact, Patrick O'Brian's mother *did* die when he was only three. Like most children who lose a parent so early, he retained little conscious memory of it—yet perhaps his dreams preserved, in the symbolic language of the Old Brain, some of what he had experienced all those years before. Another small boy, just a year older than Patrick, lost both his father and his older sister within a single year. Much later, he described a fictional hero, also aged four, in the following words: 'all at once he found himself alone and frightened in a vast unfriendly world'. We will meet this little boy, and his fictional alter ego 'James', in Chapter 7. And here is how a fictional ten-year-old describes her realisation that her dear school friend Helen Burns is about to die:

> 'And then my mind made its first earnest effort to comprehend what had been infused into it concerning heaven and hell: and for the first time it recoiled, baffled; and for the first time glancing behind, on each side, and before it, it saw all round *an unfathomed gulf*: it felt the one point where it

> stood—the present; all the rest was *formless* cloud and *vacant* depth: and it shuddered at the thought of tottering, and *plunging amid that chaos*.'[23] [italics mine]

The speaker of this passage is Jane Eyre, heroine of Charlotte Brontë's novel of the same name. That Charlotte based this passage on her own experience is beyond doubt. The figure of Helen Burns, saintly and compassionate, is modelled on Charlotte's older sister Maria, who had protected little Charlotte when she first went to boarding school and who subsequently died, along with her other sister, Elizabeth, when Charlotte was only nine. Even earlier than these later, more fully recollected losses, a five-year-old Charlotte had experienced the death of her mother, a more profound loss, one would imagine, and probably only partly comprehended. Here again, the image of the void is associated with the sudden, shocking removal through death of a loved person who has provided security and belonging—a 'lifeline' indeed. Carol White, and the other preschool children whose parents observed their responses to stories and pictures, seems to have enjoyed a secure, loving family life, with no obvious losses. Yet the images that provoke their distress are similar to Charlotte Brontë's—falls from great heights; 'thin air' and emptiness; vast distances compared which the child feels tiny and insignificant. Robert Louis Stevenson remembered his terror when afflicted by fever as a young child in very similar terms: 'a horror of infinite distance and infinite littleness'.[24] *The Old Brain does not distinguish a real loss from an imagined or fictional one*: the left hemisphere might express it in abstract language ('A feeling of annihilation') but the right hemisphere will present, instead, an *image* of falling into a great emptiness, an image which expresses fear and loss analogically, without the need for words.

In the face of perceived losses and threats in famous picture books like Marjorie Flack's *The Story about Ping*, young children will typically comfort themselves by suggesting that the young duck's mother will find him.[25] But as children grow older, they attempt to find other ways of 'putting things right', and the most clearly articulated attempts to do so come in children's fourth and fifth years of life. Some typical strategies are employed by Carol White at four-and-a-half, after her mother tells her the story of 'The Forsaken Merman', another celebrated Victorian poem, this time by Matthew Arnold:

> . . . as I should have foreseen, the desertion of the mer-children distressed her, even after I explained that mermaids were "flighty" and not at all like "real" mothers. Carol listened in silence to this gloss on the situation. Half an hour later, as we were having dinner, she told me: "You know what happened later? The mer-mummy went back".[26]

Following this 'correction' of the story's disturbing conclusion, Carol asked several questions, apparently prompted by curiosity. She asked whether it is possible to eat the fish part of mermaids, where mermaids sleep, and whether they have beds. In the middle of these questions, she asked, 'Are they comfortable like that? I don't think many mermummies would be like that—leaving their children. That's not very good, is it?'

When a younger Carol asked similar questions, we were entitled to wonder (as her mother did) whether the little girl's concerns *might* simply have represented her failure to understand how pictures work. This time, however, there can be no doubt. The 'factual' questions about the reality status of mermaids are attempts by Carol to weaken or eliminate the unpalatable idea of a mother who would abandon her children. She tries several different possibilities, including proposing that the 'mer-mummy' changed her mind, considering that mermaids might really be fish (and therefore, presumably, not have the sorts of feelings humans have), speculating that mermaids might not be human if they do not sleep, or have beds and chairs like we do. She is attempting to deal with an uncomfortable, or threatening thought, as Emily did in her monologue about the broken TV set. Shortly, we will be observing this same process of exploring alternatives to an unpalatable idea in fairy tales.

Stories, like real life, present children with deprivation, abandonment, loss, damage and death. In the second year of life, fictional loss and damage may not provoke any obvious perturbation, although real-life damage and loss certainly do (as in Melanie Klein's fifteen-month-old with the broken top). Toddlers may even laugh loudly or jump excitedly when some mishap befalls a fictional character—such reactions suggesting that they *register* threat, but express it as 'generalised arousal'—which looks to us like excitement, or even amusement. But as children move into their third year of life, their sensitivity to loss and damage within the world of story develops rapidly, and so does their ability to express it more precisely—in the form of worried questioning, angry protests, or transparent rationalisations—all of them, in one way or another, aimed at countering the threat that the pictures or the words have posed. Children at this age do broadly grasp that a story is different from 'real life'. Yet fictional threat is still 'real threat'. Even as adults, we react in exactly the same way—we are just better at concealing it.

When we 'identify' with story characters, or 'feel for' a fictional hero or heroine, what is actually happening? We now know that 'mirror neurons' in our brains fire in sympathy with what is happening to someone else, even though it is not happening to us.[27] This mechanism is what enables us to learn, not only from direct experience, but from vicarious experience (seeing something happen to someone else). Like the threat reactions which lead at the bodily level to 'fight, flight or freeze', these empathetic feelings are automatic. We cannot *not* have them. Yet they are also selective. Our mirror neurones do not fire for *everything* that happens to everyone we know, or (in stories) for everything that happens to every character. Instead, in some unconscious way, our brains 'know' who, or what, to resonate in sympathy with. Not surprisingly, Carol's feelings 'mirror' the abandoned mer-children, nottheir mother. At around the same age as Carol, I responded to Browning's 'Pied Piper of Hamelin' by identifying, not with the little lame boy—as many other children might—but with the powerful, magical Piper. Our right hemispheres instinctively recognise another person (or fictional creature) who is 'like us'—or even 'like the person we will be someday'. Sometimes these resemblances are quite literal (a fictional character who is the same age as us, or who has the same name as ours); at other times they are not (girls can recognise themselves in male characters, or boys in female ones). And to be fair, I probably empathised with the little lame boy *and* the Pied Piper, but preferred to dwell on the latter because imagining myself as powerful and magical was much more consoling than acknowledging how alone and 'left out' I sometimes felt.

As we grow up, our mirror neurones still fire without our conscious control. But we seem to gain more ability to separate ourselves from those reactions, to say to ourselves (as it were) 'this is *like* me, but it *isn't* me'. It is the brain's maturing left hemisphere which can make explicit the fact that one thing is 'like' or 'resembles' another. It is the maturing frontal lobes of both hemispheres which enable a child to inhibit automatic responses, to select, as it were, what impulses it is going to take seriously. These functions enable all of us to protect ourselves from being overwhelmed by feelings which are real, but which are not, as it were, relevant to us personally. But the same functions also enable us to distance ourselves from something that we might actually *need* to feel, or which might, at a deeper level, be relevant to us after all. 'Defence mechanisms'—a term many of us now employ glibly in everyday conversation, without really knowing what we are talking about—are examples of this distancing, in both its functional and its not-so-functional aspects. Why might 'vicarious feelings' be relevant to us? Because, as we'll see in more detail in Chapter 6, we instinctively select what or who to identify with on the basis of memories, knowledge—which in physiological terms are patterns of firing neurones—*that already exist within our brains.*

The 'Forsaken Merman' ends with the grief of the Merman and his children, as their mother departs, never to return. 'The Pied Piper' ends in a way which is ambiguous: it is entirely possible that the Hamelin children have all died, like the rats before them. Yet even when stories end 'happily', with suffering expunged, and wrongs righted, some young children may still be disturbed by the suffering, injustice and loss they contain. *A happy ending does not cancel out the distress, and the child still seeks to correct or repair it in a stronger or more efficacious way than the tale itself has done.* To the Old Brain, the threat of harm is ever-present and timeless. Now we can see even more clearly why Klein's little boy could be consoled by the 'nice doggie'—which had never suffered damage—but not reassured by the spinning top that his parents had put back together.

Let's pause now, and look again at the evidence that has been accumulating. When we looked at children's self-composed narratives, we saw signs of a structure based on a succession of statements and reversals, often driven by an underlying emotion, often (though not always) a sad or painful one. In this chapter, we have observed something similar in the ways that young children have responded to adult-made stories. Now, however, it is the (adult-created) story that makes the statement, and the child who reverses it—if the story supplies threat or damage, the child will attempt to supply the 'antidote'. When some kind of threat is involved, both self-composed narratives and text-organised responses have the same structure. The same kind of mental operation is involved, a concerted, repetitive attempt to fill the gap, repair the damage, or guard against the danger.

By now, some readers of this chapter will probably have started to protest. Am I not basing an ambitious argument on a tiny sample of children who are probably abnormally sensitive? And don't these children sound like middle class children, raised with a high level of individualised attention, the unwitting recipients of their parents' wishes and fears? And anyway, who on earth would expect a four-year-old to cope with the sadness of 'The Forsaken Merman' or a five-year-old with the death of Aslan in *The Lion, the Witch and the Wardrobe*?[28] Surely these are extreme responses to a stimulus far too 'grown up' for these preschool children, bound to provoke confusion and pain in their immature minds?

It's true that our sample has been small (the endnotes will point interested readers to further evidence), yet the children we've quoted appear to have come from stable, loving families and to have suffered no obvious trauma. It is indeed possible that the sample has been biased towards children of high temperamental sensitivity, who would register threats more intensely than others—yet these are precisely the sort of children who may well grow up to be story makers themselves. In *The Miracle at Speedy Motors*, the ninth of his immensely popular (and very funny) series about Precious Ramotswe, proprietor of the Number One Ladies' Detective Agency in Botswana, Scots author Alexander McCall Smith suddenly observes:

> 'Sometimes it seemed as if the world itself was broken, that there was something wrong with all of us, something that was broken in such a way that it might not be put together again; but the holding of hands, human hand in human hand, could help, could make the world seem less broken.'[29]

All young children—however well protected by loving parents—will sooner or later encounter things that shock, puzzle and sadden them: on the television, in their neighbourhoods, even in their own families. Why should stories be put in a separate category? James Robertson's poignant documentary film series *Children in Brief Separation*, made in the early 1950s, starkly portrays the reactions of children as young as two years old to enforced hospital stays without their parents. Nobody who has watched these films, where toddlers cry pitifully, withdraw into aching silence, or angrily reject their parents when they finally return, could ever doubt that *small children feel loss as timeless anguish*. The younger the children are, the more it is as if their parents have 'died', leaving them alone, 'in a vast, unfriendly world'. Yet when Robertson first showed his documentaries, doctors and nurses claimed that he had selected atypical children to film, or had 'edited' the footage to make the children's responses appear more 'dramatic'. We adults have never enjoyed being reminded of how vulnerable young children are, for it also reminds us of our unintentional cruelty and neglect of such tiny, defenceless beings.[30]

Like it or not, very young children can notice, and be affected by, existential threat—in stories just as in life. Damage, loss, change to what is familiar—even verbal expressions of negativity or melancholy—can trigger such reactions.[31] Adults feel exactly the same. When, at the end of the final episode of *The Sopranos* the screen went blank, viewers reacted with anger to a conclusion that seemed to them not just unsatisfactory, but unfair. Ultimately, it was *death* that they were rejecting—the death of fictional characters who had become real to them—real enough that when James Gandolfini ('Tony Soprano') came off his bike in New York, one man reportedly asked worriedly, 'Are you all right, Tony?' The Roman poet Virgil, writing in the reign of Augustus, referred to *lachrymae rerum*. The Latin words literally translate as 'the tears of things-in-general', but we would talk of 'existential sadness'—a grief that is seemingly built into the human condition by the very fact that we can envisage our own eventual deaths. Stories either acknowledge this melancholy fact (as Homer does) or defend against it with 'happy ever after' endings (as fairy tales do). So let's turn now to fairy tales—the kind of story that all of us have come to associate with 'happy ever after'.

Those Gullible Giants at the Top of the Beanstalk

Why would the woodcutter turn up just as Red Riding Hood is about to be swallowed by the wicked wolf? How could he possibly know what was happening inside the Grandmother's cottage at that moment? And why did the Giants at the top of the beanstalk allow Jack to rob them a second time? Wouldn't the Giant and his wife have been wary after his first successful theft? Questions like these are surprisingly obvious once one thinks about these well-known fairy tales, yet somehow most of us do not 'think' about them at all—at least, not when we first encounter the tales, as children. It was a British medievalist who asked what it might mean that we fail to think about such questions. When Anne Wilson began a doctoral study of the medieval English romances in the 1970s, she was not your average literary scholar. In psychoanalysis she had experienced 'free association' where the patient, at liberty to talk about anything she wishes, typically cycles backwards and forwards through multiple possibilities, admitting worrying thoughts, pushing them away, then re-engaging with them—as we saw Emily do in our last chapter. Wilson had also lived in Mozambique and Nigeria. She had witnessed how real people today can think in terms of *ritual magic*—which they saw as a very practical process for making desirable things happen, or 'unmaking' things they wished had not happened.

These varied experiences provided her with a unique perspective on the anonymous tales she wanted to study for her PhD—most of them, like the *Iliad*, originally orally transmitted. A version of her thesis was eventually published as *Traditional Romance and Tale: How Stories Mean*, but Wilson's original argument (she has since revised her theory considerably) appears most clearly and usefully (for non-medievalists) in her writing on fairy tales. For Anne Wilson, the key thing about fairy tales was not that they contained *magic* (fairies, witches and talking beasts, or spells and transformations). Rather, it was the tales' dependence on *magical thought*—a way of thinking which fails to obey the principles of logic or rationality, but which seems compelling and powerful nonetheless.[32] The fact that the tales pivot on blatant defiance of common sense suggests that they need to be understood in a very different way from adult-created stories about people in the real world—or even from fantasies like *The Golden Compass* or *The Chronicles of Narnia*, which are admittedly set in imaginary worlds, but where most of what happens follows logically from the premises set up at the beginning. In contrast, Wilson argues, fairy tales appear arbitrary and illogical all the way through. Like dreams, they are a kind of 'thinking in action'.

Wilson sees the actions that make up a fairy tale plot not as events, but as *possibilities*. They take shape in the tale as things that the protagonist, or other characters *do*, but they are really *ideas* being contemplated, *wishes and fears* being 'tried on for size'—as in 'free association'. In terms of the brain, this is because the right hemisphere on its own has no way of relating one thing to another, subordinating one thing to another, or negating something. It can only *juxtapose* images or actions, so it represents an alternative possibility by an alternative image *or even a whole alternative story*. Fairy tales are constructed on the same principle: one set of actions represents one possibility; but that is followed by a different set of actions, representing the tale's exploration of a different possible outcome. Here is the same structure we observed in preschool children's narratives in Chapter 3. The main difference is that in fairy tales, the sequence of good fortune/bad fortune or damage/repair does not continue indefinitely: it ends resoundingly, with the words that, for English-speaking people, have become synonymous with fairy tales: 'and so they lived happily ever after'.

Just as all the events of a fairy tale are alternative versions of what the protagonist might desire or dread, Wilson argues that all the *characters* in a fairy tale are simply alternative representations of its protagonist. Innocent princess and evil witch, benevolent guardian and deceitful servant, all of them are aspects of a single, childlike 'mind'. If we follow Anne Wilson's understanding of the tales, 'Cinderella' would be a story about a young woman who wants to be attractive and sought-after by a desirable man, but who is also anxious about this prospect—as many an adolescent girl is. But there is nothing in the tale about any conflicting or confused *feelings* that Cinderella has. Rather, Cinderella's self-criticism and self-doubt take the form of *people* who criticise and doubt—'step-sisters' who belittle her and abuse her. She eventually resolves her conflict in a gratifying way, by 'allowing' her true nature to be discovered by the Prince (in other words, she recognises her own attractiveness and worthiness) whereupon the ugly sisters are punished (her own self-critical thoughts are dismissed).

The brutal punishments in earlier versions of these tales (Cinderella's ugly sisters chopping bits off their feet in a desperate attempt to make them fit the slipper; the decapitation of the Princess's horse in 'The Goose-Girl') reflect the customs of a violent age, when swords and axes still dominated the battlefield and the place of execution. But although we can take them literally, they *mean* something very different. Just as a sheer cliff face *is* loneliness, emptiness and loss to the right hemisphere, so deaths and beheadings are ways the right hemisphere replaces one possibility with another (in a movie film, it would be a 'dissolve' or a 'cut'). Having served their purpose, aspects of the protagonist which are no longer relevant are 'despatched' (a word which can mean both 'sent away' and 'killed'). In 'The Frog Prince', a Princess hurls a slimy frog against the wall, whereupon he is transformed into a handsome prince. This does not mean she is a rageful murderess, only that the frog can be 'disappeared' now that his part as an undesirable lover—the *idea* of a distasteful lover—is no longer needed, and he is replaced by a more palatable possibility: a desirable human lover. (The idea that a sexual partner must necessarily be an uncouth or even monstrous being, as in 'Beauty and the Beast', makes a lot of sense when we remember that such tales were first written down at a time when it was still common for teenage virgins to be married off, in defiance of their own wishes, to hairy, smelly men old enough to be their fathers.)

As Anne Wilson continued her work over a period of some thirty years, she eventually concluded that stories embodying magical thought (including sophisticated New Brain narratives like *Hamlet*, which are built on earlier Old Brain narratives) do not simply play with different possibilities around a central conflict or dilemma. Instead, the tales' organised sequences of events closely resemble magical *rituals*, designed to ward off an unacceptable impulse, or to deal with the results of such an impulse. This structure is found in fairy tales like 'The Water of Life', where three princes in turn attempt a task (only the third and youngest succeeding), or 'The Golden Bird', where a single prince attempts three different tasks, only succeeding on his final attempt. As Wilson argued in her later work, a dream has hardly any structure, and involves no conscious control, whereas this tightly organised ritual, irrational though it is, has an element of conscious purpose.[33]

Ritual is *intended* to produce an outcome—a desired state of affairs. Fairy tale endings do produce such outcomes, whereas dreams often end inconclusively, or segue into other dream sequences, and the exploration of yet more possibilities—the true mark of the Old Brain. Indeed, the 'happy ever after' with which fairy tales often conclude functions almost like an 'Amen' at the end of a prayer, signalling that the ritual is now complete, and the desired outcome has been achieved. The fact that fairy tales 'conclude conclusively', where dreams do not, signals what I suspect is the first major impact of the left hemisphere on Old Brain story making. The left hemisphere *separates* one thing from another, and hence sees the need for clear beginnings and endings that will distinguish a story as something different from real life. Fairy tales are Old Brain narratives that have taken a key step towards a more sophisticated form of narrative—the romance, which we'll meet in Chapter 4.

'It Shouldn't Be Allowed!'

Fairy tales famously begin with some formula like 'Once upon a time'—a signal that the story is to be regarded as remote from the real-life world of those who are listening to it. When George Lucas opened *Star Wars* with the rolling text 'A long time ago, in a galaxy far, far away . . . ', he jokingly employed a similar convention. But when American educator Lucy Sprague Mitchell chose a title for her influential 1921 volume of stories for young children, she called it *Here and Now Story Book*,[34] deliberately announcing her *departure* from what she saw as the 'far away and long ago' nature of fairy tales. Mitchell argued passionately that fairy tales were not suitable for young children. Although child listeners responded strongly to them, she said, it was with 'excitement and confusion'—reactions which came from trying to cope with a stimulus too overwhelming for them. Instead, she maintained that preschool children should be given tales that reflected their own daily lives and that embodied their literary preferences: lists of objects and actions, repeated, rhythmic refrains, plots that alternated 'movement and rest, lost and found, home and away'.

Mitchell was an acute observer of young children, and her manifesto accurately captured much of what they most enjoy. But her four-year-olds were children in her own image: 'little scientists'—rational beings, albeit with a limited knowledge of the world. And despite having all the right ingredients, the stories she wrote, carefully tailored to the minds and worlds of the preschool children of her day, have not lasted. They fail to compel our attention, *because they do not draw on the powerful energies of the Old Brain*. Fairy tales—for all their logical inconsistency and emotional overload—do. Lucy Sprague Mitchell was a great educator, but she was not a great story maker. In terms of the two categories we'll shortly introduce, she was an 'interrogator', not a 'performer'. Yet even the 'age-appropriate' stories she insisted upon do *not* protect young children from 'excitement and confusion', or from the threat of loss, damage and discontinuity.[35] Let's see how this plays out in the case of a more recent example of 'here and now' storytelling.

Richard Scarry's 'Busytown' books were immensely popular during the latter decades of the twentieth century, selling in millions worldwide. As in the world of the Teletubbies, nothing really bad or worrying ever seems to happen to the inhabitants of 'Busytown'. Scarry's many titles are full of everyday events, with drama confined to minor accidents and misunderstandings, and characters who are almost all well-intentioned—although sometimes rather dumb! Yet however much Scarry may attempt to minimise harm, loss and damage, some children will still pick up the slightest hint of it. For example, five-year-old Morwenna was deeply distressed (in Scarry's *What Do People Do All Day?*) by a tiny detail showing a kitten dropping her ice cream into the water (perhaps it is not coincidental that the kitten is leaning over a dam wall when she does so—'the horror of the void' again?). For her, this tragedy coloured the whole story, even though (like every Scarry story) it ended happily. At nine years of age, she mentioned how strongly affected she had been by the incident, adding that such sad events shouldn't be allowed in books. She also commented, 'I don't really like *Rapunzel* because the mother never gets to see her child again'. Both the harsh fairy tale and Scarry's sanitised 'here and now story' had exactly the same effect on her.[36]

Scarry's books are told in a kind of staccato, commentator-style prose, without the rhythm and flow we associate with true storytelling. When listening to Scarry texts read aloud, more than one child has objected to this, insisting, '*Read* it, Mummy, don't *say* it!'[37] These children had instantly picked up the resemblance between Scarry's style, and the stop-start, conversational manner of an adult *talking* to a child *about* a book, as opposed to actually reading the author's words. None of this means that texts like Scarry's have not been popular with many small children—they have. But such narratives contain no *music*—a sure sign of right hemisphere involvement—hardly ever are their words remembered later, and very rarely do they go on to form part of the emotional landscape of their young listeners' minds. Scarry's books are also overtly moralistic, and children soon sense when they are being 'taught a lesson'. At the age of three or four, I was read Gertrude Crampton's *Tootle*, a moral tale if ever there was one. Though I memorised the rhythmic command, 'And stay on the rails NO MATTER WHAT!') I never bothered to re-read *Tootle* as an older child or adolescent, as I did with my old favourites, and (looking back on the course of my adult life) probably didn't do all that well at 'staying on the rails' either![38]

Performers and Interrogators

All the preschool children we have been studying in this chapter interacted with stories in a range of predictable ways. All of them asked questions about things they didn't understand, all of them made statements in response to the story (judgements, admonitions to characters, exclamations of like and dislike), all of them repeated or memorised key lines of text, and all of them asked for particular stories to be repeated many times. Yet one group of children seem mostly to stand *outside* the story, questioning it and commenting on it. The other group seem to go right *inside* the story, 'becoming' its characters and playing out its events. I have called these two types of child the 'interrogator' and the 'performer', and the existence of these two types of response provides further evidence for the roles played in early childhood by the brain's two separate-yet-conjoined hemispheres.[39]

Performers do exactly what the word implies—they 'enact' stories as their way of deepening their pleasurable involvement *and* as a means of understanding them. One way of performing is to *memorise and recite* parts of a story, or even entire stories. By repeating the words that have meant so much, the child becomes the *teller* of the story, 'calling it into being' for an audience, even if that audience is only herself. In fact, the reciter becomes an *aoidos*, a miniature Homer. Many parents have marvelled at their two- or three-year-old's ability to quote, word for word, entire story texts that have been read to them repeatedly. When texts are too long to be memorised in their entirety, the child's choice of what *sections* to commit to memory often turns out to be significant. At two and a half, listening to Browning's 'The Pied Piper', I presumably memorised 'rats/they fought the dogs and killed the cats/and bit the babies in the cradles' simply because the verses were so catchy. Yet why would I have remembered verbatim 'Into the street the Piper stept/smiling first a little smile/as if some kind of magic slept/In his quiet pipe the while'? Something in me, even at two and three, already resonated with the idea of a powerful adult figure who could, by his art, compel others to attend and obey. Fifteen years later, as an adolescent, I was drawn to Shakespeare's Prospero in *The Tempest* for exactly the same reason. In my subsequent life, as I now perceive, I attempted in various ways to make myself into such a figure—an aspiration as risky as it was attractive.

Our parent diaries supply a good deal of information about the rise and fall of 'quoting', which for most children seems to reach a peak somewhere in the third year of life, and then declines, to be replaced by 'paraphrasing' (where the child retells a known story in her *own* words). Most of the observed children memorised and quoted, but only the 'performers' did so as their *preferred* method of interacting with a text, reciting key phrases again and again, as if by doing so they could take the story inside them, and make it a part of their own lives. At six, Hilary Mantel amazed her mother by retelling the entire story of *The Secret Garden*—'narrative, dialogue and commentary'—in a single sitting, after seeing it serialised over several weeks on a friend's television.[40] However, a more dramatic and explicit version of this same impulse occurs in the form of what early childhood educators call 'pretend play'.

Award-winning American picturebook artist Trina Schart Hyman, who died in 2004, describes how, as a four-year-old, she 'became' Red Riding Hood for days on end, in an ongoing role-playing game instigated by Trina herself, but supported by her mother, who 'sewed me a red satin cape with a hood' and gave her a 'basket of goodies' to 'take to grandmother's house' (in the backyard—her real grandmother lived hundreds of miles away). Trina's dog stood in (safely) for the wolf, and her father stood in for the woodcutter.[41] Much later, now an accomplished illustrator, Trina produced her own version of 'Red Riding Hood' along with illustrations to several other fairy tale classics, including a powerful, brooding version of 'Rapunzel'. Three-and-a-half-year-old Lindsay Wolf became preoccupied with Hyman's 'Rapunzel'.[42] Lindsay's hair became Rapunzel's hair, and she repeatedly replayed the scene where the Prince climbs Rapunzel's long braids to enter the forest tower. She *was* Rapunzel. In Melbourne, Australia, four-year-old Rebecca identified deeply with Tove Jannson's *Moomin* books, and in particular with Snufkin, the 'loner' who lives in a tent, and prefers journeying to a settled communal life. Although she did not 'perform' any part of the stories about Snufkin, for months she insisted on being *called* 'Snufkin', and constantly carried around her collection of paperback *Moomin* books in a tiny suitcase.[43]

Most preschool children (and not just girls) engage in 'pretend play', with or without the assistance of books they've been read, or movies they've watched. There is no necessary connection between literary stories and pretend play, but from very early in their lives, our 'performers' centred much of their imaginative play on stories. These little girls—Trina, Lindsay, Rebecca—sought to recreate a story that had impressed or puzzled them by selecting a single character and then playing her or his role. By doing so, they must somehow have felt that they were participating in the story, becoming a part of it, while simultaneously making it a part of them. Their repeated actions give a concrete, literal shape to the notion of 'identification'. When we identify, we are not standing outside the tale and consciously *recognising* that a character is *similar* to ourselves—'interrogators' do that, as we'll shortly see. No, we *become* the character, *merge with* that character, as every good actor does, as every enthralled reader does.

Preschoolers' tiny 're-enactments' are usually only partial. Lindsay did not perform the entire story of 'Rapunzel', and little Trina Schart (as she then was) left out the terrifying final scene of 'Red Riding Hood'. Piaget, who made a lifetime study of children's cognitive development, basing many of his initial observations on his own children, hypothesised that between approximately three and five (the stage he called 'pre-operational') preschoolers 'centre' their attention on a single facet of any phenomenon, seemingly ignoring the 'bigger picture' of which it forms a part.[44] Replaying a single scene or incident from a known story seems to be an instance of this. It is as if this scene or incident 'stands for' the whole. As children grow beyond this stage, and into the next, they can take in a number of aspects at once, and can relate each of these parts to the whole—something that requires the full co-operation of *both* the left and the right hemispheres of the brain. So too does the appreciation that a happy ending may cancel out earlier misfortunes. A singular focus on one aspect of a story or picture, then, is the equivalent of the preoperational child's expectation that everything that happens in her world is somehow related to herself—egocentricity—for a young child learns about her own limitations concurrently by realising that other people are separate beings, not extensions of herself—Piaget called this 'decentering'. The distinction between 'self' and 'other' evolves between two and five in parallel with the distinction between 'part' and 'whole'.

Another way of comprehending this is to say that a preschool child cannot grasp a *whole* story because she does not yet have a clear sense of what a *conclusion* actually means—which fits perfectly with what we noticed in Chapter 1: most two- and three-year-old children find it difficult to 'end' their self-created narratives in anything other than an arbitrary fashion. In a well-formed story, the conclusion places earlier story incidents in perspective, reducing them to cogs in the wheel, components that helped the story 'go somewhere'. A strong conclusion forces a reader or listener to see earlier incidents anew, qualifying the emotional impact they would have had if they had stood alone. It 'contains' that impact, making the story 'tolerable'. A conclusion is not just an *ending*, it is *an ending logically linked to the events which lead up to it*, one which 'makes sense', one that we can recognise as implicit in the story from its very beginning. To produce a convincing conclusion in a self-composed story, or to accept the validity of a conclusion in a story heard or read, a child needs the assistance of the left hemisphere. Although the left hemisphere begins to catches up with the right from the second year of life, it is not until around the seventh that left hemisphere cause-effect thinking reliably supplants 'magical' thinking, a transition that Piaget called the 'five to seven shift'. And—with a predictable 'lag'—it is not until adolescence that most children are able to *create* story conclusions that we adults can recognise as 'proper endings'.

Exactly as with the quoting of memorised sections of story text, the child's selection of particular incidents for pretend play may be governed in part by how *easy* the incident is to re-enact—hence Lindsay's own hair assisted her to take the role of Rapunzel, and a staircase in her family home became the witch's forest tower. Yet the incidents selected may also suggest something about the *meaning* of the incident for the child concerned, since there is a distinct tendency for 'performers' to select incidents that are puzzling, frightening, and yet somehow significant. Here again, as we saw in the last chapter, *emotion organises response*. Hair long and strong enough for someone to climb up it is, after all, a surprising, hyperbolic image, one that does not correspond to the reality a child knows. Had Lindsay been an 'interrogator', she would have asked, 'Oodn't it hurt her, Miss?' (as a fictional six-year-old asks her teacher in Dennis Potter's TV drama *Pennies from Heaven*).[45] Instead, Lindsay *shows* us her concern by enacting it.[46]

Interrogators seem to stand 'outside' the story experience, entering into dialogue with it, asking questions, and consciously weighing up possibilities. Responding in language rather than in actions, and preferring analysis to emotion, the interrogator evinces a more prominent role for the left hemisphere. While both Lindsay Wolf and Rebecca Lowe were performers, Lindsay's younger sister Ashley seems to have been more of an interrogator. Her mother writes:

> 'To Ashley, storybook characters stayed more firmly in the pages of the book—they could be discussed, referred to and even called upon in the context of everyday events [*when accused of some misdemeanour, Ashley retorted, "Maybe Snow White did it!"*], but their personalities could not be donned with the ease of a costume. Once as she played Little Red Riding Hood . . . I addressed her as "Little Red". She rolled her eyes in exasperation: "I'm *Ashley*, Mama! I'm *Ashley*!"'[47]

Although Ashley enjoyed many of the same stories as Lindsay, she favoured non-fiction books, and showed a consistent interest in *words* and their meanings, deliberately altering Maurice Sendak's words in *Where the Wild Things Are* and *In the Night Kitchen* for humorous effect. Her mother notes that Ashley seemed strongly drawn to the musicality of texts (which would normally suggest right hemisphere dominance) but closer attention to the nature of Ashley's behaviour indicates otherwise: she wanted to 'reshape texts to match her own rhythms', and asserted her individual will over a poem or a story instead of simply 'taking part in it', or reproducing it. This is clearly left brain activity: self-conscious, verbal, contrasting fiction with reality. Where performers *merge* with story characters, interrogators *enter story as themselves*, and interact with its characters from that position. Often, they argue with the story, or propose ways that it could have been better. They are literary critics in the making.

Compare another pair of siblings, Australian brothers Ben and Dan.[48] Here it is the elder sibling, Ben, who is the 'interrogator', and the younger, Dan, who is the 'performer'. Dan initiated many games based on stories, and wanted to re-enact gratifying incidents or objects in his own play. Ben would join in his younger brother's games, but rarely started them by himself. When he did so, the stimulus seems often to have been a frightening incident in a story. But Ben's unaided way of 'working through' such incidents was to request that those sections be read again and again until (presumably) he had 'desensitised himself' and no longer felt so scared. Thus, in *The Lion, the Witch and the Wardrobe*, the alarming incidents of Aslan's death and the battle with the White Witch were the ones he wanted to hear again and again at five and six. Overwhelmingly, Ben's focus was cognitive: he wanted to 'understand', and he demanded repetitions of texts until he had that understanding. Probably, like Carol White's, his questions reflected an underlying anxiety, but he did not reveal this openly. By contrast Dan (nineteen months younger) simply refused to hear stories that he found disturbing. Instead, he focussed on happy and gratifying stories, where his preferred mode of interaction was to talk about the characters, and reproduce their activities in his pretend play—although without claiming to 'be' them. Somewhat similarly, Ashley joined in Lindsay's performances, but rarely initiating them. Without the influence of their siblings, Ashley and Ben may never have played in this way. It may also be that younger siblings adopt a different style from older sisters and brothers in order to establish their own 'niche', as suggested by Sulloway in his magisterial study of the implications of birth order.[49]

What we can say with some certainty is that our performers are showing right-hemisphere dominance; in interrogators the left hemisphere seems more prominent. While it is normal for the two sides of the brain to balance out as human beings mature, some people continue to show a slight dominance of one hemisphere throughout their adult lives. My guess is that story makers do begin as children whose right hemisphere functions are never fully balanced by those of the left. In other words, the part of the cerebral cortex that represents and speaks for the holistic, emotion-governed, pattern-driven Old Brain continues to assert itself powerfully in them. British novelist John Fowles referred to a 'golden flaw' in the makeup of the creative artist—for whom, he thought, the distinction between real and imaginary is never fully established, so that the imagined continues to demand real world re-enactment long after others have outgrown pretend play.[50]

What was lacking in Lucy Mitchell's *Here and Now Stories* will remain alive in right hemisphere dominant children. If they are to succeed in their creative endeavours, however, they will need the contribution of the left hemisphere as well. It is the way the right and left hemispheres *co-operate* that makes the difference between a story (or any creative product) that may be highly significant to its maker but means little to anybody else, and one that can mysteriously reach out, across cultures and even centuries, to find an audience far wider than its originator could ever have dreamed.

****

As our brains mature, a curious phenomenon Freud called 'early childhood amnesia' ensures that we will *forget* much of the timeless anguish (and stormy rage) we felt in the years before five, leaving many of us with a gradually-receding image of happiness and content.[51] But German novelist Thomas Mann was surely right when, in his family chronicle *Buddenbrooks*, he characterised early childhood as a time when 'we are allowed to see, hear, wonder and dream'.[52] Mann points out that this timeless absorption in our own fantasies cannot last. The preschool child's uncensored outpouring of comments and questions on fictional events and characters, her chanting of memorable phrases, and the acting-out of characters and scenes that are so deeply meaningful to her, begins to dry up. Stories still affect six- and seven-year-olds profoundly, but less of their response is on public display. What has been uttered openly since the child achieved language fluency now goes underground: it becomes 'internal speech', known only to the child herself. A private world is being created, as the maturing frontal lobes of the cerebral cortex enable children to begin to *choose* how much of what they think and feel is safe to share with others. A storied world, rich in emotion, identification and inspiration, will still exist within many children's minds, will continue to exist as they journey towards old age, but few parents and teachers will glimpse it more than occasionally. We may as well be standing in the cold and rain, gazing at the unyielding face of the mountainside.

Where We've Come From, Where We're Going

Longitudinal studies of individual children's reactions to adult-composed stories show three- and four-year-olds responding with dismay to perceived damage and loss, and this sensibility extends even to verbal expressions of negativity. Rather than assuming that these children are traumatised, hypersensitive, or unrepresentative of their peers, I see them simply as expressing *existential anxiety* far earlier than most adults would expect.

The 'statement/reversal' pattern we observed in self-composed 'songstries' now appears in a wider context. When listening to stories specifically designed for their interests and level of understanding, the children's comments display the same pattern, attempting to *reverse* events that trouble them, protesting at apparent 'damage', and suggesting conclusions that will 'double lock' the door that the story has, for them, opened onto fear and doubt. I have highlighted the way that emotion organises their *response* to narratives, just as it organises the *making* of the songstries we quoted in Chapter 1. 'Pretend play' shows how preschool children enact the themes that concern them, replaying parts of a disturbing story in order to control it and, perhaps, make it end differently. Similarly, fairy tales enact particular wishes and fears through the imagined actions of characters all of whom represent aspects of the protagonist.

All of this suggests the continuing dominance of the right hemisphere of the brain—suffused with fear and melancholy, *enacting* feelings rather than *articulating* them, 'thinking' by presenting images of actions, and negating as fairy tales do, not by saying 'I was wrong' but by *presenting a different set of actions*. The 'performers' of the preschool years show these right hemisphere dominated characteristics most clearly. They will not necessarily become the story makers of the future, but it seems highly probable that every adult story maker is someone whose right hemisphere has remained slightly dominant over the left. In our next chapter, we will show how the strengthening of left hemisphere influence from the age of seven produces story making that conforms more closely to adult expectations of what a story should be, yet in other ways preserves the magical thought of fairy tales.

Chapter Three

'A Place of Greater Safety'

Stories in Middle Childhood

Opening Doors

For the first eight years of my life, my family lived in modest homes in Sydney's affluent North Shore. My mother's mother, the only grandmother I knew, lived several suburbs away. But when I was nine years old, in my third year of school and beginning to be able to read fluently, my family moved to a little seaside town far to the north of Sydney. The big city, the school, and my old surroundings receded rapidly into the past. Every summer thereafter for the next ten years, my parents would drive back to Sydney so we could spend the Christmas holidays (a luxurious six weeks long) with my grandmother. Each time we arrived there, cold, stiff and tired after the five-hundred-mile drive, we would carry our luggage up three flights of steep stairs to my grandmother's apartment in a dark brick building which seemed unimaginably old to me, though in fact it had been built only fifteen years before I was born, and unimaginably tall (even though it was only three storeys at the back, and two at the front). The foyer smelled of plaster, concrete steps and metal railings; the apartment doors were of dark, polished wood and had cast iron rings to knock with. Each time my grandmother opened her heavy front door, it was as if the magic portal had opened in 'The Pied Piper'. We must have visited her apartment when we had still lived in Sydney, just a few suburbs away, but I *noticed* my grandmother's place for the first time when I was nine, and we had to travel through the night to get there: an arduous journey, ending in the discovery of a strange new world. New, yet somehow familiar. *Déjà vu.*

To me, in those slow-moving childhood years, the feelings I experienced when entering my grandmother's apartment were connected with the place itself. It seemed to trap mysteries within its faded fabrics, its worn carpets, its dust-laden pine and oak surfaces. And then there were the books: recent best-sellers jostling the cheap, uniformly-bound sets of Scott and Dickens which bowed the shelves in the heavy, glass-fronted bookcase, alongside Sir Winston Churchill's *History of the Second World War.* My Uncle Hugh had fought in that war, I knew, but since we never saw him, he was as unreal to me as the still-living and still-famous Sir Winston Churchill—or the long-dead Scott and Dickens, for that matter. In the cupboard beneath the book-case were piles of old children's books some of which had once (I deduced much later) belonged to my mother (*The Children's Blue Bird.*) Others, like *Coppernob, Second Mate* must have belonged to her brother, the mysterious Uncle Hugh. Some, older still, like W.H.G. Kingston's *Old Jack*, may well have belonged to my grandfather, who had 'died long before you were born' (those words were said with such finality that I knew, as children do, not to ask any more about him).[1]

Though old, these books were new to me. Some (like Arthur Mee's *Children's Encyclopedia*) became familiar with repeated visits[2], while others remained adult, baffling or boring until much later. Like many story-oriented children before and since, I sampled books as avidly as if they had been boxes of splendidly wrapped chocolates. Some I would put down after only a few sentences, unable to comprehend them; some I devoured immediately; others I knew I would read one day, but not now. Among those that I read immediately was *The Children's Blue Bird*, a version of Maurice Maeterlinck's 1909 'fairy play' for adults, retold for children by Maeterlinck's wife, Georgette Leblanc. I was fascinated by the volume's large format, the watery colours of its Art Deco illustrations, and its thick, discoloured pages (poor quality paper of this kind was commonly used for children's 'reward' books in the 1920s and 1930s). I did not understand Maeterlinck's allegory, but I eagerly journeyed with Mytyl and Tyltyl in their search for the Blue Bird—into the Land of Memory, where the little hero and heroine meet their dead grandparents; into the frightening Forest, where talking trees and unpleasant animals menace them; and into a blue-lit Future where they meet the busy, excited children who are waiting to be born (nowadays these yet-to-be-borns would undoubtedly be diagnosed as suffering from ADHD). Above all, I was gripped and horrified by what happened in the Palace of Night. Tall and statuesque, dark-robed Night warns the children not to touch the huge bronze doors that stand closed around her throne-room, but, in another attempt to find the Blue Bird, the boy Tyltyl insists on opening one of the doors—the door that leads, Night tells him, to 'the Wars':

> 'He tried in vain to shut the door which he had opened: an invincible force was pushing it from the other side; streams of blood flowed through

> the cracks, flames shot forth; shouts, oaths and groans mingled with the roar of cannon and the rattle of musketry . . .
>
> "Well?" asked Night, harshly. "Have you had enough? Did you see them?"
>
> "Yes, yes", replied the little fellow, sobbing. "They are hideous and awful . . . "'[3]

I read these words with a feeling of sick horror, almost as if it was *I* who had opened the forbidden door, and glimpsed the unspeakable. Like the small children in our last chapter, I reacted to fictional threat and damage as if they were real. My mirror neurones were firing in sympathy with Tyltyl (an impulsive, risk-taking person like myself—though of course I would not have so labeled myself until adulthood).

What Tyltyl sees through the opened door does not (I now know) form part of the original stage production. Maeterlinck's script (his play was as popular with adults as *Phantom of the Opera* has been in our own time and was filmed in 1940 with Shirley Temple as Mytyl) has Tyltyl simply opening the door, and then trying, with the help of the others, to push it shut again.[4] The final two lines of dialogue come direct from the play; the remainder is Leblanc's elaboration, presumably an attempt to spell out on the printed page what had been suggested onstage by lighting and sound effects. She had 'filled in a gap', and I had, unerringly, reacted to her attempt to fill it, as if somehow aware that this particular scene was problematic—just as Lindsay had been puzzled and captivated by 'let down your hair' in *Rapunzel*. But why did I select just that one scene, when Leblanc had filled out the stage dialogue in many other places? Was I already sensitised to the idea of battle, an experience I knew both my uncle and my grandfather had had, the former in the Second and the latter in the First World War? One was dead, I had never met the other, yet their photographs, in officer's uniform, gazed at me every time I entered my grandmother's lounge room.

There was a deeper significance to that scene in the Palace of Night, something to do with innocent curiosity leading to terror. Maybe it resonated with the Greek myth of Pandora opening the forbidden box (a steel engraving of which also hung in my grandmother's apartment)? And maybe the image of Night's doors was so 'real' because of my grandmother's dark, heavy front door? For I was already 'seeing', 'hearing' and feeling what I read about in books, my memories of real-world experiences supplying dim but effective sights and sounds to match the fictional ones. Most children who become fluent readers do this of course—and adults do it too. The process is only semi-conscious, and (at least until the last thirty years) little talked about by literary scholars or psychologists. It is most certainly *not* a matter of readers 'deciding' to give meaning to certain words and phrases by consciously calling up particular experiences of their own—as an actor might deliberately recall a personal experience in order to recreate a particular emotion on stage.

Rather, as we read, the memories of particular experiences well up *automatically* to supply the missing dimension of meaning, the whole process occurring instantaneously and smoothly, as if some Fairy Godmother had waved her magic wand.

TV dramatist Dennis Potter, who died in 1996, put it well, remembering the Bible stories, hymns and folk tales he heard in his early years:

> 'As a child—aged four, five, six or seven—it is natural to see the surrounding landscape as the landscape one reads about. So I thought of the big ponds near the pit where Dad worked as Galilee. The Valley of the Shadow of Death was a lane descending between overhanging hedges where you tended to want to whistle—but I was a timid child anyway, and the Forest itself was a labyrinth of old oaks and beeches and ash trees. The words both of those hymns and the Bible, and fairy stories too, fitted very happily into that landscape.'[5]

When nine- or ten-year-olds are asked about their experience of stories, they cannot usually talk about the sort of process Potter has just described, and no more, probably, could I have done at that age. When adult investigators ask their leaden-footed questions ('You said you liked 'Cinderella'? Why?), the answers they receive do not really engage with the question, or simply retell a part of the story: 'Cinderella is a grile [*girl*] that has very nies [*nice*] invengeras [*adventures*]' says Barbara, aged 9 years and one month. 'I like *The Lion, the Witch and the Wardrobe* because when the children were playing Hide-in-seek one hid in the wardrobe and hid behind the clothes and found herself in a cold snowy land' is the response of Helen at ten years and one month.[6]

It is easy to propose a steady developmental process in which the left hemisphere gradually takes its place as the equal of the right, and in Chapter 2 this is the kind of view I presented, but the reactions of these children to researcher Arthur Applebee's questions about 'Cinderella' shows the limitations of such an approach. Nine- and ten-year-olds may have undergone Piaget's 'five to seven shift', they may have reached 'the age of reason', but 'Why?' is a left-hemisphere question, and most of them can only answer it in a right-hemisphere way. 'Re-*doing*' the story is the closest they can come to *explaining* why it is important to them. They cannot tell us, but they can *show* us—just as our three- and four-year-olds in our last chapter showed us what 'Rapunzel' or 'Red Riding Hood' meant to them by acting out an incident from those tales. Yet an exceptional nine-year-old—perhaps a left-hemisphere-dominant one—can manage something that goes beyond this—a glimpse of *pattern*, the first signs of the ability to 'generalise' and even 'abstract' that Piaget associates with adolescence. Richard, at nine years and three months, is one such child: 'I think that the Famous Five stori's are quite good. In the storis there is a lot of adventure and a lot of things happen. They get bad luke [*luck*] at the beginning and thing all kam out all right in the end.'

Despite his somewhat rudimentary spelling and grammar, Richard is aware that there is a common 'shape' to the Famous Five books, and that initial misfortune ('bad luke') is predictably transformed by the end, when 'thing kam out all right'. In his own way, he has recognised the Old Brain pattern of threat/threat averted or misfortune/misfortune rectified that we discussed in Chapter 1, and he can state it as a *generalisation* about the series as a whole. Once Piaget's 'five to seven shift' has run its course, children employ the standard of realism ('Does this detail correspond to the world I know?') in a more focussed and consistent way than before. It is around this age that story-wise children notice that fictional characters, although they eat and drink, never seem to need to use the bathroom! The same pragmatic awareness leads them to critique earlier favourites. Thus nine-year-old Morwenna made a series of disparaging comments during a reading of *The Magic Faraway Tree*, indicating her amused awareness of various aspects of the 'Blyton formula': 'They're always saying, "No more adventures for me!" and they always do [have more adventures]!' Her scornful criticisms alternated with indications that she still found the series gratifying.[7]

But responses like Richard's or Morwenna's are unlikely to come when educational psychologists ask their 'cold call' questions. Insightful responses are far more likely when the child has just heard (or read) the story in question, when the child is 'in the presence of the story', so to speak. Children need the actual *experience* of the story to activate the abilities of their left hemisphere. That is what Piaget meant by 'concrete [mental] operations'. Only years later—and sometimes not even then—will the average child be able to abstract from a story the pattern that makes it appealing to her, to know that *The Lion, the Witch and the Wardrobe* makes such an impact not because its heroine crawls into a wardrobe and finds herself in a 'cold snowy land' (the literal 'surface' of the story's events) but because Lewis' story is 'about' being transported out of mundane reality into somewhere exciting and meaningful—something many of us crave, though only a minority of us, perhaps, articulate it.

****

One of the books I noticed on my grandmother's bookshelves, long before I could actually read it, was Charles Dickens' *Great Expectations*. The Old Brain responds to the concrete and the literal—what is 'in front of our noses'. *Great Expectations* stood out for me from the rest of the Dickens volumes because its title was *not* (like *David Copperfield*, *Nicholas Nickleby*, *Martin Chuzzlewit* or *Little Dorrit*) also the name of its protagonist. Yet the Old Brain also instinctively grasps underlying similarities, and although I had only a vague idea of what 'great expectations' might be, I somehow knew that I had them too. At nine and ten, I could not get much beyond the first page. Yet, despite the Victorian complexity of Dickens' sentences and its many long and unfamiliar words, I kept returning, year after year, to those opening paragraphs, as if already I knew that here was a story that was *mine*:

> 'As *I never saw my father or my mother*, and *never saw any likeness of either of them* (for their days were long before the days of photographs), my first fancies regarding what they were like, were unreasonably derived from their tombstones. The shape of the letters on my father's, gave me an odd idea that he was a square, stout, dark man, with curly black hair. From the character and turn of the inscription, *'Also Georgiana, Wife of the Above'*, I drew a childish conclusion that my mother was freckled and sickly. To five little stone lozenges, each about a foot and a half long, which were arranged in a neat row beside their grave, and were sacred to the memory of five little brothers of mine—who *gave up trying to get a living exceedingly early in that universal struggle*—I am indebted for a belief I religiously entertained that they had all been born on their backs with their hands in their pockets, and *had never taken them out in this state of existence.*' [Italics mine]

The word 'never', three times repeated in a paragraph about death, seems to have affected me somewhat similarly to the way that expressions of negation seem to have affected the much younger children I quoted in the last chapter. I remember that I responded far more to the 'dying fall' of this passage than to its humour (indeed, I did not perceive any humour at all). Loss and loneliness pervades the next paragraph too. It is one of Dickens' most impressively controlled and moving pieces of writing, and it would become a highly significant one for me:

> 'Ours was the marsh country, down by the river, within, as the river wound, twenty miles of the sea. My first most vivid and broad impression of the identity of things, seems to me to have been gained on a memorable raw afternoon towards evening. At such a time I found out for certain, that this bleak place overgrown with nettles was a churchyard; and that Philip Pirrip, late of this parish, and also Georgiana, wife of the above, were dead and buried; and that Alexander, Bartholomew, Abraham, Tobias, and Roger, infant children of the aforesaid, were also dead and buried; and that the dark flat wilderness beyond the churchyard, intersected with dykes and mounds and gates, with scattered cattle feeding on it, was the marshes; and that the low leaden line beyond was the river; and that the distant savage lair from which the wind was rushing, was the sea; and that the small bundle of shivers growing afraid of it all, and beginning to cry, was Pip.'[1]

The brain's right hemisphere responds instinctively to the threat posed by darkness and 'immensity', flooding Pip with the primitive emotion of fear—and we start to feel it too. Significantly, it is Pip's apprehension of what death means that precedes this fear, and precipitates his dawning awareness of his own identity—something typical of many children as they reach school age

('I'm *me!*' realised one six-year-old girl—who later became my wife). Consciousness of one's identity goes hand in hand with heightened awareness of the identity of others, of others' difference from oneself, of new places, and unfamiliar experiences. As the left hemisphere of the cerebral cortex comes into its own, these things can be not simply *experienced*, but *thought about* and their components examined. And some of those new and different experiences are literary ones.

Even at ten or eleven, this passage, 'Ours was the marsh country . . . ' was already rich in associations for me, associations both personal and literary. Since our move from Sydney, I myself had been living in a small fishing town on the north coast of New South Wales. It was very different from the Chatham to which Dickens' family moved when he was five, but I now had seaside smells, sights and sounds to bring to Dickens' words. More significantly still, I had previous *literary* experiences, in the form of two children's books whose settings and images were somewhat similar: Hugh Lofting's *The Voyages of Doctor Dolittle*, which my mother had read to me before I learned to read myself, and Enid Blyton's *Five Go to Smuggler's Top*, which remained my favourite of the entire *Five* series.[2] In both books, there were marshes, loneliness, and melancholy; in both, these images and feelings were associated with a hidden, secret past, and people who were not what they seemed (though I would not then have been able to 'abstract' those themes). At nine, I did not realise that Lofting certainly, and Blyton probably, had themselves read *Great Expectations* as young people, and had incorporated traces of its ambience (in Lofting's case traces of its actual wording) into their own stories. The right hemisphere instinctively recognises images, patterns, feelings that correspond with those it already knows. We're about to see a striking example of this in one future writer's early response to fairy tales.

Janet and Charlie in Fairyland

Around the age of eight, New Zealand poet and novelist Janet Frame was introduced to *Grimm's Fairy Tales* by her friend Poppy. (Janet's parents ended the budding friendship when Poppy also introduced Janet to the facts of life!). The Grimm volume was a revelation to Janet, who excitedly read 'The Twelve Dancing Princesses' aloud to her sisters and brother:

> ' . . . and as I read and they listened, I knew and they knew, gloriously, that *we* were the dancing princesses—not twelve, but four; and as I read, I saw in my mind the place in the coat cupboard in the corner of the bedroom where we could vanish to an underground world and the orchard that was 'our' orchard along the gully where the boughs of the trees honked and cried out when they were broken, silver and gold trees . . . And the shoes, danced each morning to shreds, we knew about these, with our own shoe

> soles flapping away from the uppers, and Dad sitting carefully marking and cutting the leather, and with the tacks in his mouth, bending over the boot-last while he half-soled and heeled our shoes, complaining, like the king in the story, 'Where have you been that your toes are scuffed and your soles are worn through?' Where indeed!'[3]

For shy, self-doubting Janet, growing up in cheerful poverty in 1930s New Zealand, the Grimms' fanciful and poetic tale was a major intervention. She did not simply associate the events and scenes in the story with ones already familiar to her, as I did with *Great Expectations.* Almost, she seems to have experienced the tale as *merging* with her daily life, *elevating* the tattered shoes and the bedroom cupboard into things of high significance and intense delight. For Janet, the words of the fairy tale contained the power that magically transformed her world; in fact, that power came from within *her.* Freud says that we unconsciously 'put' our own psychic energy into someone or something (cathexis) and in so doing, we *lend* it that magic which then (in turn) casts its glamour over the mundane events and characters of our own lives. But the 'lending' is not something any of us *decides* to do—conscious decisions are largely a function of the left hemisphere: rather, it happens automatically and instantly, when the right hemisphere responds to a similarity between a new experience, and a pattern that is already familiar. But how, exactly, are such links made?

English language versions of the Grimm story mention the highly improbable detail that all twelve princesses slept in a single room.[4] Details like this are 'fault lines' in the story's bedrock, fissures that open momentarily, prompting readers–often quite unconsciously–to engage in a special kind of investment like Janet's: 'Grimm's Fairy Tales was everybody's story seen in a special way, with something new added to the ordinary rules of observation'.[5] Her realisation was prompted by the fact that she and her three sisters slept, top to tail, in one bed: the family could not afford separate beds, let alone separate rooms—a solid similarity within an otherwise exotic, fairy tale world. At eight, few of us see this quite as clearly as Frame (and to be fair, she is writing as an adult, *reconstructing* her eight-year-old experience). We can listen with deep absorption to a story of princesses who escape from the King, their father, and dance the night away in a wondrous underground palace without consciously recognising ourselves as rebellious 'princesses' or the King as our overprotective father. Instead, we experience a compelling stream of events and images, sweeping us along, saturating us with a sense of something meaningful, while that meaning remains one that we cannot rationally grasp. If the tale were to make the meaning conscious ('This is about your own boredom and your own longing to get away from your family') then it would lose most of its power, and in fact, most of us would energetically reject such an interpretation. The magic inheres in the fact that we do *not* understand how it works, we only feel its effects. That is the power of Story, and it is a power that belongs to the brain's right hemisphere.

A century before Janet, a young Charlie Dickens experienced the world of fairy tales similarly, yet subtly differently. In 1821, when Dickens was nine, the first English translation of *Grimm's Tales* was still two years away. He did know Perrault's 'Red Riding Hood' though. He was a highly impressionable and sensitive little boy, yet the horror of Red Riding Hood's ending (prettied-up versions had not yet appeared) did not appear (at least in his hindsight) to have distressed him at all, and, like little Trina Schart Hyman, he 'fell in love' with Red Riding Hood herself. For Charlie, she seems to have been a very early version of that idealised feminine figure (Jung calls it an 'anima') he sought throughout his life.

> 'Little Red Riding Hood trips through the forest with her basket and comes to me one Christmas Eve to give me information about the cruelty and treachery of that dissembling Wolf who ate her grandmother, without making any impression on his appetite, and then ate her, after making that ferocious joke about his teeth. She was my first love. I felt that if I could have married Little Red Riding Hood, I should have known perfect bliss. But, it was not to be; and there was nothing for it but to look out the wolf in the Noah's Ark there, and put him late in the procession on the table, as a monster who was to be degraded.'[6]

But the tales that fired the young Dickens' imagination most of all were those from a completely different source, the collection we know in English as *The Arabian Nights*, and from eighteenth-century pastiches of the *Nights*, like James Ridley's *Tales of the Genii*.[7] For Dickens, as for many other literate children of the late eighteenth and early nineteenth centuries, the *Arabian Nights* occupied a place that the Grimms were soon to usurp: as a touchstone of magical imagery, impossible gratification—and shocking, startling cruelty:

> 'Hush! Again a forest, and somebody up in a tree . . . an Eastern King with a glittering scimitar and a turban. By Allah, *two* Eastern Kings, for I see another, looking over his shoulder! Down upon the grass, at the tree's foot, lies the full length of a coal-black Giant, stretched asleep, with his head in a lady's lap; and near them is a glass box, fastened with four locks of shining steel, in which he keeps the lady prisoner when he is awake. I see the four keys at his girdle now. The lady makes signs to the two kings in the tree, who softly descend. It is the setting of the bright *Arabian Nights*, all about scimitars and slippers and turbans, and dwarfs and giants and genii and fairies, and bluebeards and riches and caverns, all new and all true.'[8]

'All new and all true'. Again, this is an *adult* Dickens, recreating what he first experienced many years earlier, but again, he does so in a way that speaks for every nine-year-old reader. When the right hemisphere is left to itself, with the left hemisphere temporarily 'on hold'—as in dreams, or trance states—there is no question about whether things are 'real' or not, for that is the left hemisphere's question. To the unaided right hemisphere, everything is both *new* (experienced for the first time) and *true*. Like Frame, Dickens tells us that the language and imagery of those magical tales infused startling new possibilities into the everyday things around him. Notice that even though he's describing his boyhood, his account is in the present tense—the tense that represents the right hemisphere because it tells us that 'this is happening right now, as we speak':

> 'Oh, now all common things become uncommon and enchanted to me. All lamps are wonderful; all rings are talismans. Common flower-pots are full of treasure, with a little earth scattered on the top; trees are for Ali Baba to hide in; beefsteaks are to throw down into the Valley of Diamonds, that the precious stones may stick to them, and be carried by eagles to their nests, whence the traders, with loud cries, will scare them . . . Any iron ring let into stone is the entrance to a cave which only waits for the magician, and the little fire, and the necromancy, that will make the earth shake . . . My very rocking-horse—there he is, with his nostrils turned completely inside-out, indicative of Blood!—should have a peg in his neck, by virtue thereof to fly away with me, as the wooden horse did with the Prince of Persia, in the sight of all his father's Court'.

Both Frame and Dickens focus on the objects in their own lives that correspond with their magically transformed fictional equivalents, but Dickens, at least in hindsight, seems to have consciously *used* the images and possibilities of the tales to transform his own life, to achieve 'the hope of something beyond that place and time'—a process more reminiscent of the left hemisphere than the right. In this he resembled University of Chicago classical scholar David Grene, who said that at the age of eight or nine, 'the strongest sense of pleasure I enjoyed was . . . in trying to interchange the content of books into real facts of my own life'—a process which included retelling the great stories of history, 'to suit my notion of how things *ought* to have come out'.[9]

As we shall see, children who will later become storytellers often have a low tolerance for the boring and the humdrum, as well as for the distressing and unsatisfying. Nine-year-old Dickens yearns for something higher, something more meaningful and special, than the disappointingly ordinary world of reality—and he finds it in the words and images of fairy tales. No doubt it was this same yearning that was operating when his father showed him a large house on the outskirts of Rochester called Gad's Hill Place, and told him that one day, if he worked very hard, he himself might live in such a house. At the time, the Dickens family lived in narrow little rented terraces, but the image of Gad's Hill Place stayed in eight-year-old Charlie's mind until, as his biographer Peter Ackroyd says, 'thirty-six years later, he bought it'[10]—not just any grand house, but *the exact same house his father had pointed out to him all those years ago*, for the right hemisphere can be astonishingly literal in its need to 'make real' or 're-do' key people, places and events.

> 'In all these golden fables there was never gold enough for me. I always wanted more. I saw no reason why there should not be mountains and rivers of gold, instead of paltry little caverns and olive pots . . . for when imagination does begin to deal with what is so hard of attainment in reality, it might at least get out of bounds for once in a way, and let us have enough.'[11]

The twentieth century's two most successful writers for children, Enid Blyton and Roald Dahl (Rowling's *Harry Potter* series really belongs to the twenty-first) seem to have felt much the same way, and ensured that their own modern fairy tales would always have 'enough'—enough adventures, enough sweets, and most certainly, enough *chocolate*. As if metaphorically following his own prescription for 'mountains and rivers of gold', Dickens himself became famous for a style of description that tended to excess—a careless delight in language for its own sake, epithet piled upon epithet, a torrent of vivid, dramatic speech that generations of readers loved, but some critics thought undignified and exaggerated. Beneath that manic exuberance we can glimpse, perhaps, a boy of twelve who craved the security and opportunities that his father's bankruptcy had denied him. And behind that twelve year old (though in fact he seems to have been both loved and admired within his family) we can discern a much younger boy, who longed, painfully and lifelong, for a more total and encompassing love than the one his parents offered him, and who, at midlife, tried desperately to find that love in a woman young enough to be his daughter, a quest as forlorn as his early wish to marry Red Riding Hood.

What do Dickens' and Frame's reconstructed responses to fairy tales help us to see about the tales themselves? Both writers note the strong impression made on them by the wondrous *images*–yet these images are really few in number, and their 'wonder' is curiously matter of fact. Silver and gold trees, a spindle that sends you to sleep for a hundred years, a glass box fastened by four locks of shining steel, a cottage made of gingerbread—all are unusual and striking when we first meet them, but their 'magic' is not elaborated or enhanced in words. Similarly with fairy tale *characters*: we know nothing about Snow White except that she has black hair and white skin, and that her stepmother is jealous of her beauty. The dwarfs are just 'seven little men' (Disney's animated movie gave them individual names and habits, consciously filling the gap left by the fairy tale itself). In fact, if we try too hard to imagine how fairy tale characters, settings and objects *look*, we may lose their magic in literal details that somehow fail to match the tale's baldly powerful words. As we saw in Chapter 2, fairy tales work in the same way as dreams. The contents of dreams, whether recognisable or bizarre, strike us as new-minted and 'real' while we are dreaming. This is because there is no observing consciousness (the left hemisphere) to come between the images and us, no inner voice that says, 'Oh, this is preposterous!' or 'Wait a minute, such things can't exist'. Similarly, fairy tales have no space for description because description presupposes a self which not only *sees* an object, but *reflects* upon what it sees, and because (for self-conscious writers) description also presupposes an empathic awareness of readers or listeners other than ourselves. If we are only talking to ourselves (which is, in a way, what we are doing in dreams, and what Anthony and Emily were doing in Chapter 3), then we do not need to describe anything, because *we* can see it, and we are the only audience. Dreaming is the Old Brain 'thinking' in the right hemisphere's analogical mode, not in the left hemisphere's 'digital' (languaged) communication, which has a different kind of logic, and a different function.

Similarly, the sense of *time* is properly the domain of the left hemisphere. Fairy tales begin abruptly, flinging us into a world that we are *expected* to understand. They do not bother to locate it geographically or chronologically except in the vaguest way: 'In a certain country there lived a widow and her three daughters', or 'Once there lived a King who had three sons . . . ' Unlike dreams, fairy tales do end conclusively, but their conclusions seem (to an adult reader) abrupt and unrealistic. I have speculated that it is the maturing left hemisphere which imposes these conclusions on a narrative that might otherwise continue indefinitely, but they speak to a part of us that has only the most primitive sense of time. The curious, truncated way in which the tales typically conclude—the good rewarded by riches and marriage, the evil punished or destroyed—is another clue to fairy tales' status as Old Brain narratives. They cannot envisage much beyond gratified desire and the elimination of threat, and conclude when these things have been accomplished. The long journey of human life towards old age and death is not a part of the fairy tale view, any more than a preschool child can fully grasp the concept that it will one day cease to exist. Human beings rarely, if ever, 'live happily ever after'. We all learn that eventually, although some of us take a very long time over the learning of it, especially where 'love' is concerned.

By the age of seven or so, a child's left hemisphere has matured sufficiently to enable them to question the hyperbolic images of fairy tale—as a young Hilary Mantel does with 'Cinderella':

> 'It is such a treacherous object to wear, splintering, cutting the curved, tender sole of the dancing foot . . . the whole situation was too precarious, you were too dependent on irresponsible agents like pumpkins and mice, and there was always midnight, approaching tick-tock, the minutes shaving away, the minutes before you were reduced to ashes and rags.'[12]

This is the exact thing that Lucy Sprague Mitchell fiercely objected to in fairy tales: the fact that they do not teach children 'how the world actually works'.

Bruno Bettelheim, on the contrary, defended fairy tales just as fiercely in his controversial 1976 book *The Uses of Enchantment*. Bettelheim saw them as devices for teaching young children important lessons about life—but in a way that bypassed consciousness. The great child psychoanalyst was a bit of a confidence trickster who claimed qualifications he did not possess and arrogantly dismissed *Where the Wild Things Are* without bothering to read it first. However, on the subject of fairy tales, he was may have got it right.[13] In fact, *both* Bettleheim and Mitchell are right. We experience the world in two almost separate ways, because our two hemispheres experience it separately. Both insist on their own 'reality'. Yet, as with binocular vision, we need to merge both 'halves' in order to grasp the world in its totality and complexity. Our functioning depends on the co-operation of the two realities, as the brain transmits impulses back and forth in nano-seconds, from the right hemisphere to the left, and then back to the right. Most of the time, this *entente cordiale* works reasonably well. But as we've seen, the entities our brain yokes together still retain powerful, separate loyalties—as when Robert E. Lee refused command of the Union armies in 1861 because his deeper loyalty was to his 'old Virginia'. The place where we were born, the place we grew up in, exerts a stronger pull on us than any subsequent one, and can transcend 'higher' loyalties: *Heimat* trumps 'nation state'.[14] And in a similar way, the Old Brain tugs at our feelings, for all the newer left hemisphere's logical persuasion, because it came first, at the very beginning of our lives.

The Stories Nine-Year-Olds Write

In the light of what we've been saying, it should not surprise us that when eight-, nine- and ten-year-olds compose stories of their own, their narratives are in some ways similar to fairy tales—not in their content (what they are about) but in their process: the way they are told. The stories of elementary school children have protagonists to whom the events of the story happen, but we see these heroes or heroines only from the outside, learning hardly anything about what they think or how they feel; and the same holds true for the other characters as well. Settings are barely described. The young storytellers assume that we will know what they are talking about, with little or no introduction. The stories, however, *do* have clear beginnings and (less often) clear conclusions too. This is a dramatic leap forward from the endless, cyclic compositions of two and three year year-olds' time. It is no longer Old Brain Time—yet (as in fairy tales) it is not New Brain time either. Let's look at one such story, painstakingly handwritten by a ten-year-old girl 150 years ago:

> 'There was once a little girl and her name was Anne. She was born at a little village named Thornton and by and by she grew a good girl. Her father

> and mother were both very rich. Mr and Mrs Wood were their names and she was their only child, but she was not too much indulged.
>
> Once little Anne and her mother went to see a fine castle near London, about ten miles from it. Anne was very much pleased with it.
>
> Once Anne and her papa and her Mama went to sea in a ship and they had very fine weather all the way, but Anne's Mama was very sick and Anne attended her with so much care. She gave her her medicine'.[15]

This brief narrative has a fairy tale-like beginning ('There was once a little girl . . .'), and as in a fairy tale, she is the 'only child' of wealthy parents (a fairy tale would have made them King and Queen). This is a gratifying detail, because the girl who composed this story had never known wealth. Contrary to fairy tale practice, however, the heroine and her parents are 'introduced' and we are told where they live, in a named place in the real world. There follows a fairly coherent sequence of events, all centred on the protagonist, Anne—although there is no link between the visit to the 'fine castle near London' and the later sea voyage, except that in both cases, Anne and her mother are present. Anne's father plays no part after the first paragraph. Nor do the details (that Anne's parents are 'very rich', that Anne 'is not too much indulged') become significant later. The story does not grow organically out of its introductory section, in the way that we adults expect. Rather (as a dream might) it simply moves to another scene without 'filling in' what might logically come between this scene and its predecessor. Could it be that the narrator is secretly worried that little Anne *has* been 'too much indulged', and needs to ensure that Anne is speedily given the opportunity to reverse this 'negative' by giving her sick mother 'so much care'? We can only guess.

The ten-year-old narrator tells us that 'Anne was very much pleased with [the castle]') but later, where we might expect Anne to be distressed at her mother's illness, there is no mention of her feelings. Only her actions are recorded ('She attended her with so much care. She gave her her medicine'). It is on this abrupt note that the story ends, as suddenly as any preschooler's monologue, after a reversal of fortune has been 'made right' (or apparently so, for we are not actually told that the mother recovered from her illness). Quite possibly, the juvenile author intended to write more, but was distracted, or lost interest. Although at nine or ten the vast majority of children are aware of how 'proper stories' end, few of them are unable to duplicate these conclusions in a convincing way. In place of verbal description of people and settings, our child author accompanied the story with six small paintings, but some of these 'illustrations' depict things that are not mentioned in the story itself. The story was produced as a tiny 'book', with two supplementary pages that include a detailed map of several imaginary countries, lists of regions, and population figures for two towns. None of these details appears to be related to the narrative itself.[16] The storyteller does not firmly or finally distinguish 'story' from other imaginative activities. If this seems 'childish', consider the case of Tolkien's appendices to *The Lord of the Rings*—Hobbit genealogical tables, discourses on the Elvish language, chronologies—all of only tangential relevance to the story itself, and skipped by many readers. But for Tolkien himself it was the other way around. The *world* of Middle-Earth was what counted, the *story* of Frodo and the Ring of Power was simply an outgrowth of that world—a world which existed long before Tolkien wrote *The Hobbit*, and on which he continued to labour long after *The Lord of the Rings* had appeared. (It is precisely because of this that the trilogy's world has a solidity lacking in the creations of most of Tolkien's imitators.)

'There was once a little girl and her name was Anne' is the earliest surviving composition by one Charlotte Brontë, later to attain lasting fame as the author of *Jane Eyre*. The tale was written for her younger sister Anne (later the author of *Agnes Grey* and *The Tenant of Wildfell Hall*) and it may be that the seasickness of the fictional Anne's 'Mama' was a much softened allusion to the illness from which the sisters' real mother had died, soon after Anne's birth. Is this why the story ends without any certainty that 'Mama' did in fact recover? In the light of the biographical facts, it may well be that Charlotte's story originates in a wish to repair loss and damage, depicting the life her sister *could* have had, had their mother survived.

A century and a half later, in the summer of 1976, three eight-year-old schoolgirls collaborated on the writing of a story called 'The Tidy House'.[17] Their story is about a young adult couple, Jo and Mark, who are still childless (that's why their house is tidy!) and their adult friends Jamie (a female one) and Jason, who already have a child. During the story, Jo gets pregnant (not without some effort—the doctor tells her and Mark to 'do the—harder'!) and has a baby son. All of this sounds extraordinarily 'grown up' subject matter for three little girls, and but Carla, Lindie and Melissa are writing about the life that goes on in their own homes: 'The Tidy House' is *truly* a 'here and now story'. In many ways, it seems very different from Charlotte's. First and most obviously, it is a composite product (the girls took turns to write episodes, and argued earnestly about the process of composition). Secondly, the authors are writing in a classroom. Yet from the beginning, 'The Tidy House' was driven by the girls' own imperatives, particularly those of Carla. Like Charlotte Brontë, Carla started writing because she had something she wanted to express, not simply because her teacher had instructed her to. Thirdly, much of 'The Tidy House' consists of dialogue (Carla's contributions entirely so). These are children for whom television shows have provided the major model of story, rather than books read aloud (the model encountered by most of the preschool storytellers we met in Chapter 3) or the adult language of novels and newspapers (which was the model for the young Brontës). Charlotte, like most children of her age (both then and now) writes in the simple past tense, the conventional tense of storytelling. Lindie, Carla and Melissa often abandon it in favour of the 'historic present', which as we mentioned above, is a way that language can represent the right hemisphere's 'here and now' consciousness:

> 'Now, outside their house/
> it is brown on the walls/
> and has blue curtains on the right side/
> and brown cord on the left . . . '[18]

Yet despite important differences, there is a surprising continuity between 'The Tidy House' and Charlotte's story for Anne. 'The Tidy House' gets straight into the action, and no attempt is made to introduce the characters, or to set the scene. Proportional to its length, it contains even less description than Charlotte's. Melissa is *capable* of integrating written description into a story; but like Charlotte, she prefers to draw pictures (she and Lindie made an elaborate collage picture of the Tidy House). Despite being so much longer than Charlotte's story, 'The Tidy House' contains even less acknowledgment of the characters' inner lives. We can *hear* what the characters say to each other and *observe* what they do, but as in fairy tales, *we are hardly ever told what they think or feel*. Of course the girls are writing about their parents and siblings, whose words they can reproduce very accurately, but whose actual feelings and thoughts they may not (at nine or ten years old) understand or share. However, the girls do not portray their *own* feelings either: the main characters are all adults. Carla, Lindie and Melissa create a fictional world that is, or at least appears to be, external to them, revealing their personal emotions and perspectives only implicitly. As Charlotte Brontë (now thirty, but describing her ten-year-old heroine Jane) acutely observes: 'Children can feel, but they cannot analyse their feelings; and if the analysis is partly effected in thought, they know not how to express the result of the process in words.'[19]

'The Tidy House' unfolds in time but the narrators pay little attention to its passing, and simply skip from one 'scene' to the next (which may be several years later) with only rapid, superficial marking of the change:

> 'Jamie was soon pregnant
> and soon she was in the hospital
> and soon had a baby
> another boy it was.
> "What can we call it, Jason?"
> "I don't know, dear. What about Darren?"
> "All right".'[20]

When a new plot development needs to be introduced (little Darren and his brother Carl don't get on well), the narrative skips straight from Darren as a baby ('He was lovely') to Darren as a four-year-old. The only acknowledgement of time's passing is the word 'soon'. There is nothing about what has happened to Carl (or to his parents Jo and Jamie) in these four years. Darren becomes an 'instant four-year-old' *because Carla and her co-authors need him to be.* Their need to 'get on with the story' trumps their ability to imagine what their *characters* might experience. And, like preschool songstries, 'The Tidy House' has no proper ending, simply breaking off at an arbitrary point: 'So they went home and had tea and went to bed and—'. Charlotte Bronte's tale, too, ends less than conclusively, as if the youthful narrator had been interrupted and never returned to the tale.

In most other ways, though, both 'There was once a little girl' and 'The Tidy House' represent a very different sort of narrative from the two- and three-year-olds' compositions we examined in Chapter 1. A clear 'I am me' awareness unifies an elementary school child's actions and experiences, enabling her to narrate a story with a consistent hero or protagonist. There can be a bevy of characters other than the protagonist, although few or none of these will be described either in terms of their external appearance, or their personalities. What none of our child narrators can do, what is utterly beyond them all, is to create any real sense of mystery or suspense. None of them imitates the tricks and 'hooks' that older writers employ to evoke the thrill of mystery, perhaps because these devices require a level of self-conscious artistry that will only come with further left hemisphere maturation, in adolescence. Even a nine-year-old C.S. Lewis, who in his 'Animal Land' narratives'[21] so fluently imitates the adult language of the boys' stories and Shakespearian plays he had read, could not create suspense or mystery, as he later would in *The Chronicles of Narnia.*

On Being a Good Noticer

1920s children's author Hugh Lofting's second book, *The Voyages of Doctor Dolittle,* introduces the character of Tommy Stubbins. At the age of nine-and-a-half, Tommy confides to Polynesia the Parrot that he would like to be a naturalist like his hero, the great John Dolittle. 'Are you a good noticer?' she immediately asks.[22] In other words, does Tommy go through life with his eyes and ears open? Does he pay attention to the tiny, changing details of everything around him? Tommy is indeed a 'good noticer'—and so are all children who will later become story makers. Later in his life, Tommy sets out to record everything he has learned of John Dolittle, his animal friends, and their adventures. Even as an adult, he retains the 'cataloguing imagination' of the nine-year-old, which means that his narrative is at times quite prosaic, not unlike that of *The Tidy House.* Apart from the first, every story in the series is told by Tommy in the first person.

I was not the only child reader to resent the presence of the worthy but boring Stubbins, and to long for the third person narrative of *The Story of Doctor Dolittle.*[23] Like much younger children, I felt uncomfortable with a first person narrative, which invited me to identify with the person telling the story, instead of simply immersing myself in the tale. (I didn't like the first person narrative in *Great Expectations* either, but felt compelled to read it nonetheless.) Worse still, I myself was close to Tommy's age—so I felt I *ought* to identify with him, even though I didn't want to. A story told by a named, individual narrator is a step further towards a left hemisphere dominated literary experience, a step away from a story that comes from somewhere else, and for whom an anonymous narrator is merely the vehicle. I was in the same position as Homer's audience: to me, the *story* was what counted, and it existed independently of any author, any singer of tales.[24]

As a child, John Fowles was a 'good noticer' in exactly the sense Polynesia meant. Growing up in the 1930s, Fowles kept notebooks in which he meticulously documented the flora and fauna of the moorland around his family's home in Devon. Typically of many school-aged children, his imagination seemed to be focused more on nature than on people. Not surprisingly, his favourite book was Richard Jefferies' *Bevis*, whose hero (an incisive portrait of Jefferies himself as a child) also immerses himself in nature, playing elaborate 'pretend' games in the countryside around his home and describing with loving fidelity the changing seasons, birdlife and other wild creatures.[25] Although *Bevis* is regarded as a classic of Victorian children's literature, it is quintessentially a New Brain narrative, in which Jefferies writes about Bevis like an adult telling another adult *about* a child—with detachment and occasional amusement. And it is interesting that when he himself grew up, Fowles would also become a 'New Brain' writer, for all his best-known novels were for most of his readers synonymous with mystery and romantic longing.

Where Jefferies observed and described the world of nature, young Charlie Dickens, a child of the city if ever there was one, noticed *human beings* above all else: how they spoke, how they dressed, what they did. Even when he was too young to understand what any of it meant, his camera-like mind recorded every detail, as if on film. The first time she read *Dombey and Son*, Dickens' older sister Fanny immediately recognised Mrs Pipchin, the unpleasant landlady with whom the sickly Paul Dombey is sent to board. The fictional character was, Fanny realised, the Dickens family's own landlady in Hawk Street, Portsmouth. Her brother had been only two years old when the family lodged with her, yet as a thirty-four-year-old adult he had (according to Fanny) recalled and reproduced her clothing and manner exactly:

> 'This celebrated Mrs Pipchin was a marvellous ill-favoured, ill-conditioned old lady, of a stooping figure, with a mottled face, like bad marble, a hook nose, and a hard grey eye, that looked as if it might have been hammered at on an anvil without sustaining any injury. Forty years at least had elapsed since the Peruvian mines had been the death of Mr Pipchin; but his relict still wore black bombazeen, of such a lustreless, deep, dead, sombre shade, that gas itself couldn't light her up after dark, and her presence was a quencher of any number of candles.'[26]

As two-year-old Charlie had noticed 'a mottled face, like bad marble', so little Roald Dahl noticed with disgust the tiny fragments of food lodged in the beards of grown-up men he disliked. Thirty years later, they emerged, exaggerated and intensified, in children's stories like *The Twits.* The details recorded by the mind of a preschool child are isolated close-ups, shorn of context. Each sense impression, registered with such fidelity, is 'new' even if it has been experienced before; and every impression—whether it be something in the real world, or something encountered in a story—is equally 'true'. When the poet William Wordsworth sadly wrote about the passing of the 'glory' he had experienced as a child, he was reflecting a literal truth.[27] Even as late as nine or ten, we really *do* see the world more clearly, more vividly, than we will ever see it again, for visual acuity peaks at around this age. Nine-year-olds certainly are good noticers, but as we have seen, they cannot put the results of their observations to use in story making—not yet.

Sharp, focused detail is one of the things that distinguishes New Brain narratives from Old Brain ones, because the left hemisphere pays close attention to individual 'bits' of the whole picture, and selects precise words to convey what it sees. Yet precise detail is not sufficient in itself, and indeed, too much of it can render a scene or a character *less* credible and 'realistic' than too little, because the 'parts' get in the way of the whole. It is impossible to imagine a nine-year-old Dickens being able to create the description of Mrs Pipchin he wrote in his thirties, because in *Dombey and Son* each detail is subordinate to a coherent sense of this malevolent woman as a *person*, a sense that an adult Dickens consciously works to create in his readers, readers who, he knows, need this assistance to 'see' what he himself sees. By contrast, Thomas Hardy can be 'too good a noticer'—his descriptions of characters' faces in *The Return of the Native* and *The Mayor of Casterbridge* sometimes fail to subordinate the details to the whole, and despite the realistic details, the portrait does not cohere into a face we can easily envisage.

Pip's childish images of his parents in *Great Expectations* are based on the appearance of the *lettering* on their tombstone. *Form comes before meaning, imitation before understanding, the concrete before the abstract, the right hemisphere before the left.* Little Charlie Dickens, little John Fowles—and little Richard Jefferies as well—were sensitive children. They had an extremely low threshold for stimulus (in other words, it did not take much to make an impression on them). They registered sights, sounds, smells (in the real world) and words, names, chants and stories (in the world of language) with equal intensity and excitement. Janet Frame particularly comments on how as a child she took words 'literally'. Millions of English-speaking children have initially pronounced the word 'island' as 'is-land', but who—except for Janet Frame—stubbornly clung to their seven-year-old pronunciation of the word, insisted on understanding it as about 'being in the present'? Much later, Frame created the expression 'Was-land' to match it.[28]

In her novel *Owls Do Cry*, Frame would speak of 'firm and red words like holly berries, and smelling like bread and primroses and the inside of a teapot'.[29] Similarly, Dennis Potter wrote, 'I love the sound of words. "Elbow" was my favourite word, and "elastic" and "slither". I used to say them over and over to myself in bed.'[30] Here is the need to mimic, to 'act out' the words that we will shortly see in Dickens and other young storytellers. Interestingly, all three of the words Potter mentions as his favourites contain the consonant 'l', and two of them contain both 'l' and 's', 'slither' and 'elastic' reversing the order of the two in much the same way as toddler Anthony Weir did when he chanted 'blanket like a lipstick'. More than the actual meaning of the words, it seems to have been the formal arrangement of their sounds (their *music*), and their *feel* in the mouth, that appealed to all these children—the right hemisphere's perceptions of 'is-ness' precede, and shape, the left hemisphere's attributions of semantic meaning.

Children like Dickens, Frame and Potter also notice (and worry away at) the adult mysteries that surround them. In her 1939 memoir *Confessions and Impressions* British novelist Ethel Mannin described how she 'would lie in bed and hear the curious hum of their voices going on ceaselessly, and sometimes their silly, loud, grown up laughter, and I would lie there in the dark, resentful and angry, with great dark tides of hatred sweeping through me, and feeling terribly alone.'[31] Or, as Janet Frame put it,

> 'There were so many ways of talking about people, of admiring them or scorning them for the strangest reasons, sometimes just because they were dead, or lived in another country . . . even if you didn't know people, you decided about them and arranged your feelings for them, and told everyone how you felt . . . in your lofty, adult voice; while below, we children caught all the travelling opinions, like falling stars, keeping some and letting some slip through.'[32]

All children grow up listening to such conversations—repetitive, assured, sometimes inane—but our writers-to-be do not simply remember the words and gestures of adults, they are driven to *do* something with what they notice, to imitate it, to 'perform' it. Many years afterwards, the 'lofty adult voices' they silently endured as children re-emerge in their novels—often savagely parodied, as if the writer delights in punishing those who, long ago, inflicted their stupidity and cruelty upon a powerless child. When an oyster grows a pearl around a tiny, irritating piece of grit or sand, its self-protective mechanism generates something that we, a form of life far removed from the oyster, see as beautiful. Children like Charlie Dickens, Charlotte Brontë and Janet Frame must endure many irritants and minor traumas, and almost instinctively, they seem driven to *imitate the very things that hurt, annoy and puzzle them*. Like oysters, human storytellers find themselves building layer upon layer of mimicry, precise observation, and creative modification around the gritty realities of their daily lives, as a way of coping with the tedium they feel, or the wounding to which they have been subjected. When sufficient layers accumulate, years later, the child's mundane or painful experience can be transmuted into a fiction that strikes others as funny, beautiful, or profound. But what drives these sensitive, intelligent, inventive children to want to turn their experience into *stories*? I suspect it is their own experience of stories created by others.

Making Stories Our Own

Charles Dickens said later that he 'dreamed his first dream of authorship' when he was eight years old.[33] His first documented work of fiction was a tiny play called 'Misnar', adapted from a story in *Tales of the Genii*, and intended for performance in his cardboard toy theatre. In middle life, he would refer to the same story in *Great Expectations*. Toy theatres, purchased or home-made, feature prominently in the childhoods of many famous nineteenth-century writers, including Robert Louis Stevenson and Henrik Ibsen.[34] In the first quarter of the twentieth century, Paul Scott and his brother Peter substituted a home-made cinema, with 'movies' drawn on paper, featuring the film stars of the day.[35] Creative children appropriate whatever technology is available to them; today's equivalent would be young programmers who, not content with existing interactive computer games, devise their own.

When Dickens was ten, his parents moved to a small house in St Mary's Place, Chatham. He associated the beginning of his career *as a reader* with one particular house, and specifically with a collection of eighteenth-century novels, which (after the move) his father kept in a room next to his own. It is a benchmark that probably has more to do with Dickens' rapidly evolving self-consciousness than it does with the particulars of place or the individual texts involved. Just as the rows of Scott and Dickens I first saw at nine in my grandmother's apartment seemed different and special to me, so did a ten-year-old Dickens locate his crossing-over into a wider world of fiction in *that* room in *that* house at St Mary's Place. (Interestingly, like my grandmother's sets, John Dickens' were cheap reprints—the kind of set that sold to lower middle class buyers who wanted to appear 'cultured'.) Like many novelists-to-be, Dickens read far ahead of his chronological age. In the novels of Smollett and Fielding, he found rollicking, picaresque narratives full of larger-than-life characters—very similar to the stories he would himself create in *The Pickwick Papers*. Yet never too far beneath the surface of his novels would lurk a strong sense of the mysterious, the mythical and the irrational—the influences he had already absorbed from *The Arabian Nights*, *Tales of the Genii*, 'Red Riding Hood' and other fairy tales.

Mary Weller, the Dickens family maid, later remembered how little Charlie used to closet himself with a book in an upstairs room at St Mary's Place, sometimes acting out the stories for his own delight. Dickens, said Mary, was 'a terrible boy to read' (she meant 'a great reader'). Almost all children have literal imaginations at this stage—Melissa and Lindie needed actual illustrations to body forth their 'Tidy House'; so did the young Charlotte Brontë. Charlie Dickens needed to perform the events and 'become' the characters. He once had his ears boxed for pointing out to a visitor that the marbled paper covering an ornamental object 'wasn't marble'. It is as if he had a painful awareness of how greatly appearance and reality could differ, and almost a sense of shame over anything that pretended to be what it was not (*as Dickens himself, perhaps, would much later pretend to be something he was not?*). For his imagination to work, he needed to turn a purely mental image into a real object he could manipulate with real-world actions. He 'punished' the wolf who had devoured his beloved Red Riding Hood by placing it last in the procession of toy animals entering the Ark, and twenty years later, in the act of composing, felt compelled to imitate his characters' voices and facial expressions in front of a mirror. His daughter saw him do it. He had to 'be' them, in order to write about them with full conviction.[36]

Before he even went to school, the German novelist Thomas Mann, author of *Buddenbrooks* and, later, the Nobel–prize-winning *The Magic Mountain*, was similarly attracted to acting. Many of Mann's games were based on the stories of Homer and Virgil which his mother had read him from her own school anthology. From a table (Mount Olympus), little Thomas (Zeus) would fling down 'lightning bolts' at those below, or (now taking the role of Achilles) drag his sister (Hector) three times around the walls of Troy. Later, he and his older brother Heinrich would collaborate on performances in their puppet theatre, with musical accompaniment: 'It was a game Tommy never tired of, long after his brother had given it up'. Or, he would decide that he was 'really' an eighteen-year-old prince named Karl, and spend the day 'proud and happy in the secret of my dignity'.[37]

Growing up in the sleepy, Southern town of Oxford, Mississippi, young Billie Falkner [sic], too, seemed to need to act out the stories that mattered to him. As a schoolboy, he would sometimes walk around the streets of the town wearing an old Confederate cap.[38] He wasted a great deal of time daydreaming, and neither his schoolmates nor his teachers had much time for him. In Atlanta, Georgia, a young Margaret Mitchell insisted on being called 'Jimmy' by her child companions, dressed like a boy, and worried her parents by accompanying a troupe of disreputable Civil War veterans around the streets of the city.[39] Her first stories featured male protagonists. The child who somehow needs to 'be' the people she has read about, or heard about, to dress in their clothes, to walk like them, to try out, in her mind, how she might even sound like them—surely the right hemisphere-dominant 'performer' of our last chapter is alive and well inside her? While most children simply revolve possible futures within their own minds, story makers of the future seem extend 'pretend play' all the way into adulthood.

In Chapter 2 I proposed that stories are catalysed by painful or puzzling feelings. But Richard Jefferies' *Bevis* acknowledges that pretend play (the cradle of creativity) may be triggered by a different kind of 'pain'—the feeling of *boredom*: Bevis and his friend Mark are playing near the New Sea (as they have creatively retitled the prosaically named 'Longpond'):

> '"We ought to be something", said Mark discontentedly.
> "Of course we ought", said Bevis. "Things are very stupid unless you are something".
> "Lions and tigers", said Mark, growling, and showing his teeth.
> "Pooh!"
> "Shipwrecked people on an island."
> "Fiddle! They have plenty to do, and are always happy, and we are not".'[40]

Things are very stupid unless you are *something.* 'Stupid' is Bevis's private word for 'tedious', 'humdrum' or 'boring'. To 'be' something means to '*pretend* to be' something. Creative play (and later, creative writing) enables a child to remake the world into something desirable and exciting instead of routine and dull, to conjure stimulus when none seems present. Australian novelist Patrick White specifically mentioned boredom as a stimulus to his writing in adolescence.[41] But 'stupid' is also a word that hints at shame, as when adults say, 'It made me feel so *stupid*'. The critical importance of shame in the early experience of story makers is something we'll return to later in this volume.

****

Like Charles Dickens, Jack Lewis consciously noticed his father's books for the first time after a move to a different house. In Lewis' case, the new home was substantially larger, and outside of the town. To seven-year-old 'Jackie', it seemed as full of books as it was of rooms: 'in the seemingly endless rainy afternoons, I took volume after volume from the shelves . . . where all these books had been before we came to the New House is a problem that never occurred to me . . . '[42] In fact, the books had been there all along; it was the change of location—along with his own maturing brain—that had suddenly highlighted them for Jack Lewis, as the move to St Mary's Place had drawn Dickens' attention to his own father's collection. Lewis senior, whose laboured jokes and self-indulgent emotionality Jack increasingly despised, was at work, and there were long hours for Jack and his brother to spend in reading and imaginative play. Though the details are very different, the *feeling* of silent spaces, empty rooms, and the excited discovery of a new world would appear, many years later, in the opening chapter of *The Lion, the Witch and the Wardrobe.*

Jack's older brother Warren (always called 'Warnie') seems to have led the way in their joint games, creating an imaginary 'India' when he was around eight or nine, and Jack some three years younger. Jack's imaginary world (which was in existence at least as early his sixth year) was called 'Animal Land'. It eventually acquired a history covering several centuries and an elaborate geography, with mountains, rivers, castles, and towns. Such was the two boys' need for order and system that Animal Land came to be part of the same imaginary world as Warnie's 'India' (which had to be turned into an island in order to achieve this geopolitical feat). Many of the characters of Animal Land were in fact based on old toys with which the boys had played, hence the oddness of some of their names. Others owed their origins to influential storybooks of their early childhood, like Beatrix Potter's *The Tale of Benjamin Bunny*: 'Benjamin (surnamed 'The Bunny'), Duke of Rabbit-Land', as Jack introduced him in Chapter 3 of his *History of Animal-Land*. The young Robert Louis Stevenson and his cousin Bob created similar imaginary countries, 'Nosingtonia' and 'Encyclopedia' ('where we ruled and made wars and inventions, and of which we were perpetually drawing maps'.)[43] In British-ruled India during the First World War, Rumer Godden (born in 1908) and her older sister Jon created a 'serial tale, never written down, called "Big Girls", in which they were the wealthy parents . . . of a family of glamorous girls who had wonderful clothes and exciting love affairs'.[44]

But the most celebrated siblings to create interlocking fictional worlds were of course the Brontës. Like the Lewises, the Brontë siblings grew up in a bookish household, with a father who himself had had literary ambitions as a young man. Like the Lewis brothers, whose mother died only two years after the family had moved to the New House, Charlotte, Emily, Branwell, and Anne had suffered the early loss of their mother (at the time, Charlotte was five), and then, a few years later, of their two older sisters. Then, one evening in June, 1826, when Charlotte was ten, Branwell nine, Emily eight, and Anne seven, the children's father came home from Leeds with a box of toy soldiers for Branwell. It was as if some Djinn had materialised in their midst, with the exact magical gift they needed to defeat the dull pain of loss. In Charlotte's famous words,

> 'When Papa came home it was night and we were in bed, so next morning Branwell came to our door with a box of soldiers. Emily and I jumped out of bed and I snatched up one and exclaimed, "This is the Duke of Wellington! It shall be mine!" When I said this Emily likewise took one and said it should be hers. When Anne came down she took one also. Mine was the prettiest of the whole and perfect in every part. Emily's was a grave-looking fellow. We called him "Gravey". Anne's was a queer little thing, very much like herself. He was called "Waiting Boy". Branwell chose "Bonaparte"'.[45]

Of course the Brontës had been excitedly making up stories long before the arrival of the toy soldiers but, as we saw in our last chapter, some 'performers' need props to catalyse their imagination, and here, suddenly and definitively, were those props. Instead of just *playing* with the toys, the Brontë siblings *wrote* about them, the characters expanding and developing along with the imaginary world in which they now had their being. Key figures like Wellington and Bonaparte acquired new names and titles (Branwell's Bonaparte figure became Alexander Percy, a.k.a 'Rogue', and then 'Lord Northangerland'). Like Homer's heroes with their doubled and tripled names, or the ever-expanding history of the Time Lords and the Daleks in *Dr Who*, these changes reflect the fact that the developing saga was the product of several 'singers of tales' rather than a single author.

As Charlotte represents them, each Brontë child's choice hints broadly at his or her individual personality. Emily's 'grave-looking fellow' seems appropriate to her inward-turned demeanour and her preoccupation with suffering, loss and death. Charlotte is dismissive of her youngest sister's choice ('a queer little thing very much like herself') yet in 'Waiting Boy' Anne chose a symbol of her own youngest sibling status: she would indeed wait, although when it came, her turn on the stage of adulthood would be cruelly short.

The Brontës' choice of toys, and their names for them, typifies a process that is not confined to talented, precocious children, nor specific to stories. As Charlotte and her siblings felt drawn to one particular toy soldier, so many of us feel drawn to particular objects, pictures, movies, stage or screen stars. In every case, the attraction, or the choice, is made before we 'know' at a conscious level where the root of our attraction lies. The right hemisphere will respond while the left is puzzled as to why we are so invested in that person, that object, that piece of music, that story. These 'chosen stories' are essentially *images of ourselves*—not images of ourselves as we *consciously* know ourselves, but images of the 'deep structure' of our personalities. And those personalities will later unfold in a pattern that may eerily resemble the characters and even the plot of the stories we have chosen.

Hence Charlotte's choice of a toy soldier whom she immediately dubbed 'The Duke of Wellington' reflected not only her devotion to the hero of Waterloo (and then Prime Minister), but also her own need *to be in command*. It is she who instigates the choosing of individual toy figures and who comments on the names the others choose (if we are to trust her account, that is). This is the Charlotte who would, after the early deaths of Emily and Anne, destroy much of their unpublished work, apparently to ensure that their reputations would be secure—or possibly so that their work could not compete with her own. It was she who introduced her sisters' published novels with her own comments, apologising for the defects of *Wuthering Heights*, and subtly suggesting to its readers how they should respond to it. In these ambivalent relationships we can vividly see why psychologist Dorothy Rowe called her book about siblings *My Dearest Enemy, My Dangerous Friend*.[46]

Most dramatic of all was Branwell's naming his soldier 'Bonaparte'. He was identifying himself with an outsider who makes good, a flamboyant Man of Destiny who ultimately crashes to disastrous defeat. Napoleon had died in captivity on St Helena in 1821, five years before the arrival of 'the young men' (as they called the soldiers) at the Brontë children's home, but his shadow still lay heavily over many Englishmen after long years of warfare. Ruthless and egotistical, Napoleon was nevertheless a gifted man who left some constructive reforms as part of his legacy. That is not how most Englishmen saw him at the time. What Hitler's life has become since his death in 1945—a story of the Rise and Fall of Evil retold again and again—Napoleon's was for English people in the first half of the nineteenth century. For Branwell, we might say, the *career* and the *personality* of Bonaparte became a 'chosen story': a narrative selected because of its personal significance to the little boy. At just nine years of age, Branwell could hardly know the inexorable way in which that story would predict his own 'decline and fall'.

Loss, Shame and Longing

All of the children we have discussed so far in this chapter lived intensely in a world conjured up by their imaginations on the basis of stories read and heard. And the Brontës were not the only ones who, by their tenth year, had already experienced significant loss. Like Pip in *Great Expectations*, Janet Frame, whose paternal grandfather died in her family's home when she was seven, learned about earlier losses through reading family tombstones—including one 'Janet Frame', an aunt who had died at '13 months, 22 days', and after whom she herself had been named.[47] Thomas Mann gives us a 'close up vision' of death for a child of this age: little Hanno Buddenbrook's first encounter with the laid-out body of his dead grandmother:

> 'That was not Grandmama. That was her Sunday bonnet with the white silk ribbons, and the reddish-brown hair beneath it was hers, too. But that pointed nose, those lips that had collapsed inward, that protruding chin, those yellow, transparent hands, folded in prayer and yet looking so cold and stiff—those were not hers. This was a strange wax doll, and there was something gruesome about the way they had dressed it up for this ceremonial occasion. And he looked across to the landscape room, as if he expected his real grandmama to appear at any moment. But she didn't—she was dead. Death had come and exchanged her forever for this wax doll, with its tightly closed, forbidding, unapproachable lips and eyelids.'[48]

This kind of reaction to a death is very typical of the child at the stage of Piaget's 'concrete operations'. It is almost as if the *emotion* of grief is not present at all, or if it is, has been diverted into a search for some way of *understanding* death that makes sense to the child's here and now imagination. We saw in the last chapter how strongly a child as young as two or three can react to damage and loss. Yet we also saw how the *conscious* memory of losses in these years is likely to have disappeared. Partly because of this, an early loss will appear to have much less impact than a later one, when in fact it may have had *more*, precisely because it is no longer available to conscious recall. The young Jack Lewis lost his mother at nine. The young Sam Coleridge, later to create that great verse narrative, 'The Ancient Mariner', lost his beloved father at nine. The young 'Billie' Falkner lost his grandmother at nine, recreating the night she died in *The Sound and the Fury.* Of the storytellers we will revisit again and again throughout this book, only Dickens, Dennis Potter, and Enid Blyton escaped the death of a close family member in or before middle childhood. For these three, however, a deeply shaming experience seems to have taken the place of the death. Shame is experienced as a kind of death, for it represents the loss of that boundless, joyous conviction of one's own goodness and rightness which most of us are born with, but which does not survive the chiding, the scorn, the horrified exclamations, of the adults who mean most to us ('I had to have *stitches* when you were born!'; 'Your father would never have left me if it hadn't been for *you*!'). Least of all does it survive when adult needs force themselves upon a child's young and vulnerable body, leaving him or her with a lifelong sense of worthlessness.

Dennis Potter was sexually abused at the age of ten—an event which, in various fictional transformations, hovers around most of his adult writing, like a dark stain at which he rubbed obsessively. For the Blyton and Dickens, a different, but somehow comparable experience of shame came when they were on the cusp of adolescence. Dickens, as everybody now knows, was sent to paste labels on pots of blacking (for boots) at twelve, in the company of 'common labouring boys', a degradation that seems to have lasted only a few months, but which he never forgot, although he told almost nobody about it. This ignominy (as Dickens experienced it) was brought about by his father's imprisonment for debt, which meant Dickens was taken from school, while his older sister Fanny was permitted to remain at her studies. He seems to have felt this double unfairness so intensely that it is almost as if he personally bore the shame of the entire family. Similarly, it was when she was twelve that Blyton's father left the family to take up with another woman, leaving Enid, his favourite, with a terrible sense of betrayal and the whole family with an embarrassment that must at all costs be concealed from the world.

Is creativity, then, catalysed by early loss and shame? Not simply or solely. Countless children have experienced the loss of a loved one at an early age without developing into writers, and few children have escaped shame. But when a loss or a shaming event is experienced by a highly sensitive, highly intelligent child—a 'good noticer'—it will be experienced more acutely and painfully than by a child whose threshold for stimulus is higher, and who is less disposed to introversion. 'Performers', who are already drawn to the plasticity of the world of words, will naturally turn to storytelling as a way of coping with whatever happens to them. To such children, words seem magical: you can make them say whatever you want. Through words you can re-make your world. You can 'disappear' a loss or a shame, or keep it at bay outside strong walls. You can journey, in your imagination, to a 'place of greater safety'.

Hardly any of the gifted children we have been describing here had much to say later in life about their childhood losses. They endured their pain in silence. It is not that latency-age children do not *feel*, for they most certainly do; rather, as Charlotte Brontë pointed out, they cannot express those feelings directly. And in the mind's alchemy, the real person they have lost (along with the sense of security, warmth and specialness that they may once have felt from that person) is transmuted into images that seem to have nothing to do with any person at all—images of places, landscapes, even *seasons*. Thus Jack Lewis describes a particular kind of longing,[49] which he locates in his early experience of Beatrix Potter's *The Tale of Squirrel Nutkin*: He 'loved all the Beatrix Potter books', but

> 'The rest of them were merely entertaining. [*Squirrel Nutkin*] administered a shock, it was a trouble. It troubled me with what I can only describe as the Idea of Autumn. It sounds fantastic to say that one can be enamoured of a season, but that is something like what happened . . . and one went back to the book, not to gratify the desire (that was impossible—how can one *possess* Autumn?) but to re-awake it. And in this experience also there was the same surprise and the same sense of incalculable importance. It was something quite different from ordinary life and even from ordinary pleasure; something, as they would say now, "in another dimension".'[50]

As always, Lewis writes about the experience of literature with a willingness (rare at the time among professional critics) to reveal the extent of his own emotional investment. In his words we can glimpse the same sentiment Dickens expressed in his *Arabian Nights* musings, when he spoke of 'the hope of something beyond that place and time'. This is the principle I call 'outlift'—the experience of being 'taken out of oneself' or 'taken out of the familiar' into something strange, intense, and gratifying. It is what Dickens and Frame found in fairy tales, it is what I found in my grandmother's apartment. *All new and all true*. For Lewis, it would emerge (in a different form) as the basis of the Christianity he first rejected, and then, reluctantly, embraced in young adulthood: a sense of being compelled by something greater and more meaningful than self, something that transcends the petty little business of daily pain and daily pleasure.

How could *Squirrel Nutkin* have evoked 'the Idea of Autumn' for a young Lewis? Beatrix Potter, a pragmatic countrywoman in spirit well before she became a sheep farmer in her own right, offers us no lyrical descriptions of brightly-coloured leaves drifting down from trees, no 'mists and mellow fruitfulness': nothing is mentioned that is not of practical importance to the squirrel community. (It is very similar, in that regard, to Lewis' own youthful stories of 'Animal Land'). However, behind the squirrels' repeated journey to Old Brown's island lies the powerful idea of *preparation*: laying in stores for the winter to come. Although Potter never says it in so many words, we are aware that threatening Winter is on its way, that Autumn itself is fleeting, and that it must be spent purposefully. An elementary school child comforts and delights himself by *collecting* things, putting them in order, adding new items to the collection. Children do not comfort themselves in this way for no reason: there is always within them an awareness, however dimly glimpsed, of a painful or threatening reality against which they must protect themselves. *No threat, no story.* Carol White felt it at four-and-a-half. Perhaps we might call it the fear of 'the end of all the worlds' as Lewis put it in *The Magician's Nephew.*

Lewis himself seizes upon 'the idea of Autumn' as responsible for his reaction to *Squirrel Nutkin*, but might there not be other reasons for this particular tale to become a 'chosen story' for him? *Squirrel Nutkin* features two named brothers, Nutkin and Twinkleberry (Lewis and Warnie?), along with numerous unnamed 'cousins'. And the squirrels conduct nutting expeditions to an island presided over by a large, sleepy (but potentially dangerous) owl called Old Brown, whom most of the squirrels treat with great respect, bringing him gifts of food so that he will allow them to go about their business. Nutkin himself rebels against this diplomatic attitude, making fun of Old Brown, instead of propitiating him. Could it be that in the sleepy, potentially dangerous father-figure of Old Brown, Jack unconsciously recognised his own potentially volatile father? Tormenting an imposing adult with jokes and riddles may well have been an appealing idea to a boy who certainly laughed and joked about his father behind his back. By contrast, the more staid Twinkleberry (Warnie?) conforms to the squirrel 'norm', and is dismayed at Nutkin's irreverence. Last but not least, *Squirrel Nutkin* creates an all-male world. It has no females, a 'father', but no 'mother', two brothers, but no sisters. It is as if the very idea of a 'mother' has never existed. And when, as a fifty-year-old man, Lewis came to create the magical realm of Narnia, he too would put into it beautiful, malevolent witches and innocent prepuberal girls (like Lucy) but (apart from a tiny vignette in *The Magician's Nephew*) no *mothers.* It would be in *places*, not *people* that he would embody the longing he associated first with *The Tale of Squirrel Nutkin.*

A Place of Greater Safety

For many creative children, story makers of the future, the longing of which Lewis speaks so eloquently takes concrete shape in the form of a *place*—not just any place, but a *delightful* place, a *locus amoenus.* In medieval literature, the *locus amoenus* was typically a walled garden full of flourishing plants, with a fountain or pool by which sat a beautiful woman waiting for a knightly adventurer to arrive. Guillaume de Lorris and Jean de Meung's thirteenth-century *Roman de la Rose* ('The Story of the Rose') was the work that did most to popularise this image with medieval audiences, and C.S. Lewis wrote about it in the book that made his scholarly reputation, *The Allegory of Love* (1936). John Fowles would play with the concept not only in *The Magus* but in his later novella *The Ebony Tower.* The *locus amoenus* evokes wonder and delight, yet it combines these with a sense of safety and enclosure. It is sensuous, but pre-sexual, giving it a special 'pure' magic that is lost in dreams and longings driven by mature sexuality. I have called it the 'place of greater safety', borrowing the memorable title of Hilary Mantel's 1992 novel of the French Revolution. The Committee of Public Safety that tyrannised France in 1793 claimed to assure the 'security' of the nation by imprisoning and executing anyone at all that its paranoid rulers considered a threat. Our young story makers are not paranoid or destructive in this way, but their 'good places' still aim to eliminate threat. What they discover, both in fiction and in their own real lives, combines the appeal of the familiar and the exotic, mixes delight with protection from danger. Beatrix Potter's description of her aunt Burton's garden at Gwaynynog is a low-keyed example of this appeal:

> 'The garden is very large, two thirds surrounded by an old red-brick wall with many apricots, and an inner circle of old grey apple trees on wooden espaliers. It is very productive but not tidy, the prettiest kind of garden, where bright old-fashioned flowers grow amongst the current bushes.'[51]

In Beatrix's imagination, this garden blended with her grandparents' garden at Camfield Place to produce the 'idealised and universalised garden' in *The Tale of Peter Rabbit.*[52] The gardens that fascinate such children as Beatrix include only 'good' things; the 'bad' ones are kept safely at bay—by an 'outer' wall and an 'inner circle' of trees, in this case. British dramatist Harold Pinter discovered 'the first of a whole series of private Edens that were to haunt his later work' at the age of eight or nine. It was a piece of overgrown garden, in which he met imaginary friends, all boys: 'I had this total fantasy life in which we talked aloud and held conversations beyond the lilac tree'.[53] For Patrick White, growing up in Sydney in 1916, 'safety' was a central element in another overgrown garden:

> 'Down a flight of stone steps—"the moss so thick in places that his feet felt they were trampling flesh"—was a wild garden which became the boy's private territory . . . Through the undergrowth the boy stalked cats stalking lizards and, hidden in the summer house, said prayers to the god of the great bunya bunya [tree] . . . The tree was Paddy White's protector. If the larrikins of Darlinghurst were shouting at him through the privet hedge, all he had to do was run to the bunya bunya and he was safe. He wondered if paradise was somewhere in its branches.'[54]

Patrick was only four when he discovered this place, and the account makes clear the link between the fear and loneliness experienced by the preschool children we met in the last chapter, and the need for a 'good place' which keeps these disturbing feelings at bay. What exactly is so 'good' about this special place is hard to define, for it wells up from the Old Brain. Robert Louis Stevenson captures it perfectly when he describes his grandfather's home, the Minister's residence at Colinton, where he regularly spent holidays:

> 'I have not space to tell of my pleasures at the manse. I have been happier since; for I think most people exaggerate the capacity for happiness of a child; but I have never again been happy in the same way. For indeed, it was scarce a happiness of this world, as we conceive it when we are grown up, and was more akin to that of an animal than that of a man. The sense of sunshine, of green leaves, and of the singing of birds, seems never to have been so strong in me as in that place. The deodar upon the lawn, the laurel thickets, the mills, the river, the church bell, the sight of people ploughing, the Indian curiosities with which my uncles had stocked the house, the sharp contrast between this place and the city where I spent the other portion of my time, all these took hold of me, and still remain upon my memory, with a peculiar sparkle and sensuous excitement.'[55]

****

In 1913, a young Frenchman, Henri Alban, published his novel *Le Grand Meaulnes*, under the pseudonym of 'Henri Alain-Fournier'. 'The Great Meaulnes' is the slightly mocking nickname by which his schoolmates refer to seventeen-year-old Augustin Meaulnes, whom we first meet as a confident, adventurous adolescent boy. English translators (there have been half a dozen) have generally preferred romantic-sounding titles like *The Lost Domain*, *The Lost Estate* or *The Wanderer*. In the midst of a marshy wilderness, Meaulnes stumbles upon a chateau, a *domaine perdu* ('lost domain'), a fairy tale place, seemingly, though few of its details are particularly magical. There he falls in love with a beautiful young girl. Subsequently, as an adult, Meaulnes rediscovers and marries the girl, Yvonne, but abandons her, driven by his quest for some impossible perfection. Meaulnes epitomises the kind of person who becomes a story maker—always searching, never satisfied. Alain-Fournier himself did not survive to replicate the adult life of his hero. He was killed in the opening battles of 1914, which historian Barbara Tuchman would later describe in her masterly narrative, *The Guns of August*. But, as we'll see in our next chapter, his haunting novel would so greatly impress English writer John Fowles that Fowles would later claim that he had read it as a child, when in fact he discovered it only as an adult. He wanted to believe that it had always been a part of him.

Every 'lost world', every paradise garden, offers the promise of return to our first place, a 'good place' where all of us have been before, but which none of us consciously remember. My own experience in my grandmother's apartment, with which we began this chapter, was very similar. The apartment was safe, but different; exciting, but comforting. Like Meaulnes' *domaine perdue*, it opened doors onto a world of new possibilities. This, I suspect, is what Lewis felt in the 'little end room', what Dickens felt in the little room containing his father's books at St Mary's Place, what Paul Scott felt in his father's and aunts' attic studio, and what Rumer Godden and Rudyard Kipling both felt in the loving, protected world of their Indian childhoods, remembered later amidst the physical and emotional coldness of England. In time, the images of these real places merged for them with images of more remote and exotic places derived from the world of fiction. The possibilities created for these children by the 'delightful place' fused with the possibilities they themselves had created in their imaginative play and daydreaming *inspired* by that place. And for the remainder of their lives, these *loci amoeni* would stay with them, longed for, and re-created in their own stories—the closest they, or any of us, can come to re-experiencing the womb. For story makers can't let go of these images of safety and delight, any more than they can let go of their early apprehension of loss, pain and death.

Their creative energy takes shape, first in pretend play, later, as early as nine, in daydreaming. Our daydreams, like our earlier pretend games, are entirely under our own control. Nobody can tell us how to order the realm of our private imaginings, or our intense, absorbing games. We are 'monarchs of all we survey'. For the story makers of the future are above all, boys and girls who need desperately to *control* their worlds. If they cannot do it in the real world of people and events, they can at least do it in the worlds of their imagination—as Charlie Dickens did, after the sudden end of his formal schooling at the age of ten. He would spend hours gazing down at the city of London spread out below him, not really seeing it, but indulging instead in 'vague reflection'[56]—a state of trance that we'll say more about later. Looking down from above, being a detached observer of the wide world that others inhabit, can be a consoling experience. You are alone, but not 'lonely', different, yet superior, cut off from others, yet secure. You have reached a place of greater safety.

Where We've Come From, Where We're Going

Self-consciousness evolves gradually, but by eight, nine or ten, it has taken a huge step forward. Now a child is not only *aware* of its individuality, but able to *think about* itself, and plan its individual future. Charles Dickens, Janet Frame, and Iris Murdoch all report making the decision to be writers around the age of eight or nine. It is the age when children *notice and reflect upon* the new homes to which their families move, or the boarding schools to which they are reluctantly sent. As with places and people, so with fiction. For many children, the same age marks the first articulated awareness of literary conventions, the first inklings of understanding of the mechanics and conventions of stories. All of this signals the growing influence of the left hemisphere in middle childhood, even while the vast majority of children at this stage—including most future story makers—are still producing a modified form of Old Brain narrative: logically connected sequences of events, linked by recognisable, consistent characters, but displaying little or no ability to project themselves inside those characters, and little realisation of what others might need in order to become absorbed in those narratives. And we've seen that most children of elementary school age seem to struggle to end their stories in a way that adults would find convincing. It is only with the advance of adolescence that these adult-level capacities will start to become evident, as we'll see in Chapter 4.

Middle childhood, conventionally stretching from the seventh year of life to the onset of puberty, sees mental play ('daydreaming') supplement or even replace the pretend play of early childhood. Typically of the child at the stage of Piaget's 'concrete operations', this daydreaming is most often associated with a real place, although the child may invest it with the allure of fictional imagery. Often the place seems *new and different* in the child's experience, yet (in one of those paradoxes in which story abounds) what seems exotic may also be familiar. The right hemisphere represents *time* in terms of *space*: the wonderful garden, so secure and gratifying, reaches back far into infancy—even, perhaps, to the womb. The right hemisphere automatically associates like with like, responds powerfully to whatever reminds it of something prior.

At this developmental stage, creative daydreaming is simply enjoyable—a respite from pain, worry or threat, and asserts the child's ability to control his or her world. But it lays the foundations for later story making, and in right hemisphere dominant children like Janet Frame, Charles Dickens and Charlotte Brontë we see the revelatory impact of *stories*, an impact which will later direct their creativity towards the forging of fictions. These highly intelligent, highly sensitive children respond powerfully to loss and shame, and the story form somehow *contains and transforms* those painful experiences, as in the *Arabian Nights* a brass bottle contains, and potentially releases, the awesome power of a Djinn—although it will not be for another twenty years (as we'll see in Chapter 5) that most of them will finally realise their potential as story makers.

Chapter Four

The Age of Romance

Self and Story in Adolescence

The Knight Rides Forth[1]

Somewhere in the West Midlands of England, sometime towards the end of the fourteenth century, a poet whose name we have never known produced a masterpiece. *Sir Gawain and the Green Knight* is a strange story of magic, desire and self-discipline, in which Celtic myth gleams dully through the sumptuous fabric of courtly storytelling. Formal and mannered after the fashion of its time (the reign of Richard II) we can occasionally glimpse in *Gawain*—three hundred years before the novel emerged—the consciousness of a modern writer. But for a speaker of twenty-first-century English, reading *Sir Gawain and the Green Knight* is like plunging headlong into the dense forest of thorn-bushes that barred the way to the Sleeping Beauty's palace. Try the lines that precede Chapter 1 of this volume: you will recognise many of the words despite their uncouth spelling, but in almost every line you'll stumble over obscure dialect, and verb forms that have long since passed out of the language. *Gawain* is set at the time of King Arthur, but it begins with a brief reference to the *Iliad*, explaining how Arthur is descended from a (mythical) Trojan hero who fled to Gaul and then Britain after the Greeks took the city. Since Arthur's 'ancestor' arrived here, the poet tells us, Britain has been a place of 'war and woe and wonder'—with successive invasions from the Romans, the Saxons, the Danes and finally, the Norman French, 'war and woe' is no exaggeration, and the story the poet is about to tell is certainly one of 'wonder'.

It is mid-winter, and Arthur and his court sit celebrating the Christmas season when suddenly a huge figure rides his horse into their hall. He is enormous, well-proportioned, splendidly dressed, and carries a great battle axe, but

> 'They wondered at his skin—
> A sight they'd never seen—
> A man, a bold one too,
> Except his face was green.'[2]

The green skin indicates that the creature is supernatural—green is still the colour movies use for aliens (including Shrek!), though ours mostly come from Outer Space, not out of the Fairy Hill. There follow no less than three verse paragraphs describing in vivid detail the Green Knight's appearance, horse and armour. Homer's *Iliad* contains many similar passages, but *Gawain* is a very different kind of narrative from Homer's. No Goddess is telling this tale. And although *Gawain*'s narrator claims that he will tell the story 'as I heard it told in [the] town' (suggesting an oral tradition), he is not, in fact, composing orally, in the manner of a Homeric 'singer of tales', nor is he writing down an oral epic from memory. *Sir Gawain and the Green Knight* does not feature multiple protagonists and shifting points of view, like the *Iliad*. It has a single hero, a single antagonist, and a consistent focus on an individual's quest: this is the world of *romance*.

The Old French word *romaunt* originally meant a story 'like the Romans told', but it gradually came to mean a 'story of love and chivalry' ('*chevalerie*' meant the 'way of the mounted warrior'). While armoured knights have vanished from our world, a 'romance' still means a story about love. We have even made it into a verb, and speak of one celebrity 'romancing' another, meaning that they are 'going out' with each other (which, as some witty person pointed out, usually means 'staying in'). As a literary form, the romance involves a good deal more than love, as we'll shortly see, but nevertheless, there is a strong continuity between what a *romaunt* was to medieval listeners, and what a 'romance' is to today's readers. And there is a special affinity between romance and adolescence, as we'll see later in this chapter.

The giant, green-clad figure arrogantly demands to speak to 'the boss of this mob', thereby confirming, if we needed any confirmation, that he is a creature from right outside the civilised society of the court. But where the monster Grendel, in the Anglo-Saxon epic *Beowulf*, breaks into the King's hall by night and simply devours the sleeping warriors, the Green Knight offers a more civilised form of aggression—a knightly challenge: one of the knights is to strike off the Knight's head; but in return, he must undertake to meet the Green Knight a year hence, at the 'Green Chapel'—and offer his own head in return. Initially, nobody steps forward (by implication, they are hanging back from fear) so Arthur himself accepts the challenge, but Sir Gawain, a model of courtesy, offers to take his place. He duly beheads the Green Knight—fully aware that in doing so, he is probably giving himself just one year to live. In an odd, telling little detail, the poet tells us that when the creature's head rolls on the floor, the courtiers push at it with their feet. Their behaviour suggests both distaste and relief: it is the reaction of civilised people faced with a barbaric act that belongs to an earlier age. Whoever composed fairy tales or epics would not have included such a detail, nor thought it important. It depends on a kind of consciousness that delights in how precisely literature can echo what happens in real life. It depends on the left hemisphere's way of paying attention to the world. Then, in a horrific touch, the Green Knight—still living—bends down, picks up his severed head, puts it under his arm, and stalks out of the Arthur's hall, reminding Gawain to meet him at the Green Chapel, in twelve months' time.

As the end of the year approaches, Gawain duly sets out, and journeys alone into the wild country of North Wales to meet his doom. The journey itself is a masterpiece of descriptive writing. Most fourteenth-century romances describe landscapes only in an 'essentialist' manner, the literate equivalent of Homer's 'formulas': woods are 'wild', fields are 'rich', castles are 'strong'). *This* romance wants to conjure up for us what half-frozen streams sound like, what the cold feels like:

> 'Combat he could cope with, but winter confounded him
> When icy rain poured from the clouds—
> Frozen it fell to the frosted ground—
> Slashed at by sleet, he slept in his mail,
> Night after night, on naked rocks,
> Where cold streams chattered through ice-clenched teeth,
> And icicles inched down over his head.'

How readers or listeners of Richard II's time might have reacted to such writing is anybody's guess (and perhaps few ever did, since *Sir Gawain and the Green Knight* survives in only a single manuscript, along with three other poems that are probably by the same author). But we moderns greet such passages like old friends. This precise, evocative description, so unusual in medieval literature—less unusual in medieval *painting*[3]—bridges the gap between our experience and Gawain's, making it possible for *us* to imagine what *he* is seeing. The Gawain poet can do what the nine-year-old narrators in our last chapter could not: he can reach out to readers and command their *empathy*: assist them to 'know how a fictional hero feels'. And so, as we'll see later, can adolescent story makers.

Just three days before he is due to meet his fate at the hand of the Green Knight, Gawain comes upon a castle which looks, the poet tells us, as if it were 'cut out of paper'—again, a surprisingly modern-sounding description, and certainly not a predictable formula (of which there are plenty in *Gawain*, though not nearly as many as in the *Iliad*). The owner of the castle is a big, confident man, who welcomes Gawain with open arms, inviting him to stay until he must ride out to meet his strange adversary. Since his host claims the Green Chapel is close by, Gawain now has several days up his sleeve. The lord of the castle is called Sir Bertilak (although significantly, we only learn his name much later). As in fairy tale, most romance characters are 'functional' (they are there to play a part in moving the story along), and so their given names matter relatively little—except of course for the heroes themselves (Gawain, Arthur, Lancelot, and the rest). It is only in the era of the novel that we have come to expect that every character, even minor ones, will have a name and a unique personality—part of the triumph of the New Brain which we'll examine in Chapter 5.

Gawain particularly notices two ladies at dinner that first night, one ancient and ugly, the other young and beautiful. Neither of them is named, but the younger one is clearly the host's wife. A hail-fellow-well-met host, a wrinkled old crone and a desirable young woman—we are back in the world of fairy tale, it seems. The host suggests a semi-serious 'bargain' with his guest. For each of the next three days, he, Bertilak, will get up early to go hunting, and undertakes to give Gawain whatever he catches. Gawain, however, is to rise at his leisure, and spend the day at the castle in the company of the lord's wife. But he, too, must promise to give his host whatever he 'catches'. So Bertilak goes out hunting each morning while Gawain slumbers. But each time, the beautiful lady comes to Gawain's room, insinuating that she would happily join him in bed. Clearly, a different kind of 'hunt' is going on here! Gawain, as a guest, cannot possibly sleep with Bertilak's wife, but the rules of 'courtly love' (about which C. S. Lewis wrote in *The Allegory of Love*) dictate that he must not discourteously reject her either. For the first two nights, he manages to fob the Lady off with kisses and clever compliments. It is a test of Gawain's virtue as a Christian knight (Agamamnon or Achilles would not have felt such scruples!) The final morning, however, fearing his impending fate, Gawain does accept something from the Lady—her girdle (which at the time meant a belt or sash, not an undergarment) which she claims will make him invulnerable to any blow.

What, exactly, has he accepted? Gawain knows he has done wrong, because when Bertilak presents him with the spoils of that day's hunt—suggestively, it is a fox—Gawain does not confess to what *he* has 'caught'—the girdle. Is this a hint? Gawain has resisted the 'foxy lady', yet has he, after all, allowed himself to be seduced in another way? We are left wondering. As we have seen, fairy tales involve many unanswered questions, and things that 'do not add up' in a logical way. But romance is different: the puzzle itself may depend on a buried layer of magical thought, but the author of *Gawain* consciously sets out to tease and intrigue us, enjoying the process of creating 'mystery', enjoying the double meanings and suggestions of sexual intrigue as Gawain and the Lady walk through a 'courtship dance' without consummating it. The New Brain, as well as the Old, is at work in this kind of story.

We are all familiar with courtship dances in the bird kingdom: the gorgeously-plumed male prances before the rather drabber female, she turns away, he approaches again, is rebuffed again, and so on, until eventually she accepts his advances and they become a nesting pair. Dress codes may be different among humankind—medieval ladies were arrayed as gorgeously as their menfolk, and today's young people rely on vivid purple hair or facial piercings to make them 'hot'—but the courtship dance is still with us. The romance contains its own equivalent, the 'mating plot': a stylised sequence of moves and counter-moves in which approach is followed by avoidance, temporary union leads to separation, until eventually the 'dance' is resolved in marriage (*Gawain* is unusual in that the 'dance' does not come to this expected consummation.) Many Hollywood stars live their lives in this spirit, while the gossip-columnists and paparazzi document every step in their endless cyclic pairings, infidelities and re-pairings.

The 'mating plot' can only be fully meaningful to those who have reached the age of puberty, who themselves have felt sexual desire and yearned for an idealised beloved. Where fairy tales present the idea of love and marriage as a child would see them—a bald, asexual view without empathy or understanding of what is involved—romance *begins* to show us what must actually happen between potential partners, what it might 'feel like' for the actual participants. Of course, in *Gawain* it is all very formal and polite by our modern standards, and sex is only hinted at. But it is there all right, and every medieval reader would have been aware of it. So *Sir Gawain and the Green Knight* combines a muted survival plot (depending on fear and aggression) that corresponds with the 'reptile brain' with a more fully-realised mating plot centred on desire and playful interaction, and reflecting the priorities of the limbic system or 'mammal brain'.

Gawain says nothing to his host about the girdle, and rides off alone to the Green Chapel. As it turns out, this is not a 'chapel' at all, but a mound in a hidden valley, described as vaguely as Homer's Troy, but with details which suggest a Celtic holy place or a Fairy Hill. Gawain hears a whirring sound nearby, and realises to his horror that the Green Knight is honing his great axe ready to kill him. Yet the frightful challenge is quickly resolved. Gawain bares his neck, the Knight brings down his monstrous weapon—but the blow only scratches the knight. Has the magic girdle saved Gawain's life? Or has the Green Knight deliberately avoided killing him? The hero gets a slight wound—probably to signify that he ought not to have accepted the Lady's gift in the first place—but he retains his head because although he has accepted her gift, he has refused to 'go all the way'. Perhaps Gawain should have realised all along that if the Green Knight could walk and talk despite the loss of his head, his own 'test of courage' might not be as final as he had feared. But of course, romance heroes (like fairy tale protagonists) do not think in this logical, real-world way, and nor do we, as we read about them.

Fear is not something that most medieval romance protagonists indulge in (all armour is bright, all heroes are fearless). In allowing the possibility that the great Gawain might have feared for his life, the poet again shows us how ordinary mortals—as opposed to legendary heroes—react to the challenges that life throws at them. Yet the Old Brain element in the story remains strong. The Green Knight now reveals all. He and Bertilak are one and the same. The old woman, we are told, is Morgan Le Fay, the enchantress who haunts the Arthurian legends. It was she who put Bertilak under a spell, turning him periodically into a green monster—a spell that could only be broken when someone willingly risked his life in response to the Green Knight's challenge. And so the story ends, with Gawain's return to Camelot amidst great praise and rejoicing. It all 'makes sense'—more or less. As Anne Wilson shows in her analysis, magical thought and logical, reality-based thought are present simultaneously in *Gawain*, and this uneasy combination makes for a tale that is both baffling and yet mysteriously powerful.[4]

In *Gawain and the Green Knight*, as in fairy tales, two apparently different characters can turn out to be the same character, and the cutting off of heads is not to be taken literally. But the concerns of *this* storyteller—how to behave properly in difficult, ambiguous circumstances; whether to resist temptation, or save one's life by giving in to it—are *thought about*, rather than simply *enacted*. They are the subjects of conscious awareness, rather than presented (as in fairy tales) as a simple sequence of events. This 'grown up fairy tale' shows us the story-making capacities that come on stream from puberty onwards: the realization that a successful story (as we have come to see it) must 'bridge the gap' between the reader's (or listener's) world and the teller's, must consciously work to create a sense of mystery, and must to some degree evoke the characters' individual experience, their 'inner life'. *Gawain* is suspended evenly between the Old Brain and the New, appealing to both 'by turns' and offering 'bothe blysse and blunder' to all those who, after six centuries, are still willing to open themselves to its charm. But though it is unique in several ways, this does not prevent *Gawain* from showing us most of the things that make *any* romance what it is.

Three Faces of Romance

Gawain rides forth on his winter journey *by himself*: romance features autonomous individuals, not groups, clans or armies. The heroes of the *Iliad* are mighty men with strong wills and superhuman courage; but they are not 'on their own' in the same sense as the heroes of romance are. Proud and competitive, excelling in single combat, they are nevertheless part of a team effort (even when, like Achilles, they sulk and turn their backs on the team). But in Homer's other epic, *The Odyssey*, Odysseus behaves more like the 'lone rangers' of romance—his companions scarcely figure as individuals and part way through the story, they perish. *The Odyssey* may well have been the prototype from which medieval romance later developed. The heroes of romance typically set out without even a single companion, and their capacity to cope on their own with any eventuality is one of the things we are asked to admire about them. No wonder, then, that as the value placed by Western society on the self-sufficient *individual* has steadily increased over the last five centuries, the romance form has flourished, although it has taken on many different guises.

Romance belongs to a world where (at least for the aristocracy) play has become sharply demarcated from work, and where people can enjoy day-dreams, hypothetical possibilities. Romance is about *mystery*: unlike the *Iliad* where the outcome was already known to Homer's listeners (although not to the characters), neither Gawain nor we can guess what is going to happen. In Homer, it is the Immortals who decide everything (and this is as true of the *Odyssey* as it is of the *Iliad*). Both the strings that pull the puppets, and the puppeteers, are clearly visible at all times. In *Gawain*, implacable fate, imposed by the Gods, has been replaced by 'magic'—powerful and unpredictable, but able to be mastered by those who are '*preu et cortois*' (brave and chivalrous).[5] Homer's heroes could not change their fate, however much they conformed to Bronze Age equivalents of *preu et cortois*. Romance heroes, like Gawain, can. The possibility of *change* is something that preoccupies our contemporary world, indeed, we *overvalue* the new, the 'innovative', the 'evolving'. Reflecting traditional, conservative values in many ways, romance does celebrate change. It invites us to dream of something better, something 'perfect'. And as we shall see, perfection has a special appeal for those who become story makers.

The world of the *Iliad* is a world where life is oriented towards inevitable death. To die well is vital, because it will ensure reputation. Epic heroes, for the most part, die young—like Hector in *The Iliad*, Siegfried (around whose exploits Wagner based his *Ring* cycle), and Roland (in the Old French *Chanson de Roland*). In romance, reputation is still enormously important, but it depends much less on how a hero dies, for overwhelmingly, *romance protagonists do not die*. They live, pass the 'tests' that they encounter, and marry the lady to whom they have given their hearts. In this respect, romance is a form that belongs to youth, a time when death is so far away as to be almost unreal. In this romance world, a somewhat safer one than the one inhabited by Homer's heroes, an adventure is something to be looked forward to, and there is the expectation that mysteries can be solved, the unexpected tackled and mastered. Thus Gawain is perfectly prepared to ride off in search of the Green Chapel, despite his knowledge that he, as a mere human, will not survive the 'return blow' that the supernatural Knight will impose on him. He must accept the challenge *because this is part of being chivalrous*. Even though he shows signs of fear later in the story (as we have seen) we 'know' that Gawain will survive the encounter, and that all will end happily. The real question is, 'How will this be accomplished? What magic, cleverness or correct conduct will enable him to survive?' This is the concept of *unpredictable events within a predictable framework* that lies at the heart not just of medieval romance, but of what we now call 'whodunnits', 'thrillers' or just 'mysteries' (all modern variants of romance).

Similarly, while epic may begin and end at any point within an already-familiar cycle of tales, romance begins with an introduction that locates the story (albeit briefly and conventionally) in space and time, and ends in a conclusive fashion with the full resolution of any threats, and the completion of the quest—which, in most romances (though not in *Gawain*) means that the hero and the heroine are united—become a 'mating pair'. Epic acknowledges the reality of death, indeed, the death of one or more heroes is an expected event. *Romance, on the other hand, seems to deny death*, and in order to do so, must normally end on a note of achievement and fulfilment. Like fairy tale, romance does not look beyond a 'happy ever after' ending, and in that regard it shows the Old Brain still intact, still dictating an important aspect of storytelling. Thus, although we've speculated that the 'happy ever after' ending is the first significant modification that the left hemisphere makes to the right hemisphere's endless alternation of 'bliss and blunder', 'happy ever after' endings still embody the spirit of the Old Brain. Paradoxically, they invite us back into a world without death, the 'acre of the undying' as William Morris called it in his late nineteenth-century romance, *The Story of the Glittering Plain*, even while they tacitly acknowledge the inevitability of death by insisting on a conclusion that denies it.

A Search after Hapiness

Just four years after she wrote 'There was once a little girl called Anne', Charlotte Bronte's story making capacities had developed considerably. At thirteen, she produced a much longer and (in some ways) more 'adult' story grandly titled (if somewhat incompetently spelled) *The Search after Hapiness* (today we would say, 'The Search *for* Happiness'). It was strongly influenced by the fashionable poems of Lord Byron and by the *Arabian Nights* stories that she, like Dickens, had absorbed from an early age. In its very first sentences, Charlotte introduces her chief character, a character we will find very familiar:

> 'Not many years ago there lived in a certain city a person of the name of Henry O'Donnell, in figure he was tall of a dark complexion and searching black eye, his mind was strong and unbending his disposition unsociable and though respected by many, he was loved by few.'[6] [Author's punctuation unaltered]

Henry O'Donnell is a 'stereotype'. We recognise him not so much as an individual, but as a representative of a *class* of individuals: the tall, dark, handsome (but reserved or temperamental) hero who became popular in the early nineteenth century, and has continued to hold sway over the popular imagination ever since. For, since the time of *Sir Gawain and the Green Knight*, a massive change had occurred in the typical romance hero. The new stereotype was partly based on Lord Byron (a 'celeb' of the early nineteenth century, whose glamorous life and impetuous love affairs attracted widespread attention, while the manic-depressive mood-swings that propelled his adventures were less well known).[7] Like his medieval counterparts, the 'Byronic hero' was autonomous, he still pursued quests into the unknown, and he still searched for true love (or lasting 'hapiness'). But he was no longer a template of chivalrous virtue and courage. Instead, he was a flawed human being, and his attributes were now defined, if only superficially, in *psychological* terms (Henry O'Donnell is alone *because he is 'unsociable'* and 'though respected by many, he [is] loved by few'). These attributes remain constant. From the youthful Charlotte's O'Donnell to James Bond in our own day, the heroes of modern romance will continue to be seen more from the outside than the inside, and their appeal to readers and viewers will continue to lie in the 'adventures' that befall them, rather than in the struggles and realisations of their interior worlds. Their female counterparts, however, are drawn more 'from the inside'. The modern romance heroine is closer to the kind of fully-realised character we meet in the psychological novel than to the sketchy 'ladies' and 'demoisels' of medieval romance.

Two famous nineteenth-century novels established the romance hero as we know him today. Charlotte's younger sister Emily created one in her 1848 novel, *Wuthering Heights*. Her Heathcliff supplied much of the power behind the 'darker' version of the figure: he is obstinate, unforgiving, and manipulative, yet harbours an enduring passion for a woman he can never have. Darcy, in *Pride and Prejudice* (first published in 1813, although Jane Austen wrote a version of it at least ten years earlier) supplies the template for the more optimistic version of this same figure. Darcy's reserve and apparent rudeness turn out to be his ways of protecting himself against stupidity and insensitivity. He is in fact honest and forthright, and beneath his apparent arrogance and aloofness, he is actually vulnerable and sensitive.

The beguiling combination of masterful and frightening (on the one hand) and deliciously nurturable (on the other), of 'male' hardness and 'womanly' weakness, has inspired countless romance novels since, and is responsible for an entire genre—the Mills & Boon romance.[8] Though Mills & Boon novelettes are written by individual authors, the writers work to strict guidelines. Intending authors today are told that the man should be older than the woman (though not 'old enough to be her father'!) and more sexually experienced, while she, though not a virgin (not these days, anyway!) is 'innocent'. Would-be authors are specifically instructed to present a rounded portrait of the woman's personality, but to draw the man more sketchily. The clear intention is that *she* should emerge as the one to identify with (Mills & Boon readers are overwhelmingly female), while the man remains more remote, more mysterious, an outline to be 'coloured in' with the individual reader's fantasies (an exact reversal of the situation in medieval romance). *'Though respected by many, he was loved by few'*—but those few will include the heroine, whose role is to tame him, to bring him back within the bounds of common humanity, as nymphs and witches could heal the wounded heroes of myth and legend.

The heroine of a Mills & Boon or Silhouette romance must be attracted to the masterful, intense hero from the start, yet she must have strong reservations about him as well. The hero must initially seem proud, remote, unattainable (like Darcy) or callous, unreliable and rageful (like Heathcliff). After several moves back and forth, the heroine gives in to her overwhelming feelings, and the lovers have passionate sex (the original Mills & Boon formula has been modified to keep up with changing sexual mores). Then they are torn apart by misunderstandings, or by the hero's thoughtless behaviour. This is pretty much what occurs in Chrestien de Troyes' twelfth-century romance *Yvain* (where the knight Yvain, caught up in jousting contests, completely forgets his promise to his lady, Laudine, and goes temporarily insane when he realises that he has forfeited her love). The brief Mills & Boon stories (approximately half the length of a shortish modern novel) resolve when the hero 'softens' emotionally, or proves himself more loyal and dependable than he originally appeared. The lovers are eventually united, with marriage and a family on the horizon.

It is not hard to see how the Mills & Boon pattern would speak to generations of 'traditional women', raised to believe that their destiny is to be discovered and courted by their 'one true love'. Nor is it difficult to understand why the modern romance hero, as we have been describing him, would fit many women's experience of 'traditional men': controlling, out of touch with their feelings, and prone to use their superior strength and 'masculine rationality' to avoid vulnerability and shame. Indeed, as feminist scholars have repeatedly pointed out, this modern romance plot can be seen as validating dysfunctional relationship patterns such as occur with painful regularity in marriages characterised by domestic violence (*'But I love him—and I know that some day he'll realise what he's done, and beg me for forgiveness'*). Dangerous though such plots may be as models for some of the women who read them, they continue to enjoy a mass audience. From the evolutionary point of view, they speak to the powerful biological need to find a 'strong' mate whose genes will ensure that one's children will survive. On the emotional level, the mating plot speaks to a need to be sought after, to be loved and understood. Every time we fall in love, we enter this Old Brain world, governed by the limbic system—the part of the brain that we share with all warm-blooded creatures who suckle their young. The emotions that correspond with the mammal brain are the ones that researcher Jaak Panksepp calls 'care' and 'panic/grief.[9] 'Care' is that strong pull to be with, and look after, a partner or a child—the one we are 'attached to'. 'Panic/grief' kicks in when we lose (or believe we have lost) that person, when an attachment bond is severed. This painful feeling is triggered by fear of abandonment, and quite distinct from fear, the reptile-level reaction to a predator, just as love combines *care*—strong attachment to an individual—with the reptile level feeling of *lust*. 'Mating plots' seem to oscillate between these two poles—the quest to be with, and the fear of being without, a person who seems vital to our own emotional well-being.

In a subsidiary role, however, the mating plot also calls upon the emotional systems typically evoked by the survival plot—most notably the one that Panksepp calls 'seeking' (which in humans takes the form of a conviction that we are engaged upon a meaningful, purposeful activity—whether its goal be finding food or shelter, searching for a loved one, or any other endeavour). Romances are *quests*, and while we are reading, listening or viewing a quest narrative, we experience that same exciting sense of forward movement that the heroes and heroines do—even though we may have no idea of where we're going, or what is going to happen. I call it 'onrush'. Along the way, the survival-oriented emotional systems that produce protective fear and self-defensive rage may also be activated—as when our hero is in danger, or our heroine is cruelly treated—but they do not dominate our experience of the story as they would in a story driven by the reptile brain's concerns.

Making Stories Our Own

In the 2003 movie *Cold Mountain*, Ada (Nicole Kidman) reads aloud from *Wuthering Heights* to her 'white trash' companion Ruby Lu (Renée Zwellinger) the famous passage in which Cathy explains the difference between the passionate, instinctive attachment she feels to her foster-brother Heathcliff, and her adult feelings for the handsome, chivalrous Edgar Linton:

> 'My love for Linton is like the foliage in the woods: time will change it, I'm well aware, as winter changes the trees. My love for Heathcliff resembles the eternal rocks beneath: a source of little visible delight, but necessary. Nelly, I *am* Heathcliff. He's always, always in my mind: not as a pleasure, any more than I am always a pleasure to myself, but as my own being.'[10]

Ruby, whose reading ability is still rudimentary, is so entranced that she seizes the book and starts to sound out the words for herself. Since its first publication more than 150 years ago, *Wuthering Heights* has spoken to generations of teenage girls, putting into words what many of them feel, but cannot express (perhaps it has also expressed what they have *not* felt, but deeply *wished* they could!). Kate Bush, who in 1978 turned *Wuthering Heights* into a hit song, sang it in a high-pitched, immature voice which later embarrassed her, but that voice was highly appropriate. Typical of many entranced adolescents is novelist Jennifer Donnelly. At sixteen, she reluctantly began to read Emily Bronte's classic for a high school English assignment:

> 'A few pages in, I was no longer grumbling. I was gone. Hooked. Totally blown away.
>
> I *knew* this place Wuthering Heights. I knew the moors and the towering crags, and the aching sense of isolation they imparted. I knew the gray, melancholy skies. The deep nights. The wind sighing in the fir trees.
>
> It scared me, this knowing. It made me sit up straight. Made my heart beat faster and my hands shake. Because I had no idea *how* I knew . . . My life was lived in a little town of green lawns, picket fences, and golden retrievers named Kyle. It was sunny there, not stormy and windswept. I didn't go for walks on any moors.'[11]

Donnelly's rapturous words and short, exclamatory sentences could not be more different from the leisurely, formal opening chapters of *Wuthering Heights* itself, which many teenagers would describe as 'boring' or 'longwinded'—if they could be bothered to read them at all. And the landscape Donnelly describes so passionately is not the landscape that we glimpse in those chapters, either. There are no 'towering crags' in those chapters, just deep snow and fierce winds which make travelling even short distances risky. In fact, there is far less set piece description in *Wuthering Heights*, proportional to the book's length, than there is in *Sir Gawain and the Green Knight*. Similarly, Donnelly's description of Cathy and Heathcliff as 'head cases' who are 'totally out of control' is exaggerated. But although she may not be factually correct, she is onto something.

In *Wuthering Heights*, everything that we know about the lives of Cathy and Heathcliff comes to us through the matter-of-fact voices of a naive middle-class visitor (Mr Lockwood) and an intelligent, pragmatic serving woman (Nelly Dean). It takes a long time for us to sort out exactly what is going on, since, as we come to realise, all the key events actually took place years *before* the novel begins. The celebrated words that so attract Ruby Lu in *Cold Mountain* only occur in a single short passage of dialogue. Yet it is those words, those *feelings*, which Donnelly has remembered, and around which she has built her entire mental picture of the novel, in which 'towering crags' and 'wind sighing in the fir trees' are right-hemisphere representations of the rage and longing of the central characters. What sixteen-year-old Donnelly responded to is not so much the verbal surface of a work of fiction by a long-dead, reclusive Victorian woman, but a felt sense of the emotions behind it—she is responding to the author's *being*. Parts of Donnelly resonate in sympathy with the parts of Emily Brontë that drove her to create *Wuthering Heights*. Donnelly's involvement, like so many others', stems from an identification with Emily's 'inside', not with the 'outside' of the novel in which Emily embodied her jealously guarded emotions. It is a kind of instinctive recognition, typical of the right hemisphere, in which one 'soul' calls to a like-minded soul, across place and time.

Donnelly's preface encapsulates much of what is involved in what I call the 'chosen story' phenomenon. First, there is the uncanny sense of 'recognition' in which the landscape or the characters of a story seem somehow familiar. Donnelly is shocked when she realises that the landscape she seems to 'know' (*déjà vu*?) is one that she has actually *never* known. Then there is the experience of 'becoming' the characters, perhaps just one central character, perhaps (as in Donnelly's case) all of them. Merging with them, *being* them. This is what, in previous chapters, we have seen our young 'performers' do: taking something *inside* of them that was originally *outside* of them. The reader comes to share the *writer's* experience of being fused with her creation, simultaneously both 'inside' and 'outside' it. When critic James Stern read Patrick White's novel *The Aunt's Story*, he described the experience in very similar terms to Donnelly's. He'd never visited Australia, 'yet here was prose which . . . made an unknown landscape so real that I felt I could walk out into it as into country I had been brought up in. I could see the black volcanic rocks, the dead skeleton trees . . . '[12] As it later turned out, key details of Stern's own childhood and family background echoed White's—another part of the 'chosen story' phenomenon which we'll shortly examine.

We do not know exactly what parts of Jennifer Donnelly's 'soul' were called up by Emily Bronte's words. But as it happens, I have my own experience of 'knowing this place' to set alongside Donnelly's, my own sense of deep connection with a story first experienced in adolescence. I was around seventeen when I read John Fowles' beguiling, puzzling second novel *The Magus*.[13] Fowles' hero, Nicholas Urfe, is a self-preoccupied young Oxford graduate who has taken a job teaching English at a private school on a small Greek island, partly to escape from the messy breakup of his relationship with an airline stewardess called Alison (to whom upper-class Nicholas feels comfortably superior). Hearing about a mysterious, well-to-do Athenian called Conchis who sometimes stays at a villa on the far side of the island, Nicholas wanders *alone* in that direction, and observes Conchis' house from a distance. He hears a bell ring, the sound appearing to come from the villa. (All of this is actually a modern version of what happens at the beginning of Chrestien's romance *Yvain*, also known as 'The Knight with the Lion').[14] A week later, without really knowing why, Nicholas determines to introduce himself to the mysterious Conchis. Here is how Fowles describes his hero's arrival:

> '*I walked up the small flight of steps* to the red-tiled side colonnade. There was *a closed door with an iron knocker* cast in the shape of a dolphin. The windows beside it were heavily shuttered. I knocked on the door; the knocks barked sharply over stone floors. But no one came. The house and I stood silently in a sea of insect sound. I went along the colonnade to the corner of the southern front of the house. . . . I looked out over the treetops and the sea to the languishing ash-lilac mountains . . . *a déjà vu feeling of having stood in the same place before*, something in that particular

> proportion of the arches, something in that particular contrast of shade and burning landscape outside—I couldn't say.' [Italics mine][15]

Nicholas notices a tea-table set for two, and a bell hanging from a bracket by open French windows. This, he realises, must be the same bell he heard in the distance on the earlier visit. Then Conchis himself appears, a tanned, wrinkled old man. As if (like Sir Bertilak) he has known all along that Nicholas was planning to arrive, he invites him to tea. Conchis says enough mysterious things to thoroughly intrigue the young schoolteacher, and he is only too happy to accept an invitation to an overnight stay the following weekend. On this second visit, the mystery deepens. After a long conversation in which Conchis talks about his experiences in the trenches of the First World War, makes joking references to himself as 'Prospero' (Shakespeare's aristocratic magician in *The Tempest*) and hints that he possesses psychic powers, Conchis shows Nicholas to a guest bedroom and leaves him alone. But Nicholas has been there only a short time when overtly strange things begin to happen, as if the war stories that Conchis told him an hour earlier were actually coming to life. He hears the sounds of singing soldiers, and there is a sudden stench of decaying corpses. Nicholas goes out exploring, but can find nothing. It is at this point that he comments, 'I had entered the *domaine*'.

Those words ('I had entered the *domaine*') immediately brought back my feelings on walking inside my grandmother's crowded, musty-smelling hallway. To me, the French spelling 'domaine' made the word enigmatic and mysterious—a 'special kind of domain', I thought, or a 'magic domain'. It seemed to sum up everything I felt each year that my grandmother's door opened. My own vivid experience, strengthened by yearly repetition, welled up instinctively, giving personal meaning to the words of the Fowles' novel. I did not know then that Fowles had borrowed the words from Alain-Fournier's *Le Grand Meaulnes*, nor that he had only read it when *The Magus* was almost complete, adding that particular phrase as an afterthought. But I registered the phrase as somehow different from the rest of the passage in which it occurred, and 'remembered' them as forming part of Nicholas' first arrival at Conchis' mysterious villa (quoted above), even though they actually occur many pages later. Like three-year-old Lindsay with Rapunzel, I memorised that sentence and 'worried away' at it, as if somehow *knowing* that it signified a fault line in Fowles' seamless narrative, a tiny 'hole' that had been 'patched over' with something that seemed to Fowles new and better than what he'd originally drafted.

There were some literal resemblances between the colonnade of Conchis' villa, bathed in silent, Mediterranean sunlight, and the cool, dark foyer leading to my grandmother's apartment, at which (now I come to think of it) we always arrived in high summer. The actual similarities are italicised in the passage I quoted earlier. But there were not many of them, and I was not aware of them when I first read *The Magus*. What linked the two, for me, was simply the aura of mystery as the hero stands before a strange door opening into—something (the Pied Piper's door into the mountain?). But today, I can see that something else might have cued me to respond so strongly: the sentence about *déjà vu*. The hero feels as if he has 'been here before', and so, in the strangest way, I, the reader, conjured up a parallel experience from *my* past, almost as if following an 'instruction'. Such embedded 'instructions' are not uncommon in stories, and perhaps exert a silent influence that is not generally recognised.

I did not consciously impose my childhood memories on Fowles' description of the villa. I could not do that anyway, because the novel provided its own, quite specific descriptions, and Conchis' sundrenched, whitewashed villa with its *al fresco* dining table, its sense of quiet space, and the sound of a distant harpsichord, was quite different from the Edwardian ambiance of my grandmother's apartment. Yet intriguingly, that apartment had contained visible reminders of the Great War, potent symbols and images of my grandfather's time under fire on the Somme that connected me with Maurice Conchis's Western Front stories. When I read that small section, near the start of *The Magus*, I had my own mysteries to bring to it: my wonderings about a war that had ended long before I was born, but in which I knew that my grandfather had fought. What I did *not* know then was that my grandfather had actually written a story (later expanded into an unpublished novel) set on the Western Front. I had heard my mother speak of her father's novel (long since destroyed), but of the story itself I knew nothing. It was only after my mother's death in 1991 that a single surviving copy surfaced from among old papers long forgotten in my parents' garage. I read it with growing wonder. My grandfather had been a journalist before the Great War, but he was certainly no great undiscovered author. The language of his brief story, 'A Last Request', was clichéd, and its plot melodramatic: a British officer, Captain Hugh Gordon, encounters a dying German officer in No-Man's-Land. The German shows him a photograph of a 'beautiful English nurse' with whom he had been in love, and asks Captain Gordon to give her his dying message. The Englishman, however, recognizes the woman in the photograph: she is the same nurse with whom he himself had been in love before the war. She has been trapped in Cologne by the outbreak of hostilities. The brief story ends with the lovers reunited, and Captain Gordon promising, 'Never again will I leave you'. This story had a particular meaning to my grandfather, who seems to have had an affair with his own 'beautiful nurse' during his years of enforced exile from my grandmother between 1915 and 1919. And he named his son, born in 1919, after his fictional hero. But the *domaine perdu* extended still further.

What I did not know when I discovered my grandfather's story, and worked out its significance, was that *John Fowles' own father had written a very similar story*—a novel arising out of his own Great War experiences—also unpublished, and also built around a trio of an Englishman, a German, and a woman loved by both.[16] (Stories with such plots were predictable enough for former soldiers, and even General Helmut von Moltke, architect of Germany's victory in the Franco-Prussian War of 1870–1871, had written one.)[17] Fowles himself knew nothing of his father's story as a child or adolescent, discovering it only much later. To repeat, I knew nothing of these parallels at the time I read *The Magus.* Instead, *my own memories and speculations provided a set of feelings that fused with those of the novel*: vague, un-pin-downable feelings, yet all the more potent for that, feelings about magic and mystery, feelings that combined the alien and the familiar, the comforting and the puzzling. As I've made clear in Chapter 3, I did not deliberately connect my memories and my responses to the text in order to make meaning out of the story. Instead, at a level far below conscious awareness, I 'knew' what I was reading about, because I had experienced it (or something like it) myself once. Yet simultaneously, I knew that I was reading about something I had never experienced at all, reading about a fictional hero, Nicholas—a narcissistic man who dreams of love but cannot tolerate intimacy when he finds it, who is pulled into a world of mystery and 'magic' which teaches him, slowly and painfully, to realise his own incapacity for love.

The first sense of 'knowing' (like Jennifer Donnelly's) came to me from the right hemisphere of my brain: it occurred automatically, without conscious decision or thought, creating a direct link between me and Nicholas Urfe. The second kind of 'knowing', of course, originated in the left hemisphere. I *consciously* compared myself with Nicholas, and decided that he was quite unlike me. In fact, I disliked him (which is exactly what Fowles intended). Yet I kept reading the novel because I was enthralled. I wanted to know what would happen to Nicholas, and how the mystery would unfold. What I could not know then was that *the first 'knowing' was the truer.* I was much more like Nicholas than I realised, indeed, I was also like Augustin Meaulnes in Alain-Fournier's novel (which I had not read then), who was seventeen—the same age as I was when I first read *The Magus.* It would be another forty years before I would be ready to acknowledge those deeper and more painful resemblances.

At seventeen, I was confused and disappointed by the way *The Magus* ended. I read and re-read the final paragraphs: Nicholas and Alison are brought together in an empty public square in Paris, both expecting 'something' to happen—the final act of the 'masque' that Conchis and his collaborators have scripted for them, which Nicholas calls the 'Godgame'. They gaze up at the windows above them, but nobody appears, and nothing happens. There is no 'game', Nicholas realises. There is no hidden meaning. And realizing this, he turns and walks away from Alison, 'not looking back'. Part of me had hoped for a 'happy ever after' ending to *The Magus.* I felt disappointed, even abandoned. When, at the same age, I finally read the whole of *Great Expectations*, its conclusion provoked similar feelings of disappointment. I felt cheated.

Yet isn't this what life does to all of us? The grand illusions we sustain in youth come eventually to seem false and empty, including our illusions about ourselves. We are left with the empty square, with a 'ruined place' where we must confront our own responsibility for our lives—along with our own mortality. As Fowles himself admitted much later, *Great Expectations* had been a key influence on *The Magus*, even though he was not consciously aware of the parallels at the time he was writing his own novel.[18] Stories have a way of remaking themselves, transmitting themselves from writer to reader, and so back to writer again (as the original reader becomes the author of a new fiction inspired by the first). Often, however, they remake themselves very differently, and the dreams they inspire drive real-world actions. Instead of harmless fictions that a young story maker 'performs' for his or her own delight, some individuals enact their chosen stories on a real-world stage with all 'the fire and the fury' at their command. This was certainly, and monstrously, the case with Wagner's operas, which became the 'chosen stories' of another lonely, dream-obsessed seventeen-year-old in an Austrian provincial city in 1905.

It is often said that Adolf Hitler had no friends. However, between the ages of sixteen and twenty, Hitler did have a confidant—an apprentice upholsterer and aspiring musician named August Kubizek, who first met Hitler at the Linz opera house, and later became his roommate in Vienna. The two boys shared a passion for Wagner, but Kubizek realised that the great composer held a significance for Adolf that went far beyond anything he himself could relate to: 'I can only say that he "put on" the personality of Wagner just as though it were possible for his ghost to possess him'. In four-year-olds, we call it 'pretend play'. In late adolescence, the desire to 'put on' the personality of another takes the apparently more adult form of biographical investigation—the young Hitler read everything he could find about his hero. Yet the appearance of intellectual objectivity is deceptive. Hitler read, *not to learn the truth about Wagner, but to confirm his beliefs about himself.* Kubizek tried to reason with his friend: Wagner, he said, had lived to be seventy, and experienced many ups and downs in his life—could such a man really be compared with a seventeen-year-old who had accomplished, as yet, virtually nothing? Predictably, Adolf simply dismissed such objections: 'Wagner went through it just like I have', he told Kubizek. 'All the time he had to tackle the ignorance of his surroundings'.[19]

As Jennifer Donnelly did with *Wuthering Heights*, as I did with *The Magus*, Hitler spanned the yawning gap between his own life and Wagner's by way of a shimmering rainbow bridge artfully constructed on the basis of a handful of similarities. Wagner had had to put up with 'ignorant' people who failed to understand his genius; Hitler felt the same way about the people he was surrounded by. Wagner shared Hitler's obsession with the historic destiny of the Germanic peoples, and both turned to Germanic mythology for inspiration. Pan-German feelings were everywhere at the time, and a great many people (both talented and talentless) feel that they are 'surrounded by idiots'. But for Adolf, these very general parallels, elevated into 'outlift' by the lustrous tone-colour, seductive harmonies and heroic themes of *Lohengrin*, *Tannhauser* and *Der Ring des Niebelungen*, were quite sufficient to convince him that he and

Wagner were one and the same ('Nellie, I *am* Heathcliff!'). Richard Wagner, with his overlarge head and Jewish-looking beaky nose, had overcome ignorance and prejudice, and had achieved the great works of art of which he had always dreamed; so, therefore, would thin, pale-faced Adolf, with his piercing blue eyes, his torrent of self-obsessed talk, and his secret shame.

As Kubizek tells it, one particular opera of Wagner's spoke most eloquently to the young Hitler, and it was the composer's early work, *Rienzi*. He describes how, when the performance was over, he walked with Hitler out of the city, silent, until they climbed the peak called the Frienberg which looked out over Linz:

> 'Adolf stood in front of me and now he gripped both my hands and held them tight. He had never made such a gesture before. I felt from the grasp of his hands how deeply moved he was. His eyes were feverish with excitement. The words did not come smoothly from his mouth, as they usually did, but rather erupted, harsh and raucous . . . It was as if a second ego spoke from within him, and moved him as much as it did me. It was not at all the case of a speaker being carried away by his own words. On the contrary, I rather felt as though he himself listened with astonishment and emotion to what burst forth from him with elementary force . . . it was a state of complete ecstasy and rapture, in which he transferred the character of Rienzi, without even mentioning him as a model or example with visionary power, to the plane of his own ambitions . . . He conjured up in grandiose, inspiring pictures his own future and that of his people . . . He spoke of a special mission which one day would be entrusted to him and I, his only listener, could hardly understand what he meant. Many years had to pass before I realised the significance of this enraptured hour for my friend.'[20]

This passage has drawn its fair share of skepticism from Hitler experts.[21] Kubizek wrote his memoir many years after his youthful friendship with the dictator. The first, awkwardly-written draft was written at Nazi Party suggestion; the final, greatly enlarged version (almost certainly 'ghosted' by a professional writer or editor) was only published after Hitler's death. There was ample temptation for Kubizek (or his collaborator) to embroider events, even to fabricate whole incidents and conversations, in the light of later knowledge. Yet if this particular incident is a fabrication, it is a highly sophisticated one. Psychologically, Kubizek's account of Hitler's first encounter with *Rienzi* rings true. The way a 'second ego' seems to 'speak through' him, the unacknowledged leap from Rienzi's career to his own, and the final insistence on being alone: all chime with what we know of narcissistic disorder and its convictions of 'special destiny'. Hitler himself endorsed the story in 1939, when Kubizek reminded him of it in conversation with the dictator at Beyreuth. Furthermore, the account echoes key features of what I call the 'chosen story' phenomenon at its most eerie. When Hitler identified so strongly with the Roman politician Rienzi, it was as if, in Rienzi, he *glimpsed his own future*, recognising a life path that he had not yet trodden, not even imagined. No wonder that the experience moved him so profoundly, and that he needed first to share it with his friend, and then, dismissing Kubizek, to return to the mountain to savour it *completely alone, from a high place*: 'silent, upon a peak in Darien'.

Three features of this 'recognition' or 'foreknowing' deserve special attention. First, one would have expected that a young Hitler would have selected a Wagner opera set in a mythical or medieval Teutonic past, yet he selected one from Renaissance Italy. As we saw in the case of fairy tales, our unconscious identification with a story is strengthened when the external details of that story *conceal* the resemblance between its themes and those of our own psyche. Second, Hitler selected a story that revolved around political power, at a time when (so far as we know), he dreamed only of future glory as an artist or architect. Finally, the future that Adolf Hitler glimpsed in *Rienzi* included not only a spectacular rise to power, as 'tribune of the people' (a role which Hitler could later claim to have validly described his own career as leader of the extremist but undeniably popular National Socialist party) but also *a dramatic and total fall*. Rienzi becomes the victim of the powerful factions he has sought to overturn, and dies amidst the ruin of his hopes. It is difficult to avoid the conclusion that in some way the left hemisphere cannot fathom, Hitler had 'seen' his own future. Again, this is counter-intuitive. A wish-fulfilling daydream would certainly have included gratifying images of power and popular acclaim, but surely not a 'descent into the abyss' of defeat and death. A 'chosen story', to my way of thinking, includes strong elements of unconscious 'knowing', as if the right hemisphere (which largely drives such identifications) were aware of what is latent within us, what will only unfold far in the future. We will return to this in Chapter 6.

I said earlier that Hitler's 'merging' of himself with Wagner was based on slight foundations. And this is true enough, if we include only those facts about Wagner that Hitler himself was aware of. But now, a hundred years later, we have access to vastly more biographical information about Wagner than was available to Hitler, and for that matter, a great deal of information about Hitler himself than was available to Kubizek. The privilege of hindsight enables us to see significant resemblances between the two men's histories and even their *family backgrounds* which provide a fuller context for the young Hitler's identification with Wagner and his operas, and with *Rienzi* in particular.[22] As schoolboys, both Hitler (at twelve) and Wagner (at fifteen) were literally 'degraded' ('degraded', 'humiliated' or 'demeaned' are words narcissists frequently use to describe experiences of shame)—either forced to repeat a grade, or required to start a new school in a lower grade than the one they had left. Like the young Hitler, who failed to gain entrance to the Academy in Vienna, the young Richard Wagner was resistant to formal education, insistent on learning only what he wished, and in his own way. Both young men 'talked at' their listeners, expecting assent and admiration, not debate or critique. Both the adolescent Wagner and the adolescent Hitler attempted to write grandiose dramas, and both failed to realise their ambitions, to their own humiliation.

Most intriguing of all, both Hitler and Wagner came from families where there was a murky sexual history, partly or wholly unknown to them. Wagner's biological father was a young actor called Ludwig Geyer, who had an affair with Wagner's mother Joanna. After Carl Friedrich Wagner's convenient death, Geyer married Joanna, adopting his own biological son Richard along with Joanna's children by Carl Friedrich. Suspecting Jewish blood in Geyer, Richard, who had been brought up as 'Wilhelm Richard Geyer', insisted on returning to the surname 'Wagner' as an adolescent. There was in fact no Jewish intermarriage in Geyer's family, but the young Wagner did not know that, and his own 'Jewish nose' must have heightened his suspicions. Despite the fact that his first romantic attachment was to a Jewish girl, and despite his friendship with individual Jews in later years, Richard Wagner remained a lifelong anti-Semite.

If Kubizek is to be believed Hitler, too, had an adolescent 'crush' on a wealthy girl named Stefanie, to whom he never spoke, but whom he simply gazed at as she passed by, convincing himself that she knew of his interest, and would be his once he declared his love for her (something he never dared to do).[23] And this Stefanie, like Wagner's real father, had a Jewish-sounding surname, which cast doubts over her 'racial purity'. Hitler's father Alois was born illegitimate as Alois Schickelgruber, and had married three times, always to women much younger than himself. Hitler's mother, Klara (twenty-three years younger than her husband) was also Alois' cousin and (at one remove) his niece. While some of these resemblances may easily be dismissed as coincidental, I think it makes more sense to assume that Hitler's 'choice' of Wagner as his adolescent hero stemmed not only from consciously-perceived resemblances, but from a much more complex matching of family contexts: two families produce a talented 'misfit' offspring, who convinces himself of his special destiny, perhaps, in part, as an unconscious reaction to family shame. As any artist does, Wagner wrote his personal preoccupations and family themes into every work he created—albeit often unconsciously. When Hitler encountered that work, he (again unconsciously) recognised in it the themes that animated his own personality. Hence, his belief that he and Wagner were deeply similar is not as far-fetched as it appears to Kubizek, or indeed to any rational observer.

By writing about Hitler in the context of the childhood and adolescence of individuals like John Fowles and Emily Brontë, I do not wish to suggest that Hitler was somehow their equal. Hitler's one attempt to produce a narrative (*Mein Kampf*) is notoriously a 'rant' rather than an autobiography (though it starts out as one) and so tedious, repetitive and chaotic that even dedicated Nazi Party members only pretended to read it. I have included the

Wagner-Hitler connection because it is a famous example of how profoundly stories can influence the lives of individual readers, listeners or viewers. Hitler was in no sense a literary figure, but he *was* an 'entranced reader'. My argument throughout this book is that stories can have this kind of influence, not just on future writers, but on anyone at all. The parallels between Hitler's family history and Wagner's constitute another instance of wider family patterns supplying a context for the intense connection that can form between a particular reader and a particular story.

How Teenagers Write

None of the Brontë children had even been to London, let alone Paris or Rome, but by the fireside in a vicarage in rural Yorkshire they could live vicariously in 'Great Glass Town' or (as they later named it, using their newfound awareness of Latin and Greek) 'Verdopolis'. Charlotte and Branwell shared, and increasingly tussled over, the Kingdom of Angria, while the two younger sisters, Emily and Anne, created their own secondary world, Gondal. By mid-adolescence, the original characters they'd based on Branwell's toy soldiers had mutated into more complex identities, requiring frequent rethinking to accommodate the siblings' conflicts over the direction their world should take. Charlotte's *The Search after Hapiness*, from which we quoted her description of O'Donnell earlier in this chapter, is a romance in its own right, with strong influences from the *Arabian Nights*, but she is careful to link it with the Glass Town world, explaining in her preface that

> 'The persons meant by the Chief of the city and his Sons are the Duke of Wellington, the Marquis of Douro and Lord Wellesly. The city is the Glass Town. Henry O'Donell and Alexander Delaney are Captain Tarry-not-at-home and Monsieur Like-to-live-in-lonely-places.'[24]

A similar need to systematise and synthesise their imaginary worlds was also felt by the Lewis brothers, Warnie and Jack. Hence Jack's several attempts (as an adolescent) to create a consistent chronology for his Animal Land saga, and to bring later stories and characters into line with versions of events he'd written as a child. We are seeing early stirrings of one of the left hemisphere's most vital roles in story making: the 'inner critic' which insists that everything in a well-made story must fit together logically. Some authors revise and improve someone else's work; most revise and improve their own. In thirteenth-century France, Guillaume de Lorris left his *Roman de la Rose* unfinished: the Lover had not won his Rose. Forty years later, Jean de Meung, who had never liked de Lorris' approach to the story, completed what Lorris had left unfinished—totally changing the story's nature in the process. In mid-twentieth-century England, J. R. R. Tolkien endlessly revised the sagas and tales he had created long before *The Lord of the Rings*, so that they would dovetail better with the chronologies and nomenclatures that he had later decided upon in the trilogy.

Unlike the Brontës, Jennifer and June Gibbons (the twin daughters of Jamaican immigrants, who grew up in Wales in the 1970s) did not start their elaborate private fantasy play as children.[25] June and Jennifer had been late learning to speak (not uncommon with identical twins), and when they did learn, were sparing in their communication to other family members. Yet they chattered away fluently to each other in a private 'language' which (as professionals realised much later) was simply ordinary English spoken in rapid bursts, with slurred consonants and an unconventional intonation. (There is an intriguing parallel with the minuscule handwriting in which Charlotte and her siblings wrote their 'books' and 'newspapers', too tiny and cramped-up for their father Patrick to read.) At school, June and Jennifer simply refused to speak at all, driving their teachers to distraction and attracting bullying and teasing from other children. Like both Wagner and Hitler, the twins resisted all attempts to educate them and eventually left school at sixteen, to live comfortably if reclusively at home, using social security payments to indulge their enthusiasms. The twins had long established their bedroom as their private domain, off limits to other family members, and in this room they created a sophisticated world based on several interrelated doll families whom they dressed, educated, sent to church, disciplined and hospitalised, meantime documenting all these activities in chronicles, stories and 'radio plays'.

As Charlotte, Branwell, Emily and Anne imitated the style and content of *Blackwoods Magazine* and their father's newspapers, as a fifteen-year-old Mary Anne Evans (who later published her novels as 'George Eliot') imitated the style and subject matter of Sir Walter Scott,[26] so June and Jennifer imitated the style and content of commercial radio, schoolgirl comic strips, novelettes and TV. The Brontës' imitations sound more impressively 'literary', but in fact both sets of siblings simply used the cultural exemplars which was most readily available to them. Charlotte's devotion to 'high life' (see below) was no different to the twins' absorption in the 'high life' of their own social class and historical era. The 'Silent Twins' (as journalists later dubbed them, when their names became household words) were locked in a desperately over-close relationship with each other. They felt compelled to do exactly the same things, yet simultaneously, they struggled for supremacy, and fought to maintain some sense of separateness. Despite their lack of formal education, they signed up for correspondence lessons, embarking on a program of reading classics (including *Pride and Prejudice*) in their quest to become published writers. It seemed a dream as grandiose and unrealistic as young Adolf Hitler's aspirations to write a great music-drama about Weland the Smith, when he could not even read music—let alone compose it.

Many a Western teenager, restricted in spending power, chained to tedious high school studies and longing for adult freedom, lives vicariously through the famous, but very human, individuals today's media call 'celebs'. These individuals are surrounded by luxury, have 'adventures', succumb to despair, and fall in and out of love constantly. As human beings, they are no different from the rest of us, yet they *live* in the world of romance. Though the details and the names are different, it is the same world that Charlotte Brontë, now seventeen years old, wrote about so gaily a century ago:

> 'I like high life. I like its manners, its splendors, its luxuries, the beings which move in its enchanted sphere. I like to consider the habits of those beings, their way of thinking, speaking, acting. Let fools talk about the artificial, voluptuous, idle existences spun out by Dukes, Lords, Ladies, Knights and Squires of high degree. Such cant is not for me; I despise it.'[27]

For Jennifer and June, living on a housing estate in a drab Welsh provincial town, 'high life' meant middle-class teenage America, where 'cool' kids partied, fell in love (or at least in lust), danced in discos, got high on the drugs of the day, and drove around in fast cars. The twins assiduously copied the speech of the American boys they knew on the air force base where their father worked. By seventeen, June and Jennifer had graduated from chronicles of their dolls' imaginary lives to more grown up themes. June began her first novel, *Pepsi-Cola Addict*, with a note of gritty realism that reflected her own existence more than her gratifying fantasies of 'America':

> 'The tenement in which he lived was alternately too hot or too cold. This room remained suffocatingly hot with the contained heat of the day. Preston was thinking he was cold. His head felt neurotic and dizzy. It resembled ice. He thought he wouldn't mind if he lived in Arizona or even Hawaii; they lived on cool beverages, and didn't care what you did. Sitting in his own pad, and sipping 300 cans of Pepsi-Cola every day. The thought made him thirsty. He was thirsty. He swallowed some more Pepsi, shifted his position, and his eyes began to wander around.
>
> There was subtle colour in his bedroom, sable bricks beside yellow brimstone drawers, beside wood painted livid red. There was colour in the faces, too, overlapping, blending and clashing so that the entire room displayed a world of zany popsingers. Style impassioned his thoughts in the form of pink graffiti that illuminated the name, PEGGY ten times on the freshly painted white door.'[28]

Some of this writing is awkward, and it 'tries too hard' to sound grown-up, but June has made an attempt to bridge the gap between what is familiar to her and what her potential readers might be expected to know—the very thing that was lacking in 'The Tidy House' and the other narratives written by nine- and ten-year-olds considered in our last chapter. Isolated and pathological though Jennifer and June undoubtedly were, they showed signs of developing into competent storytellers. They were starting to use their own experience, real and vicarious, to create credible imagined worlds that go *beyond* that experience. In the overwhelming majority of children, this ability only develops during adolescence, and, like the ability to empathise with the needs of potential readers, seems to depend on the continuing maturation of both the right and left hemispheres. For, while it is the left hemisphere which seems responsible for observing precise details and expressing them in language, it is the right which attends to feelings, both our own, and those that we observe in others. In adolescent story making, the two hemispheres begin to work together in a new way. Worlds apart though they are, the adolescent writings of the Brontës and the Silent Twins have some important things in common. Both sets of siblings are adept at imitating the manner and content of their dominant stylistic models. Both capture the details—the speech mannerisms and the settings of the 'high life' of their day—while simultaneously writing, with some level of realistic detail, about things they have never experienced themselves.

However, Jennifer and June's obsession with becoming authors declined sharply when they discovered the real-life excitements of sex, drugs and crime. Now they could *live* the things that they had hitherto only imagined, they seemed to feel less need to give written form to their dreams of freedom, romance and excitement. It did not help that they had failed to get any of their writing accepted, except by vanity publishers. Ignorant of so many things, even June and Jennifer were not impressed to be asked to pay six hundred pounds towards the publication of their novel (the Brontë sisters had fallen into that trap with their first collection of poems). Where the Twins withdrew energy from their writing to pursue boys, light fires and steal from supermarkets, the Brontës clung to their imaginary worlds and their shared storytelling even while trying (with only modest success) to establish lives as independent adults. Charlotte pined for Angria while attempting to be a teacher, and resented the fact that her brother Branwell, still at Haworth, was doing his best to instigate rebellions, scandals and armed incursions in the world of Verdopolis. It was Branwell, in fact, whose life course in adolescence and early adulthood most closely resembled the Silent Twins'. He had dreamed of fame as strongly as Charlotte, Emily and Anne—although interestingly, he saw himself as a painter rather than a writer. Like the young Hitler, he failed to persist when his drawings met with criticism or rejection, and, although he had a few poems accepted by magazines, literary fame seemed equally out of his reach. Branwell relied more and more heavily on drink, lost his job, and became entangled in a 'Mrs Robinson' love affair with a much older woman. From this point, he seems to have sunk into depression, self-medicated by alcohol. He began to *live* the personality he had imagined for his character 'Rogue' or 'Badman.' Likewise, the Twins' literary preoccupation with suicide, murder and drugs prefigured their careers as shoplifters, arsonists and glue sniffers. What are we to make of this? 'Don't dream it, do it' runs the famous line from *The Rocky Horror* Show. Dreamers can certainly turn into 'doers', but do 'doers' bother to translate their dreams into writing when they can make them come true in reality? We'll return to this theme in the final two chapters of this book.

Bright, well-read adolescents, even those whose own life experience has been limited, can produce writing that is almost indistinguishable from that of an adult, provided it falls within a recognisable popular 'genre': the Mills & Boon romance, the boys' adventure tale, the *Schoolgirls' Own Library* strip cartoon, or the magazine account of celebrity life. Adolescent authors can also *parody* such genre writing quite successfully. Like nine-year-old Richard in Chapter 3, but in a far fuller way, they can see beyond specifics to a general pattern, a 'recipe' or 'formula', and genre fiction depends on formulas—somewhat different from those that Homer employed, but serving a broadly similar purpose: to supply predictable developments within a predictably unfolding plot. The recently-discovered *Lost Laysen*, a complete novella that Margaret Mitchell wrote 'in the summer of her sixteenth year', is a perfect imitation of the sort of adult short stories its youthful author had read in popular magazines. It flows smoothly and assuredly from cliché to cliché, from beginning to end. As we saw earlier, imitation is the precursor of understanding. We copy the outside—the 'letter', as people used to say, before comprehending the inside—the 'spirit'. But even when following a recipe, adolescent story makers often anticipate the adult fictions that are latent within them—Mitchell's Billy Duncan is in some respects an earlier version of Rhett Butler in *Gone with the Wind*, and the heroine's gentlemanly lover Doug Steele anticipates Ashley Wilkes. Significantly, much of *Lost Laysen* is told *in the first person*, by one of its characters—the rough-and-tough Duncan—for the maturing brain enables adolescents to imagine themselves as someone else, to 'take the role' of that person.

Adolescence is that stage of life when, apparently, we are most nakedly preoccupied with our own uniqueness, our own individuality. Yet, paradoxically, it mostly produces writing that is somehow *lacking* in true uniqueness. What most adolescent writers have in common (the inevitable concomitants of their developmental stage) is still stronger than what defines them as individuals. The adolescent ego, strident though it may be in its relentless self-affirmation, cannot yet form a reliable resource for creating characters who will strike us as 'realistically individual'. Even Margaret Mitchell can only create a 'Duncan' who speaks in the language of *Saturday Evening Post* characters:

> 'Charley boy, I sure did love that little woman. I couldn't help it, tho I knew I never had a chance—she wasn't my kind. I wonder why it's always the little women who appeal to us big fellows? She wasn't much over five feet, and she couldn't have weighed 115! Why I could have carried her in one hand and never known it! But I wouldn't have lain hands on her for all the world. Her eyes would have kept anyone from doing that. They were grey-blue eyes and she looked at you as straight and steady as a

> man without any coquetry or anything like that. She had a strong straight nose and a Cupid's bow mouth. You don't see mouths like that very often, Charley boy, the kind that were made for kissing.'[29]

Think for a minute outside the framework of storytelling, to how adolescent 'loners' attempt to assert their individuality. Mostly, it is *not* through 'being themselves', but through belonging to a collective identity. By choosing to be a Mod or a Rocker, a Goth or an Emo, they can choose an acceptable stereotype identity that expresses alienation, dissent or black despair, converting dysphoria into pride. Dressing and presenting their bodies according to the rules of such groups gives adolescents a sense of individuality, while still permitting them to belong to the subculture of their choice. All this will, of course, change over the next ten to fifteen years, as we shall see in our next chapter: the individual personality will emerge from hiding in the cave of 'cool', and the New Brain will come into its own.

A Space for Selfhood

An adolescent Enid Blyton kept a diary in her bedroom. The diary was the one place where she felt safe to express her anguish at her father's desertion of the family, her anger at her mother's failure to understand and support her, and her growing ambitions to become a successful writer. At some point between her thirteenth and her eighteenth years, however, Enid's mother, suspicious and intrusive by nature, read these diaries, which Enid had assumed were sacrosanct. Enid countered by demanding a lock on her bedroom door. She destroyed the existing diaries and vowed that in future she would never record more than a factual summary of the day's events—a resolve that with rare exceptions, she seems to have stuck to for the rest of her life.[30] The Silent Twins may have withdrawn energy from their dreams of authorship, yet they continued to write daily in the red-bound five-year diaries their mother had given them on their sixteenth birthday. For, despite the fact that they were now willing to speak (at least to some degree) they remained cruelly restricted in their ability to make the real and lasting relationships that they craved. All the feelings they could not talk about with the boys they met for casual sex, all the complexities of their dark entanglement with each other, were expressed without constraint in their diaries. When, eventually, June and Jennifer were sentenced to prison terms, they continued to write daily entries, and much of what we know about them comes directly from that source.

Not all young diarists are so self-revealing as the Twins, or Enid. John Fowles' adolescent diary contained records of his nature observations, and, later, lists of the birds and animals he shot for sport. As a prefect at boarding school, he even diarised the beatings he reluctantly administered! Not a prepossessing start to a novelist's career, one might think. One thing John did not confide to his diaries, however, was his recurrent daydream of kidnapping desirable young women and keeping them prisoner so that they would be his alone. Twenty years later, this adolescent fantasy would suddenly re-emerge, in a new and sinister form, in the novel that catapulted him to success: *The Collector.* Nobody would have dreamt that the retiring, intellectual Fowles, happily married by that time, could once have shared his unpleasant hero's dark obsession, but he had—and perhaps still did.

Today's adolescents express their individuality through their rooms. Their unmade beds, the posters and pin-ups, the mess of clean and dirty clothes strewn across the floor—all these things express more than they know: the hot desperation under the cool exterior, the inner confusion that is mirrored in the messy floor. Within contemporary teenagers' rooms, the hidden diary of Blyton's day has been replaced by a computer, but whether a handwritten diary or password-protected electronic files are involved is immaterial: here is the heart of the adolescent's private space, a miniature planet Krypton within a Fortress of Solitude—apparently off limits to outsiders, yet shockingly vulnerable, nonetheless.

The act of writing down one's inner thoughts and feelings (which implies that, potentially at least, they might be read by someone else) is less challenging than speaking them aloud to another person, yet potentially just as compromising. Writing in a diary can be a tiny, cautious step towards sharing one's inner life with others, the adolescent equivalent, perhaps, of the songstries we encountered in Chapter 1, declaimed when alone, yet seemed to imply some kind of 'audience'—if only an audience of the child herself. Writing *makes the inner world real*, and it offers more control over how that inner world is expressed than a spoken conversation in which another person is participating (unless that person is content to keep her own response to a minimum). Yet it also enables the *discovery* of thoughts and feelings that may have been inaccessible to consciousness before the writing began. What Ken Wilber calls 'egoic consciousness' (that is, culturally-validated self-awareness) seems to have developed along with the first diaries.[31] When, around the seventeenth century, men and (increasingly) women began to confide their private thoughts to journals intended for their own eyes only, they began the articulation of 'inner space' which would lead, within a century or two, to the psychological novel, in which the main interest lies in the protagonists' inner worlds, and in the contrast between these inner worlds, and the outer world of actions. This is the sort of writing that typically emerges in young adulthood, and it is the theme of our next chapter.

At the time I am writing, the stunning triumph of digital social networking appears to have radically altered the old boundaries between private and public. Teenagers now post for their Facebook 'friends' photographs and text that would only a generation or two ago have seemed extremely self-revealing. The nature of writing itself seems to be altering, with emphasis shifting to shorter and shorter written communications (although the mobile phone has ensured that oral communication continues, more volubly and impulsively than ever).

However, it is hard to imagine that adolescents will not go on craving private spaces to exploring selfhood—even if those spaces are very different from the bedrooms and handwritten diaries of the past.

Where We've Come From, Where We're Going

In this chapter, we've seen how the rapidly maturing left hemisphere enables adolescent story makers to acquire almost all of the capacities that they lacked only a few short years before: an adolescent Charlotte Brontë, or an adolescent Jennifer Gibbons can situate her characters in a credibly described place and time, can take us 'inside' those characters to witness their thoughts and feelings, and she can fluently imitate the specific styles of a variety of adult genres. Yet while the adolescent story maker can 'perform' the role of adult writer, she cannot yet fully inhabit it from the inside. In our next chapter, we will see the importance of the early thirties in writers' acquisition of that particular voice which is unique to them.

If adolescents' rooms express their need for autonomy, and diaries are vehicles through which they can explore the mysteries of their inner worlds, the mystery they most typically want to explore is that of love. For adolescents, love is the great unknown, the great adventure, the Seven Cities of Cibola, the Well at the World's End. Today, sexual experience comes early to many adolescents, but love is a greater mystery than sex. Is what I feel 'really' love? How am I *supposed* to feel when I'm in love? Does he feel the same about me? Is our love going to last? Do I still have feelings for her? Will I ever feel this way with anyone else? In the final words of Dodie Smith's *I Capture the Castle,* an adult novel cast in the form of an adolescent girl's diary: *Only the margin left to write on now. I love you, I love you, I love you.*[32]

Romance is the literary form that speaks most eloquently to us when we are adolescents because it corresponds so well with our stage of life and of consciousness. Like Scarlett O'Hara, many romance heroines are adolescents when their stories begin. Although the age of medieval romance heroes is never mentioned, we may assume that they also are very young, since this was an era when a boy could be made a knight at sixteen, and a girl could be married even younger. If we want to understand the essence of romance, we need to think about what adolescents can, and can't do: they desperately want to feel separate and independent, though in truth they know they are not; they can look forward as far as being united with the object of their desire, but not far beyond it; they are preoccupied with boredom, and seek to escape into adventure—whether through chivalrous quests, computerised virtual worlds or the excitements of drugs and crime. Despite very real pressures, adolescents are in a sense a leisured class. Life, seemingly unlimited, stretches ahead of them, unknown and beckoning. For most of them, in the words of perhaps the most famous romance heroine of our own time, 'Tomorrow is another day'.

Chapter Five

'I Would Build That Dome in Air'

Story Making in Young Adulthood

'Twixt Twelve and Thirty'

> 'That punctual servant of all work, the sun, had just risen, and begun to strike a light on the morning of the thirteenth of May, one thousand, eight hundred and twenty-seven, when Mr Samuel Pickwick burst like another sun from his slumbers, threw open his chamber window, and looked out upon the world beneath. Goswell Street was at his feet, Goswell Street was on his right hand—as far as the eye could reach, Goswell Street extended on his left; and the opposite side of Goswell Street was over the way. "Such", thought Mr Pickwick, "are the narrow views of those philosophers who, content with examining the things before them, look not to the truths which lie hidden beyond. As well might I be content to gaze upon Goswell Street for ever, without one effort to penetrate to the hidden countries which on every side surround it." And having given vent to this beautiful reflection, Mr Pickwick proceeded to put himself into his clothes, and his clothes into his portmanteau. Great men are seldom over-scrupulous in the arrangement of their attire; the operation of shaving, dressing, and coffee-imbibing was soon performed; and in another hour, Mr Pickwick, with his portmanteau in his hand, his telescope in his great-coat pocket, and his note-book in his waistcoat, ready for the reception of any discoveries worthy of being noted down, had arrived at the coach stand in St Martin's-le-Grand.'[1]

Whatever age Mr Pickwick is supposed to be, a twenty-four-year-old Charles Dickens has given him the ebullience, the optimism, and the self-confidence of young adulthood. The rising sun that shines on Pickwick is the rising sun of Dickens' own youth. If adolescents typically long for adventure, young adults have the capacity to undertake it. Energetic and impatient like his barely-adult creator, Pickwick sees past the mundane realities of a London street to the 'truths beyond'—a vista that, for Dickens himself, would almost certainly have encompassed thoughts of his own future, but also, perhaps, 'hidden countries' in the past. For our past has a habit of becoming our future, even though at twenty-four we are rarely aware of that.

More than a century later, the spirit of young adulthood shines equally brightly in Iris Murdoch's second novel, *The Flight from the Enchanter*:

> 'Annette walked quickly, taking long strides, and breaking now and then into a run. She swung her arms about a lot as she walked, occasionally cuffing passers-by. She felt herself to be tall and slim and fresh, and she read this again in the faces of the people who eyed her as she approached, and turned to stare after her when she passed. As she went, her breast was filled to bursting with a vague expectancy of bliss, the force of which, rising in her sometimes almost intolerably, made her catch her breath and close her eyes.'[2]

'Vague expectancy of bliss' is exactly right: many young adults feel an optimism that need not be tied to any particular person or looked-for event. Rather, it reflects a general conviction that their future will be rosy—a conviction rooted in the strength and resilience of their own bodies. Think of the great E-flat major arpeggio which swells repeatedly throughout the overture to Richard Wagner's opera *Rheingold*. Here, in the language of music, are the themes of emerging adulthood: generativity—the ability to create and procreate; serene confidence in one's ability to surmount obstacles and achieve dreams; the irresistible surge of the life-force, on which our little lives soar as effortlessly as board-riders on a great wave.

Young adulthood begins somewhere between the late teens and the early twenties, so modern theorists say, and lasts until the mid-thirties or even, perhaps, the early forties.[3] These elastic boundaries indicate that 'stages of life'—especially once we leave childhood behind—are as much determined by culture as by biology. In Dickens' time, young people were often required (as he was) to start earning a living much earlier than they do now, and for many, disease and poor nutrition brought youth to a premature end. Instead of the 'adolescence' and 'young adulthood' now distinguished by developmentalists, perhaps it would make more sense to speak of a single era of *youth*, spanning the period 'twixt twelve and thirty' (to alter the lyrics of Pat Boone's popular song of the 1950s). This era would begin with puberty, and would not end until myelination—the 'sheathing' of the brain's neurones with fatty tissue—is largely (though not wholly) complete by the early thirties.

Beatrix Potter, Edwardian creator of C. S. Lewis' childhood favourite, *Squirrel Nutkin*, provides a neat example. At fourteen, Beatrix began a diary in code, which was never read by another living soul until long after her death. She kept that diary for sixteen years, ceasing abruptly at 30. A year later, at the age of 31, her first book, *The Tale of Peter Rabbit*, became an overnight success, and her career as a published writer had begun.[4] Give or take a few years, the period from fourteen to 31 corresponds well with the span we've allotted to 'youth'. It also corresponds with the time that often seems necessary for the incubation of the capacity for story making—from its hidden beginnings in the adolescent's 'fortress of solitude' to its emergence as publishable fiction.

Freed from adolescent restrictions, young adults typically aspire to mastery. They want to achieve, to win, to learn, to accumulate knowledge and skills, to make money, to create a family. Very real limitations of social class and education may prevent their attaining some of those things, but they continue to believe in themselves, for good biological reasons—their physical strength and endurance are now at their peak. Like Iris Murdoch's Annette, many young adults feel, to all intents and purposes, as immortal as Homer's Gods and Goddesses. Whatever bad things may happen to others, they are convinced they themselves will never experience such misfortunes. Joseph Conrad's middle-aged narrator Marlow talks about this feeling in his celebrated story, 'Youth':

> '[T]he feeling that I could last for ever, outlast the sea, the earth and all men; the deceitful feeling that lures us on to joys, to perils, to love, to vain effort—to death; the triumphant conviction of strength, the heat of life in the handful of dust . . . '[5]

'Ah, youth!' exclaims Marlow at intervals throughout his story—marvelling at the way he once clung to his dreams (or illusions) no matter how great the obstacles he faced. For many story makers, this is the age at which they reshape their histories and even their own names, in defiance of the realities of their lives and families. Eighteen-year-old Robert Lewis Stevenson decided to adopt the French spelling 'Louis' for his second name (perhaps reflecting his fascination with Alexandre Dumas' swashbuckling stories set in the reigns of Louis XIII and XIV). Young Billie Falkner respelled his father's name, so that he would appear in print as 'William Faulkner'. And when he left his family behind in Ireland, never to return, young Patrick Branty altered his surname to 'Brontë', the Greek word for 'thunder': it didn't sound Irish! 'Making up stories' did not start with his children Charlotte and Branwell.

Secrets and Lies

Story makers seem to 'delete', 'cut' and 'paste' their *lives* from quite early on, severing connections with their families, or with parts of their own past, and fabricating 'facts' to replace what they have deleted. Mississippi-born William Faulkner constructed a fictitious past as a fox-hunting Englishman when applying to join the Royal Air Force in Canada in 1918. He even practised a British accent to lend credibility to his claim. In Atlanta, Georgia, Margaret (now 'Peggy') Mitchell got her first job in journalism by talking knowledgeably about her experience on the *Birmingham Times*—only it wasn't she who had gained that experience, but her friend Aggie. Enid Blyton turned her back on her family of origin, telling friends that she was an orphan. For story makers the boundaries between real and make believe remain fluid long after the age of pretend play, justified in their own minds by their need for psychic survival, their craving for an autonomy they do not feel, or their wish to rectify long-ago deficits and losses.

There can be no more dramatic example of 'creative editing' of a writer's own life than that of Patrick Russ. In 1945, at the significant age of thirty-one, Russ altered his name by deed poll to the one by which we now know him—Patrick O'Brian. Simultaneously, he cut off contact with most of the Russ family. He had just married Mary Tolstoi, the great love of his life, whom he had met five years earlier, and the couple were about to leave London for rural Wales, where Patrick hoped to live by his writing—a young adult 'adventure' if ever there was one. There is every reason to believe that Patrick felt considerable guilt at the way he had left his first wife and their two young children some time before he met Mary, but guilt alone fails to explain why he would take the drastic step of assuming a completely new identity. As O'Brian's biographer explains,[6] the roots of Patrick's attempt to re-invent himself lie much earlier in his life. Like Roald Dahl, Patrick had lost a parent at a very early age—his mother Jessie had died when Patrick was only three. Five years later, when his father remarried, Patrick formed a close bond with his new stepmother, Zoe. But, as we saw in Chapter 2, the impact of early losses can be registered by primitive parts of the brain even before a child learns to speak, 'holes in the world' that can never be filled. Remember Melanie Klein's little boy? The 'nice doggie' could restore his equanimity, but it could not make him trust the spinning top, even after its repair.

For five long years, little Patrick Russ had been motherless. His father, Charles, was an overbearing man who seems to have been blinded to his children's feelings by his own grief. (C. S. Lewis's father had behaved very similarly after his wife's death.) Although in some respects Patrick received privileged treatment from his father, the sensitive little boy still experienced Charles as a huge, punitive presence, eventually writing him into the Aubrey-Maturin series as General Aubrey (Jack's father)—a monster of egotism. So, as Patrick grew up, he cultivated the belief that he 'took after' his mother's family, that he was not really a Russ at all. Working for Intelligence during the war years, he had spelled his name 'Ross'. To impress his graduate colleagues, he claimed to have earned a doctorate from an Italian university. In fact, Patrick had not completed grammar school. His failure to gain entry to university was, he believed, his father's fault, and so perhaps he felt entitled to 'make it right' in much the same way as four-year-old Carol felt entitled to create a new and more consoling ending to the story of the forsaken merman. So when Richard Patrick Russ changed his name to Richard Patrick O'Brian in 1945, he was simply taking one more step in a process of distancing himself from his father, a process that had been going on since childhood. The choice of an Irish surname seems to have reflected Patrick's fond feelings for that country (he had never lived there) and for the Irishman Edward Taaffe, possibly Patrick's first real friend.

It is also significant that Patrick's remarriage to Mary took place five years after he left his first wife, the same interval as the one between the death of Jessie and his father's remarriage to Zoe. Patrick's own son Richard (by his first wife) was then eight years old—the same age that Patrick himself had been when Zoe entered his life. Despite the hostility Patrick felt towards his father, he had *re-enacted a key part of his father's story*—almost certainly unconsciously—*to an almost identical timetable.* Such age-related repeats of dramatic events in the previous generation are not uncommon in families. The paradox is that if we read about them in a novel by Thomas Hardy, we would probably scoff 'That's a bit far-fetched!', or 'Just too neat to be true!'

As so often with the story makers chronicled in this book, one protective falsehood led O'Brian to another, and eventually, as the successful author of *Master and Commander* (1969) and its successors, Patrick allowed interviewers to believe that he had been born in Ireland, and been to sea on a square-rigged sailing vessel. He claimed that he'd first read the story of Commodore Anson's great voyages in eighteenth-century copies of *The Gentleman's Magazine,* which (he said) he'd found as a child in a cellar. Patrick had indeed found old copies of *The Gentleman's Magazine* in a cellar, but they were of much later date. He read Anson's account (on which he had based his book *The Golden Ocean*) only as an adult. As John Fowles did with *Le Grand Meaulnes*, O'Brian *backdated* his first acquaintance with a story that had become part of him—as if to insist to himself that he had 'always known it'.

The Importance of Being Thirty

As we saw in our last chapter, sixteen- and seventeen-year-olds can duplicate almost all the features of a well-formed story, but it is only as the fourth decade of life begins that the majority of writers find their own voice—that voice that seems lacking in their earlier fluent imitations of someone else's style or subject matter. Between the late twenties and the middle thirties, writers break through into story making that can convince publishers of its value, and command an audience wider than their own families and friends. Scott Fitzgerald published *The Great Gatsby* when he was twenty-nine. Charlotte Brontë was thirty-one when *Jane Eyre* appeared. It was at thirty-three that

William Faulkner published *The Sound and the Fury.* Hugh Lofting was thirty-four when he published *The Story of Doctor Dolittle*, and Iris Murdoch was the same age when she published her first novel, *Under the Net.* John Fowles began work on *The Collector* at thirty-four (although it was not published until two years later). Jules Verne was thirty-five when he published *Five Weeks in a Balloon*, the first of his celebrated science fiction adventure stories. And Margaret Mitchell was thirty-five when she finally published *Gone with the Wind*, her sole novel. Every one of these stories was a resounding success. Of course, publication dates can falsify the true order in which stories were written, and belie the length of their gestation. Most of the authors I've just listed had been writing for years (Scott Fitzgerald and William Faulkner had both published two novels in their twenties, Margaret Mitchell had been working on *Gone with the Wind* since the age of twenty-six) but for each of them, the 'breakthrough age' was the period between thirty and thirty-five. Dickens, too, had been a best-seller since his early twenties, but in his first novels he had in many senses 'made his stories up as he went along'—a grown-up version of a preschool songstry. It wasn't until *Martin Chuzzlewit* that he started a novel with a clear sense of a unifying theme that would run right through it.[7] His age when the story appeared? He was thirty.

Why do these developments cluster so predictably around this age? What do they signify? It seems absurdly obvious, but the first thing a unique voice demands is a necessary minimum of life experience—enough for story makers to *feel grown up.* This is typically because they have negotiated an intimate relationship (or several intimate relationships); because they have made important life decisions and experienced the consequences of those decisions; or because they have started a family of their own. Of course, simply having lived for thirty-odd years and experienced some 'marker events' is not sufficient in itself. It is the advancing maturation of the brain, especially the frontal lobes of both left and right hemispheres, that appears to be related to a growing capacity in all of us (not just story makers) for *reflective thought*—the ability to be a dispassionate observer of self. Story makers need the mental capacity to stand back from what they have lived through, to see their own experience as if from the outside—as 'she' or 'he' rather than as 'I'.

A successful story (even if strongly autobiographical and told in the first person) needs a degree of separation between the self of the author and the self of the narrator. A story must seem to happen *'outside'* ourselves, however much its raw material comes from *inside* us. By thirty (plus or minus a few years), story makers are *increasingly aware of their own emotional functioning.* The previously unconscious patterns in their lives are becoming more visible. Awareness of the implicit patterning of one's own life is vital for the ability to shape a fictional world. With the ripening of self-awareness comes, in varying degrees, that honesty in laying bare hidden motivations (one's own, and others'), that sense of what is possible and impossible in human lives, which can transform one person's experience into something that speaks to human beings in general.

Finally, what seems to propel many (not, of course, all) story makers into maturity around the age of 30 is *a personal experience of loss*—either a recent loss, experienced as an adult, or the memory of a childhood loss, now revisited and re-imagined with the help of the brain's expanded capacities for empathy and understanding. In Chapters 2 and 3 we saw how many story makers experienced significant losses in early or middle childhood, but acknowledged that the full impact of those losses was usually outside of their awareness. But when young adult story makers, in the full flush of energetic youth, are confronted suddenly and shockingly with the possibility that any life (including their own) may be brutally cut short, the result is very different. It happened to Iris Murdoch at thirty-three, when her much older lover Franz Steiner dropped dead of a heart attack shortly after she had been with him. Such experiences, I have come to believe, provide many story makers with 'the sense of an ending'—the ability to make a story conclude convincingly, even when that conclusion does not embody the actual death of any fictional character. Do you have to 'live it before you can write it'? Not necessarily, but it seems to help.

Autobiography Is Not Enough

Notoriously, many first novels are autobiographical, sometimes transparently so, like Fitzgerald's *This Side of Paradise*.[8] Like preschool children, adults create stories as a way of dealing with emotional perturbation—but simply having been through some momentous experience and feeling driven to write about it is rarely sufficient to create a memorable story. At the age of twenty-six, while teaching at a girls' school in Brussels, Charlotte Brontë became infatuated with Monsieur Héger, who had showed a kindly interest in her. Héger was seven years older than Charlotte, and married to her headmistress: her passion had no future. Following her return to England, Charlotte wrote about the experience in her first novel, *The Professor*. Eager to disguise a potentially inflammatory theme, Charlotte clumsily cast herself as a male teacher in love with one of his senior pupils, and awkwardness multiplied as a result. Publishers said 'No', and *The Professor* did not see print until after Charlotte's death. But only a year after its rejection, Charlotte gained lasting fame with *Jane Eyre*. It was clearly inspired by the same experience—a young woman without prospects falls desperately in love with an older man—but in *Jane Eyre* Charlotte approached her theme differently.

First, she made her fictional alter ego a woman instead of a man—enabling herself to speak in her own voice about matters of the heart. Second, and more crucially, instead of casting herself as an adult from the commencement of the story, she created that celebrated opening chapter in which a ten-year-old Jane is miserably alone, bullied and humiliated by her wealthy cousins. So moving and convincing are the surface details that we do not perceive the fairy tale template that lies behind it. Instead, we are compelled by Jane's narrative to enter the consciousness of a lonely, unhappy child, locked up with her fears in a menacing room at night. The opening chapters engage us, as readers, in a *psychological* adventure ('Cinderella' only describes what the Ugly Sisters *do* to Cinderella: what she thinks, and how she feels, are left to our imaginations). When *Jane Eyre* 'cuts' to the same young girl on the threshold of adulthood, we follow her story eagerly. Memories of how Charlotte must herself have sometimes felt as a child fuel the creation of a partly fictional adult self—a process that Dennis Potter relied upon in writing his television plays more than a century later: "I decided, as I often have in the past, to use the outward *form* of autobiography to give the engine-power *Karaoke* needed.'[9] Potter did not simply 'write his own story': he *consciously used* elements of his life, recognising that only a revisiting of the pain and longing of his child self could supply 'engine power' to his creations.

If we thought carefully about what happens in *Jane Eyre*, we would find its plot unconvincing and far-fetched. Yet most readers, myself among them, are spellbound by its dramatic coincidences and melodramatic revelations—features which indicate that Jane's narrative is actually a dreamlike creation, playing with the heroine's hopes and fears as she contemplates the idea of an intimate relationship with a man old enough to be her father. As Anne Wilson's analysis suggests, the various episodes in *Jane Eyre* are not to be read as taking place in a 'real' time sequence, but instead, indicate the heroine *thinking about* one possible outcome after another.[10] Eventually, Jane's mind settles on a resolution that satisfies her—she, plain, ordinary Jane, can only feel that she is 'allowed' to marry her gentleman lover, Edward Rochester, after he has lost his wealth and been blinded—the same plot (when we think about it) as in 'Rapunzel'. It is an ending more acceptable to the reality-oriented left hemisphere than Cinderella's slipper test, but Charlotte has *brought it about* by magical thought—engineering the mad wife, the fire, St John's intervention, and so on, in order to bring her hero and heroine together at last, both of them 'older and wiser', with more realistic expectations. When Jane announces suddenly at the very end of the novel, 'Reader, I married him', we are gratified at two distinct levels: the Old Brain feels that this is 'right': the loss has been made good, Rapunzel has found her lost Prince; the New Brain tells us that such a match is now credible (just), because Jane is no longer impossibly 'beneath' Edward in terms of the class system of the day. Yet the breaking through of the second person, in direct address to the reader, indicates that a certain uneasiness remains in the author's mind.

Melanie Klein's map of early childhood included the cognitive and emotional landmark she called 'attaining the depressive position'.[11] This occurs when an infant begins to understand that Mother is a single person who is sometimes comforting and sometimes not. Prior to this, Klein theorised, the child experiences its mother as *two separate beings*, one all good (like a fairy godmother), and the other, all bad (a malevolent witch). In terms of the evolution of the brain, this earlier phase (which Klein called the 'paranoid-schizoid position') would seem to belong to the survival-oriented reptile brain, which programs the child to see the world in terms of 'friend' or 'foe'. Of course, attaining the more mature 'depressive position' in early childhood is only the first step in a much longer process. Full adult acceptance that all human beings are a mix of good and bad can take decades. Learning the painful lesson that there is no 'good place', no 'perfect partner', no 'happy ever after' may take us the rest of our lives. And in many ways, the learning of that lesson is the distinct province of the psychological novel—the literary form which belongs to the New Brain, to the cerebral cortex, to our mature ability to self-reflect. The psychological novel presents us with a sense of life as shadowed—and humbled—by the adult awareness that death lies ahead for all of us. And though *Jane Eyre* is a romance in its underlying structure and motivation, it simultaneously offers its readers a view of life that is tempered by suffering and by the inevitable loss of youthful illusions.

What we've seen happening with Charlotte Bronte's first two novels helps us to understand what occurred in the case of John Fowles. Published second, *The Magus*—which so enthralled me as a late adolescent—was actually Fowles' first novel—his equivalent of *The Professor.* It started life as a manuscript called *An Island and Greece*—a thinly-disguised account of the young Fowles, who in the early 1950s taught English at a boys' school on the Greek island of Spetsai, and fell in love with his best friend's wife. His affair with Elizabeth was the defining event of his twenties, a mixture of wild excitement and massive guilt. The autobiographical core of *The Magus* is there, but when he saw the manuscript, Fowles' literary agent—a man named Paul Scott, who would later write novels himself—immediately perceived what was wrong with it:

> 'It lacks *the power of compelling unresisting attention* . . . he is so close to writing a good book, but I am sure that he lacks *that touch of magic* which would have brought real life and sparkle to his admiration for beauty, his feeling for the past, his sense of *drama in strange places.*' [Italics mine][12]

I've italicised those phrases of Scott's that acknowledge the need for an Old Brain element in *An Island and Greece.* It needed a title that didn't sound like a travelogue—and it needed to be more than just an account of an intense emotional experience in an exotic landscape. The wealthy Athenian, Conchis, and the mysteries of his villa, the tinkle of the harpsichord, and two beautiful young women who bewitch the self-centred hero, Nicholas—all these 'touches of magic' were still to be incorporated. They would owe much to Fowles' post-Spetsai experiences (after he returned to England, he taught at a girls' finishing school and became successively infatuated with two of his senior pupils), but they would owe just as much, at a deeper level, to two stories that had deeply influenced him, and in whose protagonists he had seen himself. As we saw in the last chapter, these were Alain-Fournier's *Le Grand*

Meaulnes and Dickens' *Great Expectations*. Just as 'Cinderella' and 'Rapunzel' provided a deep structure for *Jane Eyre*, so Alain-Fournier and Dickens provided the motifs that could help him reshape *An Island and Greece*—the 'lost domain' and the 'magical benefactor'. In line with these, Fowles came up with a new title, *The Magus*—'The Magician'—and played with the idea of the occult throughout the novel, almost as if deliberately following his agent's advice to include 'more magic'. In Chapter 1 I suggested that in the process of story making, form comes before content, shape before meaning. Once Fowles had his shape (courtesy of *Le Grand Meaulnes* and *Great Expectations*) he had his novel, one that could, as the agent had demanded, 'compel unresisting attention'. But it was not until Fowles' late thirties that *The Magus* would finally achieve publication.

Like Charlotte Brontë after the failure of *The Professor*, John Fowles had to step *away from* his recent adult experience, and return to something from *earlier* in his life—that sinister adolescent daydream in which he'd imagined capturing a young girl and making her his 'slave'. By casting himself in the role of a psychopathic middle-aged man, Fowles could distance himself from this fantasy ('It isn't me, it's him') sufficiently to enter into it with frightening conviction. Written rapidly and at a white heat, *The Collector* achieved instant success. Only then could Fowles return to *The Magus*, and rework it sufficiently for it to be published. Yet he never ceased to tinker with 'this endlessly tortured and recast cripple', as he called *The Magus*, and many years later published a revised version, restoring sexually explicit passages that his editors had censored from the first edition, and subtly re-writing others. He had, he said, learned to accept that *The Magus* was more fascinating to readers than any of his other books, despite his own dissatisfaction with it.[13] That fascination, I have no doubt, depended on the same Old Brain 'magic' Fowles had woven into 'An Island and Greece' to transform it into *The Magus*.

The emotional core of Janet Frame's *Owls Do Cry*—commenced in 1955 when she was thirty-one, and published two years later—lies in childhood experiences of pain and confusion—most notably the tragic early death of Janet's older sister Myrtle ('Francie' in the novel). The opening section, like the corresponding part of *Jane Eyre*, echoes the spirit of the fairy tales that had so enthralled Janet as a child. As 'Daphne' tells her story, the prose 'swings' almost like a verse epic: 'And then . . . and then . . . and so . . . '. What is going to happen? We, Daphne's readers, keenly want to know—but in a way, we *already* know. It is clear enough that something terrible is going to happen, and quite soon it does—Francie, Daphne's older sister, who exists unreflectingly in a world of clothes, makeup, and boys, suddenly and shockingly dies. And a void opens in Daphne's world: 'I had a blue ribbon in my hair that day, and *it kept coming undone, and there was no one to tie it for me*; *it is like a kind of gap in my life*. What nonsense I talk'. [Italics mine][14]

Frame's wording echoes the repeated negatives that had such an impact on the preschool children we met in Chapter 4. It is not 'nonsense' that

Daphne talks, but *death*—the death of an older sister, which perhaps echoed an even earlier death, a death that came at the very beginning of Frame's life. Janet's twin brother had died at birth; though she never says so, it is possible that her awareness of this history not only enhanced her sensitivity to loss, but also drove her need to succeed, to 'live for' the twin whose life had ended as hers began—an imperative that has been well documented in the lives of many twins.[15]

Like the famous first section of Faulkner's *The Sound and the Fury* (by which Frame may well have been influenced) the opening pages of *Owls Do Cry* place us right inside the limited consciousness of a very young child, a child who is looking out, as if through an open door, on a miraculous, dirty, delicious, savage world. Then, as also happens in *The Sound and the Fury*, Frame's novel suddenly expands beyond this child vision and compels us to inhabit two very different inner worlds—the chillingly conventional thoughts and feelings of Chicks, Daphne's younger sister; and the narrow, self-serving ruminations of Toby, her disabled brother. We are shown three siblings' reactions to the untimely death of their sister in the most confronting way possible. It is distressing to read *Owls Do Cry*, yet impossible not to keep reading. When, in her late fifties Frame 'told the true story' behind *Owls Do Cry* in the first volume of her autobiography, she created a strong, moving narrative which inspired Jane Campion's award-winning movie *An Angel At My Table*. But for all their fine qualities, neither the autobiographical trilogy nor the movie based on it takes us by the scruff of our neck and thrusts us bodily into the pity and the pain of life in the way that the novel does. *Owls Do Cry* confronts us all with the shabby bargains that human beings make with themselves in order to keep living.

This is what a psychological novel can do that an epic or a romance cannot, this is its special contribution to humanity's contemplation of itself. The novel's voice is the voice of the New Brain, forcing us to *think about* what we experience, not just *live through* it. The technique of telling a dramatic story from the viewpoints of several different characters (*Wuthering Heights*, *The Sound and the Fury*, Paul Scott's *The Jewel in the Crown* and David Mitchell's *Cloud Atlas*) compels every reader to be *consciously aware* in a way that a continuous third-person narrative does not. Placing us 'inside' several characters one after another makes it impossible for us to identify in a simple, single-minded way with any one of them—by the end, we find ourselves simultaneously both 'inside' and 'outside'—something that the 'oral style' of the Old Brain simply cannot do.

Owls Do Cry was not a novel that I read as an adolescent or as a young adult. It was not one of my 'chosen stories'. In fact, I was never attracted to it, and read it for the first time only a few years ago. Yet when I did, I felt a shock, like diving into cold water. I had read Frame's autobiography, *To the Is-land*, and Michael King's detailed, compassionate account of Frame's life, *Wrestling with the Angel*, yet it was not until I actually read *Owls Do Cry* that I realised how closely Janet's family resembled my own. I don't mean the family I grew up in, in 1950s Australia. No, Janet's family, growing up in New Zealand in the 1920s, corresponded with my *father's* family of origin, growing up in Australia at the same time. Janet's hard working, intensely anxious, emotionally inadequate father, overwhelmed by fears of 'not being able to pay the bills'; and prone to fits of fear-driven rage was my paternal grandfather, Albert. Her passionate, tearful mother, absorbed in cooking and child rearing yet dreaming of poetry and romance, and hoping against hope that 'The Lord' would provide a refuge against pain and loss, was my paternal grandmother, Ethel. And Janet herself, with her pathological shyness, her introspection, her intense shame and her compensatory smug pride, was my father's younger sister Beth—who died while I was working on this book. Exactly as Janet had, Beth embarked on a teaching career as a young woman, only to abandon it, despite her obvious talent. Although Beth married and adopted two children, she contrived to live a life quite apart from the world, again as Janet did. The difference was that my aunt, a great reader as a child, was not driven to write in the way that Janet Frame was. And where Frame used her writing to transform her life, to bolster her sanity and self-esteem, and to provide her with a precarious financial independence, my aunt would, I think, have said that she had no need of any of those things, because the Lord provided all that she needed.

If *Owls Do Cry* is driven by childhood loss, the career of Charles Dickens shows us a different pattern. In his early twenties, when *The Pickwick Papers* was gaining him a growing following, Dickens had already experienced both the shame of his father's bankruptcy (at twelve) and the pain of rejection by his first love, Maria Beadnell (at nineteen). Yet hardly any of his suffering is visible in the sunlit world of *The Pickwick Papers*. Structurally, *Pickwick* is the adult equivalent of those two-year-old 'songstries' we met in Chapter 1—an endless, timeless succession of happenings linked loosely by the presence of Mr Pickwick and his friends, who travel around the English countryside like a bunch of overgrown schoolboys. There is no 'secret' which the narrative will eventually reveal, no developing conflict which will eventually engulf the characters. The novel could have continued forever, and when eventually the young author had to bring it to an end, he did so in a way that reminds us of two- and three-year-old narrators who simply tire of storytelling and blithely exclaim, 'The End'.

Oliver Twist was already well underway while Dickens was completing *Pickwick*—for at this stage of his career, his manic energy could support the writing of two novels simultaneously—and it began life, like its predecessor, as a loosely constructed narrative which, like its hero, 'twisted' and turned without much conscious pre-planning. But then something changed, and what changed was that while still in the middle of *Oliver*, Dickens experienced the death of his wife's younger sister, Mary Hogarth. Mary had actually lived with Charles and his wife Catherine (rather as Minna Bernays had lived with Sigmund Freud and his wife) and (also like Freud) Dickens seems to have felt more sympathised with by his sister-in-law than by his wife. Mary's untimely death (she was seventeen) occurred when Dickens himself was just twenty-four. 'Beautiful, loving and good', Mary became for him a symbol of ideal womanhood. He clung to her memory in ways that modern psychiatrists would regard as quite pathological—indeed, he behaved in almost as bizarre and exaggerated a way as Miss Havisham, the memorable 'madwoman' he created twenty years later in *Great Expectations*. However, as Dickens' biographer Peter Ackroyd points out, Mary's death seems to have been crucial to the transformation of *Oliver Twist* from a picaresque narrative into a novel that ends conclusively and even relatively believably.[16] Mary's death had moved the young writer decisively out of the 'endless' narrative of the reptile brain (*Pickwick*), provided it with that *sense of an ending* that is the first step towards the narratives of the New Brain.

The New Brain Triumphant

In the wish-fulfilling closure of the romance, wrongs are righted and dreams become realities. Even *Jane Eyre* presents a modified version of this kind of conclusion. But in novels like *Owls Do Cry*, *Le Grand Meaulnes* and *Gone with the Wind* (for all the latter's 'romantic' reputation) wrongs are not righted, dreams do not become reality, and what is 'attained' is *acceptance* of reality. As Mick Jagger reminded us, we can't always get what we want, but sometimes we get what we need. Psychological novels often end ambiguously or disappointingly. Waste, folly or tragedy may remain, but something has been realised, something hidden has been revealed, and so an ending of sorts has been achieved. We can put the book down *feeling* this sense of achievement, alongside the author. However, many readers 'twixt twelve and thirty' do not enjoy such endings, or see the point of them. At twenty, I still wanted Pip to win Estella in *Great Expectations*, in *The Magus* I wanted Nicholas and Alison to be back together, and above all, I wanted there to be Someone, or something, that conferred significance and value on their suffering. Psychological novels are novels without Immortals, novels shadowed by human aloneness in the face of inevitable death. In the most confronting of them, the 'hole in the world' is a constant, disquieting presence.

The title of Faulkner's 'breakthrough novel' *The Sound and the Fury* comes from Act V of Shakespeare's *Macbeth*, where the tyrant, facing his fate, sourly describes human life as 'a tale told by an idiot, full of sound and fury, signifying nothing'. We are constantly invited to believe that the story of the doomed Compson family, too, 'signifies nothing'. Yet the shape Faulker chooses for his narrative gives the lie to that. It begins with a 'tale told by an idiot'—literally, since Benjy, the 'speaker' in the first section, is a grown man with the mental age of a preschool child. Its second section is told by a different kind of 'idiot'—Benjy's highly intelligent but increasingly deranged brother Quentin, who eventually takes his own life. But in the final two sections of *The Sound and the Fury*, what emerges is *meaning*. We begin to understand what has happened in the past, and how that past connects with the present: how Benjy lost his beloved sister Caddy, and how Quentin lost her too, and so lost his own grip on reality. It is a grim awakening, but an awakening nonetheless. Left hemisphere *understanding* is finally substituted for right hemisphere *mystery*. The ending of *The Sound and the Fury* presents us with a meaning that the analytical, reflective part of our brain can appreciate as 'credible', even though the older part wants to reject its bleakness. Caddy will never return, Quentin is dead, Benjy will always have the mind of a three-year-old, the mean-spirited brother Jason will never feel compassion: life will simply continue. No wonder Faulkner drank himself into a stupor when he completed *The Sound and the Fury*; it cannot have been easy for a man just short of thirty to contemplate what he had created, or to live with such a view of life. But then, he had almost certainly been one of those children for whom the breaking of a beloved toy was final: there could be no repair, and no substitute could take its place.

As we saw in our last chapter, the hero or heroine of romance experiences 'adventures'—exciting, mysterious events which *happen to* him or her, something psychologists call 'having an external locus of control'. Often, these adventures occur in the course of a journey into exotic or alien places, and end with a return home. Homer's characters adopt new courses of action, wonder what they should do, or act in odd ways, but they do these things because a God has *put* particular impulses *into them*, or 'instructed' them to act differently. However in a psychological novel new thoughts and feelings are portrayed as arising *within the conscious mind of the hero or heroine*, and we are shown the *internal* thought process by which decisions and realisations occur ('internal locus of control'). As Anne Wilson shows, the 'deep structure' of *Jane Eyre* is dictated by fairy tale patterns—but unlike Cinderella, Rapunzel or Snow White, Jane ponders her experiences, comes to terms with her emotions, realises things about herself and others. Her 'adventure' is a process of understanding more fully who she is and what she wants from life. It is as if a 'New Brain layer' has been added, *on top of* the fairy tale stratum—a layer that directs the reader's conscious attention to the protagonist's reflections on action, rather than inviting the reader to simply be *caught up in the actions themselves*. To be sure, Jane makes several journeys, and uncovers several mysteries—exactly as in a romance. But these are paralleled by the journeys within her own mind.

Description plays a crucial role in the psychological novel—not just description of the protagonist's thoughts and feelings, but also description of the setting in which the fictional events take place. We saw in earlier chapters how in epic and romance, description was normally limited to a narrow range of 'appropriate' subjects, designed to glorify the heroic protagonists. The coming of the novel vastly widened the scope of what a story maker might expect to describe, including things previously seen as highly inappropriate—in *Ulysses*, James Joyce notoriously described his hero Bloom using the toilet—and most novel-readers today anticipate at least some description—indeed, they may feel bereft (as I did when reading *Wolf Hall*) if there is very little. Paradoxically, as story making consciousness has moved *inside* the individual, it has simultaneously permitted a broader focus of attention *outside* of the individual.

What does this mean? In the nineteenth century, readers of novels came to expect a kind of verbal 'picturing' of the story—and even now, when the motion picture has supplanted the novel as the dominant form of Story, readers still expect it. More subtly, descriptions can serve to create *mood* (background music plays this role in movies) or to suggest, unconsciously, what a story cannot literally acknowledge. They also contribute to an illusion peculiar to the New Brain novel—the reader's illusion that 'real world time' (the time spent in reading a novel) somehow corresponds with fictional time—the time taken by the events that the novel purports to narrate. As every child knows, descriptions slow down the forward movement of a story, and many child readers skip them in order to get on to the next 'exciting bit'—the 'reptile brain' is geared to *action*, and when there is no action, it seems that nothing is happening. But the fact that descriptions literally *take time to read* can serve a story maker's purposes.

Herman Melville occupies page after page in *Moby-Dick* with mock-scholarly accounts of various aspects of whales and whale-hunting. While his meticulously documented details are interesting (if you're interested in whales) and funny (even if you're not), they do not advance the action of the novel in any way—indeed, they slow it down, and that is one good reason for their being there. Melville, after all, has to convince us that the voyage of the 'Pequod' is taking months and years, and all those chapters about whales and whaling fill in time while we are waiting for the much-anticipated clash between Ahab and Moby Dick. When the malevolent white whale finally makes his dramatic reappearance, we can feel relief and anticipation that finally, after so 'long', either Ahab will triumph, or the creature will destroy him. In Thomas Mann's *Buddenbrooks*, a detailed description of a lavish family dinner is not just a way of showing us the bourgeois comfort (and hidden tensions) with which the young Thomas Buddenbrook has grown up—it also requires us to read more slowly in order to absorb the detail, to mentally picture the furnishings, dishes and dinner guests. This description, along with others scattered throughout the long novel, creates a kind of 'buffer' between one episode and the next, one *time* and the next, giving the reader the chance to 'live in' one generation before being asked to move to another—for the novel's events span almost a century.

So far in this chapter we've examined the rise of the 'New Brain' narrative, while simultaneously acknowledging the continuing importance of the Old Brain—even within quintessentially New Brain stories. We've seen how story makers like Charlotte Bronte, Charles Dickens, Janet Frame and John Fowles all depended heavily on myths and fairy tales to supply the structure and the 'emotional fuel' behind their psychologically sophisticated novels. We've seen how often story makers' adult experiences of love and loss built upon childhood 'memories of love and loss'.[17] And we've observed how the deep structure of a novel can, in its strong, simple shape, belie its carefully observed, naturalistic surface. Now is the time, then, for us to turn back to the 'Old Brain—to the right hemisphere and the more primitive brain structures that it subsumes—and to re-examine the mysteries of the story-making process itself, as it appears, full-fledged, in young adults. And here we will find that, while both hemispheres of the brain are involved in the creation of a fully successful story, it is the right that necessarily calls the tune.

'I Would Build that Dome in Air'

Unlike the more conflicted aspects of her inner world, which she kept concealed from everyone, Enid Blyton's method of writing stories is well documented, because academic psychologist Peter McKellar drew on her letters to him for his 1957 scholarly book *Imagination and Thinking* (still well worth reading). Blyton was proud of her creative process, and described what she called her 'private cinema screen' in apparently authentic detail:

> 'I have no idea at all what the characters will be, where the story will happen, or what adventures or events will occur. All I know is that the book will be an 'Adventure' tale, or a 'Mystery' or a 'fairy-tale' and so on, and that it must be a certain length—say 40,000 words. I shut my eyes for a few minutes, with my portable typewriter on my knee—I make my mind a blank and wait—and then, as clearly as I would see real children, my characters stand before me in my mind's eye. I see them in detail—hair, eyes, feet, clothes, face, expression—and I always know their Christian names, but never their surname (I get these out of a telephone directory afterwards!). More than that, I know their characters—good, bad, mean, generous, brave, loyal, hot-tempered, and so on. I don't know how I know that—it's as instinctive as sizing up a person in real life, at which I am quite good. As I look at them, the characters take on movement and life—they talk and laugh (I hear them), and perhaps I see that one of them has a dog, or a parrot, and I think—"Ah, that's good. That will liven up the story". Then behind the characters appears the setting, in colour, of course—of an old house—a ruined castle—an island—a row of houses. That's enough for me. My hands go down on my typewriter keys, and I begin. The first sentence comes straight into my mind, I don't have to think of it—I don't have to think of anything.'[18]

As with a fairy tale, the more we think about Enid's account, the less reliable it seems. She states that she 'does not know who her characters will be'—this may have been true of the late 1930s and early 1940s, which is when she first established the individual series on which her later popularity depended. But after that, the bulk of her novels were simply sequels, and she knew before she began that she was beginning a new 'Famous Five', a new 'Secret Seven', a new 'Malory Towers' or whatever—with characters and interactions that would have been predictable and familiar—almost 'formulaic' in the Homeric sense. A dog was already an integral part of both the Famous Five and the Five Find-Outers, a parrot was already part of the 'Adventure' gang: the appearance of such pets would hardly constitute a surprise to her. Blyton may have 'seen' her characters 'in detail', but if so, very little of this detail reached her writing, for her characters are sketchy at the best of times ('Susan was a dark-haired little girl with a sulky expression'). Likewise, she claims that 'even smells' were part of her 'movie', yet actual references to smells hardly ever occur in her stories.

Would the setting *always* appear *behind* the characters, as if in a book-jacket illustration? Unlikely in itself, this would also be incompatible with many of Blyton's series novels, in which the story's main setting does not appear until the second or third chapter. Why 'in colour, *of course*'? Did Blyton want McKellar to believe that her mental imagery kept up with the latest cinema technology? And doesn't her whole account read like a deliberate imitation of Coleridge's famous description of the writing of 'Kubla Khan'—a description Blyton almost certainly knew? All of this suggests that when the bestselling children's author corresponded with McKellar, she produced, not an objective description of a remembered experience, but a 'repisodic memory'—one conflated from numerous similar-but-not identical incidents.[19]

Yet Blyton's stress on the 'automatic' aspect of her creative process does help to explain how she could continue, in story after story, to present well-established characters as if neither she, nor the reader, knew anything about them, repeating similar epithets and descriptive formulas again and again. A more conscious craftsperson would have varied the wording, introduced new angles on the characters—but Blyton rarely did so, even though she knew full well that the vast majority of her child readers would be reading her new book precisely *because* it was about characters they already knew and loved. For her, every story really *was* 'new', even when it followed a well-tested formula. That may be why her enormous body of work, despite its manifest weaknesses, has retained its appeal better than series that were actually written by a syndicate—like the *Nancy Drew* and *Hardy Boys* stories. In left hemisphere terms, Blyton was a poor writer, but she was not a hack writer. She *believed* in her own stories and, like many more accomplished authors, she *lived in them*, during the time she was engaged in composing them. What she told McKellar was imprecise and misleading in many ways, but it was true to the *spirit* of her compositional process.

Her account also sheds light on the stereotyped characters that adult critics disliked in her books. Smugly, she tells McKellar that she is adept at 'sizing people up'. It does not seem to occur to her that what she saw on the surface might not be the whole truth about them, that they might be complex mixtures of good and bad (Melanie Klein might remark that Blyton had never attained the 'depressive position'!). Hence, her fictional characters were 'kind', 'mean', 'weak' or 'plucky', and once this was established, their subsequent behaviour would nearly always confirm the author's initial adjectives. As we've seen, this is how elementary-school children describe people when talking or writing about them, and of course, it was children of this age (between approximately seven and twelve) who constituted the great bulk of Blyton's audience. Her characters were *essentialist*, like those of epic and fairy tale—one-dimensional, uncomplicated, predictable. In the *Famous Five* novels, the tomboy George will always be impulsive and fiercely loyal; Julian will always be the sensible, protective older brother—just as Odysseus is always 'wily', and Agamemnon is always 'King of men'.

It is easy for educated adults to dismiss an account of the creative process written by an author almost all of whose work was for children, an author critics almost universally regarded as beneath contempt. But key aspects of Blyton's compositional process can be found in reports by writers of much higher critical reputations, many of whom never wrote for children at all. Paul Scott, who once told the young John Fowles that *An Island and Greece* needed more 'magic', maintained that his own novels often came to him as 'images materialising on a blank screen'. *The Jewel in the Crown*, for example, started life as a mental image of a girl running. He had no idea of who she was, or why she was running. William Golding's classic *Lord of the Flies* started as two 'pictures', one of a little boy doing handstands on a tropical beach, the other of the same little boy fleeing for his life from other boys. Dickens, in an 1841 letter to his friend John Forster, explained that when he wrote, 'I don't invent it—really do not—but *see* it, and write it down'.[20]

Robert Louis Stevenson, in a famous essay, explains his own creativity as 'magically' as Blyton does—though unlike her, he presents his account jokingly, as if to disown the mystery which remains at its core. First, he tells the story of a 'dreamer' who discovers that 'little people' (i.e. fairies, brownies) are composing stories for him while he sleeps—he borrows the idea, of course, from the Grimm fairy tale 'The Elves and the Shoemaker'. Then, shrugging off his temporary disguise, he admits,

> 'Well, as regards he dreamer . . . he is no less a person than myself . . . and for the Little People, what shall I say they are but just my Brownies, God bless them! Who do one-half my work for me while I am fast asleep, and in all human likelihood, do the rest for me as well, when I am wide awake, and fondly suppose I do it for myself . . . '[21]

Later in the same essay, Stevenson gives a more detailed account of how he programmed his mental computer to shift from wish-fulfilling pre-sleep fantasies to stories that were commercially viable—a shift that Blyton performed as well:

> 'But presently my dreamer . . . began to write and sell his tales . . . The stories must now be trimmed and pared and set upon all fours, *they must run from a beginning to an end* and *fit* (after a manner) *with the laws of life*, the pleasure, in one word, had become a business, and that not only for the dreamer, but for the little people of his theatre. These understood the change as well as he. When he lay down to prepare himself for sleep, he no longer sought amusement, but printable and profitable tales; and after he had dozed off on his box-seat, his little people continued their evolutions with the same mercantile designs.' [Italics mine]

What Stevenson is telling us is that it is perfectly possible for a writer to instruct his 'under-mind' to produce stories to a certain length, in a certain style, even to conform to left hemisphere requirements like 'fitting with the laws of life' (that is, appearing 'realistic')—and yet the resulting stories will still appear to have 'created themselves' in an automatic fashion. We notice, too, that Stevenson's 'instructions' include the requirement that the compositions should have a beginning and an ending—strongly implying that the personal fantasies out of which they emerged were shapeless and endless—no different from the 'songstries' he had composed as a young child. As we have seen, it is the left hemisphere that demands *limits* and *boundaries*, that wants to mark off a story as separate, different from 'reality'.

C. S. Lewis outlined the interaction of conscious and unconscious aspects of creativity in a somewhat different way:

> 'I have never exactly 'made' a story. With me the process is much more like bird-watching than either talking or building. I see pictures. Some of these pictures have *a common flavour, almost a common smell*, which groups them together. Keep quiet and watch and they will begin joining themselves up. If you were very lucky (I have never been as lucky as all that) a whole set might join themselves so consistently that there you had a complete story: without doing anything yourself. But more often (in my experience always) there are gaps. Then at last you have to do some deliberate inventing, have to contrive reasons why these characters should be in these various places doing these various things. I have no idea whether this is the usual way of writing stories, still less whether it is the best. It is the only one I know.[22] [Italics mine]

Like Stevenson, Lewis acknowledges that the unsought, automatic or 'God-given' (as Homer would have said) inspiration provided by the right hemisphere only goes part of the way towards making a complete story. Purposeful, conscious activity (left hemisphere activity) is required as well, to 'fill the gaps'. The story maker's right hemisphere produces pictures or scenes as if from nowhere; but it is the left hemisphere that must bridge the gaps between them, supply those logical connections without which they would remain merely a series of personally significant vignettes—a 'story' in the two-year-old vein.

Even Margaret Mitchell whose writing process was clearly dominated by the left hemisphere rather than the right, reports at least one experience of effortless creativity. That episode was responsible for three crucial chapters of *Gone with the Wind*, the ones that start with Scarlett leaving the burning city of Atlanta, and end with her discovery that her plantation home 'Tara' has been looted and that her mother is dead. Of this part of the novel, Mitchell said,

> 'I prowled around it mentally for a long time, looking at it from all angles and not getting anywhere. I could never write a line of it and never made a try at it on paper. I didn't seem able to capture the smell of the cedars; the smell of the swamp; the barnyard odours, and pack them into these chapters.'[23]

Once again, in this passage, we find Mitchell (like Lewis, like Blyton) invoking 'smells'. It is as if all these writers call on the metaphor of smell when they need to suggest something powerful but intractable, something that is real and present, but which resists conscious control. As writers like T. S. Eliot knew and researchers have confirmed, smell has a special place in human remembering.[24] Our earliest memories are often (though not by any means always) of smells. A smell, or a 'flavour' (for smell and taste are closely associated physiologically) can bring back an entire episode from the distant past, as in the opening paragraphs of Marcel Proust's *Combray*. This may explain why Enid Blyton claimed that her private 'movies' contained 'smells', even though her published stories rarely mention them. Perhaps she meant that her mental experience was so vivid that it was *as if* she could smell the flowers, or the 'come and eat me' odour of baking bread, or the salty tang of the waves on the beach at Kirrin Island?

However, we need to finish the story of how Mitchell wrote the 'road to Tara' chapters of *Gone with the Wind*. The twenty-nine-year-old would-be author of 'the great American novel' (as she semi-jokingly called her manuscript—she hid it under the bath whenever a visitor called) was actually in Atlantic City, New Jersey, and in the middle of winter, when everything she needed for the episode suddenly flooded into her mind. 'I could see clearly how dusty and stifling a red clay road in Georgia looks and feels in September', she wrote. She fled back to Atlanta to start writing, explaining, 'These three chapters are about the only ones in the book that I did not re-write at least twenty times. As they appear in the book, they are substantially as they were first written'. They were, in fact, written in what I am going to call the 'writer's trance'—rapidly, easily, with a sense of completeness and deep satisfaction that comes from following the 'dictation' of the right hemisphere, with the left hemisphere temporarily 'asleep' or 'anaesthetised'. Significantly, Mitchell had to journey to a far-off city in order to access the memories she needed (journey in space=journey in time), and then needed to return to Atlanta in order to 'make them real' by writing them down. Right hemisphere processes are heavily implicated in this whole account.

What Mitchell found herself 'flooded' with may have been prompted by a particular childhood episode. According to her biographer, the images probably dated from her sixth year, when the little Margaret, a 'Johnny Reb' from the beginning, had refused point blank to go to school. Her mother had driven her out of Atlanta, along a red dust road lined with the decaying shapes of once-great plantation houses where ageing Southern belles lived on amidst the ruin of the world they had inhabited as young women. Mitchell's mother, a convinced feminist, scornfully told her daughter that this is what happened to women who refused to take control of their own destinies. May Belle Mitchell's message was very clear: You must get a proper education, or—? Could she have added '—you'll be gone with the wind'?[25] Of course this is mere speculation, but memory can be extraordinarily literal, and the Old Brain has a seemingly limitless power to re-create the past, down to the tiniest, long-forgotten detail, as we'll see in our next chapter.

There is more to 'inspired' writing than we've seen so far. Writer after writer talks about the way characters 'take on a life of their own'. William Faulkner described how, once he had 'invented' Caddy (in a short story called 'Twilight'), she became a 'person he 'could not ignore'[26], and though she never appears in *The Sound and the Fury*, she became the pivot on which this great novel would turn. Paul Scott claimed that Barbie Bachelor, originally conceived as a minor character, 'ran away with' *The Towers of Silence*, so that the third novel of the *Raj Quartet* became her tragedy.[27] In such phrasing there is a consistent sense of disconnection between one part of the brain and another, a disconnection which feels to the story maker as if an image, a character, or even a series of actions, were coming from 'outside' him or herself, interfering with, or even replacing conscious planning. For when the right hemisphere is 'dictating' in this way, story makers feel like silent witnesses to something happening—something over which they feel no control, but something that is intensely absorbing and meaningful, even though they do not know what that meaning is—at least, not at the time. One part of their brain becomes an *audience* to the stories that another part is '*singing*'—exactly as in Homer.

The 'split brain experiments' of the 1970s suggest a possible physiological basis for this phenomenon. We know that when the *corpus callosum*, the band of neuronal matter that transmits information back and forth between the hemispheres, is either severed or temporarily anaesthetised, each hemisphere proves to have a distinct, separate way of viewing the world, processes information differently, and expresses itself in its own 'language'. The right hemisphere typically *does* produce images of events or people 'with the setting behind them', as Blyton claims (its holistic view does not separate 'figure' from 'ground'), and its analogical communications are immediate and meaningful, although that meaning is never spelled out in words. They are 'just there'. All of this corresponds exactly with what creative writers describe. Frank Harris (author of the scandalously explicit memoir *My Life and Loves*) criticised the sudden appearance of an Indian with a cart at the very end of one of Kipling's short stories—an appearance which Harris found unconvincing. Kipling replied simply, '*I see the Indian*'.[28] That is (as it were) the right hemisphere speaking. For this inspired vision to occur, the connection to the left hemisphere must be temporarily dulled or paralysed, and in 'writer's trance' something of this sort seems to happen, even though no surgical or anaesthetic procedures are involved. Illness may trigger it: struggling for breath during asthma attacks, Patrick White 'heard' his characters Voss and Laura conversing, even 'became' each of them in turn.[29] He knew that he had to start writing a novel when the conversations in his head became too insistent to ignore. Nearly all writers agree with Stevenson that the (left hemisphere's) conscious, planful contribution to the story making process seems to come 'later' in time, and, vital though it is, it is right hemisphere's 'inspiration' that story makers value most highly and long to experience.

John Fowles was so entranced by the magical welling-up of long-forgotten images that he felt bitter disappointment when his writing did not 'come to him' in the easy, gratifying way he had come to crave. When anyone (even her own children) broke in on her 'private cinema', Enid Blyton would fly into a rage. Most celebrated of all reactions to the abrupt ending of the writer's trance is that written by the Romantic poet, Samuel Taylor Coleridge. His account has been quoted times without number, but it bears quoting again, partly because Coleridge was such a wonderfully precise observer of his own experiences, and partly because it takes us further into the complexities of the writer's trance, for Coleridge's 'altered state' was induced by an intoxicant:

> 'The Author continued for about three hours in a profound sleep, at least of the external senses, during which time he has the most vivid confidence, that he could not have composed less than from two to three hundred lines, if that indeed can be called composition in which all the images rose up before him as things, with a parallel production of the correspondent expressions, without any sensation or consciousness of effort. On awakening he appeared to himself to have a distinct recollection of the whole, and taking his pen, ink, and paper, instantly wrote down the lines that are here preserved. At this moment he was unfortunately called out by a person on business from Porlock, and detained by him above an hour, and on his return to his room, found, to his no small surprise and mortification, that though he still retained some vague and dim recollection of the general purport of the vision, yet, with the exception of some eight or ten scattered lines and images, all the rest had passed away like images on the surface of a stream into which a stone has been cast . . . '[30]

Coleridge reports images 'rising up before him as things' (very similar to Blyton's and Paul Scott's 'cinema screen'). When he talks of 'the parallel production of the correspondent expressions', he may mean that the actual words appeared *in the form of images* (which would be consistent with how the right hemisphere operates) or he may mean that the words appeared *concurrently with the images*, again, like Blyton, 'without any sensation or consciousness of effort'. This vision, induced by laudanum (opium dissolved in alcohol, a commonly-used medication at the time) illustrates the way in which night dreams work. What one has experienced during the day (in Coleridge's case, words from the book he'd just read about Kubla Khan's pleasure garden) are bodied forth by the right hemisphere in concrete images, all informed by an *intense sense of presentness* (Dickens' 'All new and all true'; Potter's 'First person, present tense'). The result is an experience akin to a 'waking dream'—unshadowed by any intrusive 'What does it mean?' or 'Is it true?' Mystics report their experiences in a very similar way: the question of veracity does not arise for them: what they have seen, heard and felt is self-evidently real. For writers, the easy, gratifying trance is usually only the first stage in a much longer process—but it justifies the mental effort that will necessarily follow, in much the same way as the intense, sufficient-unto-itself state of 'in love' remains a vivid memory that sustains us through the hard work of forging a viable partnership with someone who is (most likely) very different from ourselves, at least in some key ways.

Margaret Mitchell frankly described the pain of trying to construct stories when access to the 'hyper-reality' of the right hemisphere is denied: 'After I had re-written a chapter ten or twelve times and had what I thought was a workable "first draft", I'd put it away for a month. When I dug it out again I beat my breast and snatched out my hair because it was so lousy.'[31] Beating one's breast and tearing one's hair are actions associated with *mourning* in traditional societies like Homer's. It is as if a central, highly-valued part of Mitchell has died. She thought 'most' writers wrote easily and naturally, and regarded herself as an exception. Blyton thought 'most' writers composed with conscious effort and deliberate control and regarded herself as the exception. The truth is somewhere in between. While the raw material may appear to come from a 'Goddess', from 'Brownies' or from a 'private cinema screen', it nearly always requires conscious, careful revision to become lastingly appreciated by others—indeed, to be publishable at all.

So intense and desirable is the experience of writer's trance that it is hardly surprising if many story makers use drugs of some kind (alcohol, opiates, cocaine, hashish, even caffeine) as a way of triggering, enhancing or even replacing it. Hemingway and Faulkner were both alcoholics. Paul Scott: 'could not settle at the typewriter without a glass to hand, his first act on waking was the finish the glass of whisky or vodka poured out the night before, then light up the first of the day's sixty or seventy cigarettes.'[32] In fact, the triggering of a creative trance does not depend on any external chemical stimulus. As most of us now know, even the rhythmic act of walking can trigger the release of endorphins, resulting in a (very mild) 'high', and lifting depression, if one is depressed. The rhythmic striking of the lyre with which Homeric poets commenced and punctuated their performances would have served a similar function, helping to induce the trancelike state in which the singers could continue to produce line after line. The importance of something rhythmic, something repeated, reminds us that *song* (the 'first language of the right hemisphere') may have preceded speech in human beings: doing something that approximates to music 'primes' the right hemisphere to do its creative work. Patrick White relied on listening to recordings of classical music not only to help him compose, but also to sort out impasses in existing drafts.

The story maker walks to his favourite writing place, the almost automatic rhythm of his steps freeing his mind from its surroundings. Immediately he begins to feel that 'flow' of words and ideas that marks the writer's trance. Thomas Mann, Carlos Fuentes, Thornton Wilder, and Erskine Caldwell are among the many writers who used physical movement to stimulate creativity; Dickens, Trollope and Blyton are representative of many who employed the principle of 'classical conditioning', by writing every day at a set time, in an established place.[33] In his latter years at Gads Hill Place, Dickens erected a little chalet, reached via a tunnel under the road that ran through his property. In summer, this became his favoured writing refuge—a place where he could be completely alone with his thoughts, free to rush to the mirror and perform the facial expressions and gestures of his characters. A century later, Roald Dahl used a shed in his backyard in a similar way, fitting it out with an ancient, comfortable chair, and cherished possessions from his childhood. Closing the door and surrounding himself with a comforting fug of cigarette smoke, Dahl could feel much as he had felt when smoking and daydreaming in the photography shed where he'd spent so many stolen hours at boarding school. As adults, story makers re-create key aspects of the 'place of greater safety' they first encountered as children.

Story makers already know how to 'go somewhere else' within their own minds (dissociate) perhaps originally as an escape from painful or distressing environments, but increasingly, as a substitute for a reality that they perceive as boring, tedious or mundane. Adopting the use of some substance simply makes accessing the 'place of greater safety' easier and more reliable. Thus the daydreaming of childhood transforms itself into a central part of the creative process of the mature story maker. No longer is it simply 'hours of vague reflection' (as Dickens experienced when gazing out over the city of London); now the writer's thoughts are focussed on the world of his latest story. Paul Scott once said that 'nothing could match the excitement and absorption of the images that flickered and unrolled in his mind's eye'. He would walk though a storm and arrive home drenched, without being aware of it. His mind, he said, was not 'absent' but present—only his 'present' was the novel on which he was engaged.[34]

The Language of the Right Hemisphere

Enid Blyton likened her compositional method to that of Dickens and Homer—comparisons that seem grandiose in the extreme. Yet Blyton scholar David Rudd argues that we should take the comparison seriously, and he is right.[35] Blyton and Dickens wrote in prose, in isolation from their audience, where Homer performed directly to a hall full of listeners, but their styles share important features. Both Blyton and Dickens write *as if in conversation with their readers*, involving them in the story as it goes along. Dickens—fascinated by the stage as a child, and a keen amateur actor in adulthood—came to rely more and more in the final years of his career on public appearances in which he would perform excerpts from his novels for a live audience. Their smiles, tears and gales of laughter confirmed to him the dramatic impact of his own words. For this purpose, Dickens extensively re-wrote his published texts.[36] Sentences were shortened and made more active (it was immediately clear *who* was doing *what* to *whom*), lively conversation was substituted for narrative, and key information was presented again and again, just as in the *Iliad* and the *Odyssey*. In oral storytelling, as we saw in Chapter 3, events follow one another in a simple, linear order, and clauses are strung together with 'and', 'but' or 'then'.

This creates 'onrush'—that forward movement of the narrative which encourages us to keep listening (or reading) and 'onrush' corresponds with the neuronal pathway Panksepp calls 'seeking'—in which an animal experiences an exciting sense of being engaged on a meaningful quest. We humans do not count 'seeking' as an emotion, but it may well be a primitive version of what we would term 'elevation'.[37] Similarly, in oral narrative, the actual vocabulary is simple and predictable (all maidens have lovely hair, George is always plucky): the narrator's choice of words does not draw attention to itself, and therefore distract the audience from what is happening in the story. Rather, the audience is invited to merge with the events and characters of the story, to become part of what is happening. There is little here to suggest to listeners or readers that this is a fictional construction, 'just a story', instead it is experienced as 'real'. The audience itself becomes part of the storyteller's trance—they too enter a state of altered consciousness, taken up and swept away by what they are hearing or reading. The oral style maximises right hemisphere functioning, and minimises left hemisphere invitations to stand *outside* the story, critiquing its plausibility, or consciously noticing 'stereotyped' characters and 'clichéd' language. So Blyton was quite correct in likening her *way of writing* to that of Homer and Dickens. The key issue is not whether a work of fiction is actually 'orally delivered' or written for print publication, not whether it is composed in verse or prose, but the *state of mind in which its composition takes place.* With the Old Brain in command, the words will roll forth as if independent of any merely human presence:

> 'Sing rage through me, Oh Goddess . . . '
>
> 'It was the best of times, it was the worst of times . . . '
>
> 'On a fine day right at the beginning of the Easter holidays, four children and a dog travelled by train together.'

Needless to say, the comparison cannot be pushed too far. For all that the *Iliad* and the *Odyssey* were originally told in oral performance, the written versions in which we know them today show much evidence of careful, conscious thought.[38] Even in his early works, Dickens was much more consciously involved in the choice of words and the arrangement of effects than Blyton ever was. From *Martin Chuzzlewit* and *Dombey and Son* onwards, Dickens' plots were planned in advance, his prose became denser and more reflective, and his central characters more complex. Blyton's work shows no such development over time—if anything, her earliest novels are stronger and more convincing than the later ones; increasingly, she depended on simply re-running characters she had created years before, and plots that re-worked the same motifs, increasingly tiredly. Where Dickens was able to mature as an artist (less so as a man), Blyton remained the child she had always been internally, and if anything, her fictions showed *less* willingness to acknowledge life's sadness and cruelty. Like J.M. Barrie's Peter Pan, she 'never grew up', and as we'll see in our next chapter, she was not alone in that regard.

Despite being composed in a trance-like state, Blyton's prose did not include exactly-repeated verbal 'formulas' like those from which an oral poet builds a narrative, but it is formulaic in a more general sense: she employs the same narrow range of adjectives over and over again, perfectly exemplified in this passage from her nineteenth 'Five' adventure, *Five Go to Demon's Rocks*:

> '"The rocks that the light-house is built on used to wreck many ships", said Tinker. "Wreckers used to work along that coast, you know—they would shine a light as if to guide them along the coast, and make them go on the rocks. Crash! They'd be broken to pieces and everyone drowned—and the wreckers would wait until the ship was washed up on the shore, and then take everything they could from her."
>
> "The wicked wretches!" said Dick, horrified.
>
> "There's a wrecker's cave there too, where the wreckers stored the things they stole from the wrecked ships," said Tinker. "I haven't been very far into it—I'm too scared to. They do say there's an old wrecker or two there still"'.[39]

The word 'wreck' or 'wrecker' occurs no less than seven times in this short passage (and Dick's exclamation, 'The wretches!' is an obvious variant, suggesting itself to the author simply because it sounds so similar to 'wreck'. If this reminds us of the preschool 'songstries' discussed in Chapter 3, it should—exactly the same compositional method is involved, with one word or phrase suggesting the next, and the main subject of the whole passage—'wrecked' and 'broken' ships—recalls the anxieties of two- and three-year-olds about 'holes in the world'. None of this is any co-incidence, for a careful study of Blyton's work from *The Adventurous Four* (1941) onwards reveals that she alternates damage and repair, threat and reassurance, in highly predictable patterned sequences.[40] The same themes occur when Blyton is describing places rather than people—indeed, her descriptions of ruined castles and deserted houses and villages reveal her ongoing preoccupation with loss and damage most clearly of all (another instance of a story maker revealing emotionally-charged themes in descriptions of *settings*). Most Old Brain-dominated story makers are formulaic: a friend of bestselling sex-and-sadism novelist Harold Robbins said that Robbins 'really only [had] four adjectives' and 'didn't care if he used the same adjective three times in three consecutive sentences.')[41] In his later novels, he rarely bothered with any at all, relying almost wholly on 'tough guy' dialogue and minimal narration.

In terms of the evolutionary function of story, about which Brian Boyd has written authoritatively and persuasively, the oral style embodies the advantage of 'focussing and holding the attention' of others of one's species.[42] Homer, Dickens and Blyton all enjoyed great popularity in their lifetimes. All three—including Homer—met with critical disapproval for precisely the same reason. While Aristotle and the critics who followed him *interrogated* stories, the great majority of listeners and readers simply laughed, cried and *lived* with the characters, leaving behind the left hemisphere and its capacities for analysis and logical questioning. How does this happen? Why don't we notice the gaps, inconsistencies and non-sequiturs in Old Brain-driven stories? The answer, as I've already hinted is *because enthralled readers, like inspired writers, enter a 'projective, protective trance'*.

Making Stories Our Own

On any suburban train, sandwiched between commuters plugged into their I-pods and text messages, you can still see some people hunched over a thick book, oblivious to everything happening around them. As I write this chapter, the book is likely to be one of Stig Larsen's thrillers (*The Girl with the Dragon Tattoo*), the final volume in Rowling's *Harry Potter* saga, or perhaps a bestseller from the past, like Tolkien's *Lord of the Rings*. Although these readers have probably seen the movies based on these novels, they still want to read the actual words. They are 'addicted'. Sometimes they get so absorbed that they miss their stop. When we read in this way, not for information, but for the experience itself, we are in an altered state of consciousness—a light trance. Reading fiction (or nonfiction that has a strong storyline) can be a serious, absorbing activity for adults. Exactly like writers, they object strenuously to anyone who intrudes upon their trance, and grumble when forced to emerge from it. South African psychologist Victor Nell's laboratory research, published in 1988 as *Lost in a Book*, shows that reader's trance can be evidenced by specific patterns in brain wave activity, just as TV watching can.[43] It's a powerful pull that stories exert, a pull that has not altered since the days of *The Iliad*.

In the writer's trance, it appears that events and characters are *presenting themselves to* the writer. It is much the same in the reader's trance. The right hemisphere is to the fore, as the world of the story is 'presented'—directly by images on a movie screen, indirectly via words on a page. But of course, we must also *create* this world for ourselves, or it would have no power at all. If we did not temporarily imagine ourselves as Jane Eyre, Nicholas Urfe, or Scarlett O'Hara, we would not care what happens to them. And in order to identify with a fictional character in this way, to *empathise* with him or her, we must draw on experiences and feelings of our own—a process discussed in Chapter 4. What is inside us somehow merges with what comes from 'outside'—a story made up by someone we have never met—and the way this happens is the great mystery of the reading experience. Often, it is only when we fully emerge from the trance, and start talking *about* the story to someone else, that the left hemisphere reappears, with its characteristic ability to stand back from the story, and evaluate its credibility, message, and artistic value. 'It's a real page-turner', we might say to a friend, 'but it's actually shit writing'. If we did not expect total, Old Brain immersion in something 'bigger than we are', if we did not, however temporarily, soar with Scarlett O'Hara or Harry Potter above our everyday lives, we would not read stories at all. As soon as we read a story that provides this 'outlift' (the same feeling as experienced in dissociative day-dreaming), we want more of it—'more by the same author', or 'more about the same people'—hence the appeal of series fiction, of sequels and prequels. We don't want the story ever to end. We 'can't let go'. This has little to do with the quality of the writing, for it can be generated just as easily by J. K. Rowling or *Twilight* as it can be by Patrick O'Brian or Hilary Mantel.

Norman Holland shed light on the mystery of reader-involvement with a piece of ground- breaking research he published in 1975 as *5 Readers Reading*.[44] Holland, a professor of literature, had also trained as a psychoanalyst. He conducted extensive interviews with five male College students, all studying literature. Each young man spoke with Holland about a short story he had just read for the first time—William Faulkner's 'A Rose for Emily'.[45] Each man had previously completed a batch of standardised psychological tests, so when the same student came to respond to Faulkner's story—a New Brain narrative with a fair level of complexity and subtlety—Holland already knew about the young men's literary preferences, values and attitudes, and could compare the way they talked about *themselves* with the way they talked about the *story* (which Faulkner had written at the age of thirty-four, and which, with its horrific/pathetic image of a lover's body preserved long after death, owed more than a little to Dickens' Miss Havisham).

Each student read the same words on the printed page, but what Holland found was that each of them foregrounded some aspects of the story and hardly noticed others. Each organised his interpretation of the story around the actions, feelings or themes that were most important *to him personally.* As Holland explained it, his readers—and so by implication, readers in general—use a story as 'raw material' out of which to 're-create central fantasies' about their own lives. By 'fantasy', Holland meant an (often unconscious) shaping theme that encapsulates some key aspect of our experience. Today, cognitive psychologists would call this a 'schema', narrative therapists would speak of a 'dominant story', but it is essentially the same thing. If, for example, you deeply believe that 'You can be a really good person, and try as hard as you like, but in the end, life defeats you', then you will probably be deeply moved by Thomas Hardy's *Tess of the D'Urbervilles*, or *Jude the Obscure.* If you spend your life searching for an idealised lover, all the time ignoring or discounting the person who has offered you genuine love all along, then you will resonate with *The Magus* or *Great Expectations.*

A decade after Holland published his study, another American academic, Janice Radway, began to study a group of dedicated readers in a midwestern American community which she called 'Smithton'.[46] They had never read *Sir Gawain and the Green Knight* or *Wuthering Heights.* Some of them had probably not even read *Gone with the Wind.* Nevertheless, they read, as all enthralled readers do, for the deep satisfaction of immersing themselves in a fictional world. All of them were women, most of them were married with children under eighteen, and all of them were avid consumers of 'romances'—the kind of short, love-focussed novels popularised by publishers like Mills & Boon, and more recently, Silhouette and Harlequin. Their average age was between twenty and fifty—romance reading seems most popular among women in early adulthood—up to, and including, the transition to middle age. More than half of the Smithton women had developed the habit of reading for pleasure before the age of ten, most of the rest in adolescence: unless reading-for-pleasure becomes established in childhood, it seems rarely to take root at all.

Radway found that the Smithton women could tell from very early in a new romance novel whether or not it was 'right' for them. Like Homer's listeners, who knew exactly how a hero should act and speak, the Smithton women had expectations of a 'proper' romance heroine—the kind that they wanted to read about. They had equally clear ideas about the 'male lead' (though he mattered less to them than the heroine) and were especially clear about *how he should treat the heroine*—with respect and sensitivity (maybe not at first, but eventually). If a particular novel 'failed them'—perhaps, for example, because the hero treated the heroine too badly, or if the author's description of lovemaking was too explicit for their taste—they would stop reading. Yet some would still turn to the final pages to 'see how the story turned out'. Even readers who were satisfied that they had chosen the 'right' sort of story sometimes did this, as if unable to tolerate a state of uncertainty for long enough to read the entire novella. They needed reassurance that their initial predictions would be borne out. When asked to analyse the way a particular novel was *written* (literary critics would call this its 'style') the Smithton women would almost always start to retell its *plot*, or describe its *heroine*: style seemed invisible to them—as it is to many child readers.[47] Their attention was focussed almost entirely on the heroine, and what was happening to her. Thinking consciously about how a favourite novel 'worked' (engaging the left hemisphere) would have broken their trance.

What do Radway's findings mean? Firstly, they confirm that enthralled or 'ludic' reading (as Nell called it) was an activity in which the right hemisphere dominated, to the almost total exclusion of the left. Secondly, the Smithton women's attitude to reading was very similar to that of the preschool children described in Chapter 2. Like some of the three-year-olds we met there, the Smithton women refused to keep reading if the story upset them too much. They reacted strongly to incidents that made them uncomfortable: 'Since I'm living as the heroine, I cannot handle it [a gang rape scene] in a book', said one.[48] Some of Radway's readers literally *threw into the trashcan* a book that had 'failed them'. Such reactions might be dismissed as those of naïve and uneducated individuals—until we recall that R. L. Stevenson never finished reading *Tess of the d'Urbervilles*, outraged by the scene in which Alex D'Urberville rapes the sleeping Tess ('as false a thing as ever I perused'), and that Margaret Mitchell gave up on Thackeray's *Vanity Fair* (a novel whose heroine, Becky Sharp strikingly resembles her own later creation, Scarlett O'Hara) at the end of Chapter 1, where Becky throws an 'improving' book out of the window. In their concrete ways of 'protecting themselves', the Smithton romance readers display their continuity with the little Charlie Dickens, who 'punished' his toy wolf because of what happened to Red Riding Hood.[49] For all these readers, child and adult, 'naïve' and sophisticated, the story not only affected their emotions, but *demanded additional real-life actions* in order to 'settle' those emotions. For them, the dividing line between 'fiction' and 'life' was weak and permeable—as in the practice of 'sympathetic magic', where a real world action—driving a spear into a *picture* of a deer—can produce a parallel action in the 'spirit world' (a real deer will 'allow itself' to be killed in the next hunt).

Earlier in this book, we described the effects of right hemisphere dominance in the first two years of life: when the left hemisphere's development starts to catch up with the right's, distressing events earlier in a narrative can increasingly be understood as part of a whole, which somewhat reduces their disturbing impact, and the boundary between the story world and 'real life' gradually firms up. Yet many of Radway's adult readers still reacted as if upsetting incidents on the way through a story were not cancelled out by a happy ending.[50] Their involvement with the heroine was so total that they simply could not accept anything 'bad' happening to her. Did this sort of behaviour mean that they doubted their own capacity to cope with distress, or to survive adversity—doubted it so profoundly that they could not tolerate such things even in a work of fiction? Had their brains failed to mature past three-year-old level? Did they make any distinction at all between themselves and the heroine? Between their quotidian existence and the world of the story? Perhaps they did not.

But then, how much distinction do *any* of us make, when enthralled by a novel or movie that touches us deeply and personally? The contrast that we customarily make between the 'naïve' way that children experience stories, and the 'sophisticated' way that adults read, is misleading.[51] Most adults read in the way that children read. Absorbed reading, whether of romance novelettes or of literary classics is essentially a right-hemisphere-dominated, trance-inducing experience, in which we 'enter' a fictional world, 'live as' its hero or heroine, and feel *with* them, and *for* them. Mirror neurones fire because as Brian Boyd points out, we have evolved to pay close attention to other human beings, to imitate what they do and to value what they value.[52] This, after all, is how we *learn*, and how culture is transmitted within human societies. Whether those other human beings are real or fictional is immaterial.

Provided they've already had positive experiences of stories, very young children will listen avidly to virtually any story that is not totally beyond their comprehension. But as their personalities firm up, young people become more conscious of themselves as individuals. Now, to identify strongly with a story, many readers will need a closer fit between who they perceive they are, and who they perceive a story protagonist to be. Even within the reliable romance formula, the Smithton readers needed the heroine to be sufficiently like their *ideal* self (not their real self) to justify their spending hours reading about her. Yet those same heroines also needed to be sufficiently different from the reader—and different from each other—to make the experience new each time. In the 'sophisticated' response of Norman Holland's literature majors and in the 'naïve' conversations of the Smithton romance readers we see the heart of the reading process revealed—not just for them, but (if we are honest) for most of us. We need to be reading about *ourselves*—albeit in disguise—for the reader's trance to come into full operation.

When we fall in love, we *project* key aspects of ourselves onto our beloved, seeing him or her as a kind of mirror of ourselves ('She's like me!' we think, amazed and delighted. 'She sees the world the same way! She makes me feel good about being me!') Usually, this projection process is not a complete delusion—our lover *is* similar to us, at least in some ways. But temporarily, our excited awareness of the similarities blinds us to the significance of the ways she, or he, is *not at all* like us. The 'in love' trance *protects* us, temporarily, from the uncomfortable awareness that in fact our chosen one may strongly resemble a parent we clashed with, or wished to keep at a safe distance. The protective aspect of the trance has a powerful biological function: it keeps each of us close to our partner long enough for us to procreate—thus replicating the gene pool of our respective families, and (often, but not always) providing that the children so created between us are going to be nurtured sufficiently to grow up and procreate in their turn.

Similarly, for a work of fiction to become one of our 'chosen stories', we must fall in love, not just with its protagonist, but with its entire fictional world. We will be conscious of strong attraction, but unconsciously we will be not only re-creating our own personalities and life themes with the story's help, but also discovering *new* aspects of ourselves, our lives and our potentials that we have previously been unaware of. The 'mirror' held up by the story shows us not only the selves that are already familiar to us, but things we cannot see, do not yet know. Indeed, as we'll see in our next chapter, our chosen stories may even—like the Queen's mirror in 'Snow White'—hold up to us our own futures.

Where We've Come From, Where We're Going

While many story makers begin writing as children or adolescents, few find their unique voice until somewhere between the late twenties and the mid-thirties, and many begin to publish around the same age. The importance of being thirty is that the maturation of the cerebral cortex, now nearing completion, enables a greater understanding of self and others, a more objective sense of the patterns of one's own life. Still, brain development necessarily and inevitably interacts with life experience. The 'marker events' of early adulthood assist us to grow in wisdom and insight; adult losses sharpen our awareness of finality and shape the 'sense of an ending' that successful stories need, while a maturing brain simultaneously assists us to reflect more profoundly on earlier losses. What literary scholars call the 'psychological novel' is a type of story shadowed by the smallness and finiteness of human existence—a true product, not of the 'reptile brain' or the 'mammal brain', but of the *human* brain.

The left hemisphere is now at full stretch, demanding that characters be believably flawed instead of idealised, complex and even contradictory instead of simple and essentialist. As more and more of the brain's neurones are sheathed with myelin, so the writing of young adults 'thickens': description, too, becomes 'thicker', and takes on new functions. Yet for all this, the Old Brain remains a powerful presence in early adulthood, both for story makers, and for readers and viewers. Childhood experiences, and childhood stories, shape the fictions we associate with adulthood, lying like a substrate beneath their naturalistic surfaces. The 'oral style' of Homer, Dickens and Enid Blyton will always command wider audiences than the careful realism and self-conscious craftsmanship of left-hemisphere-dominated novels like those of Hardy, George Eliot or Flaubert. And readers automatically seek out stories that resonate with themes that originated in their own childhood, even their own infancy. 'Merging' with story protagonists is a deeply unconscious process, and in this process the right hemisphere is to the fore. It is this state in which 'domes in air' are built, illusions that seem real while they last, but which inevitably dissolve into the 'thin air' through which Harold falls in *Harold and the Purple Crayon*. The inspired state in which many stories are conceived is paralleled by the enthralled state in which some readers experience those stories. Hence another of the central paradoxes of the story experience: while we *think* we are reading about someone else, to the Old Brain, we are reading about *ourselves*. Similarly, while writers *think* they are writing about someone else, they are always, in one way or another, writing about themselves.

Chapter Six

Remembering, Repeating and Foreshadowing

Midlife and Memory

The Opening Door

C. S. Lewis was forty-one when he began work on his first children's book. But it was put aside during the long years of the war, and he did not return to it for nearly a decade. In March, 1949, when he was fifty, he read aloud to his friend Roger Lancelyn Green the complete manuscript of *The Lion, the Witch and the Wardrobe*. By the time it was published a year later, Lewis had completed several sequels. He once claimed, hyperbolically, to have written all seven Narnia books in a single year—in fact, it took him four.[1] The breakneck speed with which the stories were written, their oral style and their many inconsistencies—all of these things—strongly suggest that Lewis had, while composing the series, reverted to an earlier self, with much of his scholar's sophistication and left hemisphere sensitivity to language temporarily disabled. Just as the Pevensie children find themselves pulled back into Narnia in *Prince Caspian* and *The Voyage of the Dawn Treader*, their creator found himself pulled back into his own past. Why had this happened now, to an opinionated, childless intellectual?

During the Second World War Lewis had acquired a wide audience as a radio broadcaster on Christianity. Inspired by the possibilities of science fiction, he had also written a 'cosmic trilogy' for adults, beginning with *Out of the Silent Planet* in 1938, but apart from the abortive beginning of *The Lion, the Witch and the Wardrobe* in 1939, nothing at all for children—although he continued to re-read some of the Animal Land narratives he'd written as a boy. But when, in his middle years, Jack Lewis suddenly became a storyteller for children, his new tales could not have been more different from Animal Land. There had been no magic, no *romance* in Animal Land—just geography, politics and wars, a precocious little boy's imitation of the things adults considered important. Now, after forty years frozen under the snow of logic and intellect, Jack Lewis suddenly thawed into a different self, where the intensity of childhood perceptions could be recaptured, and the fierce, total emotions of infancy could flow freely again.

Here is his heroine Lucy (who must be about nine years old) feeling her way into Narnia at the beginning of *The Lion, the Witch and the Wardrobe*:

> 'Soon she went further in and found that there was a second row of coats hanging up behind the first one. It was almost quite dark in there and she kept her arms stretched out in front of her so as not to bump her face into the back of the wardrobe. She took a step further in—then two or three steps—always expecting to feel woodwork against the tips of her fingers. But she could not feel it.
>
> "This must be a simply enormous wardrobe!" thought Lucy, going still further in and pushing the folds of the coats aside to make room for her. Then she noticed that there was something crunching under her feet. "I wonder is that more mothballs?" she thought, stooping down to feel it with her hands. But instead of feeling the hard, smooth wood of the floor of the wardrobe, she felt something soft and powdery and extremely cold. 'This is very queer', she thought, and went on a step or two further.
>
> Next moment she found that what was rubbing against her face and hands was no longer soft fur but something hard and rough and even prickly. "Why, it is just like the branches of trees!" exclaimed Lucy. And then she saw that there was a light ahead of her; not a few inches away where the back of the wardrobe ought to have been, but a long way off. Something cold and soft was falling on her. A moment later she found that she was standing in a wood at night-time with snow under her feet and snowflakes falling through the air.'[2]

The language may be simple and concrete (the language of the Old Brain), but this passage *works*, commanding our attention in the same way that Nicholas's first visit to Conchis' villa does in *The Magus*. We crawl forwards with Lucy, touching what she touches, feeling what she feels, moving with her from enclosed darkness into light, cold, and open space.[3] Like Nicholas, like Meaulnes, Lucy has entered a '*domaine perdu*'. This is an Opening Door, an entry into Mystery. Yet despite the indications of right hemisphere dominance in Lucy's movement 'further in'—for the right hemisphere perceives and values *depth*[4]—the left hemisphere is still a significant presence. She is *expecting* the inside of a normal wardrobe and keeps trying to make sense of what she encounters in terms of mothballs, fur coats, and a wooden 'back'. The new impressions that beset her are vivid but vague—'something soft and powdery and extremely cold'. Finally, as Lucy emerges into Narnia, the two hemispheres start to co-operate: the left finds the correct verbal labels, locates the right hemisphere's perceptions in terms of its existing knowledge: 'she was standing in a wood at night-time with snow under her feet and snowflakes falling through the air'. Lewis is showing us, in miniature, and without being consciously aware of it, how our brains work when we encounter a new experience. And what he earnestly desires to show us (the right hemisphere *shows*, the left *tells*) is the startling *newness* of Lucy's experience. As Lucy is being pulled forward into Narnia, and Lewis is being pulled back into his own childhood, we, too, are being drawn into something we do not fully understand, induced into a reader's trance, into a right-hemisphere world.

First, the sequence of images tells us that *something is happening contrary to normal expectations*. It 'must be a simply enormous wardrobe', thinks Lucy. (There should not be a harpsichord, sounding in a deserted villa on a Greek island, thinks Nicholas Urfe. A big house should not be shut up and dark, except for a single candle carried by a beautiful young girl, thinks Pip in Dickens' *Great Expectations*.) Then, the sequence tells us that we are *going somewhere*, even though we do not know where it is that we are going, or what it will mean. By that time, we can hardly stop. We are gripped by the sensations of Panksepp's 'seeking' response.[5] Like Lucy, we are in the process of discovering (for this is what it felt like to Lewis) a new landscape over which, dreamlike and enormous, hover the lure of Evil—and the promise of Joy. This landscape is not new at all. It is old, very old. Only our storytellers do not know this consciously, and nor do we, as we start to *re-create our own early wonder and fear through their words*. It is almost as if, the older we grow, the more our earliest childhood experience comes to matter. Intuitively, one would think it would be the other way around.

A Darkening Sky

Somewhere in the decade between the mid-thirties and the late forties, human lives seem to experience a shift of focus and energy, sometimes gradual, sometimes sudden. A succession of psychoanalytically-influenced theorists from Carl Jung and Eric Erikson to Eliot Jacques and Daniel Levinson have agreed that this is so, although they differ as to the exact span of years involved.[6] The shift seems, more than anything, to be about a growing realisation of the reality of our own death. In young adulthood our lives seem endless, and our energies inexhaustible. By the mid-to-late thirties, however, this has begun to change. For some individuals, the shadowing effect of imminent death comes early. When Stevenson published *Treasure Island* he was in in his mid-thirties but already an unwell man; by his mid-forties, he would be dead. Richard Jefferies, whose *Bevis* so enthralled the young John Fowles, published his first story at thirty-three, and his last just four years later—the somber, adult-oriented *After London*, in which great cities have been swallowed up by forest, and humans have reverted to a primitive existence. His sudden change in mood must surely have been affected by the serious illness which would lead to his early death at thirty-eight. For the majority of us, though, awareness that our days are finite only seems to begin as the thirties shade into the forties. Turning forty while working on *The Tree of Man*, Patrick White was among those who 'felt for the first time that his own old age would inevitably happen.'[7] For some, it is possible to continue living within a comfortable, established life pattern well into middle age—as C. S. Lewis did. But sooner or later, for most of us, the sky will begin to darken.

Middle adulthood should not be seen solely in terms of gloom. For many people, a sharpened awareness of death calls forth a more poignant awareness of life (Mahler's *Das Lied von der Erde*, composed in his late forties, is a heart-wrenching evocation of this). There is a determination to live more fully, to venture forth more boldly than before. New beginnings call up a child's sense of adventure and discovery, new relationships revive hope of lasting love. But the freshness of midlife differs from the freshness of childhood. It is tempered by sober realisations of what is possible and impossible, darkened by sadness at what has been lost and damaged, edged (for some storytellers, at least) with despair. German novelist Thomas Mann gives an eloquent description of midlife depression and anxiety towards the end of his family chronicle, *Buddenbrooks*:

> 'He was empty inside, and he could see no exciting project or absorbing task into which he could throw himself with joy and satisfaction. But he had a need to keep busy, and his mind never stopped working. He was consumed by his own restless energy, which for him had always been something different from his father's natural and solid joy in work, something artificial, more like a nervous itch, practically a drug—like the pungent little Russian cigarettes he constantly smoked . . . He was harried by five hundred pointless trifles, things having mainly to do with keeping up the house and his own appearance; he would become so fed up with them that he would procrastinate and then find that he could not keep them sorted out in his mind and was more disorganized than before—all because he wasted such a disproportionate amount of time worrying about them.'[8]

These words were actually written by a twenty-four-year-old. How could Mann have described so accurately something that still lay ahead of him? In part, no doubt, because he was a 'good noticer' of the older adults in his own family; but also because he put into his fictional 'Thomas Buddenbrook' the anxiety, tension and despair *he himself had already experienced*, even in early adulthood. Just as, for many story makers, memories of the past can be re-fashioned to include experiences that never happened, so the future can be vividly imagined long before it arrives. Story makers bend the left hemisphere's linear sense of time back into the 'cyclic time' of the Old Brain.[9]

As we saw in our last chapter, many writers find a unique voice and achieve popular success between twenty-nine and thirty-four; a second group do not 'break through' (or even begin to write) until a decade or two later, the period in which researchers now believe that the final stages of brain maturation occur. For, while myelination is largely complete by the mid-thirties, a slower continuation of the process goes on into middle life, the final neuronal tissues to be coated with myelin being those that connect the right hemisphere with the 'older' areas that lie beneath it.[10]

After twenty years as a sailor, Joseph Conrad began his writing career at the age of thirty-eight. George Eliot wrote only non-fiction until *Scenes from Clerical Life*, published when she was thirty-nine. Between forty and forty-six, Enid Blyton created almost all her best-known characters. Henry Fielding produced his greatest work, *Tom Jones*, at forty-one. Ian Fleming invented that suave, ruthless spy, James Bond, at the age of forty-five. William Golding's *Lord of the Flies* burst onto the literary stage when its author was forty-three, and Richard Adams' *Watership Down* was also written in his forties, though not published until much later.

Not surprisingly, perhaps, many of these writers were New Brain ones, with authors like Conrad, Eliot and Golding producing, from the beginning of their careers, stories dominated by the reflective, analytical stance of the mature left hemisphere. Across the board, though, midlife novels tend to be longer and more complex than the novels of early adulthood, as if their writers were consciously striving to say something of significance, something that would outlive them. Marcel Proust was forty-one when he drafted the first volume of *A La Recherche du Temps Perdu*. When he died ten years later, he had completed the rest of the long sequence, although the final three volumes did not appear until after his death. Paul Scott started *The Jewel in the Crown* in his mid-forties, and published the final volume of the *Raj Quartet* in his mid-fifties. *Joseph and His Brothers*, that 'pyramid-like piece of work', was begun in Mann's fifties and completed more than a decade later. And the publication of William Faulkner's Snopes Trilogy (*The Hamlet, The Town, The Mansion*) stretched over almost twenty years, from his early forties to his early sixties.

The Bell and the Hammer

In *The Magician's Nephew*, which Lewis roughed out immediately after finishing *The Lion, the Witch and the Wardrobe*, two Edwardian children, Polly and Diggory, are magically transported to a decaying palace, lit by the 'disastrous' red light of a dying sun. Then, in a vast hall, its walls lined with statues of the Kings and Queens who once ruled there, Polly and Diggory see a small stand with a golden bell, and a hammer beside it. The cryptic legend on the base of the stand reads:

'Make your choice, adventurous stranger,
Strike the bell, and bide the danger,
Or wonder, till it drives you mad
What would have followed if you had.'[11]

Polly, pragmatic 'interrogator' that she is, knows they should leave the hammer well alone, but 'performer' Diggory cannot resist those incantatory words. It is the quintessential 'male moment', the quest that drives romance heroes like Gawain, the temptation that faces Adam in the Garden. Diggory seizes the hammer and strikes the bell. Its note persists and grows in intensity until its vibrations begin to shake the ancient palace to pieces, and the closest of the seated images rises to its feet, enormous, potent, *alive*. It is Jadis, last queen of the dead city of Charn, ready to use these human intruders to help her find a new world to rule. The whole episode is a dense palimpsest of literary influences, from Chrestien de Troyes' *Yvain* and E. Nesbit's *The Story of the Amulet* to Rider Haggard's *She* and William Hope Hodgson's *The Night Land*,[12] but given what we now know about Lewis, it is hard not to see the striking of the bell as a right hemisphere image for the re-awakening of his personal past: a painful, destructive past, which cannot any longer be denied. Like falling in love, such compulsions feel 'bigger than we are', 'meant to be'.

Lewis' most penetrating and honest biographer, A. N. Wilson, sees the germination of the entire 'Narnia' series in a single event. Lewis regularly spoke at the Socratic Club, an undergraduate debating society at Oxford, where his Christian admirers would gather to see him triumph over atheists and skeptics. But, one memorable evening in 1948, Lewis met his match in the philosopher Elizabeth Anscombe, who ran rings around Lewis' shoddy logic, and 'demolished' (his own word) his arguments for the existence of God. Lewis was not just embarrassed. He was *shamed*. (Iris Murdoch shared this response to Anscombe, writing in her journal, '[her] ruthless authenticity . . . makes me feel more and more ashamed of the vague, self-indulgent way in which I have been philosophising'). Wilson suggests that something about being humiliated by a tall, commanding woman sent Jack Lewis back to the children's story he had left unfinished nearly ten years earlier, expressing in these fantasies much of the shame and fear he had felt as a child, but been unable to articulate in his prosaic Animal Land narratives.[13]

The seven 'Narnia' books contain three powerful, frightening witch-queens. All are hungry for power—and when Lewis uses the word 'hungry' (as he does in *That Hideous Strength* and at the end of *The Screwtape Letters*) it is in a horrifyingly literal way. Like Hans Andersen's Snow Queen, Lewis's White Witch is white-skinned and white-clad, but Lewis adds the vivid red lips of a vampire, the mouth that promises delight but can suck blood or tear flesh. When it suits them, however, the witches can be alluring, persuasive, even comforting. In fact, it seems that all three are simply avatars of Jadis, Queen of Charn. The entire Narnia series is overshadowed by a manipulative, evil presence who is unmistakably feminine. No threat—no story: without Jadis , Narnia would slip into insipidity. The truth is that archetypes only command our attention if they resonate with our inner lives—inner lives that were furnished well before we heard our first bedtime story. Let's look at the real men and women in Lewis' early life.

Lewis disliked his father, Albert Lewis—in fact, he despised him. Jack never forgave his father's self-indulgent emotional outbursts, his silly jokes, his inability to talk about the things that really mattered. When Jack's mother Flora Lewis died, the nine-year-old was sent off to boarding school. It was not uncommon for a middle-class boy to be sent away to school at that age, and it had already happened to his older brother Warnie—but still the decision suggests a profound lack of empathy on Albert's part. What, then, of Flora, who died when Jack had just reached that age of heightened self-awareness which we discussed in Chapter 3? Had Jack's mother been a warm, nurturing presence who made up to the little boy for Albert's deficiencies? Seemingly not.

Several of Lewis' biographers quote an autobiographical fragment Lewis wrote earlier in the same year that his mother was taken ill. Its laconic tone bears a considerable resemblance to the young Brontës' 'diary papers', written at a similar age. As Lewis puts it: 'Mamy is like most middle-aged ladys, stout, brown hair, spectacles, kniting [*sic*] her chief industry, etc. etc.' As I showed in Chapter 3 of this volume, nine-year-olds do not typically acknowledge emotion in their stories, and this was, after all, written in 1908, in a society that valued the 'stiff upper lip' above all else. Yet even in his autobiography *Surprised by Joy*, written simultaneously with the last of the *Narnia* books, Lewis says little more than that when his mother was diagnosed with cancer, he had longed for her to comfort him in his own pain:

> 'For us boys, the real bereavement had happened before my mother died. We lost her gradually as she was gradually withdrawn from our life into the hands of nurses and delirium and morphia, and as our whole existence changed into something alien and menacing, as the house became full of strange smells and midnight noises, and sinister whispered conversations.'[14]

Typical of a nine-year-old, Lewis' emphasis is not on his *mother's* suffering—it is on his *own* loneliness and fear. The 'strange smells' and 'sinister whispered conversations' are re-created in his adult novel *That Hideous Strength*, as Mark approaches the laboratory wing of the National Institute for Co-ordinated Experiments (Lewis' version of Dr Mengele's shocking activities in Auschwitz). Were images of the alien and the menacing simply easier for Jack to remember than the images of love and comfort that belonged to the time before Mother died? Or were the love and comfort—at least in his mind—less reliably present than he craved?

Flora Lewis appears to have been a cool, controlled intellectual. She gained honours degrees in both logic and mathematics—her subject choices suggesting that, like Polly, she was left-hemisphere dominant. As a child, Flora *thought* that she might have seen a miracle—a Saint's body, displayed in a church in Rome, had opened its eyes as Flora gazed at it. But her parents refused to believe her, and Flora herself accepted that what she had witnessed was simply a trick ('I thought it was done by cords pulled by a priest behind the alter [sic]' she said). As A.N. Wilson points out, this story almost certainly lies behind the episode early in *The Lion, the Witch and the Wardobe*, where her siblings do not at first believe Lucy's account of her entry into another world.[15]

Thus, even as a child, Flora opted for a 'scientific' explanation of what she had seen, rejecting the magical and the miraculous. She was the exact opposite of her father, a parson who had been known to weep at his own sermons. Significantly, she had chosen to marry someone as emotionally ungoverned, as 'enthusiastic' (in the eighteenth-century sense), as her father—and no doubt she found Albert Lewis difficult in the same way. On her deathbed, she responded to her husband's talk of the goodness of God with the swift rejoinder: 'But what have *we* done for *Him*?' None of this means that Flora did not love her boys—only that a very young Lewis may have *experienced* her that way. Her calm, logical attitude, her rejection of enthusiasm and fantasy—might these not have seemed to little Jack like 'coldness'? For above all, he longed for 'warmth'—as Aslan says, '*Come, children, bury your faces in my mane*!'

Psychoanalysts used to describe a type of mother who substitutes words of conditional praise (when the child is 'good') for unconditional loving actions. She may be a responsible and caring parent, and she would never dream of hurting her child, but she may end up shaming him or burdening him with 'great expectations' of her own.[16] The child of such a mother may feel hollow, a 'fraud'—or deeply unworthy: 'weak' and 'bad'. He needs his mother's comfort, but to seek it feels like an unwilling surrender to a superior force. As an adult, he may be a high achiever, a charming conversationalist, and, often, a charismatic personality who can win the devotion of others. But all of these attributes began in childhood as desperate attempts *to gain love from a parent who seems unable to give it.* He is, in short, what F. Scott Fitzgerald (who was one himself) called a 'romantic egoist'.[17]

So when, forty years after his mother's death, Jack Lewis imagines a world called Narnia, he puts into it, right from the start, an emotionally remote adult woman who offers seductive praise while in fact seeking to manipulate a boy for her own selfish ends. Of course the White Witch is a wildly unfair distortion of Lewis' moral, sensible mother. But the Old Brain cannot ask, 'What experiences might have caused my mother to behave in this way?' or think, 'Maybe her behavior to me makes sense in terms of what happened to *her* as a child?' To an infant, a mother who does not want to cuddle you is a bad mother. If food does not nurture, then it is poison. For Lewis' 'defeat' at the hands of Elizabeth Anscombe was only a trigger, waking up what was already lodged like a silent, unmoving statue within his memory. Anscombe in the present merges with Flora in the past to create Jadis, Queen of Charn (the French word *jadis* means 'once' or 'in a former time', and a 'charnel house' is a place of decay and death).

But where does the seductive side of the witches come from? Am I now alleging that Flora Lewis sexually abused her son? Of course not. There is a further piece of the puzzle that now demands to be put into place—the woman Lewis always referred to formally as 'Mrs Moore'. Jack Lewis was only eighteen when in 1917 he first met Janey Moore, the mother of his friend Paddy. Janey was forty-five, and separated from her husband, whom she called 'the beast'. Jack Lewis and Paddy Moore were about to join the fighting in France, and had few illusions about their chances of coming back alive. They promised each other that if either were killed, the survivor would always look after the other's parent. By the time Paddy was listed as missing in action, Jack had already found in Janey Moore someone who seemed to care more about him than his own father did. 'Old enough to be his mother', Janey must have seen in Jack both a replacement for her own son, and a potential lover too. For his part, a newly adult Jack had discovered an older woman who offered him the spontaneous affection and *joie de vivre* that Flora had been unable to display. It is almost certain that the relationship became a sexual one. With the war over and Jack back in Oxford, Janey moved into the house he and Warnie had bought, but Jack kept the nature of the relationship secret, and continued to 'live in' at Magdalen College during the week, returning home to Janey and Warnie (who couldn't stand her) only at weekends. 'Mrs Moore' remained living with the Lewis brothers for the rest of her life, and we know that Jack did not consider himself free to marry because of their relationship—hardly likely if it had been purely platonic, though some Lewis devotees still cling to this interpretation. We know hardly anything of their relationship, but it seems that Lewis himself became uncomfortable with it, and was irritated by Janey's demands on him. Obligation persisted, mixed with distaste, even disgust.

But by the time Jack returned to *The Lion, the Witch and the Wardrobe*, Janey was old and ill, requiring constant care. When he was working on *The Magician's Nephew*, she was dying. No wonder if Janey's impending death brought back painful memories of Flora Lewis', for when she and Jack first became involved, Janey was almost exactly the same age as Flora had been when she succumbed to cancer in 1908. Of course it is unlikely Jack would have been conscious of all of these resonances. 'What we do not remember, we are compelled to repeat', wrote Freud in 1914,[18] six years after nine-year-old Jack lost his mother. And a more dramatic 'repeat' was to occur only a few years later, when Lewis, now in his fifties, found true love with divorced American poet Joy Gresham, and then lost her to cancer, at forty-five.

'All this stuff about early memories of parents may be all very well', some readers may be thinking, 'but *of course* a children's writer like Lewis would be inspired by *childhood* memories! And anyway, the Narnia books are *fantasies*—surely we expect a fantasy to be full of wildly imaginative images that have nothing to do with real life!' So let's go straight to the opening paragraphs of a story as different from *The Lion, the Witch and the Wardrobe* as it is possible to imagine, written at the age of forty-four by a man who never wrote for children and never wrote a fantasy, but whose writing was just as profoundly shaped by Old Brain images from very early in his life—Paul Scott.

The Shadow of the Bibighar

'Imagine, then, a flat landscape, *dark* for the moment, but even so conveying to the girl running in the still *deeper shadow* cast by the wall of the Bibighar Gardens an idea of *immensity*, of *distance*, such as years before Miss Crane had been conscious of, standing where a lane ended and cultivation began: a different landscape but also in the alluvial plain *between* the mountains of the north and the plateau of the south.

It is a landscape which a few hours ago, *between* the rainfall and the short twilight, extracted colour from the spectrum of the setting sun and dyed every one of its own surfaces that could absorb light: the ochre walls of the houses in the old town (which are stained too with their bloody past and uneasy present); the moving water of the river and the still water of the tanks, the shiny stubble, the ploughed earth of distant fields; the metal of the grand trunk road. In this landscape trees are sparse, except among the white bungalows of the civil lines. On the horizon there is a violet smudge of hill country.

This is the story of a rape, of *the events that led up to it and followed it* and of the place in which it happened. There are the action, the people, and the place; all of which are interrelated but in their totality incommunicable in isolation from the moral continuum of human affairs.

In the Bibighar Gardens case there were several arrests and an investigation. There was no trial in the judicial sense. Since then people have said that there was a trial of sorts going on. In fact, such people say, the affair that began on the evening of August 9, in Mayapore, ended with the spectacle of *two nations in violent opposition*, *not for the first time nor as yet for the last* because they were then still *locked in an imperial embrace* of such long standing and subtlety it was no longer possible for them to know whether they hated or loved one another, or what it was that *held them together* and seemed to have *confused the image of their separate destinies*.' [Italics mine][19]

Except for 'Imagine, then . . . '—a direct invitation to us to be part of a 'conversation' with him—Paul Scott's slow, thoughtful narration does not 'hook' us in any obvious way. For the most part, the opening two paragraphs force us to *think* about what is being said, to move between past and present, between one character and another, between one scene and another. As readers, we have to negotiate complex sentences in which things are balanced, compared, considered. In all of these ways, this is a New Brain narrative, demanding much involvement from the left hemisphere. Yet Scott offers us tantalising hints of something more primitive, more frightening. It is 'dark', and in a 'shadow' there is 'a girl running'. *Something has happened*—as yet, we don't know what. We are being invited inside a world of 'immensity' which (as in Lucy's wardrobe) has something to do with the 'past'. And hidden in that past is a dramatic, frightful event—a rape.

Here is the 'threat' without which there would be no story, and yet simultaneously, we are being told that this particular violation of a woman's body means something beyond itself, beyond 'the events that led up to it and followed it'—that the story of one crime will encapsulate and symbolise enormous violations at the level of entire nations. The 'imperial embrace' that 'locks together' England and India in the final five years of the Raj reminds its author of a conflicted relationship *between individual humans*—a particular kind of conflicted relationship that he himself had experienced. It is going to be about being 'in the middle' of two other things, between two opposing forces, between love and hate. The same idea is being conveyed over and over in the four paragraphs we quoted. Repetition, the hallmark of the Old Brain, shows us that *something is speaking through the author that the author himself is only partly aware of.* What is being conveyed is the infantile sense of having one's individual identity merge with another's—as Jim Hawkins in Chapter 3 of *Treasure Island* is pulled closer to the hideous Blind Pew, as Edmund is pulled closer to the White Witch in *The Lion, the Witch and the Wardrobe.*

We should not think for one minute that Scott sat down at his typewriter and consciously decided that it made sense to compare England and India's 'imperial embrace' to the enmeshed, conflicted relationship he himself had felt with his wife Penny, or before that, with his mother, Frances, who had praised and encouraged him, but expected him to live out her own thwarted dreams. Rather, the words ('embrace', 'loved or hated') came to him as he allowed his initial (right hemisphere) picture of a girl running in the shadows to expand into something else, something larger and more significant. Those words *rose up* from deep inside him, carrying a weight of personal meaning that had begun accumulating in early childhood. Those words connected the bright, charming little boy he had been and the savagely critical, middle-aged alcoholic he had by now become. Indeed, if he was to be true to himself, these apprehensions of the pattern of his own intimate relationships could not fail to emerge. The verbal surface of *The Jewel in the Crown* (grown up, realistic, left-hemisphere) seems very different from the language of *The Lion, the*

Witch and the Wardrobe (simple, magical, right-hemisphere) yet both offer us an 'opening door' onto a disturbing *personal* past, in which lurks a shaming thing, a betrayal, done by one man to another. For Paul Scott's deepest feelings were for his own sex, and his marriage to Penny—like Thomas Mann's to the 'boyish' Katia—concealed his true inclinations.

Scott died too soon to see his *Raj Quartet* become one of the outstanding television series of the twentieth century. Yet when it did, it was his 'villain', Ronald Merrick—ambitious and vindictive, yet inwardly tortured like Scott himself, and for much the same reasons—who would capture the popular imagination as a result of Tim Piggott-Smith's masterly performance in the role. Merrick even became, as certain fictional characters do, *independent* of the narrative that had given him birth, with Piggott-Smith being accosted in the supermarket by people demanding to know 'why he'd been so cruel to poor Hari Kumar'. Was it perhaps in Merrick that Scott achieved the immortality every writer craves?[20] For at base, most story makers are tormented, like Merrick, by hidden shame and self-doubt, and (like Merrick) prepared to manipulate others, even those they love, in their desperate quest to realise their own ambitions. For these things, too, form part of the 'romantic egotist'.

Roald and the Giant Ego[21]

By his early forties, Roald Dahl was 'running out of juice'. After a brief career as a fighter pilot in Africa and Greece in 1940–1941, he had been invalided out of the RAF, and became a British diplomat-cum-spy in the United States. When C. S. Forester, author of the 'Hornblower' novels, took Dahl under his wing, and placed one of the young writer's stories in *The Saturday Evening Post*, Roald began to realise that he could make writing a career. Over the next twenty years, he acquired a reputation for cleverly-crafted, cynical tales for adults, full of wife-swapping, outrageous fraud, and cruel trickery. Dahl's short stories, much like the White Witch's Turkish delight, create an appetite for more while failing to satisfy in any lasting way. Despite Roald's celebrity marriage to Hollywood actress Patricia Neal—and the birth of two much-loved girls, he was frustrated and worried. By 1960, he had fewer and fewer ideas for new stories, and was beginning to recycle plots, or even to 'borrow' them from tales he had read years before and forgotten—or half-forgotten. The creativity tank was showing 'empty'.

With his US publisher pressing him to produce a novel for adults, Dahl could offer nothing—except a hastily-written hundred page manuscript based on a bedtime story he'd told his own daughters, an over-the-top fantasy full of manic energy and tinged with a kid-level version of the same nastiness—there's no other word for it—that had typified his stories for adults. It was called *James and the Giant Peach*. Dahl's publisher was immediately responsive, the story was published, and at forty-five, he was airborne again. Three years later came

Charlie and the Chocolate Factory, a runaway bestseller. No matter that Dahl's writing was clichéd and careless, his ideas borrowed from anywhere and everywhere: kids loved the books, and Dahl became a wealthy man.

Almost alone among the storytellers in this book, Dahl was not driven to write until adulthood. Initially, it was not childhood memories, but his early adult experiences in wartime—in particular, *flying*—that provided the stimulus. And at first he wrote as much to make money as to satisfy some deep creative need. Lewis and Dahl were both self-preoccupied, but while Lewis was idealistic and self-critical, Dahl was cynical and opportunistic. In the words of one of the giant ducks in *The Magic Finger*, Dahl 'allowed himself' to do whatever he liked, regardless of anyone else's rules or expectations. Yet despite the differences between them, Dahl's best-known children's stories, like Lewis', emerged only in his middle years,[22] and, like Lewis', contained important clues to his own inner life as a child three decades earlier. *James and the Giant Peach* begins with the abruptness of a fairy tale. Its four-year-old hero is orphaned when his parents are eaten by 'an angry rhinoceros'. Dahl narrates this in an offhand, almost jocular manner, but it doesn't take long for pathos to come to the fore: 'The lovely house by the seaside had to be sold immediately, and the little boy, carrying nothing but a small suitcase containing a pair of pyjamas and a toothbrush, was sent away to live with his two aunts.'[23]

Behind this lies something painful and personal. Four was the very age at which Dahl himself had experienced the death of his father, preceded, in the same year, by the death of his older sister, Astri. The age-appropriate egocentricity of his four-year-old self is unmistakably present: 'in the long run it was far nastier for James than it was for them'. Of course the autobiographical elements are disguised and exaggerated, just as dream narratives disguise and exaggerate without our conscious participation. Roald still had his mother, who remained a source of comfort and security to him well into his adulthood. He was *not* sent away to live with cruel relatives and banishment to boarding school did not come until several years later. From his school dormitory in Weston-super-Mare, Roald could see the lights of Llandaff where his family home was, and this too is closely echoed in the description of James's new home with his evil aunts:

> 'They lived—Aunt Sponge, Aunt Spiker and now James as well—in a queer ramshackle house on top of a high hill in the south of England. The hill was so high that from almost anywhere in the garden, James could look down and see for miles and miles across a marvellous landscape of woods and fields; and on a very clear day, if he looked in the right direction, he could see a tiny grey dot far away on the horizon which was the house that he used to live in with his beloved mother and father. And just beyond that, he could see the ocean itself—a long, thin streak of blackish-blue, like a line of ink, beneath the rim of the sky.'[24]

In this passage, James has *a vision of the world from high above*—a vision which is common to many story makers, and which seems peculiarly important to them (remember Dickens' 'hours of vague reflection' looking out over the city of London?) The image combines loneliness with the possibility of superiority: despite being able to 'look down' on the rest of humanity, and 'see further' than they do (remember Mr Pickwick?). James is a prisoner atop his hill, craving the company of other children his own age, and a normal life.

Then, in a shameless borrowing from 'Jack and the Beanstalk', James meets an old man who offers him magic seeds, and tells him to swallow them without delay. Before he can do so, James trips and falls, dropping the seeds beneath an old peach tree. The seeds burrow into the ground, and the very next day a giant peach grows on the hitherto barren tree. Shut outside at night by the aunts, James finds a tunnel leading into the inside of the peach, where he discovers some giant insects (they have also consumed the magic seeds). At first he is terrified of them, but they turn out to be benign. The next morning, James' giant friends sever the peach from the branch to which it is still attached, and the enormous fruit rolls at speed down the hill, squashing flat the evil aunts (a cartoon touch very typical of Dahl). It rolls on across the plains, drops off a cliff into the ocean and, miraculously, floats. To escape sharks, James engineers for the peach to be *lifted into the air* by masses of seagulls—a key image for ex-pilot Dahl, who had always been fascinated by balloons, and a right hemisphere representation of 'outlift'.

This magical journey is James' liberation from his evil 'foster parents', a total transformation of circumstances such as every lonely, ill-treated child would like to imagine. As the peach travels across the Atlantic, the insects explain various 'amazing facts' to James. Being high above the world confers secret knowledge, and James is no longer alone and friendless. He and the insects fight off several attacks from the formless, featureless Cloud Men, and finally, the Peach comes to land atop a skyscraper in New York City where James and the giant insects are welcomed like heroes, and James lives happily ever after.

In Dahl's story we have a remarkably accurate metaphorical portrayal of the psychological development of many children who will later become 'romantic egotists'. They experience themselves as having *lost* something vital to them—not necessarily a loved one who has died, for other kinds of pain and shame may be involved. People do not seem to understand their pain, leaving such children feeling *alone and different*. The children numb the pain of the loss with mild forms of *dissociation*, which adults typically regard as daydreaming. They cut off from the realities of the world around them, 'float above' it, or 'observe' ordinary life as if from behind a window or a screen. They *feel superior* to those who lack this detached vision—yet are also aware that their apparent superiority is shakily based: 'It was an eerie and frightening feeling to be standing on clear glass high up in the sky. It made you feel that you weren't standing on anything at all', as Dahl later put it in *Charlie and the Chocolate Factory.*[25] Their compensation for their sense of being different, cut off from the rest of humanity, is to *live temporarily in a fantasy world*, a 'place of greater safety' where everything is brighter, better and happier, and where they magically possess the power to change their circumstances. In this altered state, they come to believe that they possess *special knowledge* which others do not share, or *special skills* which make it possible for them to do things that ordinary people cannot. In other words, they develop what psychoanalytic theory would call a *grandiose self.* The enormous peach is one image of James' 'inflated self'—a 'giant ego' that is resilient, and (apparently) invulnerable to attack. Comparable images are Charlie's inheritance of a whole factory full of chocolate, the White Witch's promise to Edmund that he will live in a palace with 'whole rooms full of Turkish Delight', and the young Dickens' dream of 'mountains and rivers of gold'. Such images reassure a child that he is extremely 'big' and important, warding off his secret fear that he is small, inadequate—or even *nothing at all* (a 'Cloud Man').

For the romantic egotist's worst fear is the *fear of annihilation*: losing his distinct identity. Adolf Hitler repeatedly claimed that the Jewish race must be *vernichtet* (literally, 'nothinged')—a doctrine that led to the notorious *Endlösung* ('Final Solution'). Unconsciously, of course, it was his *own* annihilation Hitler feared. Norwegian dramatist Henryk Ibsen admits to his fear more openly and honestly. In the final act of *Peer Gynt*, the aging con-man Peer has returned to his homeland knowing that death is not far off. He quite fancies the idea of being a major sinner, a celebrity in Hell, but the sinister Button Moulder scornfully tells Peer that he hasn't done anything nearly bad enough to deserve that honour, and will simply be 'melted down', losing everything that has made him, in life, unique and individual—a fate that horrifies Peer. In *James and the Giant Peach*, the Cloud Men are the equivalent of the Button Moulder. In Lewis' *That Hideous Strength*, the evil powers who rule our 'silent planet' drain the individuality out of their adherents, leaving only frigid, empty shells like the transparently named Wither and Frost. (Against the odds, Peer manages to escape his fate—maybe—redeemed by his long-abandoned wife Solveig's faith that he will someday return to her).

When *Charlie and the Chocolate Factory* was published in 1964, Roald Dahl was forty-eight, and life was about to repeat for him, just as it had at a similar age for Jack Lewis. First, Dahl resumed writing children's stories after a break of twenty years, drawing on deep wells of his own childhood pain, disguised and transformed into extravagant compensatory daydreams that ended reassuringly. Then, like Lewis', Roald Dahl's own 'story' started to unfold, with the terrible inevitability of *The Sound and the Fury* or *Owls Do Cry.* In 1960, his infant son Theo was severely injured in an accident, and had to have brain surgery. He was not expected to survive. Roald threw himself with energy and determination worthy of any fairy tale hero into an attempt to save his son's life. Eventually, Theo did recover most, though not all, of his functioning, but this was only the beginning of the family's suffering. Two years later, Olivia,

Dahl's elder daughter, then seven-and-a-half, died suddenly of measles. She was the same age as Roald's sister Astri had been when she had died in 1920. Dahl was being confronted, in middle age, with events that woke up memories of his childhood forty years before. When Olivia died, Roald's wife Patricia was thirty-six—Sophie Dahl (Roald's mother) had been thirty-five when her daughter Astri died. In 1965, fate struck Patricia herself. At thirty-nine, she suffered a severe stroke while filming on location. For the second time, Roald shouldered the task of organising the recovery of a loved one—albeit in a very domineering fashion. It was as if he believed that, like his own character Willy Wonka, he could control anything, engineer a 'happy ending' in life as well as in writing. But even the 'iron will' that Roald shared with Hitler was not enough to accomplish that.

'It All Comes Round Again'

Intergenerational repetitions of the kind we've been documenting are not confined to creative people. Nor do they necessarily occur during the midlife years. However, repetitions *show up* most dramatically between the late thirties and the late fifties, for these are the years in which our children are growing up, while our own parents are ageing (sometimes dying). For all our determination not to repeat our parents' mistakes, our attempts to ward off those mistakes can bring about the very thing we fear—a principle powerfully communicated in fairy tales like Hans Andersen's 'The Tinder Box'. The Old Brain has a way of subverting the conscious intentions of the New. Intergenerational repeats within families have been recognised for many years within the psychoanalytic world, but mostly in the limited form of so-called 'anniversary reactions', where an individual will experience some crisis on the anniversary of a significant event (like the death of a parent, or the death of a twin). More recently, Averil Earnshaw and Ann Schutzenberger developed fuller theories about the repetition phenomenon, in which significant 'life-changing events' in one generation (e.g. the birth of a child, a death, a divorce) are echoed in the next generation by similar (though not necessarily identical) events, as genetic legacies are reinforced by family dynamics organised around them.[26] Among the general public, there has been a longstanding acknowledgment of the pattern whereby families go from 'shirtsleeves to shirtsleeves in three generations' (wealth is acquired and then squandered), and novels like Thomas Mann's *Buddenbrooks* give that pattern a powerful fictional form. Similarly *Wuthering Heights* shows an acute awareness of how a younger generation may re-enact the conflicts and attractions of the previous one: the 'play' continues its run, even though the actors are different.

Such family patterns tend to continue, because young adults automatically and unconsciously choose partners who will replicate the family gene pool.[27] Unlike most of us, however, a future story maker will not just *experience* the repeating patterns in his or her family, but transform them into *narrative*, thus preserving them for outsiders to ponder. Story makers who achieve fame attract biographers—the facts of their families will be documented alongside the fictionalised versions that they themselves produce—all of which gives the impression that dramatic repetitions are only, or mainly, found in the lives of creative people, even though this is not the case.

When intelligent adults read novels which describe cross-generational repetitions (like Graham Swift's *Waterland*), they tend to reject them as unrealistic or unconvincing. 'It couldn't happen like that in real life', readers say, yet anyone who has studied family trees or collected family stories will know that real lives are just as full of 'coincidences' as any novel by Hardy. The lives of families across time are patterned, repetitive and endless—like Old Brain stories. 'My life is based on a true story', quipped American children's author Katharine Paterson,[28] turning on its head the common understanding that 'fiction imitates life': later in this chapter we will see how true her words can be. The complex, mysterious interaction between art and life is not to be subsumed in any simplistic formula. Our own families embody 'lived stories' that play out, largely unconsciously, across generations, and to which the intelligent but genetically sensitive child is particularly attuned. Born into such families, the story makers of the future resonate with novels that unconsciously echo the themes of their family stories, the fictions lending shape to their own genetic potentials. Then the story maker *re-creates* those stories in life, in art, or in both. But those who choose to re-create their life themes in fictional form may later find themselves living things they had only *imagined* in their work.

Portrait of the Artist as a Romantic Egotist

Charles Dickens' childhood had never been far from his thoughts, but in the decade between 1849 and 1860 childhood memories and feelings intensified, resulting in the publication of two deeply self-revealing novels. *David Copperfield* was published when Dickens was thirty-seven—the same age as Ibsen was when he wrote *Peer Gynt*. Its full title is *The Personal History of David Copperfield*, and its rather coy opening sentence reads: 'Whether I shall turn out to be the hero of my own life, or whether that station will be held by anybody else, these pages must show'. What exactly is Dickens getting at here? Is he so deeply ambivalent about revealing himself—even disguised as 'David'—that he needs to hide behind this stagey entrance line? Dickens recognised that *Copperfield* was a new kind of writing for him, and he valued it above all his other novels, calling it his 'favourite child'. No wonder he could not settle down to writing it, at the age of 36, until he had found the 'right' name for his hero (whose initials just happened to be 'D.C.'—his own, in reverse)—*David Copperfield* would be the closest Dickens would ever come to writing an autobiography. He had in fact begun an autobiography just before he started on *Copperfield*, but abandoned it, giving the first portion to his friend John Forster, and burning the rest. Much of what he handed to Forster went straight into the novel, virtually word for word, even the account of that shameful period when he had had to work alongside 'common labouring boys'.Like *James and the Giant Peach*, *Copperfield* begins with a small boy who loses his parents and acquires unpleasant, punitive step-parents, but, as in *Jane Eyre*, the fairy tale template is concealed beneath wonderfully observed realistic detail. Davy's father has died, and his mother has married again, swept off her feet by the masterful but cruel Murdstone. Dickens' 'close-up vision' focuses, with Dahl-like disgust, on the 'dotted indication of the strong black beard he [Murdstone] shaved close every day'.[29] Dickens is simply selecting a detail that *shows* us (in the manner of the right hemisphere) who Murdstone is, without needing to *tell* us—is there a hint here that growing up is something the young Dickens had wanted to avoid—like Barrie's Peter Pan? Within days, the wicked stepfather has begun subjecting David to humiliation and harsh punishment. Murdstone invites his equally unpleasant sister into the house, and the two of them bully David's mother into sending the boy, aged 'between eight and nine', away to school, 'for his own good'. And a little later, she dies. Melodramatic? Unrealistic? Yet much the same actually happened to both Jack Lewis and Roald Dahl. And although it did not literally happen to Dickens, he too had been forced to leave home and survive on his own for a few crucial months. The feelings he ascribes to David are ones that he himself had felt:

> 'Behold me, on the morrow, in a much-worn *little* white hat, with a black crape round it for my mother, a black jacket, and a pair of hard, stiff corduroy trousers—which Miss Murdstone considered the best armour for the legs in that fight with the world which was now to come off—behold me so attired, and with my *little* worldly all before me in a *small* trunk, sitting, a *lone lorn* child . . . in the post-chaise that was carrying Mr Quinion to the London coach at Yarmouth! See, how our house and church are *lessening* in the distance; how the grave beneath the tree is *blotted out* by intervening objects; how the spire points upwards from my old playground *no more*; and the sky is *empty*!' [Italics mine][30]

As usual, I have italicised the words and phrases in which we can hear the voice of the Old Brain, acutely aware of the 'sadness of things'. The passage is almost as repetitious as Enid Blyton's writing, and such is the pathos Dickens feels as he contemplates his past that the prose slips into verse. The music, and the repeated, dying fall of the words 'little', 'small', 'no more', 'empty' conjures the same sense of 'thinning'[31] and 'void' to which our preschool listeners reacted so powerfully to in Chapter 2. Here again is a diminishing vision, as the hero gazes from afar at the gradual obliteration ('blotting out') of everything he has most loved and valued. (Hitler, who may well have read *David Copperfield*, includes a very similar passage early in *Mein Kampf*!) David almost glories in his own suffering, the *unfairness* of it all. As Paul Scott would write near the end of his life, 'Poor Cinderella . . . Poor Desdemona. Poor Jane Eyre. Poor Oliver Twist. Poor Uncle Tom. Even Poor Becky Sharp. The lessons of injustice and inhumanity are learned very early, and we respond to them even as children who are surrounded by love and happiness and comfort.'[32]

Scott is on the mark. Sensitivity to loss, damage and existential anxiety will be particularly strong in a right hemisphere-dominant child, no matter how apparently safe and loving his or her early environment. David Copperfield is a wonderfully detailed portrait of any such child—highly intelligent yet highly sensitive, easily shamed yet convinced of his own worth, desperately lonely yet determined to turn his sense of difference into grand success that others will envy—the kind of 'romantic egotist' who will turn to story-making as a remedy for the sliver of ice in his or her own heart—that sense of melancholy or even despair that is present at least as far back as the age of four.[33]

'Fictional' David *does* go on to become an author, like his creator—although Dickens says hardly anything about this aspect of his hero's career, clearly needing to keep this highly-prized part of his adult self out of the novel. In early adulthood, the charming, enthusiastic David becomes totally infatuated with a pretty young woman called Dora, and marries her. Dora is immature, frivolous and attention-seeking, a 'bimbo' who cannot really understand David's work or share his inner world. David is gradually falling out of love with her, but luckily, before this process has gone too far, his 'child wife' (Dickens' words) dies, and this frees David to marry his true soul-mate, Agnes. Dora is generally believed to be a thinly disguised version of Maria Beadnell, Dickens' first love, but in David's initial infatuation and later declining interest in her, we can also see elements of Dickens' gradual disillusionment with his wife, Kate. 'Magical thought' has organised the events of the novel so that David's 'mistake' in selecting Dora as his wife can be rectified, and he can find a more suitable partner without shame. 'Blunder' has been replaced by 'bliss'. It was not to work out so painlessly in Dickens' own life.

When Dickens came to his second revisiting of childhood in *Great Expectations* (published when he was forty-eight) his marriage had irretrievably broken down. In an extraordinarily literal display of his feelings (remember his 'punishment' of the wolf?) he had resorted to having an internal wall constructed to separate his wife's part of their bedroom from his. Even that was not enough: Dickens forced her to move out in 1858. He had fallen in love with a young actress, Ellen Ternan, who was only eighteen when he met her, the same age as his favourite daughter, and only a few months younger than his first love Maria Beadnell had been at their first encounter. Ellen was no brainless 'Dora', but she seems to have been confused and distressed by the famous man's attentions, and to have become his mistress only very reluctantly (some have suspected that her 'coldness' helped to shape the haughty Estella in *Great Expectations*). Though she eventually lived with her middle-aged lover for brief periods under a secret identity in a house Dickens owned on the continent, she seems to have failed to reciprocate his extravagant affection. It was as if Jane Eyre had yielded to Edward Rochester's pleas, lived with him in the south of France, and (exactly as she feared she would) hated herself for having abandoned her own principles. Increasingly depressed and despairing, Dickens had failed to find the fairy tale happiness he had longed for. Perhaps, though he never admitted it, he also felt remorse for the brutal way he had treated his wife.

In *Great Expectations*, we again encounter a bright, sensitive child oppressed by adults who are unfeeling, manipulative or even menacing. Pip, like Davy, feels unfairly treated, but this time Dickens leaves us in no doubt that Pip is at least partly responsible for his own misery. *Great Expectations* is the product of mature, honest self-reflection. Young Pip obstinately clings to the belief that he will inherit a fortune from Miss Havisham, and that the pretty, disdainful Estella will one day be his bride. The whole novel is designed to demonstrate how very far from the mark these 'expectations' are: his benefactor, as it turns out, is not the well-born Miss Havisham, but the rough-as-bags ex-criminal Magwitch, who amidst his own suffering and toil has remained loyal to the memory of the little boy he once terrified into helping him. Miss Havisham has brought up Estella not to marry Pip, but to 'break his heart'—in fact, to break the heart of any young man who loves her. In *Great Expectations* the mature Pip sits in judgment on his young self—and especially on his grand visions of his own future, the 'inflated self' that psychotherapists associate with the narcissistic personality. Throughout, Pip's sense of entitlement ('specialness') and the shame which fuels it, are portrayed more transparently than in *David Copperfield*. And in Estella, Dickens created a figure capable of inspiring love, but incapable of returning it—like Hans Andersen's Snow Queen. This 'coldness' is in fact a key aspect of the romantic egotist himself, who (as Scott Fitzgerald memorably showed in *This Side of Paradise*) is more in love with the *idea* of love than he is with a real, flesh-and-blood person.

To Dickens' conscious mind, the 'coldness' at the heart of his personality would have been invisible. He would have seen himself as his public saw him—genial, warm, affectionate and compassionate. Indeed, he was all of these things. But his emotional abuse of his wife Kate shows another side, one that he could not admit in himself, and so, quite unconsciously, located in Estella—just as Hitler put his 'shadow self' into the Jews he feared and hated, and Enid Blyton put her shadow self into *places* like 'Castaway', the secret-filled island in *Five Go to Smuggler's Top*.[34] Romantic egotists can be 'exciting' to be with, and 'picturesque' to look at, but they are also 'rather forbidding'. They lash out in rage at those who, they sense, may shame or humiliate them. Perhaps the earliest example in Western literature is Odysseus—a key figure in the *Iliad* and undisputed hero of the *Odyssey*. As Brian Boyd points out, Odysseus is by turns wise and manipulative, idealistic and opportunistic, a truth-teller and a blatant liar.[35] In clinical terms, he combines features of the narcissistic and the sociopathic personality, like Thomas Mann's Joseph, Ibsen's Peer Gynt, Arthur Miller's Willy Loman, Paul Scott's Ronald Merrick, and Dennis Potter's Arthur Parker in *Pennies from Heaven*. Storytellers write *themselves* into their most memorable tales, for they have no choice. Right hemisphere imagery, the product of writer's trance, presents us 'whole'—both the self that we want the world to see, and our denied 'dark side' as well.

The Struggle Over Endings

Endings are rarely easy for storytellers. The timeless Old Brain—as it operates in dreams, and in the songstries of very young children—acknowledges no conclusions at all. But one of the earliest modifications the left hemisphere makes is to insist on endings—initially, 'happy ever after' endings. Such endings fulfill deep wishes for comfort and secure attachment—they look back to the womb, even. In Chapter 2 we saw how hard preschool children struggle with the unsatisfactory endings that stories present them with, how they add an extra ending which 'double-locks' the door of secure closure. Today's computer games for adults offer similar 'fail-safe mechanisms': your character suddenly dies—but with 'virtual reincarnation', you can come back into the game as a new character—perhaps a Rogue will work better than a Wizard this time? Young adults know that fairy tale endings are unrealistic, but they still struggle to know how to end stories without giving in to sentimentality. By middle adulthood, when the cortex is fully mature, the tug of war between the Old Brain and the New becomes even stronger. When story makers try to craft conclusions, they can be forgiven their ambivalence, for it is in a sense *the ending of their own lives* that they must contemplate every time they end a story, and the 'realistic' ending their conscious, rational selves can believe in is not the one that many of their readers deeply crave.

In Dickens' original conclusion to *Great Expectations*, set years after Magwitch's death, Estella stops her coach on a London street when she sees Pip walking by. Estella's abusive first husband has died, and she is now married to a better man. Pip concludes:

> 'I was very glad afterwards to have had the interview, for in her face and in her voice, and in her touch, she gave me the assurance, that suffering had been stronger than Miss Havisham's teaching, and had given her a heart to understand what my heart used to be.'[36]

This is definitely not 'Reader, I married him'. It is not even 'tomorrow is another day'. Pip and Estella are not going to resume their relationship and live 'happy ever after'. Dickens offers his readers only the consolation that Estella has now become a person *capable* of love, just as Pip himself has realised who his true friends really are. They can finally *understand* one another (the left hemisphere's priority) even though the dream of romantic love has faded. However, this was not the ending that Dickens' audience was to read when the final part of *Great Expectations* was published in 1861. The instigator of the change was Dickens' friend, Edward Bulwer Lytton (author of *Rienzi*, the novel on which Wagner based his opera). Lytton prevailed upon Dickens to soften his sober conclusion, to allow at least the possibility that Pip and Estella might yet have a life together. Dickens clearly did not need too much persuasion, and so his Old Brain desire for 'full closure' reasserted itself. In the revised ending, he has Pip and Estella meet in the grounds of the now-dead Miss Havisham's former home, and although they agree to continue 'friends apart', Pip ends his account with the hopeful words, 'I saw no shadow of another parting from her'. In David Lean's classic 1945 screen version of *Great Expectations*, Satis House is not (as in the novel) destroyed by the fire in which Miss Havisham dies. In a psychologically acute gambit, the script has Estella (played by a young Jean Simmons) establish herself there, as if to re-enact Miss Havisham's life as a lonely, embittered woman. But Lean is not prepared to leave it there. Instead he has Pip (played by a young John Mills) masterfully tear down the heavy curtains that shut the daylight from Miss Havisham's old room, commanding Estella to come outside with him: 'We belong to each other! Let's start again—together!' Lean has simply replayed Dickens' original ambivalence, in wording banal enough to have been written by Enid Blyton.

A century after Bulwer Lytton persuaded Dickens to change the ending of *Great Expectations*, Elizabeth Fowles ('Alison' in *The Magus*) persuaded her husband John to change the ending of his new novel, *The French Lieutenant's Woman*. Fowles had produced a 'limp, sentimental, conventional conclusion' but Elizabeth—who had also insisted on the ambiguous conclusion to *The Magus*—wanted him to offer readers a very different glimpse of Sarah Woodruff's future life. Fowles strengthened his original ending, and then added another, less gratifying but more credible. The published novel contains both, printed one after the other.[37] The intervention of Elizabeth, like that of Bulwer Lytton with Dickens, points to story makers' reliance on a trusted other person to resolve their own ambivalence. It was a role that Paul Scott performed for M. M. Kaye (a fellow chronicler of British India), advising her to alter the happy ending she had written for *The Far Pavilions*—though Kaye's publisher, in an intervention similar to Bulwer Lytton's, subsequently persuaded her to retain it.[38] *79 Park Avenue*, one of Harold Robbins' earlier novels, ended with his call-girl heroine sacrificing her own happiness so that her former lover Mike, an attorney, could marry a 'sweet-natured, respectable girl'. Robbins' editor at Knopf pronounced this resolution unconvincing, so Robbins (who at that point in his career still accepted criticism) invented a new ending in which Mary-Ann revealed the existence of a secret love-child she had borne to Mike. Just a few months later, in one of those life-imitates-art twists that many writers' lives contain, Robbins' own mistress revealed that she was carrying his child.[39]

In the Ruined Place

As I described at the beginning of Chapter 5, my grandmother's crowded two bedroom apartment in Sydney was, for me at nine and ten, a kind of earthly paradise like the one Stevenson found at Colington. But with each visit (and these lasted until I was seventeen) I became increasingly aware that my grandmother's crowded rooms also hinted at long-ago disappointments, secrets that could not be spoken aloud. In the real world of my family, to speak of these secrets openly seemed as terrible as Jadis' use of the Deplorable Word in *The Magician's Nephew.* And the past preserved in that apartment was sufficiently similar to Miss Havisham's to supply an additional layer of explanation for my longstanding attraction to the story.

I had always imagined Miss Havisham in the novel as looking like my grandmother (she was sixty when I was born, seventy by the time I first looked into *Great Expectations*). Somewhat like Dickens' abandoned bride, my mother's mother spent hours sitting in her rocking chair, sometimes knitting or listening to the radio, but generally doing nothing at all. As I learned much later, she had indeed been 'abandoned' by my grandfather, who had gone off to fight in the Great War, fallen in love with another woman, but returned to my grandmother—only to take to drink as a way of coping with the disappointment of his 'great expectations'. He was killed in a car accident, leaving her a widow at forty-four. There was a 'gap' there in my family history—a dead grandfather, an absent uncle—which somehow needed filling, and my right hemisphere instinctively recognised that *Great Expectations* might fill it: patterns demand completion, and fragments 'pull' wholes of which they may once have formed a part.

Less than ten years after my grandfather's death, my mother's younger brother Hugh went off to fight in the Second World War, married a woman from Scotland, and spent the rest of his life on the other side of the world, returning to Australia only twice, and then very briefly (reversing the 'untold story' of Magwitch in *Great Expectations*). He had betrayed his mother, as his father had betrayed his wife. My grandmother's final thirty years were lived amongst tangible reminders of both men—letters, photographs, discarded insignia and old cartridge cases. They could not be thrown away, yet they were never spoken about. She had lived on with my mother in that apartment—like Miss Havisham and her foster-daughter—until my parents' marriage in 1944. And there was more. Like Estella, my mother was attractive, but found it difficult to express affection in a warm and spontaneous way. *I have no heart,* Estella tells Pip. '*And I can't love*', admitted Margaret Mitchell. Both my grandfather and my uncle had once had considerable ambitions, although I only learned of those as an adult. In my turn, I formed 'expectations'—not of wealthy benefactors (like Pip) or of a glamorous military career (like my Uncle Hugh), but of intellectual distinction as a scholar and writer. When I re-read *Great Expectations* as a middle-aged adult, I had begun to accept that my own dreams were unlikely to materialise, and that I had wasted a great deal of precious time. My life had unfolded sufficiently to enable me, for the first time, to understand *Great Expectations* fully, and to appreciate Dickens' own state of mind when he wrote it.

Pip's story begins in a graveyard, and it ends in an overgrown ruin inhabited by the ghosts of childhood. A new beginning must acknowledge the past, and part of the emotional work of the midlife years is to revisit our personal past, recognising not only the wrongs and injustices that were done to us, but also the wrongs and injustices we did to others. We come to 'the ruined place' when we cease to deny our responsibility for what has happened in our lives, and in doing so, acknowledge that our lives are finite. Now, if we are to remake ourselves or live differently, it is up to us. No Fairy Godmother, no Miss Havisham, no Godlike Conchis is going to assist us. That was the message I had rejected in *The Magus*, and would have rejected in *Great Expectations*, had Dickens not bowed to pressure and softened the ending.

Remembering and Foreshadowing

Over forty years, I have read *Great Expectations* many times, but every time I go back to it, I am amazed at how much I have *forgotten*. Apart from a small number of passages that I know well, I have no recollection that I *ever* read these words, even though I know that I have. Why do we remember only certain parts of what we read? How can we see a movie again a few years after first seeing it, and find that entire scenes and sequences seem completely new? The answer lies in the nature of human memory itself, and it applies not only to memories of what we have read, but also to *all* our memories of *everything*. What research has established is that *our brains process any new experience in terms of what we already know.*[40] We would expect that something new and different would make a stronger impression on us initially, and also be remembered longer. But overall, it seems that our tendency is to preserve most securely those things that conform to patterns our brains have already registered. As the years pass, our memories of 'new' experiences are subtly re-shaped so that they become more similar to the old ones they (partially) resemble. In fact, some of our most powerful experiences of 'newness'—as apprehended by the right hemisphere, processed by the left, and then re-integrated by the right—are highly likely to prove (in the longer term) to be *refashioned* memories of deeply buried Old Brain experiences. In the case of *Great Expecations*, the events, scenes and characters that I remembered best *before* my most recent re-reading were the ones that I had registered most powerfully when I *first* read the story—most of all, the hypnotic, dreamlike scenes of Miss Havisham in her gloomy house, presiding over the rotting remains of her wedding breakfast. I formed these impressions in the first place because they reminded me people, scenes and events that I already knew—or at least, guessed at.

We customarily think of memory as 'stored' somewhere in the brain, but the metaphor is somewhat misleading. There is no mental 'memory bank', not even electronic impressions on a neuronal 'hard disk'. Instead, neurologists report, there are 'engrams'—neurons that fire in a particular pattern when something triggers them to do so. The 'patterns' come into existence only when the neurons fire. It makes sense, then, to think of memory as something that is *created anew each time we remember*, rather than stored somewhere in a definitive form for retrieval. So, to return to the experience of re-reading a book that has been significant for us—a 'chosen story'—it is possible to see how the story can simultaneously seem both 'new' and 'familiar', known and unknown. Here is how American critic Anne Fadiman describes what happened when she was reading C. S. Lewis to her eight-year-old son, and couldn't resist asking,

> 'Have you noticed that '*The Horse and His Boy* isn't really fair to girls? And that all the bad guys have dark skin?'
>
> 'Henry shot me the sort of look he might have used had I dumped a pint of vinegar into a bowl of chocolate ice-cream. And who could blame him? He didn't want to analyse, criticize, explicate or evaluate the book. He didn't want to size it up or slow it down. He wanted exactly what I had wanted at eight: to find out if Shasta and Aravis would get to Archenland in time to warn King Lune that his castle was about to be attacked by evil Prince Rabadash and two hundred Calormene horsemen. 'Mommy', he said fiercely, 'Can you just *read*?'
>
> 'And there lay the essential differences between reading and re-reading, acts which Henry and I were performing simultaneously . . . The former was more fun, the latter was more cynical. But what was remarkable about the latter was that it *contained* the former: even while, as with the upper half of a set of bifocals, I saw the book through the complicating lens of adulthood, I also saw it through the memory of the first time I'd read it, when it had seemed as swift and pure as the Winding Arrow, the river that divides Calormen from Archenland.'[41]

In her 'bifocal' analogy, Fadiman splendidly captures the re-reading experience. When re-reading a story of personal significance we are *re-creating an earlier self*, yet being concurrently *aware of our present selves*—noticing things we were not consciously aware of when we first read it. Our original experience was predominantly a right hemisphere dominated one—entranced reading. Our much later experience is monitored by the left hemisphere, interrogating, evaluating, criticising. Yet the earlier survives *within* the later.

If re-reading can generate different reactions to a loved story, it can also highlight the ways in which that story has shaped our lives *subsequent* to the original reading. Here is Jamie James, now in his early fifties, realising how his thirteen-year-old experience of Conrad's *Lord Jim* predicted his subsequent life in an amazingly literal way:

> 'On the second page, before flashing back to Jim's school days, the book describes his later career as a 'water clerk', or salesman for a ship's chandler. 'Thus in the course of years he was known successively in Bombay, in Calcutta, in Rangoon, in Penang, in Batavia'. I re-read those words sitting on the porch of my house in Jakarta—as Batavia has been known since 1949. Since my travels in Asia began sixteen years ago, I too have spent some time—been known, you might say—in those places, all except Calcutta; it's still on my 'not yet' list. I have been a party to a few after-dinner storytelling sessions at hotels in Singapore, though the verandahs are now usually glazed and airconditioned. I have slept in the jungles of Borneo, in a hut much like Jim's.'[42]

Graham Greene's splendid essay, 'The Lost Childhood' contains a similar account:

> '. . . in childhood all books are books of divination, telling us about the future . . . If it had not been for [*King Solomon's Mines*] would I at nineteen have studied the appointments list of the Colonial Office and very nearly picked on the Nigerian Navy for a career? And later, when surely I ought to have known better . . . wasn't it the incurable fascination of Gagool with her bare yellow skull, the wrinkled scalp that moved and contracted like the hood of a cobra, that led me to work all through 1942 in a little stuffy office in Freetown, Sierra Leone?'[43]

Greene was *aware* that he re-enacted his 'odd African fixation' in adult life. But as James' example shows, even when we *forget* what we read as children, we can still 'repeat' it, provided that at some time, it has made sufficient impression on us. This is what Freud was getting at: if we don't remember, we're more likely to repeat, but remembering *without* 'working through' may still compel us to 'repeat'.[44] I would contend that no story could make such an impression—becoming a sort of 'guide' to how to live our lives—had we not in some mysterious way contained *within ourselves* the potential that the story then proceeds to unlock. So, as Greene concludes, despite its impact on his subsequent life choices, *King Solomon's Mines* was *not* his most significant 'chosen story'. Rather, it was Marjorie Bowen's *The Viper of Milan*, which he first read at the age of fourteen, that made him a writer—because it offered him a template for stories in which humans were, in varying degrees, fallible, cowardly, and manipulative: it was, in other words, a New Brain story, and Greene became a New Brain novelist, for all that he wrote spy thrillers. Though Greene never says so, I have no doubt that he recognised himself in Marjorie Bowen's characters, for they are the kinds of characters we meet again and again throughout his fiction—betrayers of others, betrayers of their own principles.

Memory research shows that it is perfectly possible for us to have no conscious memory of something we have seen, or read and yet to be influenced by it. This is called 'implicit memory'[45], and it helps to explain why writers—even highly conscious, New Brain writers—can borrow from earlier writers—may in fact reproduce their exact words—without ever realising it. It almost seems as if *everything we ever read, saw, heard, tasted or felt* can potentially form part of a story we may later tell. No conscious awareness of the earlier experience need be present for us to use it in this way. Enormous slabs of what we experience are never 'encoded' into memories that we can retrieve at will, yet at some level, they can still shape us. When a lawsuit was lodged against J. K. Rowling, alleging that she had plagiarised an earlier children's story that also featured a School for Wizards, the charge was futile. Writers cannot *help* but 'borrow', and Schools for Wizards have been around for years. The *Harry Potter* series is as much a tissue of borrowings—blatant or subtle—as *The Chronicles of Narnia*.

Our earliest memories are those that date from a time before we could speak. Such infant memories exist as vague body sensations (feeling 'crowded' or 'stifled'; experiencing a sense of warmth and comfort, or cold and clammy discomfort). They are not amenable to conscious recall, but can return powerfully when 'triggered' by a particular stimulus (a smell, sunlight on a little girl's golden hair, the sound of a voice, the prickly feel of a tweed jacket), as we know from research on trauma and 'flashbacks'.[46] Such memories are almost impossible to pin down in space or time, for an infant has little sense of either. Yet there are language forms which actually *correspond* with such experiences, forms which I have, earlier in this book, loosely called 'the language of the Old Brain'. Of course the oldest parts of the brain—the brain stem and the limbic system—have no language at all, but if they did, that language would be *global*, *absolute*, and *timeless*, 'all or nothing' language, corresponding with 'all or nothing' perceptions. Such adjectives convey the right hemisphere's essentialist perceptions: 'this is how it is'. *All new and all true.*

When infant experiences are being accessed in psychotherapy, even well-educated, intelligent people will produce 'timeless' statements like, 'I've *never* felt like I mattered' or 'He *always* treats me like a child'. Vague, yet deeply felt statements such as 'It's all just *yukky*', or 'When I try to talk to her there's just *nothing there*' point to states of being that were probably first experienced in infancy—even though the speaker is talking about a current, adult relationship. Such early feeling-states are not accessible to New Brain interrogation. If a cognitive-behavioural therapist asks a client, 'What evidence do you have to support your belief that you've never mattered to anybody?' the client is likely to reply (with increasing irritation or confusion) 'I don't know, it just *feels* that way!'—just as Janice Radway found that her Smithton readers could not directly answer her questions about the author's style or skill in plot-construction, and resorted to retelling the story instead.

Jung postulated archetypal images that existed in a 'collective unconscious', and could appear in the drawings or the dreams of individuals to whom they were completely unknown. However, another way of thinking about such images is that they represent *the way the right hemisphere thinks*, the 'language' of the right hemisphere. In other words, if the right hemisphere apprehends loneliness and set-apartness, it will automatically produce images of beetling cliffs or isolated houses on top of hills (O'Brian's dreams, *James and the Giant Peach*, Enid Blyton's 'Smuggler's Top'). If the right hemisphere apprehends confusion and ambiguity, it will automatically produce images of dusk, fog and mist (as in *Great Expectations* and *Bleak House*). When it apprehends emotional distance, it will produce images of Arctic cold (as Dickens'marriage began to break down, he entertained a persistent fantasy of 'escaping to a realm of ice and snow' to write his next novel—something that he managed to achieve shortly afterwards by performing in a play called—believe it or not—*The Frozen Deep*.) It will produce such images irrespective of cultural and historical differences, and irrespective of the individual's level of formal education. For the right hemisphere, the 'abstract' is *conveyed by* the concrete and the individual. When it is aware of desolation, it will produce a 'ruined place'. 'Wisdom' might be a Wise Old Man, as Jung postulated, or a Wise Old Woman like George MacDonald's Great-great-grandmother figure in *The Princess and the Goblin*. For the right hemisphere it is not a question of something 'symbolising' something else—it is the left hemisphere that insists on separating the two, and it does so in order to think consciously about how one relates to the other.

In the case of Old Brain-dominated authors, it is possible to detect long-buried literary memories in an occasional 'breaking through' of *precise, observant* language that is not typical of the author in question. Enid Blyton's bland, formulaic prose left few indications of what, in her childhood reading, had most struck her. But every now and then, traces of things she had read—as a child, or even as an adult—would work their way to the surface, much as prehistoric potsherds occasionally surface in a newly-ploughed field. In *Adventures of the Wishing Chair*, her first full length fantasy novel, an entire passage depends on the wording of Robert Browning's 'The Pied Piper of Hamelyn', which every literate child at the time would have heard or read at school if not at home.[47]

The opening chapter of the book version of J. M. Barrie's play *Peter Pan* is titled 'Peter Breaks Through', and fantasy literature is full of situations in which the 'other world' 'breaks through' into the real world, or vice versa. Will, Philip Pullman's hero in *The Subtle Knife*, literally cuts through the invisible fabric that divides his own world from the parallel world of Cittàgazze. Though we associate these images with make believe, 'breaking through' corresponds to a real phenomenon. Any dedicated story maker tends to blur the boundary between the real and the fictional, and the price he pays is that his own life begins to take the shape he has 'imagined' for his characters in earlier stories. Alternatively, his own 'made-up creations' begin to intrude into his 'real' life. Dennis Potter memorably portrays the latter situation in his four-part TV drama, *Karaoke*, written in the shadow of his impending death. His hero, TV dramatist Daniel

Feeld, is sitting in a restaurant when he overhears people at a nearby table voicing 'dialogue' that he recognises as one of his own previously-written scripts. He tries to explain this uncanny experience to Sandra, a nightclub hostess, as they walk down an iron fire escape into the grounds of the hospital where Daniel has just been diagnosed with terminal cancer. Daniel tells her that he has called his latest drama 'Karaoke' because 'you know, the song or the story of our lives is already made up for us'. Sandra replies, 'Well in a way, yeah, I know the feeling'. Of course she doesn't—she just knows how to make men feel good—but Daniel is only too happy to believe that she really does share his experience, for almost all story makers crave understanding. He blurts out the secret fear of every writer: 'Words, all I've ever had is words'. All his life, he has used language to assert control over the seemingly uncontrollable, only now the words are no longer at his bidding, are 'taking over', becoming 'real'.[48] Normally, the left hemisphere guards the boundary between 'real' and 'pretend' as fiercely as the George Martin's Knights' Watch guard the Wall in *Game of Thrones*. But now that boundary has been breached, and the White Walkers are infiltrating the Seven Kingdoms.

At the improbably early age of six, Paul Scott devoured Elinor Glyn's Edwardian bestseller *Three Weeks*, the story of how a 'Godlike' adolescent boy is 'inducted into manhood' by a sophisticated older woman. Why exactly little Paul would have chosen a book so unsuitable for a child just starting school seems a mystery—until we remember its hero's name—*Paul*. It is at this highly individual level that the right hemisphere connects us with the world, almost as if saying, 'This man *is* you. This story is *about you. Three Weeks* would indeed prove to be 'about him', although Scott himself may not have realised it. When he embarked on young adulthood, full of excitement and optimism, Paul was mentored by Gerald Armstrong, a sophisticated older man who encouraged his writing, critiqued his poetry, introduced him to Oscar Wilde's *The Picture of Dorian Gray* (another 'coming of age' novel)—and also became his lover. The gender of the 'fairy godmother' may have been different, but the pattern set up by *Three Weeks* is very clear. Scott had *lived*, at eighteen, what he had *read* at six. And. at the very end of his life, terminally ill with colon cancer, Scott insisted on carrying on his teaching at the University of Tulsa from his hospital bed. His conduct reminded one of his students of his character Barbie Bachelor in *The Towers of Silence*, although at the time he wrote that novel, eight years earlier, Scott had not yet been diagnosed. It was as if he had first imagined Barbie's dying, and then in his own life 'played the part' he had written.[49]

At the age of forty-seven, John Fowles wrote a novella called *The Ebony Tower*, in which an ageing British artist lives in an isolated manor house in Brittany with two young female art students who care for him, cook for him, and 'don't deny him the little bit of sex life he can still manage.'[50] Twenty years later, and only months after the death of his wife Elizabeth, a pretty, volatile Oxford student, Elena van Lieshout, introduced herself to Fowles as a dedicated fan of his work. Soon they were living together. He was sixty-four, she was twenty-one. Fowles' friends said that it was a case of 'life imitating art', meaning, of course, *The Ebony Tower.*[51] By then, Fowles had become impotent as a result of a prostatectomy, and his relationship with Elena unfolded in a way that resembled not only *The Ebony Tower* but also, more disquietingly, his first novel, where the middle-aged Clegg imprisons a young student, but never touches her, and experiences *her* as manipulating *him*. Real-life Elena even accused Fowles of being 'no better than the man in *The Collector*'. He was not the only ageing artist to find himself in this vulnerable position: Dickens with Ellen Ternen—barely out of adolescence—and Ibsen, who at ninety fell passionately in love with a woman young enough to be his grandchild, are only two of many examples that could be cited. Needless to say, such partnerings are not unique to story makers—it is simply that story makers give them fictional form long before they 'become real'.

How are we to explain these examples of fiction foreshadowing the future? I suspect it is a matter of the unfolding of 'biological wisdom', a kind of parallel to the unfolding of the genetic potentials embodied in our DNA. Far below the level of conscious awareness, all of us may have some inkling of what our own future is to be. Story makers, who from an early age have blurred the boundary between 'real' and 'made up', between 'conscious' and 'unconscious', can more readily gain access to their 'under-minds' than most of us. In a semi-trance state, akin to hypnosis, they can access both the implicit memories that the rest of us have lost, and the shadow selves that most of us deny. By embodying those intimations in fiction, story makers can allow them some limited independence while still holding them at a safe distance. But as lives continue to unfold, and repeats begin to multiply, it is almost inevitable that life and fiction will begin to coincide—the theme of *Karaoke* and also of *The Singing Detective*, Potter's masterpiece. In making stories, we not only 'repeat' what we 'remember', we 'foreshadow' what is yet to come.

Where We've Come From, Where We're Going

In this chapter, we've been preoccupied with repeating patterns—in individual lives, in families and in stories—for all right-hemisphere-dominated stories reflect the deep structures of human lives over time. Whether we remember our past or not, we seem compelled to repeat it, and so our past can become our future—especially in the case of story makers, for whom the boundary between 'real' and 'pretend' has always seemed permeable. By *writing* it in words, they 'make it happen'. We've seen how middle adulthood is a time when childhood memories insist on welling up, even for writers who have previously shut them firmly away, and how this can sometimes result in a shift back in the direction of Old Brain storytelling—sometimes foreshadowing dramatic 'repeats' in the writer's own lives. Yet we've also seen how midlife marks the final stage in the maturation of the cerebral cortex, leading to the creation of stories that acknowledge more fully the shadow of death that lies over the human condition: hence story makers' wish to leave behind a 'legacy'—a statement significant enough to survive their own passing. Where C. S. Lewis and Roald Dahl channeled their early memories in the form of gratifying (yet disturbing) Old Brain stories for children, the midlife narratives of Charles Dickens, Paul Scott, and Thomas Mann were longer, denser, sadder and wiser than those of their youth. Yet *both* groups of writers are profoundly influenced by the imperatives of the Old Brain, and both draw on the right hemisphere image of the 'ruined place' to acknowledge their own egocentricity and destructiveness.

Chapter Seven
Light at the End of the Tunnel
Storytelling in Old Age

Under Alzheimer's Net: Iris Murdoch's Last Novel

When Iris Murdoch published her first novel, *Under the Net*, she was thirty-four. Her prolific output concluded with *Jackson's Dilemma*, when she was seventy-six. She was not formally diagnosed with Alzheimer's type dementia until two years later, but *Jackson's Dilemma* bears overwhelming evidence of its author's decline, and she never wrote another novel. It is confronting to have to start our chapter on storytelling in old age with this subject, but I have chosen to do so because *Jackson's Dilemma* is a striking example of a story maker whose brain can no longer sustain the capacity for creativity: the nature of that deterioration enables us to see anew some of the key things that make stories work, and in particular, to see what happens when the left hemisphere can no longer play its part in making an individual emotional experience into a viable story.

Though her reviewers mostly avoided saying so, the sad truth is that *Jackson's Dilemma* is clumsy and repetitive, its dialogue is stilted and unconvincing, and its language often clichéd. Murdoch had never been the most elegant of prose writers, but in this novel her sentences sometimes sound more like notes to herself than finished statements. Had *Jackson* not been submitted to Chatto & Windus by the much-acclaimed Dame Iris Murdoch, winner of the Booker Prize and the Golden Pen award for literature, it is hard to believe that her long-term publishers would ever have accepted it. The opening sentences of *Jackson* are as follows:

> 'Edward Lannion was sitting at his desk in his pleasant house in London, in Notting Hill. The sun was shining. It was an early morning in June, not quite midsummer. Edward was good looking. He was tall and slim and pale. He was very well dressed. His hair, slightly curling, thickly tumbling down his neck, was a dark golden brown. He had a long, firm mouth, a rather long, hawkish nose, and long light brown eyes. He was twenty-eight.'[1]

In many ways, Iris Murdoch's description of Edward reminds us of the writing of a bright twelve-year-old like Charlotte Bronte or Patrick O'Brian. Most of the adjectives ('good looking', 'tall', 'well dressed') are essentialist—speaking to the perceptions of the Old Brain. The passage is more than a little reminiscent of Edwardian novelist Elinor Glyn's initial description of Paul, the hero of her 'shocker' *Three Weeks*. Paul is 'young . . . and fair and strong. He had been in the eleven at Eton and left Oxford with a record for all that should turn a beautiful Englishman into a perfect athlete'.[2] Only Iris Murdoch was not writing in 1907, but in 1994. And intriguingly, *Jackson's Dilemma* contains hardly anything from the late twentieth century: there are telephones, cars and (distantly) airplanes, but no televisions, and only a single perfunctory mention of a 'word processing machine' (Murdoch herself wrote longhand). Very few of the characters seem to need to earn a living, and gradually it becomes clear that these are upper-middle-class people, living much as they would have done in the 1950s (or even in the 1930s, when Murdoch was growing up). All of this gives *Jackson* an almost fairy tale quality. Murdoch was well known for her tendency to the uncanny and the fantastic. Yet *The Flight from the Enchanter*, with its many fairy tale elements, is solidly realistic compared to *Jackson*, whose repetitive events and almost featureless characters seem to 'float' in space, as timeless and placeless as Doctor Who's Tardis.

The novel is full of the same interlocking love triangles Iris Murdoch had always portrayed (and which strike us as unrealistic, until we realise that they reflected her own highly secretive love life). In *A Severed Head*, published more than thirty years earlier, Murdoch had managed to carry off with aplomb these credibility-straining situations, in which A loves B, who pretends to love C but is actually infatuated with D, who secretly lusts after A, and so on. But in *Jackson's Dilemma* the situations themselves are so baldly presented that they seem like scenes from *Days of Our Lives* or *The Bold and the Beautiful*.

The many short sections of which the novel is constructed (most of them only a few pages long) give the impression of driving over a road with speed humps every few hundred yards: as a reader, you build up momentum, only to have to keep slowing down, and there is a jarring bounce if you go over a hump a bit too fast. It is as if Murdoch had stopped writing, and then started again later without remembering what she had written before: which, given her dementia, is probably exactly what happened. Sensitive editing would probably have been able to smooth out most of this, but Murdoch had always been unwilling to accept suggestions that what she had written might in *any* way be pruned, telling her publishers to 'put it all back'. The decline of her higher cognitive capacities would have meant that she herself was unable to spot the many rough patches in *Jackson* when she went through the proofs.

Once we are aware of what was happening to Iris Murdoch during the period she was working on *Jackson's Dilemma*, it is easy to see examples of her own mental state intruding into the book. The novel is full of scenes in which characters wander alone around their houses, gaze into mirrors or walk compulsively around London, often at night. They try to write, or engage in some other creative activity, but lose concentration and become easily distracted, while their work sits unfinished. They come to rest in one another's homes for brief periods, and then almost literally run away, rejecting offers of help and comfort from their friends. All of this accurately mirrors mental state of the dementia sufferer herself. To be sure, the characters in *The Message to the Planet*, published six years before *Jackson*, also run out of creative inspiration, abandon their scholarly work, or fail to achieve the grand philosophical or mystical breakthroughs they seemed to be striving for. The theme is not new for the novelist. What is new in *Jackson's Dilemma* is how all-pervasive it has become. Reading the novel is like going into room after room, only to find each room identical with the one before—a nightmare imagined by David Lynch in the chilling final episode of *Twin Peaks*. We are forced to conclude that Murdoch simply imbued *all* of her characters with the fearful, depressed condition in which her own last years were spent. Dickens, that great observer of human misery—who himself spent countless hours wandering the streets of London at night talking to prostitutes, street children and policemen—described this state perfectly (ironically in his first, and sunniest, novel):

> '... that state of partial unconsciousness when the mind wanders uneasily from scene to scene, and from place to place, without the control of reason, but still without being able to divest itself of an indescribable sense of present suffering.'[3]

There can be little doubt that Dickens was writing about feelings he had experienced personally, but they never 'take over' his characters, not even in his last, unfinished novel, *The Mystery of Edwin Drood*, where his own anguish is clearly visible. In *Jackson's Dilemma*, every character feels what Murdoch feels.

The one exception—at least for a while—is Jackson himself. Jackson is introduced as a 'manservant', but clearly he is far more than that. He claims mysterious powers (though these are never spelled out) and seems to know exactly when his presence might be required by his employer, turning up at precisely those times. Jackson is in fact a figure created by magical thought. With his appearance, we start to read on with more conviction, because we want to know more about this man, what his real purpose might be, and how his presence is going to affect the lives of the other characters. The story that begins to emerge is predictable to those who have read Murdoch's earlier novels, but at least *Jackson's Dilemma* now begins to resemble a *story—a sequence of events that unfolds with a sense of inevitability and meaning.* Shadowed by the dark, lurking presence of Alzheimer's Disease, the novelist still seems capable—just—of enlisting her readers in a quest for 'what is going to happen next.'

Yet when, suddenly, we are let into Jackson's thoughts, we find that he too, is 'exhausted', 'confused', and racked with dreadful guilt. He, too, begins to move from one place to another, as if unable to stay anywhere. This is disconcerting. His efficacy in the novel up to this point has depended precisely on his being a Godlike figure who is far removed from the lives of the others, and makes things happen for them. At the very end of the novel, Jackson talks vaguely of a 'mission', and mysterious statements to the effect that he 'cannot guarantee how long he will stay'. But even here the author's own desperation seeps into him:

> 'Sometimes, he had a sudden loss of breath, together with a momentary loss, or shift, of memory. So he was to wait, once more, forgetfulness, his and theirs. He thought, my power has left me, will it ever return, will the *indications* return? No assignment. But punishment? Madness of course always now at hand. He had forgotten where he had to go, and what he had to do . . . My powers have left me, will they return—have I simply misunderstood? . . . Is it all a *dream*, yes, perhaps a dream—yet my strength remains, and I can destroy myself at any moment. Death, its closeness. Do I after all fear those who seek me? I have forgotten them, and no-one calls. Was I in prison once? I cannot remember. At the end of what is necessary, I have come to a place where there is no road.'[4]

It feels as if the writer herself is speaking, somewhat like Charlotte Brontë's sudden 'Reader, I married him' near the end of *Jane Eyre*. In *Jackson's Dilemma* we have a very rare thing: a portrayal of Alzheimer's disease written 'from right inside' that experience, possibly more emotionally accurate because it is presented, not as autobiography, but as fiction.[5] Providing that we know the mental state of its author at the time she wrote it, reading *Jackson* becomes a deeply moving experience. Without this awareness, it is simply a very bad novel. In *Jackson*, we can *feel* the fictional process being twisted out of shape, its smooth surface fissured by gaps—as the tissue of the 'Alzheimer's brain' literally shrinks, and develops 'holes'. *My power has left me.*

Adjectives (and adverbs) are the parts of speech that, above all others, lend *feeling* to our utterances. 'It was wonderful!' or 'It was terrible!' express opposite emotional experiences. Like 'wonderful' and 'terrible', many of the adjectives in *Jackson's Dilemma* are global and imprecise. Emotion is present, but instead of Iris Murdoch's left hemisphere making conscious decisions about how to convey that emotion in the most precise way, as she would routinely do in earlier works, the emotion simply 'represents itself', often employing the language of the Old Brain to do so. The global adjectives and adverbs are, I suspect, the written equivalent of the 'flattening of affect' that afflicts the actual speech of the Alzheimer's victim (and, we should not forget, the seriously depressed or traumatised individual). The emotion is there, but the verbal shading that would convey its degrees of intensity, and its precise meaning, are gone. The prose of *Jackson's Dilemma* seems 'grown up' in its vocabulary and (to some degree) its sentence structure, but its emotional content is without nuance. There are individual passages in *Jackson* where Iris Murdoch is, briefly, writing with the full, conscious control typical of a normally-functioning partnership between right and left hemispheres. Of course her awareness of what she is doing must still be operating to *some* degree, or she would be unable to write connected prose at all! She is still a writer, though no longer a good one. But the overall feel of *Jackson* is of the 'Old Brain' taking over, as conscious control slips away.

Struggling against the failing of her New Brain, Iris Murdoch shows us in *Jackson's Dilemma* much of what is essential in the making of a viable fiction. First and foremost, *memory* is vital, because our ability to make coherent stories is of a piece with our ability to make a coherent narrative of our own lives. Robert Louis Stevenson, a much underrated commentator on human nature, expresses it eloquently:

> 'And yet conceive us robbed of it, conceive that little thread of memory that we trail behind us broken at the pocket's edge; and in what naked nullity should we be left! For we only guide ourselves, and only know ourselves, by these air-painted pictures of the past.'[6]

Second, a narrative may *repeat* a great deal of material, yet in order to hold our attention, there must be much more than repetition. An author must *feel that she is going somewhere,* and in turn, enable *us* to feel the same. As soon as we begin to sense that perhaps things will simply go round in circles, our absorption within any fictional world becomes harder and harder to sustain. We become bored and confused. We are highly likely to stop reading (or, if it is a movie, viewing). As we saw in Chapter 1, the most primitive Old Brain stories (like songstries and dreams) cycle back and back over the same themes without reaching any real conclusion. That is part of the reason so many parents (and even scholars!) dismiss them as 'babble'. But for a story to compel us, we need the sense that someone is in charge, that we have a guide on our quest. Hence the third necessity for a successful story: the teller must offer us characters who seem *different* from herself, must be able to 'stand apart' from them. The teller must be able to cast herself as a 'she' or a 'he'. In dreams, in preschool songstries and in fairy tales, all characters are simply aspects of the protagonist. So too in Iris Murdoch's final novel: there is no separation of teller from tale, of creator from character. There are only the emotions—desperate sadness, overwhelming fear—that brought the story into being. The person who must exist to tell it is being washed away like a sandcastle at the seaside.

After this chilling vision of what happens when storytellers become 'lost for words', it's a relief to return to the world of normal ageing, where, to be sure, profound changes happen in all of us, but where stories and story making are of central importance in the human endeavour of holding onto meaning.

Holding Onto Meaning

In early childhood, we tell stories to grasp a world that is vast, new and puzzling, trying to unravel its contradictions, gain some control over its unpredictability, cope with the frightening and saddening things that it seems to contain. In old age, we are more likely to tell stories to hold fast to what we already know, relying on a fund of trustworthy anecdotes in which we have invested our emotional capital. People suffering from dementia say the same thing again and again because they cannot remember what they have just said. Mentally healthy old people, however, may tell the same story over and over for a very different reason. Retelling the story reminds them who they are (and were). Like the Old-Brain-dominated narratives of early childhood, these anecdotes may not be well formed—they do not necessarily contain a clear, intriguing starting point or develop towards a satisfying conclusion. Like preschool songstries, the anecdotes of old age may fail to spell out the context necessary for listeners to understand them fully, and hence are not very compelling for the listener. Some very young children listen, entranced, to elderly relatives' anecdotes, even though they only partially understand them. William Faulkner was one such child, Janet Frame another, Patrick Russ a third. Many of those long-ago, half-understood 'stories' told by relatives, nannies and family friends turn up, half a century later, in adult fiction like Faulkner's 'The Bear', where the teller's voice is immediately audible ('There was a man and a dog too this time . . . ').[7] As with the first words of *The Jewel in the Crown*, it is as if we are overhearing a conversation *that is already in progress.* But for most of us, as we grow up, ageing relatives who tell rambling stories without any crafting or explanation are simply 'boring'—unless of course we love the teller well enough to care deeply about what matters to him or her. As Sanjay Sircar points out, there must be an age at which children's automatic interest in adult anecdotes gives way to distaste or boredom—perhaps this occurs during adolescence, when relatives become temporarily 'uncool' as part of the drive for autonomy.[8] Yet specific well-formed stories first encountered very early in our lives assert their influence right through to the end. For it isn't just a love of words or exposure to a flow of adult anecdotes that turns an intelligent, sensitive child into a story maker, but a compelling wish to re-create the whole story experience, to reproduce the *feeling* of particular narratives that have already made a deep impression. We cannot always know what those narratives were, but surprisingly often, we can, because writers themselves retain vivid memories of them.

Award-winning non-fiction writer Barbara W. Tuchman said in 1983 that she probably became a historian because of Lucy Fitch Perkins' 'Twins' books, which were popular at the time she was growing up. In particular, she remembered *The Dutch Twins*, the *Twins of the American Revolution* and *The Belgian Twins* (the latter suffered under the German occupation of Brussels). Not surprisingly, then, Tuchman's own later works included *The First Salute* (about the Revolutionary War), and *The Guns of August*, an account of the 'Battle of the Frontiers', the German invasion of Belgium and France in the late summer of 1914 in which Henri Alain-Fournier was killed. Like any story maker, the adult Tuchman was revisiting the stories that had inspired her as a child, but retelling them with the expert knowledge and insight she'd accumulated since she first read them. Significantly, Tuchman's approach to historical writing had a strong narrative flavour—her early reading of novels (including the swashbuckling tales of G. A. Henty and Alexandre Dumas) had shaped her wish to *tell stories* about the past, not simply accumulate facts and place them in meaningful order—as in Holger Helwig's *The Marne*, which covers the same period as Tuchman, but lacks the narrative 'onrush' (and occasional inaccuracy) of *The Guns of August*.[9]

My wife's uncle Gordon, now in his nineties, has no high opinion of recent screen or TV versions of *Pride and Prejudice*. For him, they are 'not a patch on' the version made in 1940, with Greer Garson as Elizabeth and Laurence Olivier as Darcy. For him that movie represents an ideal—a vision of how he wanted to see his own life and marriage. Late in his life, Gordon wrote a memoir of his days as an Australian combat soldier in New Guinea during World War Two. He recounts a series of uncomfortable and frightening experiences with charm and humour. It is the same light touch that informs both *Pride and Prejudice*, and his all-time favourite author of historical romances, Georgette Heyer. Their stories had in a sense taught him how to write—though seemingly he did not utilise this implicit knowledge until very late in life.

Of course, not all stories told (or retold) in old age are confirmatory and reassuring. Some old people return again and again to experiences that were traumatic for them, events which have left lasting scars. Typically, though, these stories are told in a way that exonerates the tellers, placing them in the best possible light, while gaining delightfully satisfactory revenge on those who may have wronged them. Such a storyteller, *par excellence*, was Mary Wesley, who leapt into publishing success at the age of seventy.

On the Terror Run

The television adaptation of Mary Wesley's *The Camomile Lawn* had my close attention right from the start.[10] At a funeral, an elderly man, his face lined and saddened, suddenly recognises a middle-aged woman, whom he last saw forty years earlier. She was ten then; he was eighteen. 'Good God! Sophy!' he exclaims, and suddenly we are flung back to the Indian Summer of 1939, as war looms over a carefree bevy of young cousins who gather in a large house overlooking the dramatic Cornish coast, just as they've done for years. Like Janet Radway's Smithton readers, I sensed from these opening moments that this story would speak to me. Why? My father's family originated in Cornwall, and the spirit of 1939—youthful innocence and hope colliding with the harsh realities of wartime—has always meant something to me, partly, no doubt, because my own parents and their relatives must have experienced something similar, though in a different country. Yet I did not particularly *like* most of the characters who appeared in that first episode of *The Camomile Lawn*, nor did I did not feel much in common with them, except, perhaps, with ten-year-old Sophy. And I did, as the story unfolded, prove to have something in common with her, though not anything I would have expected.

The cousins—Oliver, Polly, Calypso and Walter—have evolved a holiday ritual they call 'the Terror Run': it involves racing alone, at night, along a narrow cliff path, all the way from one landmark to another, with the waves crashing on the rocks below. Until this year, Sophy has always been considered too young for the Terror Run, so this is her rite of passage. Unbeknown to the young people, it is also the last year that the event will occur—a rite of passage on a far more monstrous scale is about to take its place—but for Sophy, the 'terror' will be immediate. She arrives at the finish line sobbing hysterically, gasping something incomprehensible about a 'pink snake'. The path takes all the young people past the hut where the coastguard lives, and we are given to understand that he has exposed himself to Sophy—and perhaps worse. Her first encounter with adult sexuality has been alarming, and in time, she will find her own way of dealing with the coastguard, one that will shock the others as much as the coastguard has shocked her.

I had more personal points of connection with this dramatic first episode. As a child, I too had felt the drug-like 'rush' of running fast through a night-time world, in the excited company of other children, and it was easy enough for me to imagine something genuinely frightening occurring in that same darkness. That small node of shared experience, along with the other connections I've mentioned, was enough to 'kick start' my emotional investment in the story. I followed the remaining episodes with increasing involvement, and when the series came out on DVD many years later, I immediately watched it all over again. I read Wesley's other novels, admiring their sharp humour and their confronting honesty, but only *The Camomile Lawn* has become a 'chosen story' for me.

Did *The Camomile Lawn* encapsulate the kind of life I might have had, if I had grown up with the Blitz, rather than the Beatles? Had I been more uninhibited, lived more in my body and less in my mind, might I have been one of the young people she writes about? Walter, perhaps? During those wartime years my mother's younger brother Hugh (who was almost the same age as the older cousins in Mary Wesley's tale) had embraced combat and romantic love, and by the time I myself was adult, he had reached the same point of middle-aged *anomie* as Oliver. Did I, through them, glimpse the kind of life my uncle may have had as a young man? Remember that as a child, my uncle was a mystery to me, a 'gap' that needed to be filled. By the time I viewed *The Camomile Lawn*, I'd found out quite a lot about my uncle, yet somehow the gap still existed (remember Melanie Klein's little boy and his broken spinning top?)

The Camomile Lawn begins with Sophy, at ten, hopelessly in love with nearly grown-up Oliver. Oliver, to whom Sophie is just a child at the time, lusts after the beautiful Calypso, who treats him coolly. Forty-five years pass, years of disappointment and disillusionment for Oliver. We know nothing about Sophie's life during those years (her adult life is not revealed in *The Camomile Lawn*, just as Estella's adult life is one of the 'untold stories' that hover at the edges of *Great Expectations*). Then the two meet at the funeral with which the televised version opens, and sixty-something Oliver begins to hope that perhaps their relationship, which never got off the ground in 1939, might perhaps be re-started. It is not a Mills & Boon scenario, exactly. But a 'mating plot' is definitely coming to its resolution. *The Magus*, too, turns on the reader's hope that a relationship fractured by distance and misunderstanding can somehow be resurrected. Predictably, that theme resonated with me also.

The Camomile Lawn had been Mary Wesley's second novel, and it was quickly followed by ten more in just fifteen years. The handsome, silver-haired author (given to using without the slightest embarrassment words respectable old ladies were not supposed to know) went in a few years from genteel poverty to considerable wealth—a 'rags to riches' plot in real life.[11] Mary Wesley was born Mary Farmar,[12] the daughter of a serving army officer, and a descendent on her mother's side of the Duke of Wellington's older brother. Mary escaped her family at twenty-four by marrying for money and status (exactly as Calypso does in *The Camomile Lawn*). She divorced her husband after the birth of two children (only the first of them actually being his) and, like both Polly and Calypso, enjoyed numerous romantic relationships of greater and lesser intensity, until eventually she met Eric Siepmann, the great love of her life, to whom she stayed faithful as her own heroine Rose is to Milo in *Not That Sort of Girl*.

During this second marriage, she made sporadic attempts to write both fiction and autobiography, but threw away most of them. Then her second husband Eric died. He too had been a writer, and perhaps his death, which reduced Mary to temporary despair, also freed her to take up her own efforts at storytelling. (Couples where both aspire to be writers seem quite often to operate in this way, with one, usually the woman, subordinating her own desire to write to her partner's, as if the relationship could tolerate only one 'real writer'. The marriage of Australian novelists George Johnson and Charmian Clift took an even sadder form, with Charmian eventually committing suicide when

George put a fictionalized version of her into his semi-autobiographical novel *Clean Straw for Nothing.*)[13]

By the time Eric died, Mary was in her late sixties, and her first published adult novel, *Jumping the Queue* begins with a blackly humorous scene in which its heroine methodically plans her own death. In the novels that followed, Mary mostly returned to her own early adulthood for inspiration, but the youthful thrills and pangs she remembered so vividly are all filtered through the consciousness of a woman in her seventies, achieving a double perspective on her own memories (similar to the 'double vision' involved in adult re-reading of a childhood favourite as described by Anne Fadiman) that she probably would never have accessed had she published earlier in her life. *The Camomile Lawn* shifts constantly between the protagonists' older and younger selves, as older women reminisce about 1939–1945 in the hearing of young relatives:

> '"The war was very romantic", said Helena all those years later, driving down the motorway with Calypso's son Hamish.
>
> '"Surely not, Great-aunt"
>
> "Surely yes. Why Max and I went to Covent Garden at dawn and he bought flowers as they were unloaded from lorries. He filled a taxi with roses and carnations. He was exhilarated by his first concert in London. What a success! Those flowers! I can remember the smell now. We drove back as it grew light to Polly's house, where I was staying. It wasn't so romantic when we got there."
>
> "Not enough flower vases?"
>
> "No. Someone had just woken Polly to tell her her parents had been killed by a stray bomb. They were somewhere near Godalming, near the hospital. Her father was a doctor, you know".
>
> "I didn't know".
>
> "They can't have known anything about it, but it was sad for Max after his concert".
>
> "Did he know them? Worse for Polly, surely".
>
> "No, but think of the embarrassment of all those flowers, and Polly so upset."
>
> "What happened to the flowers?"
>
> "We told the taxi driver to take them to a hospital, but I expect he sold them. I kept some roses for Polly.
>
> "Not so romantic, then."
>
> "It was when he bought them. It is those moments one remembers. Oh yes."
>
> "Nice to look back." Hamish knew old people lived in the past. He was glad poor old Helena found it enjoyable.'[14]

For Helena, being seduced by flamboyant musician Max Erstweiler (towards whose funeral she and Hamish are now driving) was a life-changing experience—something the much younger Hamish fails to understand. She knows he does not, and lets him know she knows. Many old people display this blunt honesty—they are unconcerned about the judgments others may make of them, and can take a malicious delight in exposing the pretences and hypocrisies of their listeners. Yet Mary Wesley is not just a grumpy old woman with a sharp tongue. Like Dickens, like Wordsworth, she retains a keen appreciation of the wonder of life when one is young. She famously remarked, 'God, when I think of the time I've wasted going to bed with Old Etonians!' but in fact her regrets went a good deal deeper than that. A key motivation behind the novels of her final years was her need to come to terms with her own aggression, even, perhaps, her own hate.

Patrick Marnham's biography *Wild Mary* covers the novelist's life from birth to late adolescence in a single, eight-page chapter, and presumably this reflects Mary's own emphasis in the interviews she gave during the years of her success. Mary did not dwell overmuch on a childhood she had endured rather than enjoyed. However she wrote one novel that does draw directly on the loneliness and bitterness she clearly felt at that time. *A Sensible Life* is Mary Wesley's *Jane Eyre*, her *David Copperfield*, her *Buddenbrooks.* In it we can see the way in which storytellers authentically re-create their own *feelings* as children and adolescents, while transforming the settings and relationships within which they felt those emotions—much as dreams preserve feelings intact while disguising settings, people and events. *A Sensible Life* commences with a passage which should immediately be familiar to us after our explorations of *Great Expectations* and *James and the Giant Peach* in Chapter 6:

> '*There was no wind*; sea flat as a plate met sky the same colour as the water. Only an occasional glint betrayed their meeting. The beach sloped so slowly to meet the sea it might have been an illusion that it inclined at all. Sand, dry as a biscuit near the shore, changed colour gradually, growing wetter, more sea-coloured as it smoothed close to the distant water.
>
> On an unexpectedly warm February day birds inland were rehearsing their spring song, *but the beach was silent; it stretched wide and empty.* A heron flapping its way with lazy sweeps emphasised the *emptiness* as it left the estuary to travel inland. The boy, imagining he could hear its wings, lowered his binoculars in disappointment; he had come to watch sea birds and *there were none.* He blinked into the sun, already low in the sky, and decided to go home.
>
> A movement half a mile out at the water's edge attracted his attention: a tiny figure moved. The boy screwed up his eyes against the shimmering light. The figure split in two. A child and a dog? It must have climbed down the cliff to the west and walked along the water's edge; there was *no line of footprints* from the beach, *no mark on the sand* still damp from the last tide and the fresh water sweep of the stream from the estuary seeping its clandestine way to the sea.'[15]

Isolation, disappointment, repeated negatives, the 'long view', the diminishing of individual identity: all the themes of this passage evoke the childhood experience of a romantic egotist. When *A Sensible Life* commences, its ten-year-old heroine, Flora, is living with a governess in France while awaiting the arrival of her parents, Vita and Denys. The latter are not looking forward to the reunion. They regard their daughter as a nuisance, an unwanted intrusion into their absorption in one another. This is not a factual portrait of Mary's own parents, but there are key elements in common. Mary's mother made no secret of the fact that she had not really wanted her daughter. Like my own mother's father, Mary's went off to fight at the beginning of the Great War, so she would have seen little of him until five years later. He was posted abroad again when she was eight. He could express his love for his daughter only in letters, and when she might have turned to him for emotional support, he was simply not there. Mary had, in consequence, spent long periods of time alone and bored, 'acting out' her own suffering by rescuing animals from cruelty, and later (in adolescence) discovering that she could use her sexual attractiveness to achieve a temporary feeling of being loved and wanted.

A Sensible Life takes these experiences and transforms them in the way of the Old Brain: intensifying, exaggerating, and simplifying. Mary turns *one* unloving parent into *two* handsome, narcissistic adults who callously sacrifice their child's needs to their own sexual obsession. After the holiday in France, Vita and Denys dump Flora in a boarding school in England while they go off to India. She is expected to join them there at seventeen, and their intention is to marry her off as soon as possible. However Flora, by now a forthright and independent young woman, simply walks off the steamer at Marseilles, reappearing years later as an adult who has somehow acquired poise and self-knowledge. Like most of Mary Wesley's protagonists, and long before 1960s feminism, Flora is determined to make sex work for her, but never to be enslaved by it.

Mary reproduces the parents' conversations with enough sharp-edged realism to make Vita and Denys much more credible than the crudely-presented parent figures in Virginia Andrews' bestselling *Flowers in the Attic* series—stories which seems to channel the loathing many people feel for parents who have abused or neglected them.[16] Throughout *A Sensible Life*, Flora's passionate attachments, her bewilderment, her anger towards her parents, and her growing confidence in her ability to make her way in the world, echo Mary Wesley's own life. But fiction does not simply *recreate* vivid emotional experiences, it *uses* them to create an alternative world, with significant editing, significant 'cuts'. *A Sensible Life* contains no equivalent of Mary's most enduring adult relationship—with her second husband Eric—and *The Camomile Lawn* contains virtually no details of Sophy's life between twenty and fifty. In this way, Mary manages to put a great deal of autobiography into her novels (note that both heroines are ten when their stories start—the age of dawning self-consciousness which we explored in chapter 3) yet maintain her privacy.

Once her career as a published writer had begun, Mary worked with passionate intensity as if aware that her time was limited, writing with hardly any punctuation, and sometimes without chapter divisions. Like the story makers we met in Chapter 5, Mary became irritable if interrupted her while 'taking dictation'. And what her Old Brain dictated was mostly *conversation*, welling up as if remembered, word for word, from 40 or more years in the past.

There is very little description in Wesley's novels (the passage we quoted earlier from *A Sensible Life* is exceptional) and only a necessary minimum of direct narrative. Almost everything is carried by the dialogue; crisp, funny and sometimes crude. Her books are almost 'plays in novel form'. Because Wesley's characters are rarely described, and because (like Hilary Mantel today) she does not remind us very often who is speaking to whom, a reader has to do some mental 'work'—engage the left hemisphere—to keep abreast of what is going on. What begins as 'inspired' writing for Mary becomes a New Brain activity for her readers—but only up to a point. Once the characters *are* familiar, we find ourselves reading faster and faster. We *care* about them, we want to know what happens to them: a fiction has evoked the same sense of attachment as the primitive mammal brain evokes in real children and parents. Re-reading *The Camomile Lawn* in preparation for writing this chapter, I found this happening to me all over again. My knowledge of the events that would unfold had surprisingly little power to prevent my re-immersion in 'onrush'. The trance in which Mary Wesley wrote her books is re-created in the trance that I, and other readers, experience as they become more and more invested in her characters. These characters start life as aspects of the author, or versions of people in her own life, but then become, by the alchemy of the reading process, aspects of us, and versions of people in ours. This is how literature works—across continents, even across centuries.

Because most of Mary's writing was compressed into her last two decades of life, and because her books followed one another in such rapid succession, it is easy for us to see the patterns that occur over and over again in her novels. Her biographer lists them:[17] a young woman in relationship simultaneously with two men (brothers/twins/close friends); a child born within marriage, but to another man; young girls being sexually interfered with by much older men; a heroine who commits murder or manslaughter, and a heroine who attempts suicide (in both cases by drowning). Many of these things—or at least, milder versions of them—were present in Mary's own life. She may not have murdered anyone, but perhaps she would have liked to; she may not have literally attempted to kill herself, but she certainly considered it seriously; she may not have slept with twins simultaneously (as Polly does in *The Camomile Lawn*) but clearly, there was some relationship that involved two related men (in Mary's case, they were brothers). These fictional themes represent the angers and shames, the wishes and fears of her life. They preoccupied her, troubled her. And so, in each new novel, two or three of them would be reworked, appearing in a different guises, some closer to the reality that Mary herself had known, others exaggerated or dreamlike. According to her biographer Patrick Marnham, there is no evidence that Mary was ever molested. However, I find it hard to believe Mary would have included variants of child sexual abuse in novel after novel had her own childhood or adolescence not been marked by *some* form of uninvited and unwelcome sexual intrusion. It is, after all, far more common than our society used to admit.

In fact, I have good reason to believe that my mother suffered it as a child, even though she never hinted at it until the final weeks of her life when she, like Iris Murdoch and Enid Blyton, was under Alzheimer's net. And so, perhaps, my own engagement with *The Camomile Lawn*, my own sense of connection with Sophy, may have stemmed, in part, from a fictional re-creation of a traumatic experience of my mother's. The Old Brain recognises such similarities instantly and instinctively: it is not necessary for parents to disclose traumas to their children for the children to sense their existence.

A preschool child's 'songstry' typically lasts only a few minutes. An adult novel may take years to write, and hours to read. But when we examine a *series* of novels by a single author, we can see an exact equivalent to the structure of the preschooler's monologue, as the storyteller works and reworks the themes of greatest significance for her, presenting different versions of the same theme across several narratives. This is true not just for Mary Wesley, but also for most novelists. Nobody would undertake the hard work, both mental and emotional, of writing a novel if they were not driven to do so by demons within themselves, things 'left over', unfinished, unresolved, still nagging away at them—holes in their world—but holes which might also mysteriously connect times and places: John Fowles' 'wormholes', Janette Turner Hospital's 'isobars'.[18] In 'lucid dreams', the dreamer knows he or she is dreaming, while unable to control what is happening in the dream. In storytelling, the writer knows that she or he is participating in creating something, yet remains fundamentally driven by the story that wells up from within. And perhaps, if there were *not* that 'welling up', that element of compulsion that escapes the storyteller's conscious control, it would not be possible for us, the audience, to experience the same freedom from conscious control, in reading it.

Into the Golden Ocean

Like Mary Wesley's, Patrick O'Brian's writing in old age looks back, as from a dark tunnel, at the intense emotions and brightly coloured landscape of youth. Superficially, Wesley and O'Brian seem a world away from each other, their realities divided on traditional gender lines. Hers is the world of intimate relationships, to which war (in *The Camomile Lawn*) provides only a distant, almost unimportant backdrop. In Patrick O'Brian's world, war takes centre stage, and (except in *Post Captain*) intimate relationships are relegated to the periphery. Hers is a world where girls grow up learning to live with the consequences of their own actions. In O'Brian's world, men go off on adventures, leaving behind the intractable problems of marriage, children and money for years at a time. At the start of a new novel, we typically find O'Brian's hero, Captain Jack Aubrey, on shore in England with his family, perhaps in debt, humiliated by a lack of promotion, or struggling with painful marital misunderstandings. But within a few chapters, the wind is blowing from the sea, Jack is back on board *H.M.S. Surprise*, and a new quest takes shape. Mirror neurons fire, and we are 'seeking' alongside him.

Ever since he abandoned his birth name along with his family of origin and his first wife, Patrick O'Brian had believed that his stories would only command respect from the literary world if they were *serious* and *pessimistic*. The three novels he produced between 30 and 50 (*Three Bear Witness*, also known as *Testimonies, The Catalans* and *Richard Temple*) all fictionalise shameful parts of Patrick's earlier life. All three are full of agonised self-examination and self-reproach—the marks of a man who is honest enough to acknowledge his failings, but not detached enough to see them in perspective. By 1955, O'Brian had left Wales, and was living with his second wife Mary in Collioure (the same village in the South of France that John Fowles had briefly visited a few years earlier). O'Brian was still struggling to make a name for himself as a writer. In his youth, he had contributed a few stories of seagoing adventure to *The Oxford Annual for Boys*. Now, in response to a publishers' request, he tried his hand at a full-length sea adventure for children. The pages of *The Golden Ocean* are full of exciting naval action and sudden reversals of fortune, but the novel could not be more different from the boyish stories O'Brian published in his twenties as Patrick Russ. *The Golden Ocean* is told as if from *within* the 'long eighteenth century', effortlessly creating the illusion of a Georgian world, seen through Georgian eyes. So familiar is O'Brian with its vocabulary, its syntax, and its idioms ('The Year One', for '1801', 'Give you joy of it, my dear sir') that we feel we are *there*. Even more amazingly, O'Brian describes the working of the ship, the intricate technology of its rigging, the beauty and the squalor of life on board, the complex dynamics of its officers and men, as if he had, like Joseph Conrad, spent his entire young adulthood at sea. But O'Brian's intimate knowledge of life aboard a square rigger was derived almost wholly from his reading. As a reader, he had *lived* what he read, and when he came to write, his own readers would feel they were living it too. 'And all who heard would see them there', as Coleridge put it near the end of 'Kubla Khan'.

The Golden Ocean is a quintessentially New Brain narrative. Certainly, there is excitement and suspense, but at the height of it O'Brian often intervenes, lifting us out of the ongoing action and requiring us to wait until the next chapter for a mystery to be solved, or a situation to be resolved. This does not entirely destroy the suspense—sometimes it even heightens it—but it does prevent the reader fully entering that 'reader's trance' we discussed in Chapter 5. Above all, *The Golden Ocean* is richly, compassionately humorous. Again and again, we laugh—both *with* O'Brian's characters, and *at* them. The ability to laugh at ourselves and our predicaments is a key ability of the New Brain, requiring the cortical maturity in both hemispheres to see how our own actions may be incongruous with our words or our beliefs. When *The Golden Ocean* appeared in 1956, O'Brian was forty. Rather later than the writers we followed in Chapter 5, he had finally found his unique voice. He wrote one more 'juvenile' in a very similar vein, *The Unknown Shore*, and then, after a long interval, and again at his publishers' suggestion, produced a new naval adventure, but this time for adults. Its name was *Master and Commander.*

It was as if the Aubrey-Maturin series were already there, fully formed inside O'Brian's head, needing only to be written down. Graham Greene called his own spy stories 'entertainments' to distinguish them from his serious novels, but writing 'entertainments' freed Patrick to find his true voice. By the time *Master and Commander* appeared, O'Brian was fifty-six—almost at the end of the 'middle years' as we have conventionally defined them in Chapter 6. The series itself did not become a popular success until he was in his seventies. His twenty completed Aubrey-Maturin novels are as much a product of an ageing consciousness as Wesley's ten.

'Entertainments' they may be, but in a thousand small ways, O'Brian's stories acknowledge the hard realities of life. Boys' adventure writer Charles Gilson (who had seen active service in the Boer War and whose stories Patrick had read as a youngster) never mentions that after the exhilaration and fear of combat men typically experience adrenal exhaustion, felt as depression. By contrast, O'Brian (who had never fought in any war) knew that even the 'Iron Duke' (Arthur Wellesley, Duke of Wellington, Mary Wesley's distant relative) had burst into tears as he listened to the roll call of officers killed at Waterloo—many of them known to him personally. Confident and optimistic though he is, O'Brian's hero Jack Aubrey frequently feels this leadenness of spirit after a glorious victory. Such a phenomenon has no place in the world of Gilson, Henty, or Ballantyne—though it was well known to R. L. Stevenson, who, like Lord Byron, suffered from bipolar disorder and knew all about 'the black pit'. O'Brian's Jack is a man of action, but not a man of steel. It is precisely his human side, his anxiety, his times of embarrassment and humiliation, that invite us to care about him.

It is only as the journey of adulthood progresses that most of us come to appreciate heroes uncomfortably like our actual selves. Jack Aubrey is the adventurer Patrick O'Brian wished he could have been—but imagined with the capacities of the left hemisphere fully operational. Similarly, Stephen Maturin, Jack's close confidant and O'Brian's alter-ego, is also a flawed human being. Affectionate, a highly skilled surgeon with the enquiring mind of a true scientist, he is also prone to depression and sleeplessness, which (like Coleridge) he attempts to medicate with laudanum, becoming thoroughly addicted as the series progresses. Stephen's ongoing struggle against addiction lasts almost as long as his country's on-again, off-again naval war against France. Maturin's love for the beautiful, high-spirited Diana Villiers is an example of how a marriage straight out of Georgette Heyer's romances can be described with the self-knowledge O'Brian had painfully acquired over many years. Even after Diana accepts his offer of marriage, the paranoid Stephen takes many years to trust that she will not betray him—a state of mind that Patrick knew intimately. When O'Brian married Mary Tolstoi in 1945, he chose a woman who had previously been as much a magnet for men as Mary Farmar. Despite Mary O'Brian's dedication to supporting and nurturing her struggling writer husband, her willingness to put up with his black moods and to tolerate his extreme sensitivity to anything remotely critical, Patrick still feared that she might tire of him. Into his stories he put his fear of losing her ('the horror of the void')—making Diana susceptible to indulging in romantic 'flings', even after her marriage. Similarly, Jack's constant sense of unfairness and betrayal as time and again he is passed over for promotion reflects O'Brian's own longing for literary success, good reviews, awards, and splendid sales—all of which eventually came to him, but not until very late in his life. Significantly, Patrick 'promotes' his Jack Aubrey to Admiral only in his last completed novel, *Blue at the Mizzen*.

In his own life, O'Brian was powerless to modify his faults, and those who knew him in his final years remember the way he could, over drinks or dinner, shift suddenly from *bonhomie* to savage bitterness, from realistic modesty to outrageous fabrication. His relationships with his family of origin were distant or non-existent, and towards his own son, Richard, he could be unempathic and even punitive (not all that much better than his father, Charles Russ, had been with him). Like Caesar, the 'panda-leopard' hero he had created as a youngster, Patrick conducted his personal life as if surrounded by enemies, in a kill-or-be-killed world. His twelve-year-old story had contained a deep truth about himself, one that would never really be outgrown. While most of his earlier novels had foregrounded this battle for personal survival, O'Brian's writing in the last 30 years of his life was largely compassionate. Here is how Jack and Stephen first meet, while listening to a concert in Majorca. Jack Aubrey, who himself 'scrapes away at the fiddle' as a hobby, has been enthusiastically beating time to the music:

> 'The listener farther to the left was a man of between twenty and thirty whose big form overflowed his seat, leaving only a streak of gilt wood to be seen here and there. He was wearing his best uniform—the white-lapelled blue coat, white waistcoat, breeches and stockings of a lieutenant in the Royal Navy, with the silver medal of the Nile in his buttonhole—and the deep white cuff of his gold-buttoned sleeve beat the time, while his bright blue eyes, staring from what would have been a pink and white face if it had not been so deeply tanned, gazed fixedly at the bow of the first violin. The high note came, the pause, the resolution; and with the resolution the sailor's fist swept firmly down upon his knee. He leaned back in his chair, extinguishing it entirely, sighed happily and turned towards

> his neighbour with a smile. The words, "very finely played, sir, I believe" were formed in his gullet if not quite in his mouth when he caught the cold and indeed inimical look and heard the whisper, "If you really must beat the measure, sir, let me entreat you to do so in time, and not half a beat ahead".
>
> Jack Aubrey's face instantly changed from friendly ingenuous communicative pleasure to an expression of somewhat baffled hostility; he could not but acknowledge that he *had* been beating the time; and although he had certainly done so with perfect accuracy, in itself the thing was wrong. His colour mounted; he fixed his neighbour's pale eye for a moment, said, "I trust . . . " and the opening notes of the slow movement cut him short.'[19]

What Jack Aubrey experiences here is *shame*—the way we feel when we have been engaged on some activity that appears pleasurable and unproblematic, but which we suddenly realise has violated the expectations of others.[20] As if a maleficent fairy has cast a spell on us, what seems good, right, and innocent suddenly turns to something bad and wrong. Shame is what Patrick O'Brian himself had felt repeatedly throughout his life: shame, coupled with a fierce sense of insult and wish to 'bite back' at the person who had humiliated him. *Master and Commander* and its successors are full of scenes where misunderstanding and embarrassment temporarily fracture a relationship of mutual trust and respect. At times, Jack (and others), carried away by too much wine, or by the elation of a successful action, become boastful and indiscreet, saying things they later have cause to regret, and having to be saved by others from the consequences of their own ill-judged words. The 'highs' and 'lows' of both Steven and Jack are O'Brian's own, yet the overall effect is still one of serenity and well-being. Patrick O'Brian had finally achieved—at least in his fiction—the kind of balance between hope and despair that is necessary if we are to live a full life in our declining years. That balance became his enduring gift to his readers, a *mare pacificum* across which they could glide, propelled by the steady, unvarying Trade Winds, perhaps for ever.

Patrick would not live to see Russell Crowe play his beloved Jack Aubrey in Peter Weir's movie *Master and Commander*—a movie which, despite its name, is mainly based on *The Far Side of the World*.[21] Inevitably the screen experience fails to convey the reading experience, and it would no doubt have deeply disappointed Patrick for that reason. The novels that translate best into movies are those where the characters and their actions are more important than the words in which they are described—in other words, novels shaped by the Old Brain. The movie can *show* the events and the people, bringing them to more vivid life than most readers can re-create them within the shadow-theatre of their own minds. But no movie can convey an author's distinctive 'way with words', the contribution of the left hemisphere. That is why *Jane Eyre* converts to the screen more successfully than *Pride and Prejudice*, which is so dependent on the witty, acerbic rise and fall of Jane Austen's highly individual voice, as she comments on what her characters are doing, thinking and feeling. It is also the reason why the movie versions of *Great Expectations* and *Gone with the Wind* are so much closer to readers' romantic mental reconstructions of the novels than they are to the actual texture of Dickens' and Mitchell's stories. Movies speak direct to the Old Brain of the viewer, subverting New Brain irony and self-awareness.

Just as surely as Mary Wesley's, O'Brian's stories demand mental 'work'. We are required to *think* about what is being said, and about what it means. Not the sort of style out of which we would expect an exciting narrative to emerge, and O'Brian will never be appreciated by those who demand instant action in the first few pages. Yet once we acclimatise ourselves to his world, Story takes over, sweeping the reader along in its imperious way. O'Brian's scenes of ship-to-ship combat are as vivid, exciting and involving as any in Forester's *Hornblower* novels. Patrick O'Brian had accomplished the very thing that (in his opinion) Joseph Conrad failed to do: to show readers the complexities of human nature, while still allowing a narrative to 'have its head'.[22] As the Aubrey-Maturin series progresses, the characters become familiar and loveable—loveable in their eccentricities, even in their failings. Older readers, aware that they, too, have fallen short of their own ideals, have sometimes acted despicably or stupidly, can 'forgive themselves' through Jack and Stephen—even through that memorable Able Seaman 'Awkward' Davies. This is what Aristotle meant when he spoke of catharsis—we are 'purged' of our own shame and guilt through watching others with whom we identify. Of course the purging is only temporary, but it is no less welcome for that. Temporarily, we have been raised to a higher plane of existence, 'lifted up where we belong'.

We have seen how many readers enter a state of trance while 'lost in a book', a deep connection occurring between their own unconscious world and that of the writer. When entranced readers encounter an author who also seeks to create an 'endless' experience, a powerful alliance is forged. And this is precisely what seems to have happened with the late novels of Patrick O'Brian. Jack and Stephen took on a life of their own, becoming, like Paul Scott's Ronald Merrick, almost independent of their creator, with lives that demanded to be followed year by year. And so the series ended up occupying the rest of Patrick O'Brian's life. He was about one third of the way through a first draft of his twenty-first novel when he died in 2000. No doubt, in time, we will see new 'Jack and Steven' adventures written by other hands, as we have seen new 'James Bonds', new Oz tales, sequels to *Pride and Prejudice* and *Rebecca*, German continuations of Enid Blyton's *Mallory Towers* series, and Jean Rhys' 'prequel' to *Jane Eyre*, *Wide Sargasso Sea*. The human need to keep loved stories going, to extend them forwards and backwards through time, is compelling. The struggle between Old Brain and New over conclusions continues. It is tempting to speculate that the Aubrey-Maturin sequence recreates Patrick's own experience of 'endlessness' on a real beach at Seaford, so many years before: 'the rhythm of your steps and the half-heard incessant thunder of the sea induced that trance in which one can go on and on forever, singing perhaps, or talking to the air.'[23]

The Dream of Immortality

'When I grow up, I'm going to be the first man to live for ever and ever', says a ten-year-old Philip Marlowe in episode two of Dennis Potter's *The Singing Detective*.[24] And in his final television drama, the playwright made it come true. Writing shortly before his death, Potter explains how finding that he had only a few months to live transformed his vision of the world:

> 'Already, as I sat down on that first darkly early hour of the first morning, I had been unable to avoid the strange and rather disturbing feeling that things directly in front of me were somehow *presenting* themselves to me . . .
>
> The rim of the coffee-cup, the faint seagull-wing cusp made by the slant of light on top of the coffee, and the pleasurable surprise in finding the fold of the bedsheet should be just like that. The hard edge of the continent that was my desk, the emptiness of the paper, the wonderful slithers and curls to make with the ups and downs of letters and punctuation marks, and, above all, the curious little bite as the fine-tipped pen I work with made contact with the crisply waiting paper! . . . A paring down to what was precisely here, precisely now in the very present tense itself, full stop.'[25]

Potter's words reiterate themes that should now be very familiar to us. 'Things were *presenting* themselves to me' is reminiscent of Coleridge's vision of Xanadu; 'the wonderful slithers and curls' of the letters recalls Dickens' and Jefferies' delight in the physical appearance of words on a page (or tombstone); here again is the 'close-up vision' of early childhood as conveyed by Dickens and Dahl. Here, without a shadow of doubt, is the way the unaided right hemisphere experiences the world: *here and now, present tense, all new and all true.*

Human beings can access this experience through meditation and other spiritual practices; they can experience it in episodes of fever or sensory deprivation; drugs of hallucination can replicate it to some degree; and so can the so-called 'Near Death Experience'. All of these different pathways lead to the same end: to neutralise the self-conscious left hemisphere, and to restore a state of being in which the world impacts on us directly, wonderfully, and meaningfully, without any *thinking* being involved, a state which Stevenson rightly says is essentially an 'animal' way of being, life as experienced by the Old Brain. William Golding attemptedto convey that state in his poetic vision of the Neanderthal people in his second novel, *The Inheritors*—perhaps the least appreciated of his brilliantly imaginative novels. Knowing that he would soon die restored Dennis Potter's sense of living in what Janet Frame called the 'Is-land'.

When he was first diagnosed with pancreatic cancer, Potter had been at work on a new six part TV drama, *Karaoke*. Realising that time was short, Potter reconceived the piece as the first half of a larger eight-part drama which would now be his farewell to his audience. 'Performers' perform to the very end—and so great is their need to be in control that they may even need to 'stage' their own deaths. In *Karaoke*'s devastating sequel, *Cold Lazarus*, Dennis Potter produced one of the most confronting visions of resurrection ever conceived. Its razor-sharp edge came from Potter's knowledge that he was, essentially, staying alive just long enough to finish it. A morphine pump kept him sufficiently free of pain to complete both scripts and even to discuss production details, before he died. It was 1994, and Potter had not yet reached his sixtieth year. The two linked dramas were first broadcast two years later.

Karaoke is set in the present, and as we saw in our last chapter, its protagonist is a TV scriptwriter, Daniel Feeld, who has just been diagnosed with the same cancer as Potter himself. We see Daniel actively investigate the possibility of preserving his body through cryogenic (deep freeze) technology in the hope that perhaps he might be revived at some time in the distant future. He decides to leave his money to the 'tart with a heart', Sandra, who finds it hard to believe he is serious. The final scene of *Karaoke*, where Daniel's agent and his producer join Sandra around the dying man's hospital bed, is actually seen only in the sequel, *Cold Lazarus*. *Karaoke* itself ends with a scene in which Daniel engineers the shooting of underworld boss Arthur 'Pig' Malion (a stand-in for the tramp who abused the young Daniel Feeld, himself a stand-in for Uncle Ernie, who abused the ten-year-old Dennis Potter). Like Mary Wesley, Potter was dedicated to gaining fictional revenge on those who had wronged him in life.

In *Cold Lazarus* the 'distant future' has actually arrived. It is 2394, and Daniel Feeld's attempt to engineer his own resurrection has been hideously perverted. His body has vanished, and only his head remains, preserved in a black tank hooked up to trailing wires and feed-tubes (as Potter himself was connected to a morphine pump). In their laboratory, a group of scientists are trying to access Daniel's memories by chemically stimulating key areas of his brain. Random scenes from his past come to life as 'movies' on a huge wall screen[26], and the media barons of the future (including a thinly disguised Rupert Murdoch) hover greedily, sensing the commercial possibilities in turning Daniel's most intimate moments into mass entertainment—millions worldwide can now watch 'the actual life of a human being' who lived 400 years before. The scientists realise, at first with shock and discomfort and then with fear and self-reproach, that Daniel's disembodied head is actually *aware* of what is being done to it, and that 'Daniel' even has some *control* over his memories. They are forced to accept that their experiments are not benign, that they are actively causing suffering. Daniel's wished-for immortality has become a living nightmare—much as Dean Swift's immortal 'Struldbrugs' in the Third Voyage of *Gulliver's Travels* have turned into shrivelled creatures for whom every moment of continued life is an agony.

The image of a disembodied head kept alive by technology is not one that Potter invented. One of Roald Dahl's most famous short stories—originally called 'Abide with Me' but later retitled 'William and Mary'—concerns William, an academic who (like Potter) has terminal pancreatic cancer. William makes an agreement with an eminent brain surgeon that after death, his brain will be detached from his dead body, and preserved in a bowl of fluid. William will, the surgeon believes, recover consciousness after some days and retain most of his normal brain functions. Bizarrely, he will also retain a single eye, attached by a nerve to his brain.[27] William is at first disgusted and alienated by the proposal, but surprisingly soon agrees to it. After William's death, his long-suffering wife Mary is contacted by the surgeon, who invites her to go and see 'it' (as, to her horror, the specialist calls William's brain). Mary herself calls the brain 'he', which somehow seems just as horrifying.

> 'He was far larger than she had imagined he would be, and darker in colour. With all the ridges and creases running over his surface, he reminded her of nothing so much as an enormous pickled walnut. She could see the stubs of the four big arteries and the two veins coming out from the base of him and the neat way they were joined to the plastic tubes; and with each throb of the heart machine, all the tubes gave a little jerk in unison as the blood was pushed through them.'[28]

However, Mary adapts with remarkable speed, glimpsing the possibility of taking 'him' home with her, thus gaining revenge for his years of controlling, dismissive behaviour. We are left in no doubt that William's future existence will be very different from the one he confidently expected when he arranged for his brain to be kept alive, and that in fact a kind of 'living Hell' may well be in store. Here, then, is much of the scenario Potter has imagined in *Cold Lazarus*, but the image has a more complex history still. Dahl himself probably took the disembodied brain idea from Curt Siodmak's horror movie *The Lady and the Monster* (1944) filmed again ten years later as *Donovan's Brain* (1953). Had Dahl seen either movie? Or read the crudely-written thriller (1942) on which the movies were based, and then forgotten it completely?[29] Alternatively, could he have derived the 'disembodied brain' image from C. S. Lewis' *That Hideous Strength*, published just a year after Siodmak's original movie, in 1945? As we saw in our last chapter, the nature of memory makes issues of 'originality' somewhat pointless, but what remain fascinating are the subtle ways in which the basic image alters in the hands of different writers.

Lewis's own use of the image is more overtly horrific than either Dahl's or Siodmak's. His heroine, Jane, has had a series of dreams which, it becomes increasingly obvious, are prescient. In one of them, she 'sees' through the eyes of her husband, the ambitious Mark, who has become involved with the sinister National Institute for Co-Ordinated Experiments (NICE).

> 'I thought I saw a face floating in front of me. A face, not a head, if you understand what I mean. That is, there was a beard and nose and eyes—at least, you couldn't see the eyes, because it had coloured glasses on, but *there didn't seem to be anything* above the eyes. Not at first. But as I got used to the light, I got a horrible shock. I thought the face was *a mask tied onto a kind of balloon thing. But it wasn't*, exactly. Perhaps it looked a bit like a man wearing a sort of turban . . . I'm telling this dreadfully badly. What it really was, was a head (the rest of a head) which had had the top part of the skull taken off and then . . . then . . . as if something inside had boiled over. *A great big mass* which boiled out from inside what was left of the skull. Wrapped in some kind of composition stuff, but very thin stuff. You could see it twitch. Even in my fright I can remember thinking, "Oh, kill it, kill it, put it out of its pain". But only for a second because I thought the thing was real, really. It was green looking, and the mouth was open, and quite dry . . . Yes, it had a neck and a sort of collar thing round it, but *nothing below the collar, no* shoulders or body. Only these hanging things. In the dream I thought it was some kind of new man that had only head and entrails. I thought all those tubes were its insides. But presently, I don't quite know how, I saw that they were artificial. Little rubber tubes and bulbs, and metal things too. I couldn't understand them. All the tubes went into the wall. . . . Then came the most horrible thing: the mouth began to dribble. I know it sounds silly, but in a way I felt sorry for it because *it had no hands* and couldn't wipe its mouth. [Italics mine][30]

The brain is that of a French murderer, Alcasan, kept alive in a very similar way to William's, and Donovan's (in Siodmak's thriller), so that The Head (as the leaders of the NICE call it) can actually speak, once the taps are turned on. However, the consciousness that animates The Head is not that of the dead criminal, but, chillingly, the voice of an evil spiritual power, the 'dark eldil' who rules Earth, and the instructions that it gives to its devotees are increasingly frightening. As the novel comes to its bloody climax, the Head begins to speak *without* the technology that supposedly sustains it: 'Adore', it commands the initiates who stand before it. Then it begins demanding that its worshippers 'bring me another Head'. In their frenzy to obey, they struggle to decapitate each other, until terror, fire and death overwhelm them and their whole evil enterprise.

Mary's view of William's brain has the same 'close up vision' on which we commented earlier in this volume, with its detached, factual quality ('all the tubes gave a little jerk in unison'), and the same 'moue' of disgust for the physical body ('an enormous pickled walnut') that hovers at the edge of all Dahl's writing. Lewis, whose experience of combat in 1917 had been very different to Dahl's in 1941, had probably seen the 'greenish' colour of real heads, blown from their bodies by the force of a shell and left to decay in no-man's land. Lewis's description is less detached than Dahl's, less 'coolly in control', more emotive. And, unlike Dahl's, it has embedded within it the 'dying fall' of the repeated negative, the effect of which we've seen so often in this book. However, the descriptions do have one striking common factor: *both invite pity for the poor disembodied 'thing' which is so helpless and vulnerable* ('Oh kill it, kill it, put it out of its pain!'), and this theme too is continued in *Cold Lazarus.*

In fact the image of the severed head is far older than any of these examples. Lewis himself was almost certainly influenced by H. G. Wells' novel *The First Men in the Moon* (1901), in which the chief 'Selenite' has a huge head (suggesting a monstrously developed brain) dwarfing a tiny, vestigial body, and in L. Frank Baum's *The Wonderful Wizard of Oz* which had appeared in the US the year before Wells' story, the Wizard sometimes appears as a disembodied head. In Chapter 4, we saw Gawain sever the head of the Green Knight—only to find that the body continues to function, and that the (green) head is still capable of speaking. In Greek mythology the great musician Orpheus was torn to pieces by the Maenads, but his severed head continued to prophesy. The modern versions of these traditional images simply add an element of futuristic technology to replace what authors of bygone times would have classed as 'magic' or divine intervention. But where Lewis and Dahl follow Siodmak in making their 'Heads' those of criminal or evil individuals, Potter is unique in allowing Daniel's 'head' to be that of a relatively normal person, with whom we have already established rapport and fellow-feeling. So we *must* feel compassion for it (or 'him'), not just fear and disgust at the process of artificially prolonging a grotesque parody of life.

The image of 'disembodied consciousness', from Orpheus and the Green Knight through to more modern examples, speaks to the universal human longing to survive physical death, but it has an additional, very particular meaning for story makers. As we've seen, the romantic egotist feels *cut off* from others not only by a sense of being different but also by a certain *clinical* detachment, a callous disregard for other people's feelings—Martin Lynch-Gibbon in Iris Murdoch's *A Severed Head* is a textbook example, later repeated in Charles Arrowby (narrator of *The Sea, The Sea*).[31] The creative artist's sense of entitlement to 'carve up' or 'exploit' other people as material for his or her fictional characters is one manifestation of this, a theme Patrick White highlighted in the title of his novel *The Vivisector* (1970).

In *Cold Lazarus,* Potter first invites us to feel shock and horror at the way the commercial interests of the future intend to turn Daniel's most personal memories into a sort of giant soap opera. But then we realise that Daniel himself has been professional exploiter of other people's private lives.. What

Potter wants us to understand is that writers *do* exploit others, not only by re-creating real people from their own lives as 'fictional' characters, but by exercising total *control* over these characters, deciding what they can say, and even what they think and feel, in the interests of 'art'. This is 'the Godgame', as John Fowles called it in *The Magus*.

In L. Frank Baum's fantasy, the wizard appears to Dorothy as a giant bodyless head on a throne, but the 'real' wizard is a funny little man who commands no magic at all—his power is all a sham, supported by his credulous subjects' belief in him, and the green-tinted glasses they wear that turn Oz into an illusory 'city of emeralds'. Baum's conception neatly suggests the 'inflated self' of the narcissistic personality (Oz's 'head' is in fact made of layers of paper, with a face painted onto it—as Jane first imagines in *That Hideous Strength*). Narcissists sustain their grandiosity through the adulation of others, and the 'spin' that they employ to gain it. The actual name 'Oz' probably owes its origins to Shelley's Ozymandias, in his poem of the same name.[32] Here, too, the head of the statue of the Great King has been separated from its body, but a legend on the pedestal still proclaims,

> 'I am Ozymandias, king of kings,
> Look on my works, ye mighty, and despair!'

The poem then concludes:

> 'Nothing beside remains. Round the decay
> Of that colossal wreck, boundless and bare,
> The lone and level sands stretch far away.'

Thus in Shelley's poem the severed head motif converges with the 'ruined place' image we met in Chapter 6. Both return to, and amplify, children's early preoccupation with damage, loss and negation that we discussed in Chapter 2. When this imagery of destruction and void returns in the work of romantic egotists, especially later in their lives, it suggests not only some acknowledgement of the destructive power within story makers themselves, but perhaps also an embracing of the inevitability, even the fitness, of death.

However, the image of the severed head also suggests to us a very different aspect of the romantic egotist's existence. These enlarged, exposed brains, 'boiling' out of their skulls, or 'twitching' grotesquely as serum or chemicals pump through the arteries that feed them, are Old Brain images for the extreme vulnerability felt by makers of fiction, who (as it were) amputate huge chunks of themselves and put these into their stories—then have to stand helplessly by while reviewers and readers savagely criticise, judge or condemn the thinly disguised selves they have created. Remember that story makers start life as highly sensitive children. Iris Murdoch refused to read any reviews of her many novels. William Golding made sure he was always abroad and uncontactable whenever a new work of his was to be published, and Dickens often did the same—substituting 'doing a geographical' for the purely mental process of dissociation. Many creative artists have depended enormously on the one or two totally reliable people in their world—Iris Murdoch's husband John Bayley, John Fowles' wife Elizabeth, Dickens' friend John Forster—to 'vet' the reviews, and to protect them from the judgments of what they perceive as an uncomprehending, unsympathetic world.

Whether they believe in a literal afterlife or not, most writers long for some kind of immortality. They hope that their stories will outlive them, just as most of us hope that we will live on in our children, and our children's children. But we personally will not survive our own death, nor is it right that we should do so. The message from Potter to Potter himself, and to all story makers, is as plain as Swift's: do not hope for immortality on this earth, or you may get more, terrifyingly more, than you bargained for.

Light at the End of the Tunnel

Dennis Potter allows just one glimpse of optimism in the bleak vision of *Cold Lazarus*. Fyodor, one of Emma Porlock's team, has been secretly working for an underground organisation which aims to restore 'reality' to the sanitised, controlled, commercially dominated existence of the twenty-fourth century. Fyodor manages to destroy the laboratory that has kept Daniel's head alive (another parallel with *That Hideous Strength*). Before he is gunned down himself, he shoots Daniel's head. It is not an act of violence. He has understood the agony in which Feeld now exists ('Kill it, kill it, put it out of its misery!'). As he dies, Daniel's final moments of consciousness are brought up on our TV screens (though not, presumably, on the wall screen in the laboratory, which ought not now to be functioning).[33] Though the images and memory fragments are Daniel's personal ones, the actual sequence corresponds with what those who have almost died repeatedly report. There is a very rapid 'rewind' through key moments from Daniel's life. Believably, these moments mix joy (a tender sexual encounter with 'Beth', who will become his wife) and terror (ten-year-old Daniel hiding in a tree from the tramp who is about to abuse him), interspersed with fragments of hymns learned in childhood, understood then in a half-literal way, now, achingly, given a different and final meaning:

> 'When I wake with the blest
> In the mansion of rest
> Will there be any stars
> In my crown?'

The 'stars' in the hymn are meant to be the stars in the crown of the redeemed, but in the cruel reality of Daniel's end, they are the bullet-holes that shatter his brain and end his terrible half-life. This, for him, is 'the mansion of rest', and that interpretation is apparently confirmed by the consoling images that follow, as Daniel cries out ecstatically, 'Ye-e-e-e-es! Ye-e-e-e-es! Ye-e-e-e-es!'[34]

As in much of Potter's previous work, this ending is profoundly ambiguous. These cannot be the last moments of Daniel's 'life' in the laboratory, because his death then is instantaneous. Rather, we must be witnessing 'stored' images of his first 'death', in his hospital bed, back in 2394. Is Daniel entering an endless state of orgasmic bliss? Or is he merely conjuring childhood images of Heaven to comfort himself? We do not know, we will never know. Like the ends of all good stories, *Cold Lazarus* leaves us breathless, temporarily lifted out of ourselves into some higher state of being, fleetingly in touch with the ineffable. Here is 'outlift' in its most profound form—leaving us silent after we close the book, still seated as the movie credits roll, with the real world briefly transformed into something nobler—or at least, into something more meaningful and honest: *all new, and all true.*

The common features of the NDE (Near Death Experience), charted by experts and based on hundreds of interviews, are well established.[35] Most informants report a sense of travelling down a dark tunnel and emerging into a preternaturally bright light. Sometimes (as in *Cold Lazarus*) the entry into the light is preceded by a rapid 're-run' of key memories ('my life flashed before my eyes'). In most reports the images are happy ones. The feeling throughout is one of calm, freedom from fear, and great joy. For all but a minority, the Near Death Experience is overwhelmingly positive. Most subjects have a sense of disappointment when they are 'told' (usually by spiritual presences) that they cannot stay in this blissful state, but must return to their earthly life, because it is 'not yet time' for them to enter their new life. Such an experience frequently triggers profound changes in the individual concerned: deepened spiritual awareness, heightened connection with others and, very commonly, disappearance of fear of death. The NDE usually occurs when a person has *literally* been close to death, but this need not be the case. Enid Blyton's account of what she experienced 'in her teens' under the influence of laughing gas at the dentist runs parallel with those we've been discussing, and so does William Golding's very Jungian 'big dream' towards the end of his life, in which he was 'given special knowledge' by an Old Man. Perhaps in both cases, the writers had simply converted something they had previously read about into an hallucination or a dream—it is impossible to be sure.[36]

The meaning of Near Death (and similar) experiences has been interpreted in very different ways. For those with a religious faith, the NDE proves that there is an existence beyond this earthly one. Others see the experience simply as an artifact of the dying brain, its form largely dictated by chemical changes caused by oxygen starvation. Certainly we are familiar with a process whereby the body generates endorphins to counteract extreme pain and fear, gently 'removing us' from our anguish to a place of peace and detachment—la belle *indifference.* This is what seems to happen when individuals 'dissociate' in response to trauma, and throughout this book, we have seen that something akin to dissociation may also occur even when no pain or fear is present. Such experiences form the physiological basis of 'outlift'. It is probably the endorphins called up by the dying brain that enable us—or at least some of us—to pass from life in relative peace. There is abundant evidence that hallucinations and 'spirit journeys' are shaped by the individual's *prior* beliefs and by *anticipated* images. In the case of our own culture, it may be that the Old Brain has taken a metaphorical 'cliché' ('there's light at the end of the tunnel') and transformed it back into the intense, absolute, inherently meaningful experience an infant would have felt. It is as if the right hemisphere is, in these moments, restored to its original dominance.

Of course it is possible that what actually happens may not exhibit the neat, story-like shape that witnesses report. For example, one informant comments that the NDE itself is timeless—it gets put into a sequence only as it is retold afterwards.[37] Perhaps the happy-ever-after story template is so ingrained in us that it reshapes our memories of this unique experience? Yet even extreme positivists must concede that accounts of NDEs are remarkably consistent. They normally to progress from darkness to light, from ignorance to knowledge, from fear to love and awe. It is the same underlying structure as we found in the proto-narratives of very young children in Chapter 2: from lack to abundance, from need to fulfilment, from damage to repair. But unlike those early stories, the Near Death Experience 'story' *does not then cycle back into lack, need and damage.* It has been converted into a 'proper story'. What remains with almost all of those who have been through the NDE is hope and joy. Whatever it is, and whatever it means, the Near Death Experience seems to be a story whose function is to comfort us, and what greater comfort could there be than a 'return to the beginning' of our lives as human beings, our very birth—where for the first time, we emerged from a 'profound dull tunnel' into a place of light, inhabited by mysterious, loving beings?

Even a twelve-year-old Patrick O'Brian (then Patrick Russ), precocious author of *Caesar, The Story of a Panda-Leopard*—seems to have heard about the NDE. He is able to project himself convincingly into his animal hero, Caesar, at the moment the latter realises he is dying:

> 'The light seemed to be fading, though I knew it was only afternoon, and I felt curiously aloof from my body, and felt no pain . . . my strength was ebbing fast, and I was weak like a little cub again. I looked at my wife, but I could not see her so clearly. I looked at her again, and she seemed very far off and misty, like my mother was when I saw her in the hut years before.'[38]

Patrick, a widely read boy, may simply have been imitating something he had found in a book, but it is also possible that his account contains an element of personal experience. Patrick had almost certainly experienced dissociation: his later writing is full of examples of feeling invisible and of looking at things as if from a remote vantage point. It was not a giant step for him to use these experiences to imagine the ebbing of life. Even the way that Caesar's mate seems to blend with the image of his mother from the distant past echoes the way that many survivors of the NDE report that they encounter loved ones after they have left their physical bodies behind, and recalls the way that Solveig in Ibsen's *Peer Gynt* blends the roles of wife and mother as Peer dies, cradling his head on her lap, and singing a lullaby.

In Roald Dahl's final children's story, *The Minpins*, Little Billy will soon be too grown up for magic, and is taken for a final flight on Swan's back:

> 'Swan flew through the night for what seemed like hours and hours until they came to a gigantic opening in the earth's surface, a sort of huge gaping hole in the ground, and Swan glided slowly round and round above this massive crater and then right down into it. Deeper and deeper they went into the dark hole. Suddenly there was a brightness like sunlight below them, and Little Billy could see a vast lake of water, gloriously blue, and on the surface of the lake, thousands of swans were swimming slowly about. The pure white of the swans against the blue of the water was very beautiful.'[39]

Tellingly, Dahl—writing close to the end of his own life—evokes the image of a 'hole in the world', but then makes the tunnel lead to 'brightness like sunlight'. It is almost as if this big, bullying, yet childlike man is trying to repair the great sense of loss and damage that he, and almost every other story maker, has felt lifelong, and to transform it into a vision of abundant life and beauty.

Indeed, many story makers seem, in their final years, to 'go back to the beginning' in one way or another. Paul Scott's final published work was a retelling of 'Cinderella'. Thomas Mann took up *The Confessions of Felix Krull, Confidence Trickster* (begun nearly half a century before) and published it (albeit only as 'Part One' of a work he'd originally conceived as much longer). William Faulkner's late-published *The Reivers* was a conscious revisiting of his own youth, and as his biographer says, 'All the harshness, the darkness, the violence was banished. The author was willing himself towards closure, recasting his past in a rosy glow'.[40] Now in his late seventies, British writer Alan Garner has returned to the Blytonesque protagonists of his first children's books, *The Weirdstone of Brisingamen* and *The Moon of Gomrath* and completed a 'Colin and Susan trilogy' with *Boneland* (2012), a piece of adult fiction. The drive to complete what has been left unfinished, to repair what seems somehow damaged, is very strong. Interestingly, writers who originally fictionalized their own early lives in early novels return, much later, to write actual autobiographies. Perhaps such writers experience a need to 'complete the circle' by restoring the 'facts' and making clearer the distinction between invention and literal truth in their earlier works—although, as scholars have repeatedly pointed out, 'factual' autobiographies can be as much shaped by the imperatives of story as any work of fiction.

Death and Her Brother

In his wildly inventive graphic novel series *The Sandman*,[41] Neil Gaiman creates a modern pantheon—not Gods, exactly, but personified abstractions whom he calls The Endless. Gaiman's 'immortals' (listed in birth order) are Destiny, Death, Dream, Destruction, Desire, Despair and Delirium. The operations and rivalries of this family impact on human lives in much the same way as Homer's feuding Olympians do. Gaiman's chief character is Dream (sometimes called Lord Morpheus), portrayed by successive artists as a tall, thin man in black who wanders moodily around his enormous, illusory domain, seeking happiness but never finding it. Dream is a remote figure who never gets his relationships with females right. He also manages to offend his manipulative brother Desire, leading inexorably to his own downfall in the climactic volume of the series, *The Kindly Ones* (1993). In Dream, Gaiman embodies key aspects of most story makers—for romantic egotists are betrayed by their own desire for perfection, which leads to inevitable disappointment, and alienates those who love them and try to nurture them. But story makers are not entirely defined by narcissism, for they also dreamers—visionaries, who see 'something better' than mundane reality, something new and true, a vision that can lift all of us into a heightened awareness of the nobility, as well as the tragedy, of the human condition.

Most readers would agree, though, that Gaiman's most memorable creation is not Dream, but his older sister—Death. The Endless are impressive, but (with the possible exception of Delerium, a touchingly innocent, scatter-brained little girl whose original name was 'Delight') they inspire little feeling in us. Death is different. Gaiman's masterstroke is to re-imagine the figure that we humans normally portray as gloomy and threatening—like the menacing black-hooded figure who dominates Bergman's movie *The Seventh Seal*. By contrast, Gaiman's Death is a pragmatic yet compassionate young woman with the spiked hair and tight black clothes of a 1980s 'Goth'. Almost everyone who speaks with Death becomes devoted to her, and when she reaches out her hand to them, they often take it willingly. In *Death: The Time of Your Life*, a young woman called Hazel asks Death what we would call 'existential questions': 'Look, um, *why* do we *hurt*? Why do we *die*? Why isn't life *good* all the time? Why isn't it *fair*?' Admitting that Hazel's questions are almost impossible to answer, Death nevertheless tries her best: 'If you never had the *bad* times, how would you know you had the *good* times? It's the *moments* that illuminate it [life] though . . . They make the rest of it matter.' At the end of this strange conversation, Hazel confides, 'I love you'. Death replies equably, 'I love you too', to which Hazel responds resignedly, as a patient might say to a therapist, 'Yeah, but you love *everybody*!' Death smiles and calmly replies: 'I know'.[42] Neil Gaiman's Death teaches us about life—which makes good sense, because it is knowledge of our inevitable death that gives shape and significance to our time on earth.

In a letter to his daughter Scottie, written towards the end of his life, F. Scott Fitzgerald said that what he had learned was 'the sense that life is essentially a cheat and its conditions are those of defeat, and that the redeeming things are not "happiness" and "pleasure" but the deeper satisfactions that come out of struggle.' He advised Scottie, 'You can get a hell of a lot of enjoyment out of whatever bright things come your way'.[43] I think that's what Death means too. Stories provide 'contrasts', they are 'moments out of time'. Temporarily, but sometimes unforgettably, they *make the rest of it matter.*

Conclusion

The Brain, the Tale and the Teller

The Nine Cities of Troy

In 1870 amateur archaeologist Heinrich Schliemann began to excavate a small windswept hill in Anatolia which he believed to be the site of the fabled city of Troy. He had first encountered Homer's story at the age of eight, via a book illustration, and it had stayed in his mind through his many years as a successful businessman. Schliemann's conviction was that the events of the *Iliad* had really happened, and he hoped to dig up the city that Agamemnon and his allies had besieged. Schliemann wanted the story of Troy to be real, and in this, he resembles all the inspired writers and entranced readers we have encountered in this book.

A crude and unscientific archaeologist by later standards, Schliemann drove a great trench through the hill of Hisarlik, aware that it consisted of the remnants of many cities, each superimposed upon the one before, but certain that the Trojan War and its larger-than-life, heroic participants would be found in the oldest layers. He settled on the remnants of a small, archaic citadel that we now call Troy II, the second earliest of the nine main cities that make up Hisarlik. In a shaft grave he found exquisite golden jewellery, including a magnificent headdress clearly intended for a queen, and he photographed his young Greek wife wearing the 'Jewels of Helen'. Schliemann needed to *perform* in real life the story he had first encountered as a child. We now know that the 'Jewels of Helen' were a thousand years too early for Homer's tale. Romantic egotists try their best to make life conform to story, flying in the face of the hard realities of human existence. We would not be human if we did not dream, or distort facts to fit the shape we desperately need them to have. Though he wrote no fiction, Heinrich Schliemann was a story maker. In fact the Troy of the *Iliad* was probably the city we know as Troy VI—modern dating technology, as well as its fine limestone walls, suggest it—but Schliemann would have felt deeply disappointed that 'his' Troy was not Homer's.[1]

The builders of each new 'Ilios' levelled most of the above-ground structures of the preceding city, but incorporated its building materials into their own. Because each city grew on the foundations of the preceding one, Ilios gradually grew higher—a process that happened with many ancient cities, from Mesopotamia to Yucatan. The evolution of the brain has followed somewhat similar principles. The limbic system has grown around the brain stem, the cortex around the limbic system. The older systems still function, operating in parallel with, and sometimes in conflict with, the newer and more sophisticated ones. Newer emotions (newer in evolutionary terms) use the same neural pathways as older ones. Throughout this book we have seen how human storytelling reflects this curious and sometimes contradictory structure, calling up compelling, survival-oriented feelings from our animal origins while simultaneously appealing to our 'higher' capacities for empathy, compassion, self-regulation and reflection.

It is these survival-oriented feelings which account for the primitive power of story—its ability to pull us in, and to carry us along at breathless speed towards its end, as if we were personally engaged in a quest. In the survival plot, which harnesses the primitive emotions of rage and fear, that quest is generally to escape from enemies or defeat them; in the mating plot, the quest is to win the love of a desirable partner, or cope with losing that partner—so joy, care and grief play a more prominent part. The Old Brain, lacking self-observing consciousness, 'merges us' with fictional characters: the question of their 'realness' does not arise, nor does the issue of how much they resemble (or fail to resemble) us. Once mirror neurons fire, we simply 'feel with' them. Their goal is ours, we want them to succeed, and feel devastated when they are cut down, their goal unachieved. We resonate with story characters exactly as we resonate with our team when it is winning or losing that decisive game.

Human memory in some respects also resembles the layered cities of Hisarlik. New experiences are, broadly, retained to the extent that they resemble earlier ones. Freud hypothesised that our fragmentary memories of early childhood—often of seemingly unimportant details—may act as 'screens', standing for earlier, more disturbing memories buried beyond conscious recall.[2] The 'jewels of Helen' belonged to a time far earlier than the period Homer chronicled—to a time even Schliemann would have assumed to be too crude and primitive for such consummate craftsmanship. Similarly, our earliest, un-languaged memories may be just as compelling, just as 'true', as those we can date to particular ages after we acquired the gift of speech. The emotions we feel as mature adults can momentarily re-create the infant experiences we first associated with those emotions. The very *words* we use to articulate our feelings may echo much earlier experiences, lost to conscious memory.

Few of us can remember the first stories that our parents read to us, or the first ones we saw on television, but though their content is lost without a trace, their form, repeated over and over seems to stick: it is the *shape* of story that we take with us out of childhood and never lose. What is that shape? Story seems to rise out of the simple but powerful alternation of opposite states (broken/fix it; happy/unhappy). Yet a well-formed story needs to be much more than simply a series of actions and reactions—it needs to have a *mind* at work in it. As Benjy's section of *The Sound and the Fury* shows us, baldly narrated events and sense impressions do not make a story, though they can *hint* at it. There must be a protagonist—someone with whom a listener, reader or viewer can temporarily merge—and the sequence of events in which we 'live as the protagonist' must make enough sense for us to *want* to continue to 'be' them. There must be a sense that we are 'going somewhere'—even though we won't necessarily know where. In this way, a successful story must re-create in us the sensations of 'seeking' that we share with other creatures.

Aristotle's celebrated pronouncement that a story must have a beginning, a middle and an end is more than just a statement of the obvious. An end that follows too fast upon a beginning frustrates us; a conclusion that is inconsistent with its beginning seems wrong. 'Middles'—which may extend to hundreds of pages in long psychological novels—give conclusions their impact. If we don't get lost along the way, we will not experience the relief (or sadness) that comes when we emerge from the forest and back into the cleared ground of 'real life'. Children, even adolescents, struggle with 'middles', and many writers need to have reached 'the middle of the journey of their lives' before they can make their fictional middles credible.

While story beginnings are a kind of birth—the opening of a door onto a vivid, mysterious yet also potentially overwhelming new world—endings are a kind of death. Both inspired writers and entranced readers find endings difficult—and indeed, most of us seem to find them difficult. Audiences in movie theatres get up and leave as soon as the credits start to roll, leaving themselves no time to absorb the emotional impact of the cessation of a world they have just been absorbed in. Television programmers play ads for the next week's episode over the closing credits of this week's, or run a voice-over about something completely different. Such behaviours point to a powerful wish to deny or minimise the impact of an ending, as if we are saying to ourselves, 'Well, don't worry, it was *just a story*.'

A Tale of Two Hemispheres

The differential functioning of the brain's two hemispheres explains a series of dichotomies that have succeeded one another over two millennia. The ancients contrasted 'passion' (the domain of Dionysus) with 'moderation' (the province of Apollo), valued God-given 'inspiration', yet feared it as 'madness'. Classical and medieval scholars categorised literature as *dulcis* (pleasurable) or *utile* (useful)—the start of a long tradition in which experts valued instruction over 'mere entertainment'. Bruner's and Turner's recent interpretations of narrative as a fundamental 'mode of thought'—almost a problem-solving device—are an attempt to move Story from *dulcis* to *utile*.[3] To be sure there is much to be learned from stories—at least, from *some* stories—but that is not why they come into existence. We can distil a meaning from them—as Aesop and La Fontaine did in the final lines of their fables—but that leaves the stories dead: Janet Frame's 'shrivelled skin' of something once living. Stories are *alive*; they offer us *experiences* in an analogue world. Their meaning transcends and bypasses reasoned enquiry and conscious communication.

The successive dichotomies I've just listed are not identical with one another—nor with Freud's 'unconscious' and 'conscious'—but all of them echo the underlying structure of the bicameral cortex: the holistic, emotion-suffused, survival-oriented right hemisphere, which 'performs' in order to communicate, and its partner, the analytical, reasoning, self-conscious left, which 'interrogates' instead. The right hemisphere is not *unconscious*—but it is un-*self*-conscious—its 'self' is embedded in the world. By contrast, the left hemisphere experiences itself as a *spectator* of the world, breaking down the holistic perceptions of the right in order to build up a 'truth' from the individual parts, and linking them according to logical principles. The right offers us wholes, and stories are *wholes.*

A fragment of a story—a beginning without an end, or a beginning and an end without a 'middle'—is at best tantalising, at worst frustrating and disappointing. I reject the current trend in some circles to categorise as 'stories' simple statements like 'I opened the refrigerator and found a couple of eggs'[4] or self-talk like 'I fail at everything I do.' Such statements *condense* experience, whereas stories are like Doctor Who's Tardis: bigger inside than they appear from the outside. Stories *expand* the mental spaces within which we customarily live, and in so doing, they invite our selfhood to expand too (of course we may reject their invitation, and frequently do).

Stories are driven by the right hemisphere's imperatives, and the experiences stories generate simulate a right hemisphere apprehension of the world: immersion in a dramatic, significant present-ness. Stories take us 'to the Is-land'. The observing left hemisphere knows that Story comes from somewhere 'outside' itself, which explains writers' consistent statements—literal or metaphorical—that their stories are 'dictated' to them, that their characters 'take on a life of their own'. It also helps to explain how certain successful stories (and the characters within them) become independent of the form in which they originally occurred. Highly successful stories (from the *Iliad* to *Twilight*) are told and retold; they are elaborated, and generate sequels and prequels by other hands. Rarely do the events and characters of New Brain stories become 'independent' in this way. Old Brain stories beget offspring, where those dominated by the New Brain—*Tristram Shandy, Middlemarch, Madame Bovary, Women in Love*—are left with the sterile dignity of childless adults.

But literary stories are *verbal* creations—representations *in language* of right hemisphere experience—and from its putative origins in right hemisphere patterned sound, language has evolved as a specialised function of the left hemisphere. Words must bridge the gap between individual tellers and their audience, otherwise the tale would not survive and flourish in the wider world. So left hemisphere arrangements of words must be chosen to convey right hemisphere patterns, visions, feelings. In the realm of Story, these arrangements of words are most often the ones we've called the 'oral style'—the style of Homer, of fairy tale, of romance—and of most bestselling fiction for adults. In this style, witches are wicked, princesses are beautiful and castles are strong because the Old Brain needs to recognise *any* enemy, *any* potential mate, *any* refuge. Except, perhaps, in courtship rituals, it has no time to be concerned with what differentiates one individual from another. Global, 'essentialist' language is the first one we learn, in the second and third years of life: hence *automatically* its words suggest our most basic perceptions: 'big', 'little', 'in', 'out', 'dark', 'light', 'up high', 'down low', 'clean', 'dirty', 'nasty', 'nice', 'open', 'shut', 'broken', 'fixed', 'safe', 'scary'. Such words (and phrases in which they are embedded) are foundational to Story, and recur at key moments even in highly sophisticated, New Brain novels, especially in their introductory and concluding passages.[5] When we read them as adults, these words reach back to *early* experiences, *universal* experiences—ones that few of us do not share.

So the stories of the Old Brain describe in 'formulas', expand fictional space and time by 'listing' (like the catalogue of ships in Book II of the *Iliad* and Melville's catalogue of whales in *Moby-Dick*) and populate their world with 'stereotyped' characters. They are narrated in the third person, by a narrator who 'channels' characters and events that seem to exist independently of authorial intention. Old Brain stories are told in relatively short, simple statements, with much repetition—a method that ought to strike us as 'slow' yet which actually invites 'onrush'. Reaching back to the 'first language of the right hemisphere', they tend to the rhythmical and the musical—to the mode of incantation. The ancient Greek *hystor* who stood in the marketplace and declaimed the 'news' to the gathered populace is still alive and well today, in the form of the voice-over narrators of documentary films and TV reporters reading from a teleprompter. Obviously, modern novels told in prose are much less musical, but the oldest language of the Old Brain survives in their dramatic, semi-metrical titles (often borrowed from well-known poems and journalistic clichés): *Death Comes as the End; Dreams Die First; Fame is the Spur; The Rainbow Comes and Goes; The Ebony Tower; The Jewel in the Crown.*

Art critic and historian Anton Ehrenzweig noticed many years ago that when we try to sing a piece of orchestral (or band) music, we can reproduce only the melody line and the rhythm: the bass, the harmonies, the counterpoint are impossible for a single voice to incorporate.[6] Similarly, in the grip of a successful story, we skate faster and faster over the individual words, skim over (or even skip) lengthy descriptions, notice details only subliminally, pay most attention to *what is happening*, relegate what remains of the left hemisphere's presence into *predicting what is likely to happen*. The plot, if you like, is the 'melody line'. The rest still enhances our enjoyment and participation, but we are largely oblivious of it. The New Brain, by contrast, requires that we engage with the 'orchestration' of a story rather than with its 'melody' or 'rhythm'. The New Brain notices particulars and asks how they relate to the whole. It demands the right to describe in a leisurely, attentive way, to conjure up precise pictures of anything and everything—from particular *places* to the thoughts and feelings of highly individual *characters*. It *slows us down*, instead of speeding us up. The syntax typical of New Brain stories operates in a very similar way. A complex sentence with main and subordinate clauses is a microcosm of the left hemisphere's mode of operation—synthesising a whole out of individual parts, and requiring us to 'multi-task' to make sense out of it.

Thus it is not surprising that literary criticism (a left hemisphere creation) prefers New Brain stories, and is most useful when it analyses them. The left hemisphere has little to say about Story, and if it does, often seems embarrassed by it. Literary criticism works *against* the key experiences of Story, or at least strongly modifies them: it invites us to stand apart from characters and evaluate them, instead of *feeling with* them as they undergo their trials. No wonder that students who as adolescents devoured *Wuthering Heights* or *Gone with the Wind* often claim that literary analysis 'tears stories apart'. It is perfectly possible to put stories together again, and then re-read them with enhanced appreciation, but relatively few of those who study literature in school or college achieve that semi-conscious juggling between right and left hemispheres, and the majority of adults avoid novels (and movies) that pose too much left-hemisphere challenge, or give them up after a few pages as 'too slow'. Insofar as the formal study of literature can achieve anything, it can at least help a minority of us to persist long enough with a New Brain novel to allow it to 'grow on us' and begin to feel significant—which may take a hundred pages or more.

The 'inspirational' part of the writing process remains forever beyond the grasp of the pragmatic left hemisphere. Shaped and elaborated by cognition though they inevitably are, stories arise from *experiences*. At the oldest evolutionary levels of the brain, there is no distinction between emotion and thought, 'affect' and 'cognition': they are two sides of the same coin. Stories do not arise from the conscious wish to solve a problem, or to teach a lesson, but well up automatically, taking shape in ways that remain beyond the hegemony of consciousness. Inspired writers cannot fully control 'their' stories, and nor can entranced readers control their experience of those stories. Like coming to orgasm, falling in love, giving birth or growing old, they feel as if 'meant to be': *stories unfold with a sense of inevitability.* In this way, they recapitulate or anticipate the profound experiences that we all share.

Inspired Writing

I believe that the urge to make stories arises in individuals out of a (right hemisphere-inspired) painful awareness of damage or impasse, in the same way that an oyster coats an irritating grain of sand with smoothing pearl. Stories sense loss and defend against it, recognise 'holes in the world' and fill them, acknowledge the inevitability of death and yet invest life with meaning, celebrate beauty and joy, yet grieve their inevitable loss. The formal artistry of the story grows around, and defends against, the irritants of loss, shame, ugliness and bewilderment. Without them, there would be no story. The most powerful apprehensions of these things occur early, because childhood is when we are at our most impressionable, most open to each and every event that happens to us. Most stories deal solely with adult experience, and make no overt reference to childhood—but they are *driven by* childhood experiences, whether those experiences are part of the story's content or not.

Future story makers begin life with a high level of genetic sensitivity and a high level of intelligence, a combination that lends an edge to the experiences they share with many other children. It makes them 'good noticers' of tiny, significant details, 'good rememberers' of every event, magnifies the importance of shame, fear, and joy. But almost all of these traits are typical of creative children in general. What is it that propels some creative children towards story making instead of music, painting, or scientific quest? Seemingly, these children learn very early that experiences can be mastered, though not necessarily made sense of, by *articulating them in words.* Yet despite this contribution from the language-wielding left hemisphere, these children retain lifelong the right hemisphere's preference for analogical communication, preferring to 'perform' instead of 'interrogate', to '*be* someone' instead of just reading *about* that 'someone', to daydream better worlds in a 'place of greater safety', and ultimately, to *tell a story* that reflects the themes of their own lives and personalities, but appears (both to them and to others) to be about others. I find it plausible that such children instinctively respond to the *form* of story, and that, in their pretend play, they adopt the third person ('he walks and walks until he comes to a . . . ') instead of the first person. Later, these children are entranced by the content and wording of *particular* fictions, revisiting them again and again. They strive to re-create these stories by becoming authors themselves: *stories make us make stories.*

Samuel Coleridge's 'Kubla Khan' begins in the third person, and almost, but not quite, begins to tell a story. That section breaks off at the point that the poet was interrupted, and 'lost' the inspired wording of his original vision. When he returns to the poem, he has shifted to the first person:

'A damsel with a dulcimer
In a vision once I saw'

Now the left hemisphere must 'round off' and 'complete' what the right left timeless and unfinished. But Coleridge manages to put all his longing for that 'lost domain' into his magical, musical final lines:

'Could I revive within me
Her symphony and song,
To such deep delight 'twould win me
That with music loud and long,
I would build that dome in air,
That sunny dome! Those caves of ice!'

For Coleridge, and for most story makers, the act of creation is an act of re-creation, making a 'vision' real. It is the music of patterned words—the primal language of the right hemisphere—which gives lift and life and inevitability to something that the poet originally *saw.* Significantly, too, Coleridge fuses the 'singer of tales' with his 'flashing eyes' and 'floating hair' with the mystic or the Sybil, for in the world of the right hemisphere, the divine is immanent. Godhead speaks through the singer and the maker of tales.

'Weave a circle round him thrice
And close your eyes with holy dread
For he on honey-dew hath fed,
And drunk the milk of Paradise.

Entranced readers become inspired writers. Their 'chosen stories' will channel some of their potentials (not others), and so foreshadow some aspects of their future lives. So badly do story makers need to make real what they have experienced only in imagination that they may 'remember' what never happened, and 'invent' something they once read but subsequently forgot. The nature of memory, subtly re-shaped each time it is called into being, lends itself to this plasticity, and makes 'plagiarism' an empty charge. Story makers take what they need, and may even lie and fabricate to protect the self-invented 'truths' of their lives and work.

Unlike most of us, story makers remember and document the stories that so fascinated them as children, as they remember and document *everything* of significance to them. Such activity requires a particular kind of self-preoccupation that we've called 'romantic egotism'. The narcissist we know from psychiatry believes he is supremely gifted and superior, entitled to do whatever he wants, no matter what the cost to others. Pain and emptiness may lie beneath that confident self-presentation, but they lie so deep that the narcissist is only occasionally and fleetingly aware of those black depths. By contrast, 'romantic egotists' are acutely conscious of their own pain, constantly nagged by the 'hole in the world' that signals their own imperfection. They pay close attention to their own thoughts, feelings and experiences (in a left hemisphere way) because they provide the raw material story makers can transform into a pearl—a work of art that will transcend their individual suffering, and perhaps even outlast their individual lives.

We have seen that the right hemisphere spontaneously produces images that represent emotions concretely in terms of *objects in space*. The 'door that opens' into wonder or mystery, the 'place of greater safety', the 'view from above', the 'ruined place' and the 'severed head' all represent particular experiences shared by romantic egotists and, I suspect, by their most devoted readers also. These images body forth the inner world of the romantic egotist in a way that no psychiatric textbook can ever do, and they are remarkably consistent from writer to writer, from culture to culture, and from age to age. I have little doubt that the unknown Sumerians who performed *The Epic of Gilgamesh* and the 'praise singers' who declaimed *The Iliad* were as much romantic egotists as Charlotte Brontë, Charles Dickens, F. Scott Fitzgerald or Thomas Mann—though of course this is impossible to prove. Left hemisphere imagery is specific and focussed, but right hemisphere imagery is holistic and essentialist, offering us a concrete experience that re-creates the story maker's own.

Entranced Readers

If only a fragment of a hologram is on show, that fragment will nevertheless embody the whole. When writers build their 'domes in air', the themes and dynamics of their individual personalities are embodied in each story's chapters, paragraphs, even sentences. *Le style, c'est l'homme même*: writers cannot but reveal who they are in the very *way* that they write. Essentially, each author's stories consist of the same encoded information, disguised as an evolving, ever-changing presentation of different information. Practised readers of fiction—not just Radway's romance readers—can intuit from a first paragraph something of the author's personality, and sense (intuitively) *whether it matches their own*. The brain's right hemisphere has evolved to make these kinds of matches, and it does so automatically and instantaneously, exactly as it does when we fall in love, or become addicted to heroin: the same brain chemicals and neural paths are involved in all three processes.

Of course the vast majority of stories are 'chosen' only at a general and superficial level—we pick up a novel or a DVD because we expect to be entertained for an hour, or several. Such choices involve little that is deeply personal, and the stories concerned may be rapidly forgotten. But in the case of what I've called 'chosen stories', the matching is profound. As when we fall in love, we unconsciously seek a protagonist who is both deeply similar to ourselves, and yet superficially different. What I've termed the 'projective, protective trance' operates to disguise the true nature of 'falling in love': we are drawn to someone whose deepest selfhood (secure or fragile) matches our own.[7] In the same way, when deep matching occurs in the literary domain, we are being 'pulled' towards stories that reflect *our own* personalities, our own life themes.

Romantic egotists repeatedly re-create *themselves* in their stories, from Gilgamesh and Odysseus through Coleridge's Ancient Mariner and Dickens' Pip Pirrip to Ursula Le Guin's Sparrowhawk and George Martin's Tyrion Lannister—proud, wounded wanderers who can also be egocentric and opportunistic. Often, the story maker splits him- or herself into two, as Thomas Mann does in *Joseph in Egypt*, the great novel of his middle years, where the author appears both as the gifted, manipulative young Joseph, and as Potiphar's wife, trapped within a sexless marriage to a good man, and inwardly tormented by her impossible passion for the handsome Hebrew. The world's enduring stories embody a deep split within the romantic egotist that is also a split within the human condition itself. Humans crave immortality but are denied it; long to be honourable and courageous, but fall short of their own ideals; dream of perfect love, but know it will not last. Does this split sound familiar? It should, because it echoes the split within our own brains: the epic sweep of the right hemisphere's global, essentialist vision, and the close-up self-conscious, death-conscious realism of the left.

Lifelike Stories and Storied Lives

We have seen how human lives across time resemble stories, and in turn, stories replicate the inherent structures of all organic life: bilateral symmetry, variation within limits, swings away from the norm and back to it—as Tylor suggested in 1871, and as Gregory Bateson more recently repeated, mind echoes nature.[8] Our lives are story-like, and our stories are life-like. To put it more precisely, though, *Old Brain* stories display the kinds of patterns that are displayed across time by *unexamined* lives (lives where conscious attention is not directed back onto those lives). This kind of patterning is evident in the spontaneous chants of children just mastering language; in the monologues of patients 'free associating' in psychoanalysis; and in the scripts of many television documentaries, with their free movement between past and present, their constant repetition of key themes, and their strong reliance on repetitive, emotive musical scores (Michael Wood's *In Search of the Trojan War* is an excellent example). They are displayed, too, in intergenerational family process, in which patterns recur across generations in a way that seems so eerie as it generates a kind of 'taboo'.

The stronger the influence of the left hemisphere, the less Old Brain stories—'survival plots' and 'mating plots'—will seem credible or acceptable. They will be relegated to 'cultural studies' or 'children's literature'. Under the dominance of the left hemisphere, pundits of the nineteenth and twentieth centuries evolved a conception of Story which set up 'truth to life' as its standard, while redefining 'life' to diminish its story-like features. Such a conception apes the approach of science, yet is *unscientific* in that it neglects or minimises the unconscious patterning that typifies human lives and which is mirrored in the magical thought that informs Old Brain story. While more recent postmodern approaches have eschewed unitary notions of 'truth' and avoided canonical judgements—emphasising instead the socially constructed, culturally relative, fragmented nature of human experience—they remain as much products of the left hemisphere as F. R. Leavis' 'Great Tradition' of novelists distinguished by their 'moral earnestness'.

Can Stories Teach? Can Stories Heal?

McGilchrist describes the left hemisphere of the cortex as 'pragmatic'. It is concerned with the *uses* of things, and values more highly those that it sees as serving a *purpose*. Hence society's continuing preoccupation, from Plato to Leavis, with what stories might 'teach' us—despite what we now recognise as their evolutionary origins as a form of play. My contention in this book is that we can *learn from* stories, but that what we learn will in large part be shaped by what we *bring to* them, a paradox that poet Randall Jarrell expressed eloquently in 'The Carnegie Library, Junior Division':

> 'We learned from you to understand so much about so many things
> But never what we were; and yet you made us that.'[9]

Entranced by Story has offered an argument for the powerful, largely unconscious connection that can occur between particular stories and particular readers, listeners and viewers. Yet that connection is not one that can be engineered or manipulated by teachers, librarians or therapists. Bibliotherapy will never be more than hit-or-miss.[10] Let's not be led astray by the currently fashionable proliferation of the 'narrative metaphor' in education, nursing and psychotherapy (among other disciplines). Assisting troubled individuals to fashion 'new narratives' of their own lives, ones that offer a richer understanding of self and a wider range of potential life choices, is an admirable goal. The 're-storying' of individual lives, crafted jointly by client and therapist, is a conscious, cognitive process, aimed at promoting more nourishing 'self-talk' in place of constant thoughts of negativity and failure.[11] But it is not to be equated with the unconscious, feeling-organised origins of story making as we've come to recognise them in preceding chapters. Like Lucy Sprague Mitchell's 'here and now stories' for pre-schoolers, such narratives do not draw on the powerful energies of the Old Brain. So yes, stories can heal, but not 'on demand', and the healing they offer is partial and unpredictable.

Operating alone, the left hemisphere literally has no concept of story, and at best, what it creates can only be a 'construction' in the original sense of that word.[12] Ira Levin's Stepford Wives look and sound like the flesh-and-blood women they have replaced, but when their smooth, perfumed skin is ripped open, the circuitry beneath is shockingly obvious.

Remembering and Foreshadowing

Though I am not a novelist, *Entranced by Story* has been driven by my own need to re-create beguiling, frightening and shameful experiences. In writing it, I have (I now see) been attempting to create a more perfect thought-world, to replace my own deeply felt imperfection. In my Introduction, I said that I knew roughly what this book would say before it began—in fact, I didn't. I also quoted Hans Andersen's words from 'The Snow Queen' ('When we get to the end, we will know more than we do now!') without realising how true his words would prove to be. Having written the book, I do indeed know more—far more—than I did when I began it. In this respect, at least, I've had an experience of 'inspired writing'.

Part way through the process of working on this book, I broke off to write the first half of a novel. It won't be a world-beater, but it is a story that is in me to tell. In a small, personal way, I have learned what it is like to be a maker of stories, and I hope that the readers of *Entranced by Story* will have learned something of that too. But this book is also an attempt at a unified *theory* of Story, one that will embrace the left hemisphere as well as the right, inspiration as well as analysis, the reader as well as the writer—grounded in what actual writers and readers, child and adult, have reported. I may prove to be as romantic and unscientific as Schliemann was when he excavated Troy, but I trust that, as in his case, later investigations will show that I got some important things right. Sometimes merely *remembering* a great story can elevate the spirit, *lifting us out* of our quotidian reality. Story makers' words *sing* in our heads, the images they conjure *shine* with preternatural radiance, their characters become *old friends.* Stories remind us of what being human is really about. *They make the rest of it matter.*

Notes

Notes to the Introduction

1 See René Welleck and Austin Warren. *The Theory of Literature*, Harmondsworth, Peregrine Books, 1963 [First published 1942]: 75ff.
2 See W. Hooper, Ed. *Of Other Worlds: Essays and Stories*, London, Bles, 1966: 3–21 [essay first published 1947].
3 'See 'Psycho-analysis and literary criticism' (1941) in C.S. Lewis, *They Asked for a Paper: Papers and Addresses*, London, Bles, 1962: 120–138.
4 See David Lynch, *Catching the Big Fish: Meditation, Consciousness and Creativity*, New York, Penguin, 2007: 61.
5 See Sigmund Freud, 'Creative Writers and Daydreaming' (1907) in Albert Dickson, Ed., *The Pelican Freud Library 14: Art and Literature*, Harmondsworth, Penguin, 1985; Christopher Booker, *The Seven Basic Plots: Why We Tell Stories*, London, Continuum, 2004; Simon O. Lesser, *Fiction and the Unconscious*, Boston, Beacon Press, 1957; Norman N. Holland, *The Dynamics of Literary Response*, New York, Oxford University Press, 1968.
6 See *The Origin of Consciousness in the Breakdown of the Bicameral Mind*, Princeton, Princeton University Press, 1976.
7 See *The Master and His Emissary: The Divided Brain and the Making of the Western World*, New Haven/London, Yale University Press, 2009.
8 See Paul D. MacLean: *The Triune Brain in Evolution, Role in Paleocerebral Functions*, New York, Plenum, 1990. I have also made use of Thomas Lewis, Fari Amini and Richard Lannon, *A General Theory of Love*, New York, Random, 2001; Louis Cozolino, *The Neuroscience of Psychotherapy: Building and Rebuilding the Human Brain*, New York, Norton, 2002 and R. Grant Steen, *The Evolving Brain: The Known and the Unknown*, New York, Prometheus, 2007.
9 Striking evidence of human brain stem reflexes typical of much earlier life forms is noted by Oliver Sacks in *The Island of the Colour-blind*, Sydney, Pan Macmillan Australia, 1996: 281–282.
10 See Richard Fortey, *Life: An Unauthorised Biography*, London, HarperCollins, 1997: 331–332.

11 See Leslie Rogers, *The Development of Brain and Behaviour in the Chicken*, Wallingford, CABI Publishing, 1995.
12 See Fortey, op. cit.: 67.
13 Ernest Raymond, *Through Literature to Life: An Enthusiasm and an Anthology*, London, Cassell, 1928; Roger Sale, *Fairy Tales and After: From Snow White to E. B. White*, Cambridge, MA, Harvard University Press, 1978; Francis Spufford, *The Child that Books Built: A Memoir of Childhood and Reading*, London, Faber, 2002.
14 See Jerome Bruner, *Actual Minds, Possible Worlds*, Cambridge, Harvard University Press, 1986: 14.
15 Mark Turner, *The Literary Mind*, New York and Oxford,Oxford University Press, 1996; 'story grammars' see Vladimir Propp, *Morphology of the Folk Tale*, Trans Laurence Scott; 2nd Edn, Rev and Ed. Louis A. Wagner, Austin and London, University of Texas Press, 1968. [First published in Russian, 1928.]
16 See Jaak Panksepp and Lucy Biven, *The Archaeology of Mind: Neuroevolutionary Origins of Human Emotions,* New York, Norton, 2012.
17 See Panksepp and Biven op. cit: 14.
18 See David Marr: *Patrick White: A Life*, Sydney, Random House Australia, 1991: 211.

Notes to Chapter One

1 '*War and Woe and Wonder*': my free translation of *Sir Gawain and the Green Knight*, ll. 16–20.
2 See Ruth Hirsch Weir, *Language in the Crib*, The Hague, Mouton, 1962. Excerpted in Peter Smith, *Play in Animals and Humans*, Oxford, Blackwell, 1984: 618.
3 See Richard Dawkins, *Climbing Mount Improbable*, Harmondsworth, Penguin, 1996: 33–63.
4 See Iain McGilchrist, *The Master and His Emissary: The Divided Brain and the Making of the Western World*, New Haven and London, Yale University Press, 2009: 102–105.
5 From Katherine Nelson, Ed., *Narratives from the Crib*, Cambridge, Harvard University Press, 2006: 162. [First published 1989.]
6 From 'Memoirs of Himself' in *Works of Robert Louis Stevenson,* Tusitala Edition, XXIX, 1887: 153.
7 See Shirley Brice Heath: *Ways with Words: Language, Life and Work in Communities and Classrooms*, Cambridge University Press, 1983: 86–103.
8 Such 'truncations' are common when young children retell or respond to adult-created narratives, and several examples are contained in Maureen and Hugh Crago, *Prelude to Literacy* (1983). Barbara Leondar's view is that young children do *attempt* to imitate formal beginnings and endings; see her 'Hatching Plots: Genesis of Story Making' in David Perkins and Barbara Leondar, Eds. *The Arts and Cognition*, Baltimore, Johns

Hopkins University Press, 1977: 172–190. It depends on what corpus of narratives one pays attention to: children asked to 'tell me a story' (as in Evelyn Goodenough Pitcher and Ernst Prelinger, *Children Tell Stories: An Analysis of Fantasy*, New York, International Universities Press, 1963, and Louise Bates Ames' *Children's Stories*, Genetic Psychology Monographs 73, Provincetown, MA, The Journal Press 1966) will almost certainly reproduce more aspects of 'well formed story' than are apparent in the spontaneous 'songstries' of a slightly earlier age. Brian Sutton-Smith's *The Folkstories of Children* (Philadelphia, University of Pennsylvania Press, 1981) does not specify how the stories were elicited, though it was most probably in the same way as both Pitcher and Prelinger, andAmes elicited theirs.

9 Janet Frame: *To the Is-land, Autobiography I*, London, The Women's Press, 1983: 19.

10 From Lucy Sprague Mitchell, *Here and Now Story Book*, New York, Dutton, 1921: 24.

11 See Barbara Leondar, op. cit.; Vladimir Propp, *Morphology of the Folk Tale*, Trans Laurence Scott; 2nd Edn, Rev and Ed. Louis A. Wagner, Austin and London, University of Texas Press, 1968. [First published in Russian, 1928.]

12 See Stephen A. Mitchell and Margaret J. Black: *Freud and Beyond: A History of Modern Psychoanalytic Thought*, New York, Basic Books, 1995: 174.

13 See Henri Wallon, *L'Evolution psychologique de l'enfant*, Paris, A. Colin, 1941, reissued 1974.

14 See Smith, op. cit.

15 See Brian Boyd, *On the Origin of Stories*, Cambridge, Harvard University Press, 2009: 177--187.

16 See Anne Wilson, *Magical Thought in Imaginative Writing*, Stroud, Gloucester., Thimble Press, 1983. Wilson's ideas are discussed in more detail in Chapters 2 and 3.

17 See for example Maureen Crago's evidence in *Prelude to Literacy*, Carbondale, IL, Southern Illinois University Press, 1983: 223–224; and Virginia Lowe's chart (Appendix 12) in her unpublished PhD thesis, Is This a Real Story: Young Children's Concept of the Reality Status of Stories and Pictures, La Trobe University, 1997: 448–449.

18 My comments on Homer's *Iliad* rely heavily on translations and commentators in English. I have made much use of Moses Finley: *The World of Odysseus*, 2nd Rev Edn, 1978, Harmondsworth, Penguin 1979; Albert B. Lord, *The Singer of Tales*, Cambridge, Harvard University Press, 1964; James C. Hogan, *A Guide to the Iliad, Based on the Translation by Robert Fitzgerald*, New York, Anchor Books, 1979; Bernard Knox, Introduction to *Homer: The Iliad*, translated by Robert Fagles, New York, Viking Penguin, 1990; and most recently, Andrew Dalby's *Rediscovering Homer: Inside the Origins of the Epic*, New York, Norton, 2006. Among the several

translations I have used, all with considerable virtues, I most heartily recommend Stanley Lombardo's recording of his own translation in *The Essential Iliad*, Parmenides Audio, 2006. This abridged version, on five CDs, contains approximately one-third of the complete poem.

19 My version, based on a literal English translation of *Iliad* lines 1–11.

20 See M. I. Finley, *The World of Odysseus*, Penguin 1979: 67.

21 See Andre Favat, *Child and Tale: The Origins of Interest*, Urbana, Illinois, NCTE, 1977.

22 See Finley, op. cit.: 114.

23 See Hugh Crago, 'The Unlearned Lessons of the Stories Children Tell', *Signal* 92, May, 2000: 94–118.

24 See Enid Blyton, *The Tale of Troy, The Story of the Siege of Troy* (*Stories from World History, Retold by Enid Blyton*), Kingsway Supplementary Readers. London, Evans Brothers, n.d. [1934]. Rosemary Sutcliff, *Black Ships Before Troy: The Story of the Iliad.* Illus. Alan Lee, London, Frances Lincoln, 1993.

25 See C. S. Lewis, *The Lion, the Witch and the Wardobe*, London, Bles, 1950: 122.

Notes to Chapter Two

1 Carolyn Steedman's *The Tidy House: Little Girls Writing,* London, Virago, 1982: 85ff, contains a fascinating summary of this period.

2 As Steedman, op. cit., points out, male diarists predominated prior to the twentieth century, whereas from the 1950s onwards almost all the diarists have been women.

3 White's book, first published by the New Zealand Council for Educational Research (Christchurch, Whitcombe and Tombs, 1954) was reprinted in 1984. Dorothy Butler, *Cushla and Her Books,* Auckland, Hodder & Stoughton, 1979; Maureen and Hugh Crago, *Prelude to Literacy,* Carbondale, IL, Southern Illinois University Press, 1983; Shelby Wolf and Shirley Brice Heath, *The Braid of Literature*, Cambridge, Harvard University Press, 1992; Virginia Lowe, *Stories, Pictures and Reality,* New York and London, Routledge, 2006. Article-length studies include: Virginia Lowe, 'Books and a Pre-Verbal Child, 3–18 Months', *Children's Libraries Newsletter* [Australia], *11, 3, 4*: 1975; Margaret Graetz: 'From Picture Books to Illustrated Stories: How Children Understand All Those Words, *Children's Libraries Newsletter* [Australia], *12*:3 (1976: 79–87.

4 Typically of studies by academic scholars of narrative, Katherine Nelson's edited volume *Narratives from the Crib,* Cambridge, Harvard University Press 1989, contains no reference in its index to 'stories', 'books', or 'picture books'. See also M. Baghban, *Our Daughter Learns to Read and Write: A Case Study from Birth to Three,* Newark, DE, International Reading Association, 1984; Marilyn Cochrane-Smith: *The Making of a*

Reader, Norwood, NJ, Ablex, 1984; J. A. Schickendanz, *Adam's Righting Revolutions:One Child's Literacy Development from Infancy through Grade One*, Portsmouth, NH, Heinemann, 1990: 117. Carol Fox's *At the Very Edge of the Forest*, London, Cassell, 1993, falls somewhere between the 'literary' and the 'literacy' camps, being essentially a study of young children's self-composed stories, comparable with those we examined in Chapter 1.

5 Shirley Brice Heath, *Ways with Words: Language, Life and Work in Communities and Classrooms*, Cambridge, Cambridge University Press, 1983.

6 Gabrielle Lord, *Shattered*, Sydney, Hachette Australia, 2008: 1.

7 See White, op. cit.: 22.

8 See the evidence collected in Maureen Crago, 'Incompletely Shown Objects in Children's Books: One Child's Response', *Children's Literature in Education 10* (1979): 151–157. Distress seems first to be felt in relation to real objects, then a year or more later, to be felt in relation to pictured objects. See also White op. cit.: 45–46, on Carol's reactions at age 3.6 to Lois Lenski's illustrations to Lucy Sprague Mitchell's *Fix It Please*, New York, Simon & Schuster, Little Golden Books, 1947. Contrary to her mother's interpretation, I suspect Carol was most probably made anxious by the *broken eggs* in this book!

9 See Melanie Klein, 'On Observing the Behaviour of Young Infants' (first published, 1952) in *Envy and Gratitude and Other Works*, 1946–1963, with an introduction by Hanna Segal, London, Vintage, 1997; first published by The Hogarth Press, 1975: 94–121. At various times, Klein referred to all three of her children in her case studies, under pseudonyms. See Phyllis Gross-Kurth: *Melanie Klein: Her World and Her Work*, New York, Knopf, 1986. In another paper, Klein reported on 'a child whom I know' who at the age of fourteen months exhibited a strong anxiety reaction to a headless fish, which he saw lying on the kitchen table (Gross-Kurth, op cit.: 78).

10 Klein, op. cit.: 113.

11 See M. D. S. Ainsworth, M. C. Blehar, E. Waters, and S. Wall, *Patterns of Attachment: A Psychological Study of the Strange Situation*, Hillsdale, NJ, Erlbaum, 1978.

12 This MS record (Cheshire Record Office, DSA, 75) is quoted in Steedman, op. cit.: 86.

13 See Jean Piaget, *The Child's Conception of the World*, Trans. Joan and Andrew Tomlinson, London, Paladin, 1973: 236ff [first published in French, 1926].

14 Adults whose sense of self is fragile will often smash objects. These actions do not simply express rage and frustration; such individuals seem to need to create a damaged object in the external world, as a correlate of their own sense of being 'damaged', and by doing so, somehow comfort themselves. Klein herself believed that broken or damaged toys signified adults (usually parents) in the child's life, whom the child conceived of as damaged by the child's own hostile feelings (see Gross-Kurth, op. cit.: 102).

15 Klein, op. cit.: 114.

16 'Who changeth not' is from the hymn 'Abide with Me', written by Henry Francis Lyle, 1793-1847; 'a place of greater safety': see Hilary Mantel's novel of the same name (London, Viking, 1992).

17 See Sylvia Anthony, *The Discovery of Death in Childhood and After*, Harmondsworth, Penguin, 1973: 55. [First published 1971.]

18 White, op. cit.: p. 152.

19 Enid Blyton quotation: 'Things I Don't Like', from her weekly 'From My Window' column in *Teachers' World*, Feb. 24, 1926.

20 See Crockett Johnson, *Harold and the Purple Crayon*, Hamondsworth, Penguin, 1972, openings 19, 20. [First published 1955.]

21 See Margaret R. Higonnet: 'Narrative Fractures and Fragments' *Children's Literature* 15, New Haven, Yale University Press, 1987: 37–54; Maureen and Hugh Crago, op. cit.: 206. Both children focussed on the question, 'How can he draw things in the air?'

22 See Nicolai Tolstoi, *Patrick O'Brian: The Making of the Novelist*, London, Century Books, 2004: 167–168.

23 Charlotte Brontë, *Jane Eyre*, London, The Folio Society, 1991: 83. [First published 1847.]

24 See 'A Chapter on Dreams' in *Across the Plains* (1892): 154.

25 See Marjorie Flack and Kurt Wiese, *The Story about Ping*, London, Bodley Head 1935 [first published 1933]. See also Maureen Crago, 'Missing Home, Missing Mother: One Child's Preoccupation with Their Location in Picture Books', *Orana 14*:3 (1978): 74–78.

26 White, op. cit.: 170; Carol's other comments on mermaids, ibid, 172.

27 See Louis Cozolino, *The Neuroscience of Psychotherapy*, New York, Norton, 2002: 184–186.

28 See Margaret Graetz, op. cit.: 85.

29 Alexander McCall Smith, *The Miracle at Speedy Motors*, London, Little, Brown 2008: 111.

30 See Robert Karen, *Becoming Attached: First Relationships and How They Shape Our Capacity to Love*, New York, Oxford University Press, 1998: 82–86.

31 Maureen Crago [unpublished diary] describes a child's strong emotional responses following phrases like 'they can *never be together again*' and 'the Boy sees what *no human eye will see again*' [italics mine] in Christopher Fry, *The Boy and the Magic*, London, Dobson, 1964. Similar reactions to purely verbal negativity can be found in other accounts.

32 Anne Wilson, *Traditional Romance and Tale: How Stories Mean*, Ipswich, D. and S. Brewer, 1976. See also her 'Magical Thought in Story', *Signal, 36* (1981): 138–151; 'What is Magic?' *Signal, 38* (May, 1982): 170–180.

33 See *Plots and Powers: Magical Structures in Medieval Narratives*; Gainesville, University of Florida, 2001.

34 Lucy Sprague Mitchell, *Here and Now Story Book, Two to Seven Year Olds*, New York, Dutton, 1921.

35 Thus, Carol White at four-and-a-half was greatly perturbed by the shipwreck in Edward Ardizzone's *Little Tim and the Brave Sea Captain*, loudly enjoining, 'The Engineer should have *seen* the rock!' (White op. cit.: 151) and when Lynd Ward, author of *The Little Red Lighthouse and the Great Gray Bridge* describes how the 'fat black tug' lies 'wrecked and broken', another child aged 2.6 objected, 'I don't like this picture', 'I don't like the tug coming from Albany' (Crago and Crago, op. cit.: 23). Loss and damage are still present, however 'age-appropriate' the themes, and the child reacts with distress.

36 Richard Scarry, *Please and Thank You Book*: London, Collins, 1973: 90. See Maureen and Hugh Crago, unpublished MS diary, pp. 202–203.

37 See Crago and Crago, op cit.: 234.

38 Gertrude Crampton, *Tootle*, Illus. Tibor Gergely, New York, Simon & Schuster, 1946.

39 Compare D. W. Harding's 'spectator' and 'participant' roles (concepts introduced in 1937 in his 'The Role of the Onlooker', *Scrutiny* 6: 246–258), and Howard Gardner's 'patterners' and 'dramatists'. Both categories have significant common ground with my 'interrogators' and 'performers'. See Gardner's *Artful Scribbles: The Significance of Children's Drawings*, New York, Basic Books, 1980. See also Cathy A. Malchiodi, *Understanding Children's Drawings*, New York, Guilford Press, 1998: 77–78.

40 See *Giving Up the Ghost: A Memoir*, London, Fourth Estate, 2003: 76–77.

41 See *Self-Portrait: Trina Schart Hyman*, Reading, MA, Addison-Wesley, 1981.

42 See Wolf and Heath, op. cit.: 7; *Rapunzel, from the Brothers Grimm,* retold by Barbara Rogasky with illustrations byTrina Schart Hyman, New York, Holiday House, 1984. Frustratingly, no ages are given for either child in this reference, although the bulk of Wolf's data appears to have been collected in one six-month period during Lindsay's third year (Lowe, personal correspondence, May 20, 1944.)

43 See Lowe, op. cit.: 20–21. In fact, Snufkin was simply the last in a series of such identifications; see Hugh Crago, 'Why Readers Read What Writers Write', *Children's Literature in Education*, *24*:4 (1993): 277–289.

44 In terms of fiction, Piaget's 'centration' corresponds with Anne Wilson's theory that a fairy tale embodies only a single point of view, all characters being aspects of a single character (the protagonist, with whom the listener identifies automatically).

45 See Dennis Potter, *Pennies from Heaven*, with an introduction by Kenith [sic] Trodd, London, Faber, 1996: 512. [The drama was first broadcast in 1978].

46 See Wolf and Heath, 1992: 44ff; Lowe, 2006: 68, 141–142.

47 See Wolf and Heath, op. cit.: 44. See also 38–48.

48 See Graetz, op. cit. 83-86.

49. See Frank Sulloway, *Born to Rebel: Birth Order, Family Dynamics and Creative Lives,* Boston, Little, Brown, 1996.

50 Fowles, *Diaries* Vol 12, quoted in Eileen Warburton, *John Fowles: A Life in Two Worlds*, London, Cape, 2004: 376–377.

51 Until the advent of language in the second year of life, memories cannot be encoded in words, and so are largely inaccessible to conscious attempts at retrieval. Moreover, the hippocampus, which appears to assist with conscious memory formation, only matures fully after the third year of life. Thus it seems that nearly all of us really do 'forget' some of the most momentous events of our early lives, and we cannot access them at will.

52 Thomas Mann, *Buddenbrooks*, trans. John E. Woods, London, Everyman's Library, 1994: 48. [First published in German, 1901].

Notes to Chapter Three

1 For more on *Old Jack* and *Coppernob*, see my 'Childhood Reading Revisited', *Papers* 1, 3 (1990): 99–115. My uncle's and my grandfather's stories are told in 'Gone to Soldiers Every One', a chapter in my unpublished three generation family history, *A Family in Time*.

2 I have written in detail about my childhood experience of Mee's *Children's Encyclopedia* in 'The Last Days in the Old Home', *Signal 68*, June, 1989: 51–70.

3 Georgette LeBlanc, *The Children's Blue Bird*, trans. Alexander Teixeira de Mattos, illus. Albert Rothenstein, London, Methuen, 1913 [3rd edn, 1929]: 71–72.

4 See Maurice Maeterlinck, *The Blue Bird, A Fairy Play in Six Acts*, Trans. Alexander Teixera de Mattos, London, Methuen, 1909: 47–48.

5 See Humphrey Carpenter, *Dennis Potter: The Authorised Biography*, London, Faber & Faber, 1998: 17.

6 The questions, and the following three quotations in response to them, are from Arthur Applebee, *The Child's Concept of Story*, Chicago, University of Chicago Press, 1978. : See pp. 94, 100.

7 Maureen Crago, unpublished diary of Morwenna Crago's book responses; Hugh Crago, 'Growing Out of Enid Blyton', unpublished MS, c.1989.

8 Both quotations from Charles Dickens, *Great Expectations*, 1860-1. London, Folio Society, 1981: 1.

9 See my 'Prior Expectations of *Great Expectations*: How One Child Learned to Read a Classic', *College English 58*: (October, 1996): 676–692.

10 See Janet Frame, *To the Is-land: Autobiography Vol. 1*, London, The Women's Press, 1983; reprinted London, Flamingo, 1993: 545.

11 See Brian Alderson, Transl., *The Brothers Grimm: Popular Folk Tales*, Illus. Michael Foreman, London, Gollancz, 1978: 112.

12 Frame, op. cit.: 55.

13 From 'A Christmas Tree', published in *Household Words*, 1850, quoted in Peter Rowland, comp. and ed., *Charles Dickens: My Early Times*, London,

Folio Society, 1988: 523. Dickens' 'degrading' of the wolf is physical enough to suggest Piaget's sensorimotor stage of development (approximately from birth to the onset of language), where the infant thinks through *actions*.

14 *Alf Layla wa Layla* [literally, *[A] Thousand Nights and [One] Night*] was first translated into French by Antoine Galland and published between 1704 and 1712; a number of English versions followed. James Ridley's *Tales of the Genii*, first published in 1764, was republished in 1824, claiming to be 'translations from a Persian manuscript' by 'Sir Charles Morell'.

15 This and the following quotation are from Dickens' essay, 'A Christmas Tree' in *Household Words*. Quoted in Rowland, op. cit.: 56.

16 See David Grene, *Of Farming and Classics*, Chicago, University of Chicago Press, 2007: 1. Just like the four- and five-year-olds of our last chapter, young Grene was determined not to allow an unhappy ending to 'get away with it'.

17 See Peter Ackroyd, *Dickens*, London, Sinclair-Stevenson, 1990: 32.

18 Quoted in Ackroyd, op. cit.: 46.

19 Hilary Mantel, *Giving Up the Ghost: A Memoir*, London, Fourth Estate, 2003: 523.

20 See Bruno Bettelheim: *The Uses of Enchantment: The Meaning and Importance of Fairy Tales*, New York, Knopf, 1976.

21 The German word *Heimat* conveys, as no single English word can, a sense of the 'place to which one belongs'. Edgar Reitz used it as the title for his massive film chronicle—three series, televised over fifty-three hours between 1984 and 2004—about the people of a small village in the Hundsrück region, spanning most of the twentieth century.

22 Charlotte Brontë's earliest extant story is reprinted in Christine Alexander, Ed., *An Edition of the Early Writings of Charlotte Brontë*, Vol 1, Oxford, Basil Blackwell, 1987: 3.

23 Ibid.

24 The text of the entire story is reproduced in Carolyn Steadman's academic study, *The Tidy House: Little Girls Writing*, London, Virago, 1983: 184–218.

25 Steadman, op. cit.: 44.

26 Charlotte Brontë, *Jane Eyre*, London, Folio Society, 1991: 31. [First published 1847.]

27 Steadman, op. cit.: 53.

28 See for example 'The Relief of Murry' in Walter Hooper, Ed. *Boxen: Childhood Chronicles Before Narnia*, London, HarperCollins, 2008: 24.

29 See Hugh Lofting, *The Voyages of Doctor Dolittle*, London, Bodley Head, 1923: 57.

30 See Wolfgang Schlegelmilch, 'From Fairy Tale to Children's Novel', *Bookbird 4* (1970): 14–21.

31 More confusingly still, while I was invited to identify with a 'Tommy' close to my own age, I also knew that the *author* of the story was a 'Hugh', like me. Surely, I thought, Lofting's first person narrator should have been 'Hugh'?

32 Richard Jefferies, *Bevis: The Story of a Boy*, Ed. and Abridged Brian Jackson, Harmondsworth, Penguin (Puffin Books), 1974. [First published 1882.]
33 See Ackroyd, op. cit.: 16; Charles Dickens, *Dombey and Son*, London, The Folio Society, 1984: 934. [First published 1848.]
34 'Ode: Intimations of Immortality, from Recollections of Early Childhood', l. 18. [First published 1807.] See also Douwe Draasima, *Why Life Speeds Up As You Get Older*, Trans. Arnold and Erica Pomerans, Cambridge University Press, 2004. [First published in Dutch, 2001.]
35 See Janet Frame, *To the Is-land*, London, Women's Press, 1983: 13, 41.
36 See Janet Frame, *Owls Do Cry*, London, The Women's Press, 1985: 25. [First published 1961.]
37 See Carpenter op. cit.: 22.
38 Ethel Mannin, *Confessions and Impressions*, London, Penguin Books 1936: 18. [First published 1929.]
39 Frame, *To the Is-land*: 67–68.
40 See Ackroyd, op cit.: 27, 38.
41 See Robert Louis Stevenson, 'A Penny Plain and Twopence Coloured', *Memories and Portraits*, London, Chatto & Windus, 1909: 213; Michael Meyer, *Ibsen, A Biography*, 1967; Harmondsworth, Penguin, Rev. Edn, 1974: 37.
42 See Hilary Spurling, *Paul Scott: A Life*, London, Hutchinson, 1990: 36.
43 See Ackroyd, op. cit: 38; Warburton, op. cit.: 220.
44 See Donald Prater, *Thomas Mann*, New York, Oxford University Press, 1995: 5.
45 Jay Parini, *One Matchless Time: A Life of William Faulkner*, New York, HarperCollins, 2004: 24. [In this chapter I have spelled Faulkner's name as it was spelled by his father; Faulkner later changed the spelling, as I mention in Chapter 5].
46 See Darden Asbury Pyron: *Southern Daughter: The Life of Margaret Mitchell*, New York, Oxford University Press, 1991; Harper Perennial, 1991: 36ff.
47 Jefferies, op. cit.: 1864: 81.
48 See David Marr, *Patrick White: A Life*, Sydney, Random Century Australia, 1991: 98.
49 C. S. Lewis, *Surprised by Joy, The Shape of My Early Life*, London, Bles, 1955: 14.
50 See Robert Louis Stevenson, *Memoirs of Myself*, 1887, Tusitala Edition, Vol XXIX: 156.
51 See Anne Chisolm, *Rumer Godden: A Storyteller's Life*, London, 1999: 17. [First published 1998.]
52 Quoted in Juliet Barker, *The Brontës*, London, Weidenfeld & Nicholson, 1994: 154.
53 Dorothy Rowe, *My Dearest Enemy, My Dangerous Friend: Making and Breaking Sibling Bonds*, London, Routledge, 2007.
54 See Michael King, *Wrestling With the Angel: A Life of Janet Frame*, Sydney, Pan Macmillan Australia, 2000: 29.

55 Thomas Mann, *Buddenbrooks*, Trans. John E. Woods, London, Everyman's Library, 1994: 571. [First published in German, 1901.]
56 The word Lewis chose for this feeling was the German *Sehnsucht*, which literally means 'craving for longing' or 'longing addiction'.
57 *Surprised by Joy*, op. cit.: 19ff.
58 Linda Lear, *Beatrix Potter: The Extraordinary Life of a Victorian Genius*, Harmondsworth, Penguin, 2007: 13, 154. [First published 1966.]
59 Ibid.
60 See Michael Billington, *Harold Pinter*, London, Faber, 2007: 5. [First published as *The Life and Work of Harold Pinter*, 1996.]
61 See David Marr, *Patrick White: A Life*, Sydney, HarperCollins Australia, 1991: 30–31.
62 See Robert Louis Stevenson, 'The Manse', *Memories and Portraits*: 106–119.
63 See Michael Slater, *Charles Dickens*, New Haven and London, Yale University Press, 2009: 17.

Notes to Chapter Four

1 Erich Auerbach used this phrase as a chapter title in his great study *Mimesis: The Representation of Reality in Western Literature*, Trans. Willard Trask, Princeton, NJ, Princeton University Press, 1953. [First published in German, 1946.]
2 The free translation of these and later lines is my own. For those who want a sense of what the words literally say, I recommend *Sir Gawain and the Green* Knight Ed. W. R. J. Barron, in the Manchester Medieval Texts series, New York, Barnes & Noble, 1974, which prints the original alongside a close translation.
3 Interestingly, accurate depictions of landscapes and scenes of 'everyday life' appeared in art a century or more before they became common in literature. Look at the illustration for 'February' (F2v) in the *Très Riches Heures du Duc de Berry*, Musée Condé, Chantilly, London, Thames & Hudson, 1969.
4 See Anne Wilson's analysis of the romance in *Magical Thought in Creative Writing: The Distinctive Roles of Fantasy and Imagination in Fiction*, Stroud, Glos, Thimble Press, 1983: 94ff.
5 The phrase is from Chestien de Troyes' *Yvain*, l.3, *Yvain: Le Chevalier au Lion*, The Critical Text of Wendelin Foerster, with introduction, notes and glossary by T. B. W. Reid, Manchester, University Press, 1942.
6 'A Search after Hapiness' has been reprinted as a stand-alone publication with modern illustrations: T. A. J. Burnett, Ed., *The Search after Hapiness: A Tale by Charlotte Bronte, Written at the Age of 13*, Illus. Carolyn Dinan, London, Harvill Press, 1969: 13.
7 See Kay Redfield Jamison's careful study of the relationship between bipolar disorder and creativity, *Touched with Fire: Manic-depressive Illness and the Artistic Temperament*, New York, Free Press, 1983.

8 Since the original Mills & Boon publications, the romance novelette market has expanded and diversified. The company is now 'Harlequin Mills & Boon', and there are different brand names to indicate to regular romance-readers the type of romance they are getting, and how explicit its sexual content is likely to be. For more details, see Chapter 1 of Janet A. Radway, *Reading the Romance, Women, Patriarchy and Popular Literature*, 2nd Edn, London, Verso, 1987. [First published 1984.]

9 See Jaak Panksepp and Lucy Biven, *The Archaeology of Mind: Neuroevolutionary Origins of Human Emotions*, New York, Norton, 2012, Chapters 8 and 9. Panksepp uses block capitals (e.g. CARE, FEAR) to indicate that he is talking about 'neuronal pathways' *corresponding to* emotions, not the actual emotions. I hope he will forgive me for substituting lower case to make things easier for the reader.

10 Emily Bronte, *Wuthering Heights*, London, Folio Society, 1991: 87. [First published 1847.]

11 Jennifer Donnelly, 'Why You Should Read This', Introduction to the Bloomsbury Classics reprint of *Wuthering Heights*, London, Bloomsbury, 2006: vii.

12 Quoted in David Marr, *Patrick White: A Life*, Sydney, Random House Australia, 1991: 303–304.

13 See *The Magus, A Revised Version*, London, Triad/Panther, 1977. [First published in 1966.]

14 See *Le Chevalier au Lion (Yvain)* Ed. Mario Roques, Paris, Librairie Honore Champion, 1970: ll. 370ff. Though the details of Chrestien's fairy tale-like incident are quite different from those in *The Magus*, the *feeling* is similar: an apparently deserted, mysterious place, the 'ringing of a bell', followed by the appearance of a supernatural being. In Chapter 6, we will see C. S. Lewis also re-imagining this incident.

15 Jonathan Fowles, *The Magus*, London, Jonathan Cape, 1966: 78. [Italics mine.] This is the wording of the first edition, the one that I read at seventeen. There are slight changes in second edition.

16 See Eileen Warburton, *John Fowles: A Life in Two Worlds*, London, Cape, 2004: 15; Fowles himself described that story in *The Tree*, 1978: 6.

17 See Otto Friedrich, *Blood and Iron: From Bismarck to Hitler: The von Moltke Family's Impact on German History*, Harper, 1995: 61–62.

18 See Fowles' Preface to *The Magus: A Revised Version*: 6.

19 See August Kubizek, *The Young Hitler I Knew*, Introduction by Ian Kershaw, London and St. Paul, MN, Greenhill, 2006: 84. [First published in German, 1953.]

20 See Kubizek, op. cit.: 117–118.

21 See Kershaw's Introduction, Kubizek, op. cit.: 12.

22 See Ian Kershaw, *Hitler 1889–1936: Hubris*, London, Allen Lane, The Penguin Press, 1998, Chapter 1: Fantasy and Failure; Robert W. Gutman, *Richard Wagner: The Man, His Mind and His Music*, 1968; Harmondsworth, Penguin Books, 1971. 21–44.

23 See Kubizek, op. cit.: 116–119.
24 Charlotte Brontë, op. cit.: 9.
25 For all details of June and Jennifer Gibbons, see Marjorie Wallace, *The Silent Twins*, London, Chatto & Windus, 1986; Harmondsworth, Penguin, 1987.
26 See Rosemary Ashton, *George Eliot: A Life*, London, Hamish Hamilton, 1996: 21.
27 See Christine Alexander, Ed. *An Edition of the Early Writings of Charlotte Bronte*, Vol 1, Oxford, Basil Blackwell, 1987: 3.
28 Wallace, op. cit.: 59, 62.
29 This unpublished story was written in 1916 and discovered less than twenty years ago. Margaret Mitchell, *Lost Laysen*, Ed. Debra Freer, New York Scribner, 1996: 63–64.
30 See Barbara Stoney, *Enid Blyton: The Biography*, 2nd Edn, London, Hodder, 1992: 20ff.
31 See Ken Wilber, *Up From Eden, A Transpersonal View of Human Evolution*, Boston, Shambhala, 1986; Lawrence Stone: *The Family, Sex and Marriage in England, 1500–1800*, London, Weidenfeld & Nicholson, 1977, 226–228; Charles Taylor, *Sources of the Self: The Making of Modern Identity*, Cambridge, Harvard University Press, 1989.
32 Dodie Smith, *I Capture the Castle*, London, Heinemann, 1949: 342.

Notes to Chapter Five

1 Charles Dickens, *The Pickwick Papers*, London, Folio Society, 1981: 6. [First published 1836–1837.]
2 Iris Murdoch, *The Flight from the Enchanter*, London, Chatto & Windus, 1956: 75.
3 See Elliot Jacques, 'Death and the Midlife Crisis', *International Journal of Psychoanalysis 46* (1965): 502–514; Daniel Levinson et al., *The Seasons of a Man's Life*, New York, Ballantine, 1978.
4 See Linda Lear, *Beatrix Potter: The Extraordinary Life of a Victorian Genius*, Harmondsworth, Penguin, 2008. [First published 2007.]; Leslie Linder (Transcriber), *The Journal of Beatrix Potter from 1881 to 1897*, London, Warne, 1966.
5 'Youth' in *Youth, Heart of Darkness and The End of the Tether: Three Stories by Joseph Conrad*, London, Dent, 1902: 36–37.
6 All details of O'Brian's life are from Nicolai Tolstoi, *Patrick O'Brian: The Making of the Novelist*, London, Century Books, 2004/Arrow Books, 2005. Tolstoi is the son of Mary Tolstoi by her first husband.
7 See Michael Slater, *Charles Dickens*, London, Yale University Press, 2009: 208.
8 Fitzgerald later talked of 'two or three great and moving experiences' that shape a writer's life, and which he will later rework again and again in his fiction. For Fitzgerald, all these experiences happened in young adulthood. See Matthew J. Bruccoli, *Some Sort of Epic Grandeur: The Life of F. Scott Fitzgerald*, New York, Harcourt, Brace, Jovanovic, 1981: 420.

9 See Dennis Potter, 'Introduction' to *Karaoke and Cold Lazarus*, London, Faber, 1996: xiii.

10 See Anne Wilson, *Magical Thought in Creative Writing: The Distinctive Roles of Fantasy and Imagination in Fiction*, Stroud, Gloucester., Thimble Press, 1983: 48–61.

11 See Melanie Klein, 'Some Theoretical Conclusions Regarding the Emotional Life of the Infant' in *Envy and Gratitude and Other Works 1946–1963*, London, Vintage, 1977. [Essay first published 1952.]

12 See Charles Drazin, Ed., *John Fowles: The Journals Vol 1*, London, Cape 2003/Vintage, 2004: 320. All other biographical details from Edith Warburton, *John Fowles: A Life in Two Worlds*, London, Cape, 2004: 156–177; 199[insert en dash]222

13 See Fowles' Preface to *The Magus, A Revised Version*, London, Jonathan Cape, 1977: 2.

14 Janet Frame, *Owls Do Cry*, London, The Women's Press, 1985: 100. [First published 1957.]

15 See Lawrence Wright, *Twins: Genes, Environment and the Mystery of Identity*, London, Weidenfeld & Nicholson, 1997.

16 See Peter Ackroyd: *Dickens*, London, Sinclair-Stevenson, 1990: 229.

17 See Margaret and Michael Rustin, *Narratives of Love and Loss: Studies in Modern Children's Fiction*, London and New York, Karnac, 2001. [First published 1987.]

18. See Barbara Stoney, *Enid Blyton: The Biography*, 2nd Edn, London, Hodder, 1992: 216; quoted from Peter McKellar, *Imagination and Thinking; A Psychological Analysis*, New York, Basic Books,1957: 136.

19 See Ulric Neisser, Ed. *Memory Observed*, New York, Freeman, 1991.

20 See Hilary Spurling, *Paul Scott: A Life*, London, Hutchinson, 1990: 43; C. S. Lewis, 'On Three Ways of Writing for Children' in Walter Hooper, Ed. *Of Other Worlds: Essays and Stories*, London, Bles, 1966: 32; John Carey, *William Golding: The Man Who Wrote* Lord of the Flies, London, Faber, 2009: 149; Michael Slater, op.cit.: 172.

21 See R. L. Stevenson, *Across the Plains, with other Memories and Essays*, London, Chatto & Windus, 1913: 165–166; 15–89. [First published 1892.]

22 C. S. Lewis, 'On Three Ways of Writing for Children' in W. Hooper, Ed., *Of Other Worlds: Essays and Stories by C. S. Lewis*, London, Bles, 1996: 32.

23 For this and the following Mitchell quote, see Darden Asbury Pyron, *Southern Daughter: The Life of Margaret Mitchell*, New York, HarperCollins, 1992: 362–363 [First published 1991.]

24 See Douwe Draaisma, *Why Life Speeds Up As You Get Older: How Memory Shapes Our Past*, Cambridge, Cambridge University Press, 2004: 31–44. [First published in Dutch, 2001.]

25 Pyron discusses this incident in detail on pp. 57ff.

26 See Jay Parini, *One Matchless Time: A Life of William Faulkner*, New York, HarperCollins, 2004: 112–113.

27 See Hilary Spurling op. cit.: 346.

28 See Janvier Marius, *Written Lives*, Edinburgh, Canongate Books, 2006: 104 See David Marr, *Patrick White: A Life*, Random House Australia, 1991: 301.

30 This preface to the poem dates from 1816, when 'Kubla Khan' was published alongside 'Christabel', and 'The Pains of Sleep'. The poem itself had been composed many years earlier. See Richard Holmes, Ed., *Coleridge: Selected Poems*, London, HarperCollins 1996: 229–231.

31 See Pyron, op. cit.: 303.

32 Spurling, op. cit.: 313–314.

33 See Ronald T. Kellogg: *The Psychology of Writing*, New York, Oxford University Press, 1994: Chapter 9. Kellogg also describes (1989) the use of alcohol as a stimulus to composition, with writers commonly revising when sober.

34 Spurling, op. cit: 383; see also p. 395 for Scott's need to light up when telling an anecdote.

35 See David Rudd, *Enid Blyton and the Mystery of Children's Literature*, Basingstoke, Macmillan, 2000: 165ff.

36 Dickens' revisions of the material he performed are discussed in detail in Chapter 22 of Michael Slater, op. cit.

37 See Jaak Panksepp and Lucy Biven, *The Archaeology of Mind: Neuroevolutionary Origins of Human Emotions*, New York. Norton, 2012, 95–144.

38 See Andrew Dalby, *Rediscovering Homer*, New York, Norton, 2006: 110ff.

39 Enid Blyton, *Five Go to Demon's Rocks*, Hodder, 1961/13th impression, 1980: 35–36.

40 See my 'Enid Blyton: The Greatest Adventure of her Life' in A. Mills & J. Smith, Eds., *Utter Silence: Voicing the Unspeakable*, New York, Peter Lang, 2001: 157–182.

41 See Andrew Wilson, *Harold Robbins: The Man Who Invented Sex*, London, Bloomsbury, 2007: 153.

42 See Brian Boyd, *On the Origin of Stories: Evolution, Cognition and Fiction*, Cambridge, Harvard University Press, 2009, in particular Chapter 7.

43 See *Lost in a Book: The Psychology of Reading for Pleasure*, New Haven, Yale University Press, 1988.

44 See 5 [sic] *Readers Reading*, New Haven, Yale University Press, 1975.

45 'A Rose for Emily', first published in *Forum*, April, 1930. Reprinted in Malcolm Cowley, Ed. *The Portable Faulkner*, Rev. Edn, Harmondsworth, Penguin, 1967: 392–402.

46 See her *Reading the Romance: Women, Patriarchy and Popular Literature*, University of North Carolina Press, 1984. 2nd Edn, London, Verso, 1987. Most of the details in my account come from Chapter 2 of Radway's study (pp. 46–85).

47 Radway, op. cit.: 190. See also Hugh Crago, 'Childhood Reading Revisited', *Papers 1*:3 (1990): 99–115.

48 Radway, op. cit.: 71.

49 See Claire Harman, *Robert Louis Stevenson: A Biography*, London, HarperCollins, 2005: 43; Pyron, op. cit.: 63; Dickens: See 'A Christmas Tree',

published in *Household Words*, 1850, quoted in Peter Rowland, Comp. and Ed., *Charles Dickens: My Early Times*, London, Folio Society, 1988: 523.

50 Radway, op. cit.: 81.

51 See Hugh Crago, 'Cultural Categories and the Criticism of Children's Literature', *Signal 30* (1979): 40–50.

52 See Brian Boyd, op. cit.: 395.

Notes to Chapter Six

1 All Lewis details in this chapter from A. N. Wilson, *C. S. Lewis: A Biography*, London, Collins, 1990. See also Roger Lancelyn Green and Walter Hooper, *C. S. Lewis: A Biography*, Rev. Edn, London, HarperCollins, 2002: 301–328. [First published 1974].

2 See C. S. Lewis, *The Lion, the Witch and the Wardobe: A Story for Children*, London, Bles, 1950: 12–13.

3 The same sequence of images and feelings reappears in *The Silver Chair*, London, Bles, 1953: 192ff.

4 See Iain McGilchrist, *The Master and His Emissary: The Divided Brain and the Making of the Western World*, New Haven and London, Yale University Press, 2009: 77–79.

5 See Jaak Panksepp and Lucy Biven, *The Archaeology of Mind: Neuroevolutionary Origins of Human Emotions*, New York, Norton, 2012: 95ff.

6 See Eric Erikson, 'Seven Ages of Man' in *Childhood and Society*, London, Hogarth Press 1965: 239–261 (originally published in the USA, 1950); C. J. Jung, *Memories, Dreams, Reflections*, New York, Pantheon, 1963, and *The Archetypes and the Collective Unconscious*, Collected Works, Vol 9, Part 1, Princeton, NJ, Bollingen, 1968; Eliot Jacques, 'Death and the Midlife Crisis' in *International Journal of Psychiatry 46* (1965): 502–513; Daniel Levinson et al., *The Seasons of a Man's Life*, New York, Ballantine, 1978.

7 See David Marr, *Patrick White: A Life*, Random House Australia, 1991: 292.

8 Thomas Mann: *Buddenbrooks: The Decline of a Family*, Trans. John E. Woods, London, Everyman's Library, 1994: 595.

9 See John Bleibtreu, *The Parable of the Beast*, London, Gollancz, 1968: 38–83.

10 See Kurt W. Fischer and Ellen Pruyne, 'Reflective Thinking in Adulthood' in Jack Demick and Carrie Andreotti, Eds., *Handbook of Adult Development*, NY, Springer, 2003: 169ff.

11 C. S. Lewis, *The Magician's Nephew*, London, Bles, 1955: 50.

12 See Hugh Crago, 'Such Was Charn, That Great City', *Children's Literature Association Quarterly 19*:1 (Spring, 1994): 40–44.

13 See A. N. Wilson, op. cit.: 213ff; Peter Conradi, *Iris Murdoch: A Life*, London, HarperCollins, 2001: 266.

14 C. S. Lewis, *Surprised by Joy*, London, Bles, 1955: 21.

15 Wilson, op. cit.: 2 (this account is not referenced by Wilson, and it is not clear how old Flora was at the time, nor whether Flora herself told this story; Lewis does not mention it in *Surprised by Joy*).

16 For a reliable account of contemporary conceptualisations of the narcissistic personality, see Nancy McWilliams: *Psychoanalytic Diagnosis: Understanding Personality Structure in the Clinical Process*, New York, Guilford, 1994: 168--188. I use the male pronoun because the majority of the 'romantic egotists' discussed in this book are male.

17 This was the original title of Scott Fitzgerald's first novel, published in 1920 as *This Side of Paradise.*

18 Sigmund Freud, 'Erinnern, Wiederholen und Durcharbeiten' ['Remembering, Repeating and Working Through'], *Internationale Zeitschrift fur ertzliche Psychoanalyse* 2:6, 1914. [English translation in J. Strachey, Ed. *The Standard Edition of the Complete Psychological Works of Sigmund Freud*, London, Hogarth Press, Vol 12 (1950): 145–157.

19 Paul Scott, *The Jewel in the Crown*, in *The Raj Quartet*, New York, Everyman's Library, 2007: 5 [*Jewel* first published 1966.]

20 See Hilary Spurling, *Paul Scott: A Life*, London, Hutchinson, 1990: 365–366.

21 All details of Dahl's life from Donald Sturrock, *Storyteller: The Life of Roald Dahl*, London, Harper, 2010.

22 Briefly popular, *The Gremlins* (New York, Walt Disney/Random House, 1943) was virtually forgotten by 1960.

23 Roald Dahl, *James and the Giant Peach*, London, Allen & Unwin, 1967: 7–8. [First published 1961.]

24 Dahl, op. cit.: 8.

25 Roald Dahl, *Charlie and the Chocolate Factory*, Harmondsworth, Penguin 1973: 126 [First published 1964.]

26 See Averil Earnshaw, *Family Time*, Sydney, A. and K. Publications, 1983, *Time Bombs in Families and How to Survive Them*, Sydney, Spencer Publications, 1998; Anne Ancelin Schützenberger, *The Ancestor Syndrome: Transgenerational Psychotherapy and the Hidden Links in the Family Tree*, Trans. Anne Trager, London, Routledge, 1998: 259 [First published in French, 1993.]

27 See Hugh Crago, *A Circle Unbroken: The Hidden Emotional Patterns that Shape Our Lives*, Sydney, Allen & Unwin, 1999: 108–115; 140ff.

28 See Katharine Patterson, 'My Life is Based on a True Story', *Magpies 2* (May, 1989): 5–10. [This is a revised version of 'Story of My Lives' in her *The Spying Heart*, New York, Dutton/Lodestar, 1989.]

29 See Charles Dickens, *David Copperfield*, London, Folio Society, 1983: 21. [First published 1849–1850.] Dickens employs a very similar image to characterise Jaggers in *Great Expectations.*

30 Dickens, op. cit.: 139–140.

31 See John Clute and John Grant's intelligent and scholarly *Encyclopedia of Fantasy*, London, Orbit, 1997: 942–943.

32 Paul Scott, 'After the Funeral' in Shelley C. Reece, Ed. *My Appointment with the Muse, Essays 1961–75*, London, Heinemann, 1986; quoted in Spurling, op. cit.: 15.

33 See Martin Seymour-Smith, *Hardy*, London, Bloomsbury, 1994: 16; Valerie Lawson, *Mary Poppins She Wrote: The Life of P. L. Travers*, New York, Simon & Schuster, 1999: 38.
34 See Enid Blyton, *Five Go to Smuggler's Top*, London, Hodder & Stoughton,1954: 356. [First published 1945.]
35 See Brian Boyd: *On the Origin of Stories: Evolution, Cognition and Fiction*, Cambridge, Harvard University Press, 2009: 223.
36 Charles Dickens, *Great Expectations*, London, The Folio Society, 1981: 415. [First published 1860–1861.]
37 See Eileen Warburton, *John Fowles: A Life in Two Worlds*, London, Cape, 2004: 294–295.
38 See Spurling, op. cit.: 403.
39 See Andrew Wilson, *Harold Robbins: The Man Who Invented Sex*, London, Bloomsbury, 2007: 79.
40 See Daniel Schacter, *Searching for Memory: The Brain, the Mind and the Past*, New York, Basic Books, 1996.
41 See Anne Fadiman, Ed. *Re-readings*, New York, Farrar, Strauss & Giroux, 2005: xi–xii.
42 In Fadiman, op. cit.: 121.
43 See Graham Greene, *The Lost Childhood and Other Essays*, London, Eyre & Spottiswood, 1951: 13.
44 Freud, op. cit.
45 See Daniel Schacter, op. cit.: 171.
46 See Lenore Terr, *Unchained Memories: True Stories of Traumatic Memories, Lost and Found*, New York, Basic Books, 1994.
47 See Hugh Crago, 'Is Plagiarism Inevitable? Implicit Memory in the Writing Process' [unpublished MS, 2011].
48 Dennis Potter, *Karaoke* and *Cold Lazarus*, London, Faber, 1996: 95. For earlier variants of this idea, see Muriel Spark's *The Comforters* (1957), and Flann O'Connor's *At Swim-Two-Birds* (1939).
49 See Spurling, op. cit.: 406–407.
50 John Fowles, *The Ebony Tower*, London, Cape, 1974: 38.
51 See Warburton, op. cit.: 443. Like Lily and Rose in The Magus, the 'two compliant women' echo the much younger Fowles' 'adventures' with Sanchia and Sally at Ashridge College after his return from the island of Spetsai.

Notes to Chapter Seven

1 Iris Murdoch, *Jackson's Dilemma*, London, Chatto & Windus, 1995: 1.
2 Quoted in Hilary Spurling, *Paul Scott: A Life*, London, Hutchinson, 1990: 26–27.
3 Charles Dickens, *The Pickwick Papers*, London, Folio Society, 1981: 36. [First published 1836–1837.]
4 Murdoch, op. cit.: 248–249. Interestingly, Murdoch couples 'loss of breath' with 'loss, or shift, of memory', raising the possibility that her own

dementia may have been the result of mini-strokes, and thus not Alzheimer's type dementia at all—as, most probably, Enid Blyton's was.

5 For autobiographical accounts of Alzheimer's, see for example Diana Friel McGowin, *Living in the Labyrinth*, San Francisco, Elder Books, 1993; Christine Boden, *Who Will I Be When I Die?*, Sydney, HarperCollins Religious, 1998.

6 See R. L. Stevenson, *Across the Plains, and other Memories and Essays*, London, Chatto & Windus, 1913: 153—154. [First published 1892.]

7. 'The Bear' first appeared as two short stories, and later was reworked as part of *Go Down, Moses* (1942).

8 Dr Sanjay Sircar, personal communication, March, 2013.

9 See Barbara W. Tuchman, *The March of Folly: Practising History*, London, Macmillan, 1983: 13ff. The talk on which this chapter is based was originally delivered in 1963, at which point *The First Salute* had not yet been written. See also Helger Holweg's *The Marne, 1914: The Opening of World War One and the Battle that Changed the World*, New York, Random, 2009.

10 Written by Ken Taylor, Directed by Peter Hall, Channel Four Television, 1992.

11 See Christopher Booker's *The Seven Basic Plots: Why We Tell Stories*, London/New York, Continuum, 2004.

12 All biographical details in this chapter from Patrick Marnham, *Wild Mary: The Life of Mary Wesley*, London, Vintage Books, 2007. [First published 2006.]

13 See George Johnson, *Clean Straw for Nothing*, London, Collins, 1969; see also Nadia Wheatley, *The Life and Myth of Charmian Clift*, Sydney, Flamingo, 2001.

14 Mary Wesley, *The Camomile Lawn*, London, Vintage, 2006: 105. [First published 1984.]

15 Mary Wesley, *A Sensible Life*, London, Vintage, 2006: 9. [First published, 1990.]

16 *Flowers in the Attic* was first published by Pocket Books in 1979; several sequels followed, and since Andrews' death, more sequels and 'prequels' have appeared, written by other hands.

17 See Marnham, op. cit.: 245ff.

18 See John Fowles, *Wormholes*, New York, Henry Holt, 1998. The term is an alternative name for astronomy's 'black holes', taken up by SF writers as a convenient means of allowing one time/place to 'connect' with another—a theme of obvious interest to Fowles. See John Clute and Peter Nicholls, Eds. *The Encyclopedia of Science Fiction*, London, Orbit, 1993 (Rev. Edn 1999): 129–131. See also Janette Turner Hospital, *Isobars*, Brisbane, University of Queensland Press, 1990.

19 Patrick O'Brian, *Master and Commander*, London, Fontana Books, 1979: 7. [First published 1970.]

20 See Donald Nathanson, *Shame and Pride*, New York, Norton, 1992.

21 Patrick O'Brian, *The Far Side of the World*, London, Collins, 1984.

22 See Nikolai Tolstoy, *Patrick O'Brian: The Making of the Novelist*, London, Century, 2003: 299.

23 From his autobiographical short story 'The Walker', first published in *Lying in the Sun*, 1956. In *Patrick O'Brian: Collected Short Stories*, London, Flamingo, 1995: 723.

24 Dennis Potter, *The Singing Detective*, first broadcast 1986. Potter died in 1994.

25 Dennis Potter, Introduction to *Karaoke and Cold Lazarus*, London, Faber, 1996: xii–xiii.

26 Here Potter was possibly influenced by the 1983 movie, *Brainstorm* (script by Bruce Joel Rubin) which includes a comparable conceit.

27 This detail is significant in that the romantic egotist is very much an 'observer of self', constantly scrutinising and managing the impressions he or she gives to others.

28 In *The Collected Short Stories of Roald Dahl*, Harmondsworth, Penguin, 1992: 32.

29 See Forrest J. Ackerman Presents: Curt Siodmak's *Donovan's Brain*, Pulpless, Inc, 1999. [First published 1942.]

30 C. S. Lewis, *That Hideous Strength*, London, Bodley Head, 1945. Rev. Edn London, HarperCollins, 2005: 24–56. Siodmak's brief descriptions (op. cit.: 59; 175; 179) of Donovan's brain supply significant hints that Lewis took up: the brain is artificially 'fed' and grows 'bigger' in the laboratory; it takes over the mind of the scientist who tends it and incites him to murder; and it is eventually destroyed in a bloody scene in a laboratory. The brain 'IT' in Madeleine L'Engle's children's classic *A Wrinkle in Time* (1963) similarly 'takes over' others and warps them towards evil.

31 See Iris Murdoch: *A Severed Head*, London, Chatto & Windus, 1961; *The Sea, The Sea*, London, Chatto & Windus, 1978.

32 See *The Annotated Wizard of Oz*, Centennial Edn, Ed. Michael Patrick Hearn, New York, Norton, 2000: 187. Shelley's poem was first published in 1818.

33 Here again, Potter appears to have been influenced by *Brainstorm*, see note 26.

34 Potter, *Karaoke* and *Cold Lazarus*: 392.

35 See Yvonne Kason, M. D. and Terri Degler, *A Farther Shore: How Near-death and other Extraordinary Experiences Can Change Ordinary Lives*, New York, HarperCollins, 1994.

36 Barbara Stoney, *Enid Blyton: The Biography*, 2nd Edn, London, Hodder, 1992: 224; John Carey, *William Golding: The Man Who Wrote Lord of the Flies*, London, Faber, 2009: 335.

37 Don Piper in Lisa Miller, *Heaven: Our Enduring Fascination with the Afterlife*, New York, HarperCollins, 2010: 157–158.

38 Patrick O'Brian, *Caesar: The Story of a Panda-Leopard*, 2nd Edn., The British Library, 2001: 612. [First published 1930, under the name 'Patrick Russ'.]

39 See Roald Dahl, *The Minpins*, 1991: 43; compare his much earlier short story, 'The Swan' in *The Wonderful Story of Henry Sugar and Other Stories*, London, Cape, 1977: 65–85.

40 See Jay Parini, *One Matchless Time: A Life of William Faulkner*, New York, HarperCollins 2004: 415.

42 The 'Sandman' was published in separate graphic novels, commencing with *The Doll's House* (1990), and concluding with *The Wake* (1996). [The original pieces appeared in serial format in *The Sandman* comic, published by DC Comics between 1988 and 1997.]

42 Neil Gaiman, *Death: The Time of Your Life*, Illus. Chris Bachalo, Mark Buckingham and Mark Penningham. New York, D.C. Comics, 1997: 69–70.

43 See Matthew J. Bruccoli, *Some Sort of Epic Grandeur: A Life of F. Scott Fitzgerald*, New York, Harcourt, Brace, Jovanovic, 1981: 529.

Notes to the Conclusion

1 See Michael Wood, *In Search of the Trojan War*, New York and Oxford, Facts on File, 1985. BBC Video, 1996; DVD version, 2007.

2 See Sigmund Freud, *Introductory Lectures on Psychoanalysis*, Lecture 13 in *The Pelican Freud Library*, Harmondsworth, Penguin, 1974: 236–238 [First published 1916–1917].

3 See Jerome Bruner, *Actual Minds, Possible Worlds*, Cambridge, Harvard University Press, 1986; Mark Turner, *The Literary Mind*, New York, Oxford University Press, 1996.

4 As in Daniel Stern's *The Present Moment in Psychotherapy and Everyday Life*, New York, Norton, 2004.

5 See 'First Lines of Novels' in Adrian Room, Ed., *Brewer's Dictionary of Modern Phrase and Fable*, London, Cassell, 2000.

6 Anton Erhenzweig, *The Hidden Order of Art: A Study in the Psychology of Artistic Imagination*, London, Paladin, 1970: 40. [First published 1967.]

7 This was the theory of marriage choice proposed by Murray Bowen in his *Family Therapy in Clinical Practice*, New York, Aronson, 1978: 265.

8 See Edmund Tylor, *Primitive Culture: Researches into the Development of Mythology, Philosophy, Religion, Art and Custom*. London, John Murray, 1871. Gregory Bateson, *Mind and Nature: A Necessary Unity*, New York, Ballantine Books, 1979.

9 'The Carnegie Library, Juvenile Division: ll. 44–45, in *Randall Jarrell: The Complete Poems*, London, Faber, 1971: 99.

10 See Hugh Crago, 'Bibliotherapy and Psychology' in Peter Hunt, Ed., *International Companion Encyclopedia of Children's Literature*, 2nd Rev. Edn, London, Routledge, 2004, Vol II: 826–835.

11 See Michael White, *Maps of Narrative Practice*, New York, Norton, 2007.

12 See Iain McGilchrist, *The Master and his Emissary: The Divided Brain and the Making of the Western World*, New Haven and London, Yale University Press, 2009: 75–76.

References

Ackroyd, Peter. *Charles Dickens*. London, Sinclair-Stevenson, 1990.
Ainsworth, M. D. S., Blehar, M. C., Waters E., and Wall, S. *Patterns of Attachment: A Psychological Study of the Strange Situation*, Hillsdale, NJ, Erlbaum, 1978.
Alain-Fournier, (pseud. of Henri Alban-Fournier). *The Lost Estate* ('Le Grand Meaulnes'). Trans. Robin Buss. Harmondsworth, Penguin, 2007. [First published in French, 1913.]
Alexander, Christine, Ed. *An Edition of the Early Writings of Charlotte Bronte*, Vol 1, Oxford, Basil Blackwell, 1987.
Ames, Louise Bates. Children's Stories. *Genetic Psychology Monographs 73*, Provincetown, MA, Journal Press, 1966: 337–396.
Andersen, Hans. Trans. Erik Haugaard, *Hans Andersen: His Classic Fairy Tales*. Illus. Michael Foreman, New York, Doubleday. 1976.
Andrews, Virginia. *Flowers in the Attic*, New York, Pocket Books, 1979.
Anthony, Sylvia. *The Discovery of Death in Childhood and After*, Harmondsworth, Penguin, 1973. [First published 1971.]
Applebee, Arthur. *The Child's Concept of Story*, Chicago, University of Chicago Press, 1978.
Ardizzone, Edward. *Little Tim and the Brave Sea Captain*, New York, Oxford, 1936.
Auerbach, Erich. *Mimesis: The Representation of Reality in Western Literature*. Trans. Willard Trask, Princeton, NJ, Princeton University Press, 1953. [First published in German, 1946.]
Baghban, Marcia. *Our Daughter Learns to Read and Write: A Case Study from Birth to Three*, Newark, DE, International Reading Association, 1984.
Barron, W. R. J. [Ed.] *Sir Gawain and the Green Knight, Manchester Medieval Texts*, New York, Barnes & Noble, 1974.
Baum, L. Frank. *The Annotated Wizard of Oz*, Centennial Edn, Ed. Michael Patrick Hearn, New York, Norton, 2000.
Billington, Michael. *Harold Pinter*, Rev. Edn., London, Faber, 2007. [First published as *The Life and Work of Harold Pinter*, 1997.]
Blyton, Enid. *The Tale of Troy: The Story of the Siege of Troy (Stories from World History, Retold by Enid Blyton)*, Kingsway Supplementary Readers, 1934. London, Evans Brothers, n.d. [1934].
Blyton, Enid. 'Things I Don't Like' in "From My Window"', *Teachers' World*, Feb. 24, 1926.
Blyton, Enid. *Five Go to Smuggler's Top*, London, Hodder & Stoughton, 1945.
Blyton, Enid. *Five Go to Demon's Rocks*, Hodder, 1961/13th impression, 1980.
Boden, Christine. *Who Will I Be When I Die?* Sydney, HarperCollins Religious, 1998.
Booker, Christopher. *The Seven Basic Plots: Why We Tell Stories*, London, Continuum, 2004.
Bourne, Laurence R. *Coppernob: Second Mate*, London, Humphrey Milford, 1929.
Boyd, Brian. *On the Origin of Stories: Evolution, Cognition and Fiction*, Cambridge, Harvard University Press, 2009.
Brontë, Charlotte. *Jane Eyre*, London, The Folio Society, 1991. [First published 1847.]
Brontë, Charlotte. *The Search After Hapiness: A Tale by Charlotte Bronte, Written at the Age of 13*, Ed. T. A. J. Burnett, Illus. Carolyn Dinan, London, Harvill Press, 1969.
Brontë, Charlotte. 'There Was Once a Little Girl Called Anne'. Christine Alexander Ed. *An Edition of the Early Writings of Charlotte Bronte*, Vol 1, Oxford, Basil Blackwell, 1987.
Brontë, Emily. *Wuthering Heights*, London, The Folio Society, 1991 [First published 1847].

Browning, Robert. 'The Pied Piper of Hamelin, A Child's Story' in *Dramatic Lyrics*, London, 1842.
Bruccoli, Matthew J. *Some Sort of Epic Grandeur: The Life of F. Scott Fitzgerald*, New York, Sphere Books, 1991. [First published 1981.]
Bruner, Jerome. *Actual Minds, Possible Worlds*, Cambridge, Harvard University Press, 1986.
Butler, Dorothy. *Cushla and Her Books*, London, Hodder & Stoughton, 1979.
Carpenter, Humphrey. *Dennis Potter: The Authorised Biography*, London, Faber & Faber, 1998.
Carey, John. *William Golding: The Man Who Wrote* Lord of the Flies. London, Faber, 2009.
Chretien de Troyes. *Yvain; Le Chevalier au Lion*, The Critical Text of Wendelin Foerster, with introduction, notes and glossary by T. B. W. Reid, Manchester, University Press, 1942.
Chisolm, Anne. *Rumer Godden: A Storyteller's Life*, Rev. Edn, London, Pan Books, 1999. [First published 1998.]
Clute, John and Grant, John. *The Encyclopedia of Fantasy*, London, Orbit, 1997.
Cochrane-Smith, Marilyn. *The Making of a Reader*, Norwood, NJ, Ablex, 1984.
Coleridge, Samuel Taylor. Introductory note to 'Kubla Khan' in Richard Holmes, Ed., *Coleridge: Selected Poems*, London, HarperCollins 1996: 229–231.
Conrad, Joseph. 'Youth' in *Youth, Heart of Darkness* and the *End of the Tether*, London, Dent 1902.
Conradi, Peter. *Iris Murdoch: A Life*, London, HarperCollins, 2001.
Crago, Hugh. 'Cultural Categories and the Criticism of Children's Literature' *Signal 30* (1979); 40–50.
Crago, Hugh. 'The Last Days in the Old Home', *Signal* 68, June, 1989: 51–70.
Crago, Hugh. 'Growing Out of Enid Blyton' [unpublished MS, c. 1989].
Crago, Hugh. 'Childhood Reading Revisited', *Papers 1*:3 (1990): 99–115.
Crago, Hugh. *A Family in Time*, unpublished MS, 1993.
Crago, Hugh. 'Such Was Charn, That Great City' *Children's Literature Association Quarterly 19*:1 (Spring, 1994): 40–44.
Crago, Hugh. 'Prior Expectations of *Great Expectations*: How One Child Learned to Read a Classic', *College English 58*:6 (1996): 676–692.
Crago, Hugh. *A Circle Unbroken: The Hidden Emotional Patterns That Shape Our Lives*, Sydney, Allen & Unwin, 1999.
Crago, Hugh. 'The Unlearned Lessons of the Stories Children Tell', *Signal 92* (May, 2000): 94–118.
Crago, Hugh. 'Enid Blyton: The Greatest Adventure of her Life' in A. Mills & J. Smith, Eds., *Utter Silence: Voicing the Unspeakable*, New York, Peter Lang, 2001: 157–182.
Crago, Hugh. 'Bibliotherapy and Psychology' in Peter Hunt Ed. *International Companion Encyclopedia of Children's Literature*, 2nd Rev. Edn., Vol. II, London, Routledge, 2004, 826–835.
Crago, Hugh. 'Plagiarism or Intertextual References? Implicit Memory in the Writing Process', [unpublished MS, 2011].
Crago, Hugh. 'Story' in Philip Nel and Lissa Paul Eds. *Keywords for Children's Literature*, NY, New York University Press, 2011: 207–212.
Crago, Maureen. 'Missing Home, Missing Mother: One Child's Preoccupation with their Location in Picture Books', *Orana 14*:3, (1978): 74–78.
Crago, Maureen. 'Incompletely Shown Objects in Children's Books: One Child's Response', *Children's Literature in Education 10* (1979): 151–157.
Crago, Maureen and Hugh. *Prelude to Literacy: A Preschool Child's Encounter with Picture and Story*, Carbondale, IL, Southern Illinois University Press, 1983.
Cozolino, Louis. *The Neuroscience of Psychotherapy: Building and Rebuilding the Human Brain*, New York, Norton, 2002.
Dahl, Roald. 'William and Mary', in *Roald Dahl: The Collected Short Stories*, Harmondsworth, Penguin, 1991: 12–36. [Original title, 'Abide with Me'; first published in *Kiss Kiss*, New York, Knopf, 1960.]
Dahl, Roald. *James and the Giant Peach*, New York, Knopf, 1961/London, Allen & Unwin, 1967.
Dahl, Roald. *Charlie and the Chocolate Factory*, New York, Knopf, 1964/Harmondsworth, Penguin 1973.
Dahl, Roald. 'The Swan' in *The Wonderful Story of Henry Sugar and Other Stories*, London, Cape, 1977: 65–85.
Dahl, Roald. *The Minpins*, London, Jonathan Cape, 1991.
Dalby, Andrew. *Rediscovering Homer: Inside the Origins of the Epic*, New York, Norton, 2006.
Dawkins, Richard. *Climbing Mount Improbable*, Harmondsworth, Penguin, 1996.

Dickens, Charles. *The Pickwick Papers*, London, The Folio Society, 1981.[First published 1836–7.]

Dickens, Charles. *Dombey and Son*, London, The Folio Society, 1984: 934. [First published 1848.]

Dickens, Charles. *David Copperfield*, /London, The Folio Society, 1983. [First published 1849–1850.]

Dickens, Charles. *Great Expectations*, London, The Folio Society, 1981. [First published 1860–1861.]

Donnelly, Jennifer. 'Why You Should Read This', Bloomsbury Classics reprint of *Wuthering Heights*, London, Bloomsbury, 2006.

Earnshaw, Averil. *Family Time*, Sydney, A and K Publications, 1983.

Earnshaw, Averil. *Time Bombs in Families and How to Survive Them*, Sydney, Spencer Publications, 1998.

Erikson, Eric. 'Seven Ages of Man' in *Childhood and Society*, London, Hogarth Press 1965: 239–261. [First published in the USA, 1950.]

Fadiman, Anne. *Re-readings*, New York, Farrar, Strauss & Giroux, 2005.

Faulkner, William. 'A Rose for Emily' in Malcolm Cowley, Ed., *The Portable Faulkner*, Rev. Edn, Harmondsworth, Penguin, 1967: 392–402. [Story first published in *Forum*, April 1930.]

Faulkner, William. 'The Bear' in *Go Down, Moses and Other Stories*, New York, Random House, 1942.

Faulkner, William. *The Sound and the Fury*, New York, Cape & Smith, 1929.

Favat, Andre. *Child and Tale: The Origins of Interest*, Urbana, IL, National Council for the Teaching of English, 1977.

Finley, Moses. *The World of Odysseus*, 2nd Rev. Edn, 1978; Harmondsworth, Penguin 1979.

Fischer, Kurt W. & Pruyne, Ellen. 'Reflective Thinking in Adulthood' in Jack Demick and Carrie Andreotti, Eds. *Handbook of Adult Development*, New York, Springer, 2003: 169ff.

Flack, Marjorie and Wiese, Kurt, *The Story about Ping* London, Bodley Head, 1935. [First published US, 1933.]

Fortey, Richard. *Life: An Unauthorised Biography*, London, HarperCollins, 1997.

Fowles, John. *The Collector*, London, Cape, 1963.

Fowles, John. *The Magus*, London, Cape, 1966.

Fowles, John. *The Ebony Tower*, London, Cape, 1974.

Fowles, John. *The Magus, A Revised Version*, London, Triad/Panther, 1977.

Fowles, John. *Wormholes*, New York, Henry Holt, 1998.

Fowles, John. *John Fowles: The Journals Vol 1*, London, Cape 2003/Vintage, 2004.

Fox, Carol. *At the Very Edge of the Forest*, London, Cassell, 1993.

Frame, Janet. *Owls Do Cry*, Christchurch, Pegasus Press, 1957/London, The Women's Press, 1985.

Frame, Janet. *To the Is-land, Autobiography I*, London, The Women's Press, 1983.

Freud, Sigmund. 'Creative Writers and Daydreaming' in Albert Dickson, Ed., *The Pelican Freud Library* 14: *Art and Literature*, Harmondsworth, Penguin, 1985: 131–141.[First published as 'Der Dichter und das Phantasieren', 1913.]

Freud, Sigmund. 'Erinnern, Wiederholen und Durcharbeiten' ['Remembering Repeating and Working Through'], *Internationale Zeitschrift fur ertzliche Psychoanalyse 2*: 6: (1914). English translation in J. Strachey, Ed. *The Standard Edition of the Complete Psychological Works of Sigmund Freud*, Vol 12 (1950): 145–157.

Friedrich, Otto. *Blood and Iron: From Bismarck to Hitler: The von Moltke Family's Impact on German History*, Harper, 1995.

Fry, Christopher. *The Boy and the Magic*, English version by Christopher Fry, illustrated by Gerard Hoffnung, London, Dobson, 1964. [A picturebook version of Colette's libretto for Ravel's opera *L'Enfant et les Sortilèges*.]

Gaiman, Neil. *Death: The Time of Your Life*, Illus. Chris Bachalo, Mark Buckingham and Mark Penningham, New York, D.C. Comics, 1997.

Gardner, Howard. *Artful Scribbles: The Significance of Children's Drawings*, New York, Basic Books, 1980.

Gawain and the Green Knight, Sir [medieval romance], see Barron, W. R. J.

Graetz, Margaret. 'From Picture Books to Illustrated Stories: How Children Understand All Those Words, *Children's Libraries Newsletter* [Australia] *12*: 3 (1976): 79–87.

Green, Roger Lancelyn and Walter Hooper. *C. S. Lewis: A Biography* (Collins, 1974/Rev Edn, London, HarperCollins, 2002.

Greene, Graham. *The Lost Childhood and Other Essays*, London, Eyre & Spottiswood, 1951.

Grimm, Jacob and Wilhelm. *The Brothers Grimm: Popular Folk Tales*, Trans. Brian Alderson, London, Gollancz, 1978. [*Kinder und-Hausmärchen* first published 1812, 1815; six subsequent revised editions to 1857.]

Gross-Kurth, Phyllis. *Melanie Klein: Her World and Her Work*, New York, Knopf, 1986.

Gutman, Robert W., *Richard Wagner: The Man, His Mind and His Music*, 1968.

Harding, D. W. 'The Role of the Onlooker', *Scrutiny 6*: 246–258.

Harman, Claire. *Robert Louis Stevenson: A Biography*, New York, HarperCollins, 2005.

Heath, Shirley Brice. *Ways with Words: Language, Life and Work in Communities and Classrooms*, Cambridge, Cambridge University Press, 1983.

Higonnet, Margaret R. 'Narrative Fractures and Fragments' *Children's Literature* Vol 15, Annual of the MLA Division on Children's Literature and the Children's Literature Association. Yale University Press, 1987: 37–54.

Hogan, James C. *A Guide to the Iliad, Based on the Translation by Robert Fitzgerald*, New York, Anchor Books, 1979.

Holbrook, David. 'The Problem of C. S. Lewis', *Children's Literature in Education 10* (March, 1973): 3–25.

Holland, Norman N. *The Dynamics of Literary Response*, New York, Oxford University Press, 1968.

Holland, Norman N. *5 Readers Reading*. New Haven, CT, Yale University Press, 1975.

Holweg, Helger. *The Marne, 1914: The Opening of World War One and the Battle that Changed the World*, New York, Random, 2009.

Homer. *The Iliad*, Translated and read by Stanley Lombardo in *The Essential Iliad*, Parmenides Audio, 2006.

Hooper, Walter. 'The History of Boxen', in *Boxen: Childhood Chronicles Before Narnia, C. S .Lewis and W. H. Lewis*, Introduction by Douglas Gresham, London, HarperCollins, 2008.

Hooper, Walter, Ed. *Of Other Worlds: Essays and Stories*, London, Bles, 1966: 3–21

Jacques, Elliot. 'Death and the Midlife Crisis', *International Journal of Psychoanalysis 46* (1965): 502–514.

Jamison, Kay Redfield. *Touched with Fire: Manic-Depressive Illness and the Creative Personality*, New York, Free Press, 1993.

Jaynes, Julian. *The Origin of Consciousness in the Breakdown of the Bicameral Mind*, Princeton, NJ, Princeton University Press, 1976.

Johnson, Crockett. *Harold and the Purple Crayon*, Hamondsworth, Penguin, 1972. [First published 1955.]

Johnson, George. *Clean Straw for Nothing*, London, Collins, 1969.

Jung, C. G. *Memories, Dreams, Reflections*, New York, Pantheon, 1963.

Jung, C. G. *The Archetypes and the Collective Unconscious*, Collected Works, Vol 9, Part 1, Bollingen, 1968.

Karen, Robert. *Becoming Attached: First Relationships and How They Shape Our Capacity to Love*, New York, Oxford University Press, 1998.

Kason, Yvonne, M. D. and Degler, Terri. *A Farther Shore: How Near-death and other Extraordinary Experiences Can Change Ordinary Lives*, New York, HarperCollins, 1994.

Kellogg, Ronald T. *The Psychology of Writing*, New York, Oxford University Press, 1994.

Kirshaw, Ian. *Hitler 1889–1936: Hubris*, London,Penguin, 1998.

Kirshaw, Ian. Introduction to August Kubizek's *The Young Hitler I Knew*, London and St. Paul, MN, Greenhill, 2006.

King, Michael, *Wrestling with the Angel: A Life of Janet Frame*, Harmondsworth, Penguin, 2000.

Kingston, W. H. G. *Old Jack: A Tale for Boys*, London, Ward, Lock, n.d

Klein, Melanie. 'On Observing the Behaviour of Young Infants', [first published, 1952] in *Envy and Gratitude and Other Works*, 1946–1963, with an Introduction by Hanna Segal, London, Vintage, 1997: 94–121.

Klein, Melanie. 'Some Theoretical Conclusions Regarding the Emotional Life of the Infant' in *Envy and Gratitude and Other Works 1946–1963*, London, Vintage, 1977. [Essay first published 1952.]

Knox, Bernard. Introduction to *Homer: The Iliad*, Translated by Robert Fagles, New York, Viking Penguin, 1990.

Kubizek, August. *The Young Hitler I Knew*, London and St. Paul, MN, Greenhill, 2006. [First published in German 1953 as *Adolf Hitler, Mein Jungenfreund.*]

Lancelyn Green, Roger and Hooper, Walter. *C. S. Lewis: A Biography*, Rev. Edn, London, HarperCollins, 2002. [First published 1974.]

Lawson, Valerie. *Mary Poppins She Wrote: The Life of P. L. Travers*, New York, Simon & Schuster, 1999.

Leavis, Q. D. *Fiction and the Reading Public*. London, Chatto & Windus, 1932.

LeBlanc Georgette. *The Children's Blue Bird*, Transl. Alexander Teixeira de Mattos, Illus. Albert Rothenstein, London, Methuen, 1913. 3rd Edn, 1929.

Joseph LeDoux. *The Emotional Brain: The Mysterious Underpinnings of Emotional Life*, New York, Simon & Schuster, 1998.

L'Engle, Madeleine. *A Wrinkle in Time*, London, Constable, 1963. [First published in the US, 1962.]

Leondar, Barbara. 'Hatching Plots: Genesis of Story Making' in David Perkins and Barbara Leondar, Eds., *The Arts and Cognition*, Baltimore, Johns Hopkins University Press, 1977: 172–190.

Lesser, Simon O. *Fiction and the Unconscious*, Chicago, University of Chicago Press, 1957.

Levinson, Daniel, with Darrow, Charlotte N., Klein, Edward B, Levinson, Maria H. and McKee, Braxton. *The Seasons of a Man's Life*, New York Ballantine, 1978.

Lewis, C. S. *The Allegory of Love: A Study in Medieval Tradition*, Oxford University Press, 1936.

Lewis, C. S. 'Psycho-analysis and Literary Criticism' in C. S. Lewis, *They Asked for a Paper: Papers and Addresses*, London, Bles, 1962: 120–138. [Essay first published 1941.]

Lewis, C. S. *That Hideous Strength*, London, Bodley Head, 1945; Rev. Edn, London, HarperCollins, 2005.

Lewis, C. S. 'On Stories', see Hooper, W. Ed., *Of Other Worlds: Essays and Stories by C. S. Lewis*. London, Bles, 1966: 3–21. First published, 1947.

Lewis, C. S. 'On Three Ways of Writing for Children' see Hooper, W, Ed., *Of Other Worlds: Essays and Stories by C. S. Lewis*, London, Bles, 1966: 22–34. [First published, 1952.]

Lewis, C. S. *The Lion, the Witch and the Wardobe*. London, Bles, 1950.

Lewis, C.S. *The Silver Chair*, London, Bles, 1953.

Lewis, C. S. *The Magician's Nephew*, London, Bles, 1955.

Lewis, C. S. *Surprised By Joy: The Shape of My Early Life*, London, Bles, 1955.

Lewis, Thomas, Amini, Fari, and Lannon, Richard. *A General Theory of Love*, New York, Random, 2000.

Lombardo, Stanley. *The Essential Iliad*, Las Vegas, Parmenides Audio, 2006.

Lord, Albert B. *The Singer of Tales*, Cambridge, Harvard University Press, 1964.

Lowe, Virginia. Is This a Real Story? Young Children's Concept of the Reality Status of Pictures, Unpublished PhD Thesis, La Trobe University, 1997.

Lowe, Virginia. *Stories, Pictures and Reality: Two Children Tell*, New York, Routledge, 2006.

Lowe, Virginia. 'Gaps in Read-Makers: Young Children Finding and Filling Gaps in Stories', *Double Dialogues 2* (http://www.doubledialogues.com/archive/issue_two).

Lowe, Virginia. 'Books and a Pre-Verbal Child, 3–18 Months', *Children's Libraries Newsletter* [Australia], *11, 3, 4*: 1975: 73–79; 108–112.

Lynch, David. *Catching the Big Fish: Meditation, Consciousness and Creativity*, New York, Penguin, 2007.

Malchiodi, Cathy A. *Understanding Children's Drawings*, New York, Guilford Press, 1998.

McCall Smith, Alexander. *The Miracle at Speedy Motors*, London, Little, Brown 2008.

McGowin, Diana Friel. *Living in the Labyrinth*, San Francisco, Elder Books, 1993.

McKellar, Peter. *Imagination and Thinking: A Psychological Analysis*, New York, Basic Books, 1957.

MacLean, Paul D. *The Triune Brain in Evolution: Role in Paleocerebral Functions*, New York, Plenum, 1990.

McLaren, Duncan. *Looking for Enid: The Mysterious and Inventive Life of Enid Blyton*, London, Portobello, 2007.

McGilchrist, Iain. *The Master and his Emissary: The Divided Brain and the Making of the Western World*, New Haven, CT, Yale University Press, 2009.

McWilliams, Nancy. *Psychoanalytic Diagnosis: Understanding Personality Structure in the Clinical Process*, New York, Guilford, 1994.

Maeterlinck, Maurice. *The Blue Bird, A Fairy Play in Six Acts*, Trans. Alexander Teixera de Mattos, London, Methuen, 1909. [First published in French, 1909.]

Mann, Thomas. *Buddenbrooks: The Decline of a Family*. Trans. John E. Woods, New York, Everyman's Library, 1994. [First published 1901.]

Mannin, Ethel. *Confessions and Impressions*, London, Penguin, 1929.

Mantel, Hilary. *A Place of Greater Safety*, London, Viking, 1992.

Mantel, Hilary. *Giving up the Ghost: A Memoir*, London, Fourth Estate, 2003.

Mantel, Hilary. *Wolf Hall*, London, Fourth Estate, 2009.
Marnham, Patrick. *Wild Mary: The Life of Mary Wesley*, London, Chatto & Windus, 2006/Vintage Books, 2007.
Marr, David. *Patrick White: A Life*, Sydney, Random House Australia, 1991.
Miller, Lisa. *Heaven: Our Enduring Fascination with the Afterlife*, New York, HarperCollins, 2010.
Mitchell, Lucy Sprague. *Here and Now Story Book*, New York, Dutton, 1921.
Mitchell, Lucy Sprague. *Fix It Please*, Illus. Lois Lensky, New York, Simon & Schuster, Little Golden Books, 1947.
Mitchell, Margaret. *Gone with the Wind*, London, Macmillan, 1936.
Mitchell, Margaret. *Lost Laysen*, Ed. Debra Freer, New York, Scribner, 1996.
Mitchell, Steven A., and Black, Margaret J. *Freud and Beyond: A History of Modern Psychoanalytic Thought*, New York, Basic Books, 1995.
Murdoch, Iris. *The Flight from the Enchanter*, London, Chatto & Windus, 1956.
Murdoch, Iris. *A Severed Head*, London, Chatto & Windus, 1961.
Murdoch, Iris. *The Sea, The Sea*, London, Chatto & Windus, 1978.
Murdoch, Iris. *The Message to the Planet*, London, Chatto & Windus, 1989.
Murdoch, Iris. *Jackson's Dilemma*, London, Chatto & Windus, 1995.
Nathanson, Donald. *Shame and Pride*, New York, Norton, 1992.
Neiser, Ulric, Ed. *Memory Observed*, New York, Freeman, 1991.
Nell, Victor. *Lost in a Book: The Psychology of Reading for Pleasure*, New Haven, CT, Yale University Press, 1988.
Nelson, Katherine, Ed. *Narratives from the Crib*, Cambridge, Harvard University Press, 1989.
O'Brian, Patrick. *Caesar: The Story of a Panda-Leopard* [originally published under the name Patrick Russ, London, Putnam's, 1930] 2nd Edn published by The British Library, 2001.
O'Brian, Patrick. 'The Walker', in *Patrick O'Brian: Collected Short Stories*, London, Flamingo, 1995. [First published in *Lying in the Sun*, 1956.]
O'Brian, Patrick. *Master and Commander*, London, Collins, 1970.
O'Brian, Patrick. *The Far Side of the World*, London, Collins, 1984.
Panksepp, Jaak, and Biven, Lucy. *The Archaeology of Mind: Neuroevolutionary Origins of Human Emotions*, New York. Norton, 2012.
Parini, Jay. *One Matchless Time: A Life of William Faulkner*, New York, HarperCollins, 2004.
Paterson, Katharine. 'My Life is Based on a True Story' *Magpies 2* (May, 1989): 5–10. [Revised version of 'Story of My Lives', *The Spying Heart*, New York, Dutton/Lodestar, 1989.]
Piaget, Jean. *The Child's Conception of the World*, Trans. Joan and Andrew Tomlinson, London, Paladin, 1973. [First published 1926.]
Pitcher, Evelyn Goodenough and Prelinger, Ernst. *Children Tell Stories: An Analysis of Fantasy*, New York, International Universities Press, 1963.
Potter, Beatrix. *The Journals of Beatrix Potter From 1881 to 1897*, transcribed from her code writing by Leslie Linder, London and New York, Warne, 1966.
Potter, Beatrix. *The Story of a Fierce Bad Rabbit*, London, Warne, 1906.
Potter, Beatrix. *The Tale of Squirrel Nutkin*. London, Warne, 1903.
Potter, Dennis. *Pennies from Heaven*, London, Faber, 1996. [First broadcast, March 1978.]
Potter, Dennis. *The Singing Detective*, London, Faber, 1986. [First broadcast 1986.]
Potter, Dennis. *Karaoke* and *Cold Lazarus*, London, Faber, 1996.
Propp, Vladimir. *Morphology of the Folk Tale*, Trans Laurence Scott; 2nd Edn, Rev. and Ed. Louis A. Wagner, Austin and London, University of Texas Press, 1968. [First published in Russian, 1928.]
Pyron, Darden Asbury. *Southern Daughter: The Life of Margaret Mitchell*, New York, Oxford University Press, 1991.
Radway, Janet A. *Reading the Romance, Women, Patriarchy and Popular Literature*, 2nd Edn, London, Verso, 1987. [First published 1984.]
Raymond, Ernest. Ernest Raymond. *Through Literature to Life: An Enthusiasm and an Anthology*, London, Cassell, 1928.
Ridley, James. *Tales of the Genii*. [First published in 1764, republished 1824.]
Rogasky, Barbara (reteller) *Rapunzel*, From the Brothers Grimm, Illus. Trina Schart Hyman, New York, Holiday House, 1982.
Rogers, Leslie J. *The Development of Brain and Behaviour in the Chicken*, Wallingford, CABI Publishing, 1995.
Rowland, Peter. Ed. and Comp. *Charles Dickens: My Early Times*, London, The Folio Society, 1988.

Rudd, David. *Enid Blyton and the Mystery of Children's Literature*, Basingstoke, Macmillan, 2000.

Rustin, Margaret and Michael. *Narratives of Love and Loss: Studies in Modern Children's Fiction*, London and New York, Karnac, 2001. [First published 1987].

Sacks, Oliver. *The Island of the Colour-blind*, Pan Macmillan Australia, 1996.

Sale, Roger. *Fairy Tales and After: From Snow White to E. B. White*, Cambridge, Harvard University Press, 1978.

Scarry, Richard. *Please and Thank You Book*: London, Collins, 1973.

Scarry, Richard. *What Do People Do All Day?* London, Collins n.d. [First published by Golden Books, 1968.]

Schacter, Daniel. *Searching for Memory: The Brain, the Mind and the Past*, New York, Basic Books, 1996.

Schart Hyman, Trina. *Self-Portrait*, New York, Addison-Wesley, 1981.

Schickendanz, J. A. *Adam's Righting Revolutions: One Child's Literacy Development from Infancy through Grade One*, Portsmouth, NH, Heinemann, 1990.

Schützenberger, Anne Ancelin, *The Ancestor Syndrome: Transgenerational Psychotherapy and the Hidden Links in the Family Tree*, Trans. Anne Trager, London, Routledge, 1998. [First published in French, 1993.]

Scott, Paul. *The Jewel in the Crown*, London, Heinemann, 1966.

Scott, Paul. *My Appointment with the Muse, Essays 1961–75*, Ed. Shelley C. Reece, London, Heinemann, 1986.

Seymour-Smith, Martin. *Hardy*, London, Bloomsbury, 1994.

Shakespeare, William. *The Tempest*. Ed Frank Kermode, The Arden Shakespeare, London, Methuen, 1962. [First published 1623.]

Sir Gawain and the Green Knight [anonymous medieval romance], see Barron, W.

Slater, Michael. *Charles Dickens*, New Haven and London, Yale University Press, 2009.

Smith, Dodie. *I Capture the Castle*, London, Heinemann, 1949.

Smith, Peter. *Play in Animals and Humans*, Oxford, Blackwell, 1984.

Spufford, Francis. *The Child that Books Built: A Memoir of Childhood and Reading*, London, Faber, 2002.

Spurling, Hilary. *Paul Scott: A Life*, London, Hutchinson, 1990.

Steedman, Carolyn. *The Tidy House: Little Girls Writing*, London, Virago, 1982.

Steen, R. Grant. *The Evolving Brain: The Known and the Unknown*, New York, Prometheus, 2007.

Stern, Daniel. *The Present Moment, in Psychotherapy and Everyday Life*, New York, Norton, 2004.

Stevenson, Robert Louis. 'A Chapter on Dreams' in *Across the Plains, and other Memories and Essays*, London, Chatto & Windus, 1913. [First published 1892.]

Stevenson, Robert Louis. 'Memoirs of Himself' in *Works of RLS*, Tusitala Edition, XXIX. [Collected Edn, 1887.]

Stevenson, Robert Louis. *Across the Plains, with other Memories and Essays*, Chatto & Windus, 1913 [First published 1892.]

Stone, Lawrence. *The Family, Sex and Marriage in England, 1500–1800*, London, Weidenfeld & Nicholson, 1977.

Stoney, Barbara. *Enid Blyton: The Biography*, 2nd Edn, London, Hodder, 1992.

Sturrock, Donald. *Storyteller: The Life of Roald Dahl*, London, Harper, 2010.

Sulloway, Frank. *Born to Rebel: Birth Order, Family Dynamics and Creative Lives*, Boston, Little, Brown, 1996.

Sutcliff, Rosemary. *Black Ships Before Troy: The Story of the Iliad*, Illus. Alan Lee, London, Frances Lincoln, 1993.

Sutton-Smith, Brian, with David M. Abrams, Gilbert J. Borvin, M'Lou Caring, Daniel P. Gildersgame, Daniel H.Mahoney and Thomas R. Stevens. *The Folkstories of Children*. Publications of the American Folklore Society, New Series, Vol 3, Philadelphia, University of Pennsylvania Press, 1981.

Swift, Hildegard H. and Ward, Lynd. *The Little Red Lighthouse and the Great Gray Bridge*, New York, Harcourt, Brace & World, 1942.

Terr, Lenore. *Unchained Memories: True Stories of Traumatic Memories, Lost and Found*, New York, Basic Books, 1994.

Tuchman, Barbara W. *The March of Folly: Practising History*, London, Macmillan, 1983.

Taylor, Charles. *Sources of the Self: The Making of Modern Identity*, Cambridge, Harvard University Press, 1989.

Tolstoi, Nicolai. *Patrick O'Brian: The Making of the Novelist*, London, Century Books, 2004.

Tres Riches Heures du Duc de Berry [medieval illuminated MS] Museé Condé, Chantilly; London, Thames & Hudson, 1969.
Turner, Mark. *The Literary Mind*, New York/Oxford, Oxford University Press, 1997.
Tylor, Edward B. *Primitive Culture: Researches into the Development of Mythology, Philosophy, Religion, Art and Custom*.London, John Murray, 1871.
Wallace, Marjorie. *The Silent Twins*, London, Chatto & Windus, 1986; Harmondsworth, Penguin, 1987.
Wallon, Renée. *L'évolution Psychologique de l'Enfant*, Pris, A. Colin. [Reissued 1974.]
Warburton, Eileen. *John Fowles: A Life in Two Worlds*, London, Cape, 2004.
Welleck, René and Warren, Austin. *The Theory of Literature*, Harmondsworth, Peregrin Books, 1963. [First published 1942.]
Wesley, Mary. *The Camomile Lawn*. London, Macmillan, 1984. [Television adaptation written by Ken Taylor, Directed by Peter Hall, Channel Four Television, 1992.]
Wesley, Mary. *A Sensible Life*. London, Transworld, 1990.
Weir, Ruth Hirsch. *Language in the Crib*, The Hague, Mouton, 1962.
Wheatley, Nadia. *The Life and Myth of Charmian Clift*, Sydney, Flamingo, 2001.
White, Dorothy Neal. *Books before Five*. New Zealand Council for Educational Research, 1954. Repr. Norwood, NJ, Ablex, 1984.
White, Michael. *Maps of Narrative Practice*, New York, Norton, 2007.
Wilber, Ken. *Up from Eden, A Transpersonal View of Human Evolution*, Boston, Shambhala, 1986.
Wilson, A. N. *C. S. Lewis: A Biography*, London, Collins, 1990.
Wilson, Andrew. *Harold Robbins: The Man Who Invented Sex*, London, Bloomsbury, 2007.
Wilson, Anne. *Traditional Romance and Tale, How Stories Mean*. Ipswich, D. and S. Brewer, 1976.
Wilson, Anne. 'Magical Thought in Story', *Signal 36* (September, 1981): 138–151.
Wilson, Anne. 'What is Magic?', *Signal 38* (May, 1982): 170–180.
Wilson, Anne. *Magical Thought in Imaginative Writing: The Distinctive Roles of Fantasy and Imagination inn Thinking*, Thimble Press, 1983.
Wilson, Anne. *Plots and Powers: Magical Structures in Medieval Narratives*; Gainesville, University of Florida, 2001.
Wright, Lawrence. *Twins: Genes, Environment and the Mystery of Identity*, London, Weidenfeld & Nicholson, 1997.
Wolf, Shelby and Brice Heath, Shirley. *The Braid of Literature*, Cambridge, Harvard University Press, 1992.
Yvain: Le Chevalier au Lion [medieval romance] see Chretien de Troyes.

Index

Note: In subheadings and cross-references, 'right hemisphere' is abbrieviated to 'RH' and 'left hemisphere' to 'LH']